TRAVERSING THE MINEFIELD

Best Practice:
Reducing Risk in
Funeral-Cremation Service

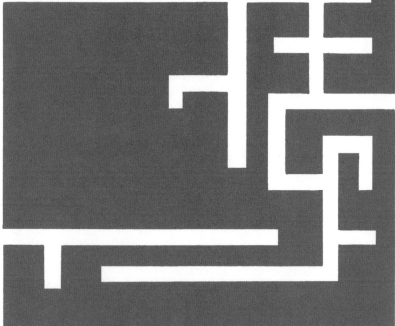

TRAVERSING THE MINEFIELD

Best Practice: Reducing Risk in Funeral-Cremation Service

by

Michael Kubasak
and
William M. Lamers, Jr., M.D.

Pasadena, California

September 2007

What others say about this book...

"Traversing the Minefield just might be the most important and direly needed book ever published for funeral-service professionals. Kubasak reveals widespread shortcomings in current practices and the dangers in sticking to the status quo. This excellent book has page after page of practical, plain-English strategies and tools to reduce lawsuits and costly, reputation-damaging mistakes. A must-read for all practitioners, as well as those who support, represent and advise them."

Doug Hernan, President, FuneralServe Enterprises, former Editor-Publisher of *Funeral Service Insider*

"This 'must read' book is for all funeral-cremation practitioners. It will be required reading for my entire staff. The information is for anyone who wants to operate ethically and safely. Inform before you perform is a great mantra!"

John Carmon, CFSP, President, Carmon Community Funeral Homes & Past President, National Funeral Directors Association

"This excellent book should be a daily desk reference. It contains practical and helpful information that every industry member should read and know."

Harvey Lapin, Esq., Harvey I. Lapin, P.C., Former General Counsel for Cremation Association of North America

"No other book, manual or guide has addressed the risk issues confronting funeral service today. Mike has insight and knowledge that most funeral directors would not encounter in a lifetime. This is critical information that every funeral director and crematory operator needs to know and employ."

Tom Snyder, Vice-President, Facultative Technologies The Americas, Past President, Cremation Association of North America

"Mike has documented policies, procedures, principals and rationale that effectively create a Best Practice manual. He sets the operations bar at a level that will earn customer trust, loyalty and accolades for a firm. This book is about 'doing the right thing' and everything is explained with examples reinforcing the premise presented. Must reading for CEO to part-time associate, from student to embalmer, cremationist and pre-need counselor."

Ernie Heffner, President, Heffner Funeral Chapels & Crematory

"Mike puts due diligence in an easy-to-follow format that will help owners avoid the minefields we read about. This book serves as a not-so-subtle reminder of what needs to be done to make sure your business does not end up on a court docket."

Edward J. Defort, Publisher & Editorial Director, *American Funeral Director &* *American Cemetery* **Magazines**

"This book is a 'strike of lightening from a clear sky!' Not available in any other book, this book covers how the funeral service provider can best serve client families. It walks the reader through the land mines of serving a client. This book should be in every funeral home, in the hands of every licensee, embalmer and sub-contractor. Mike teaches you how to document, document, document."

Robert G. Mayer, Funeral director-embalmer, author of *Embalming – History, Theory, and Practice*

"This book addresses numerous issues with an eye for preventing misunderstandings and other issues that can potentially lead to lawsuits. All in all, it is a very comprehensive 'guide' to good policies and best practices, and will likely be a valued reference for the legal community, as well as death care and funeral service providers and cremationists."

Ron A. Hast, Publisher, *Abbott & Hast Publications*

"Mike reveals the hidden woes that all funeral providers face from the initial first-call through disposition. Those who follow the recommended Best Practices will be in a much better position to defend claims and lawsuits."

David Overstreet, Esq.

"*Traversing the Minefield* levels the playing field in dealing with lawsuit-slinging lawyers and provides a step-by-step approach to avoid landmines in business today. The book is a treasure; an absolute must-read."

Rick Obadiah, President, Star Legacy Funeral Network, Inc.

"The most complete guide on the subject of cremation liability."

Scott Gilligan, Esq., General Counsel, NFDA

"Mike did it again and hit the target! This is a must read book on risk management. By implementing Best Practices, funeral directors can mitigate the perils of serving families in a litigious society."

Ric Newton, Funeral director, cremationist and cemeterian

"This book contains the most comprehensive and beneficial collection of Best Practices available to the funeral profession. The real-life stories hit home."

Mark J. Panciera, Director of Business Development, The Whitmore Group

"Kubasak & Lamers have written an important book that should be read by everyone connected with funeral service. They have addressed the problems head on and offer recommendations and solutions. This book astutely cautions us once again that to be forewarned is to be forearmed."

Robert Fulton, Ph.D., Professor of Sociology, Emeritus, Univ. of Minnesota

LMG Publishing
A subsidiary of Lamers Medical Group

LMG Publishing, 9515 Seabreeze Terrace, Malibu, CA 90265-2279

Printer: The Castle Press, Pasadena, CA

Library of Congress Catalog Control Number: 2007936750
ISBN 978-0-9669263-2-3

Cover Artist: Bill Gamm

This publication is designed to provide accurate and authoritative information in regard to the subject matter covered. It is sold with the understanding that the publisher and author are not engaged in rendering legal, accounting or similar professional services. If you require legal advice or other expert assistance, you should seek the services of a competent professional.

Printed in the United State of America.

Special Sales
This book is available at special discounts for bulk purchases and for special needs or sales promotions. For more information, contact LMG Publishing or Kubasak Associates, Inc., or email: mkubasak@aol.com

Dedication

To

Dr. William M. Lamers, Jr., M.D.

No one could be a better friend, mentor, coach and
trusted advisor than you are to me.
Thank you, big guy.

Table of Contents

Preface

I have been a funeral director for more than 42 years. During most of this time, I owned and operated my own funeral home and cremation services business. I operated the funeral home as a part of a family enterprise and as a sole practitioner. After selling the business, I worked with Service Corporation International, a major funeral service consolidator, for seven years. Over my 40-plus years in funeral-cremation service, I have seen many kinds of leaders. Some of them treated risk management and risk avoidance lightly. Some felt that training employees was an unnecessary expense, secondary to revenue generation. Some viewed disgruntled customers as people who do nothing but disrupt their daily regimen. Still, others wrongfully believed that client families do not need to know what will take place. As an owner, I viewed best practice and risk reduction as powerful tools to establish customer loyalty and differentiate myself from all competitors. In addition to improving revenue, risk management provided me an intangible benefit I call "sleep insurance." I am confident that this book will help you in the same way.

This book could have been written in many different ways. I chose to focus on important areas that challenge the funeral-cremation provider and discuss those things that follow a natural sequence of events from the time of receiving the first-call through ultimate disposition. I have drawn on examples from legal cases I have been involved in where other funeral-cremation providers did not always do the right thing.

Some readers may be uncomfortable with some of the suggestions and recommended best practices in this book. The average funeral professional and student may be overwhelmed with some of the content. I could not have made this a "soft" book that did not deal with all the harsh realities I've come to know. I have spoken to thousands of colleagues in every part of the country. The situations I describe are real. In some parts of the book, instead of using a shovel, I used a "bloody spade." The truth must be known about the dangers that exist and how lives and businesses can be changed, even destroyed, when facing a lawsuit. I have not exaggerated but have drawn from real-life examples.

In 1990, I wrote *Cremation and the Funeral Director – Successfully Meeting the Challenge*. At the time and with the exception of a couple of progressive casket manufacturers I occasionally advised, who like me, saw a drifting away from traditional funeral elements and the importance of dealing with cremation, I was not widely known outside the state of California. I vividly recall the words of Wes Horbatuck, a friend of mine, prior to writing that first book. At the time, he was the national sales manager for Casket Shells, Inc., in Eynon, Pennsylvania. After a presentation to funeral directors on the East Coast, Wes waited until he was the last person in the lecture room. After thanking me for the presentation, he said, "Mike, there is one thing you must do if you truly care about funeral service and your colleagues. You have to put what you said in a book. Funeral directors need this information *in a book* so they can study it and learn from it." Wes caught me off-guard. I was flattered but knew nothing about writing a book.

I contemplated Wes' words for several weeks. Thinking about it made me chuckle and I just shrugged it off. How does one go about writing a book? It seemed insurmountable until I received a call one day from my very good friend, Dr. William Lamers, Jr. When I told Bill about the comment from Wes, without hesitation, Bill said, "It's a good idea and you're the person to do it. I'll help you. Come over tomorrow and we'll start by making an outline."

As I look back on how much has changed since then, I realize my first book offers this lesson: Write one. If a book sells nicely, a funeral director's life changes; and then an author's life changes.

Invitations to speak about cremation came from funeral companies, professional organizations and state & national associations all over the country, from people I did not know. Some colleagues asked me to advise them with operating their business. Such a welcome response triggers a potential pitfall: It is to think I know everything now. Labeled as an "expert" or guru, the author looks inside, believing he can find all the wisdom he needs.

Traversing the Minefield is a close look "at home." What I have come to realize is that this book began shortly after publication of the first book. As an author and frequent speaker about "cremation," the consumers who choose it, and how funeral service is affected by it, I also began receiving phone calls from attorneys, asking me for advice and my opinions on various funeral, cremation and cemetery legal issues. I was asked to serve as an expert witness. In 1990, I never envisioned this type of involvement in my profession. Working as an expert witness for the past 17 years has become an unanticipated and very important part of my education and career. *Cremation and the Funeral Director* served to focus on an aspect of funeral service handled until recently, with avoidance by many colleagues, and even with contempt by a few. Cremation, while practiced for thousands of years in other parts of the world, was relatively uncommon in most areas of North America in 1990. Working as an expert witness in various lawsuits covering most aspects of the business shocked me with the realization that only a small number of funeral-cremation practitioners know about or engage in best practice in fulfilling their duties. The vast majority of funeral-cremation providers are trusting, hard-working and care-giving. Sometimes overwhelmed in serving the needs of bereaved people, many have never considered being sued as a concern and have not realized they perform their duties without a safety net. They are not aware of the minefield they are walking through in this day and age. For some of my colleagues, a lawsuit is what happens to someone else, not to them.

Traversing the Minefield, like my first book, emphasizes my experiences – as a personal service provider, a funeral director and embalmer, owner and employee, expert witness, "funeral director's coach" to colleagues and advisor to related service businesses – and reflects on ways in which the first book changed my perspective. This book shares other experiences through working with defense and plaintiff attorneys as well as plaintiffs and defendants. A quote from Dame Cicely Saunders, OBE, a founder of the modern hospice movement, is applicable here. She said of hospice care, "Nothing leaves us out from excellence." The same is true for funeral-cremation service.

I wrote this book because experience can be a tough teacher. I have seen first-hand people's lives ravaged by lawsuits. If you understand the principles in this book and adopt them in your business, you may not have to learn the hard way as some other colleagues have. Like some of them, I have also experienced the agony that accompanies being sued while owning a funeral home. Being a hands-on owner in southern California, I noticed how rapidly the legal climate and consumers were changing. The business that I learned from my father and mother was changing. Customer tolerance was replaced by higher performance expectations without defect. When something went wrong, some client families were inflexible to explanation and instead, escalated their concerns into a lawsuit. Sadly, I also learned that many practitioners put off examining their risk exposure, including their insurance coverage, until after they have been sued. After being sued, practically every funeral home, crematory, cemetery and independent contractor puts best practices in place and makes important modifications to policies and procedures. The smart ones do it ahead of time.

I wrote this book because, with the exception of experience, there are few, if any resources available to help funeral, cremation and cemetery operations assess their exposure to risk and avoid future lawsuits. In many ways, funeral-cremation businesses remain "unprotected," not because they do not have adequate amounts of insurance (many do not, however), but because they are unaware of their vulnerability. Many practitioners go about performing their duties as they have for generations. As some avoided learning about cremation, some avoid acknowledging their vulnerability today. There is no "center" where one can obtain comprehensive training about risk management. At present, no such information is included in the curriculum in schools of mortuary science. Only a few major insurance companies provide a service of this type to their clients and, because they are not familiar with the day-to-day operations of running a funeral home, crematory or cemetery, overlook many critical areas. Experience (the school of hard knocks) must not be the only teacher. Maybe this book will jump-start such a learning center and prompt some mortuary schools, professional organizations and insurance companies to focus on due diligence.

I wrote this book because over the years, I have met thousands of funeral-cremation providers who are unaware of the tremendous changes taking place among consumers and especially within the legal profession. All of these contribute to greater vulnerability for the practitioner, especially for the unknowing. It is a fact: operating a personal service business, like a funeral home or crematory, goes far beyond just meeting the requirements of the Funeral Rule, OSHA standards and your state laws and regulations. Customer service goes far beyond just satisfying a client family. The business climate and our responsibilities are fraught with obstacles that resemble a minefield that can destroy a reputation overnight that took generations to build.

I wrote this book because funeral professionals, like other personal service professionals, have become a "target" and identified as a "cash cow" by some people in the legal profession. Major settlements have put the funeral, cremation and cemetery businesses on the front burners and garnered the interest of attorneys. In addition to the usual specialties of law, there is an emerging specialty that deals with funeral, cremation and cemetery litigation. Funeral service has not only made the financial pages of the Wall Street Journal but is a topic of discussion in law-school classrooms and legal journals. In legal seminars, attorneys learn about lawsuits involving our profession and industry. As incidents of wrongdoing continue to make headlines and become more widely known among consumers and attorneys, the magnitude and number of claims will continue to escalate.

I wrote this book because as a student of the consumer, I learned that the new consumer requires a lot of information and desires to be educated. This is the age of consumerism. Client families want to know more than just how much it will cost; they want to know what is going on, who will be doing what and why certain things need to be done. Practices within the profession cannot be kept proprietary or secret. Almost as a second nature, the new consumer challenges expertise, authority, tradition, leadership, ritual, belief systems and more. People working in funeral-cremation-cemetery services are not exempt from these challenges. The new consumer expects to do business with an expert and desires active participation from their personal service providers. They do not like dealing with "order takers." Their questions can be hard-hitting and to the point. This is why you will read often throughout this book my personal mantra that I adopted years ago: *Inform before you perform.*

I wrote this book because I learned to my amazement, that as I and my staff became more conscious of risk reduction and developed best practice, we reflexively became more customer-focused. Client families liked the openness we exhibited and valued learning about many aspects of service we provided. Not only did we reduce our vulnerability, we also found it less stressful to perform our duties. Readily sharing information and making disclosures helped us become recognized as the premier funeral-cremation-shipment resource in our community.

I wrote this book because the occasional bad news is highly offensive to all of us and it must stop. Bad news about funeral, cremation and cemetery abuses reflects on all of us. What happens at a funeral home or crematory in New York City affects funeral service in Oregon, and usually overnight. Client families deserve only the best of care and service. It is not someone else's responsibility to police our profession. It is not some agency's job to make sure things are done correctly. Everyone who works in the profession shares in the responsibility of preventing bad from occurring.

Finally, I wrote this book because if I had a son or daughter entering the business, these are the things that I would want them to know to become the consummate professional expected by customers today. It is in that spirit of sharing, continuous improvement, love of the profession and best wishes for your practice that I present these proven strategies, lessons learned, case examples and risk-management tools and resources to help you safely traverse the minefield.

But enough of this Preface. It is already too long. Let's get started!

Michael Kubasak

Disclaimer

The information offered in this book is not intended to be, nor should it be construed as legal advice. It is not to be considered as a substitute for advice of an attorney. It is a compilation of experience gathered by the author from more than 40 years of practice as a licensed funeral director, embalmer, and provider of cremation, burial, and shipment services in the author's own funeral home and cremation services business, and more than 16 years experience as an expert witness in various legal cases.

All questions regarding specific situations of your own practice must only be answered by your own legal counsel. It is recommended that such an attorney be one familiar with funeral, cremation, burial, and cemetery matters.

Recommended best practices and forms, as a part of this book, are made available for sample purposes only. Adopting a best practice should only be done after you seek and receive independent legal counsel within your own State, Province, or other jurisdiction concerning that specific practice. A best practice or form should only be considered for adoption into your practice after review and independent assessment by your own legal counsel.

This publication is intended to provide you with current and accurate information about the subjects covered. But, such information may not be sufficient in dealing with a particular situation. The authors and their consultants neither warrant nor represent its suitability for that purpose. Those using this publication do so with the understanding that neither the authors nor consultants are engaged in the practice of law, and do not render legal services. The information contained in this book should not be relied upon as a substitute for your own independent research.

Michael Kubasak and William M. Lamers, Jr., M.D.

Acknowledgements

No one ever writes a book alone. Many years ago, a friend told me the only solitary thing about a book is reading it. He was right. Everything else is a collective effort.

We have been blessed with the encouragement of many wonderful people. In fact, the book could not have been completed without the support of important, and in some instances, "pivotal" people in my life. The contributors did more than "review." They inspired. All are influential in their field – their philosophy and practices serve as an example of what this book is all about.

To anyone we have overlooked and failed to mention by name, you are appreciated as a contributor – not just to this book but to the profession. We want to publicly acknowledge the following people we are particularly indebted:

Thank you, Lisa Lamers, M.A. (Malibu, CA)

You are a very special person to me. You amaze me with your patience, computer knowledge and eye for detail. Your work was often behind the scene, helping to keep the "big guy" going and helping me solve my computer problems.

Thank you, Doug Hernan (Rockville, MD)

You are the "word guru" and the master of phraseology. You became my "go to" person when I struggled. I'll never forget this. You have shown enthusiasm for this subject matter from day one. Even though you are not a funeral director, it's wonderful how much you care for funeral service. Thank you for always being there and never saying no. You are a remarkable writer and thinker.

Thank you, David Overstreet IV, Esq. (Fresno, CA)

When it comes to personal injury attorneys, you are the model and leader of the pack. From the moment we first worked together, I was impressed with your caring attitude for clients, your unwavering integrity and professional behavior. You were extremely benevolent in giving me your time and sharing your authoritative, insightful experience and organizational skills. Your numerous suggestions were always appropriate. It's your turn to write a book. Go for it!

Thank you, Mike Wildes (Garden City, NY)

We've only met once and that was briefly. But we clicked. I was immediately impressed with your knowledge of insurance and keen understanding of the challenges funeral-cremation professionals face on a day-to-day basis. I am glad to be on board with you.

Thank you, Harvey Lapin, Esq. (Northbrook, IL)

You are one of the true friends of funeral service and the premier attorney in the field. Your creative mind has helped advance legislation and laws in many states which has led to enhancing the level of professionalism throughout funeral-cremation service. For your own good, however, your golf game must begin taking precedence.

Thank you, Ernie Heffner (York, PA)

Even after a lifetime in funeral service, you gave me a new awareness for properly using the words, "deceased person." It is my hope that the principles we share will be the foundation for a lasting friendship.

Thank you, Robert G. Mayer (Pittsburgh, PA)

Your time and suggestions in improving the clarity and content of this book are deeply appreciated. You are the authority in embalming and contribute greatly in helping bereaved families assuage their grief through professional care rendered to deceased persons.

Thank you, Tom Snyder (Kingwood, TX)

For many years we have shared a passion as advocates for cremation consumers and improving the standards for cremation practitioners. Your knowledge of all aspects of the cremation process is second to none. I am grateful that you are always willing to share with me.

Thank you, John Carmon (Avon, CT)

To me you are every funeral directors role model. You conduct yourself as a true professional; your compassion for the bereaved and generosity to the profession is unexcelled. We still have a ski date to hit some Wasatch powder.

Thank you, Ric Newton (Chico, CA)

One of the finest practitioners in California, and a long-time friend, you are highly respected and recognized for service excellence. Your high level of education is an indication of your dedication to the profession and bereaved people. Thank you for sharing your knowledge and time with me.

Thank you, Ed Defort (Wall, NJ)

As the publisher and editor of *American Funeral Director* and *American Cemetery* Magazines, you have a keen awareness of the difficulties of operating a funeral home and cremation service. You have brought a high-level of professionalism and class in your award-winning publications. Thank you for allowing me to "pick your brain" to clarify many complex issues.

Thank you, Ron Hast (Tiburon, CA)

One of the most knowledgeable persons in funeral service, you bring to the forefront the ever-changing dynamics of funeral practices. You have established a reputation of telling it like it is, and through this, have helped to elevate the practices within the profession. Your knowledge of the subject matter and support is very much appreciated.

Thank you, Mark Panciera (Fort Lauderdale, FL)

Friends for a long time, you bring a unique blend of entrepreneurship, licensed funeral director and insurance background to the field. I was grateful that you made reviewing the book a priority. It is a pleasure to be a member of your team.

Thank you, Melissa Johnson (Forest Park, IL)

You see the need for raising the standards. A specialist in embalming and shipment of deceased persons, you continue to share your enthusiasm for the profession with funeral directors nationwide. I am grateful for your participation in this project.

Thank you, Robert Fulton, PhD (St. Paul, MN)

As the pre-eminent authority on funeral customs, thanatology and the history of funeral service, we cannot thank you enough for assisting us. You continuously support the value of the funeral in your writing, teaching and consulting.

Thank you, David A. Levy, PhD (Malibu, CA)

A noted psychologist whose book, *Critical Thinking*, reflects his wisdom and worldwide experience in helping others deal with grief. His background in serving as an expert witness in several major funeral-cremation lawsuits makes his contributions meaningful to our project.

Thank you, Bill Gamm (Leawood, KS)

A true friend, who graciously provided the art work and design for the cover of the book. Your creative talents as a graphic artist and artist are unmatched. Your friendship is priceless. A world traveler, I think it's time we enjoy another adventure together.

Thank you, The Whitmore Group (Garden City, NY)

In particular, thank you, James Metzger. You made your entire office available to answer my insurance questions. You did more than provide information; you opened your heart. Thank you for being so generous to funeral service. I am glad we are friends.

Thank you, Scott E. Schutzman, Esq. (Santa Ana, CA)

You taught me a great deal about serving as an expert witness. You helped to clarify many legal issues for me. As a plaintiff attorney, your comments are invaluable to my colleagues.

Thank you, Jaey Sedlacek (West Des Moines, IA)

Your tough editing helped bring the passion out in me. You taught me much about the insurance business. I think it's time we make another assault on Everest!

Also, thank you to

Judy Estrin, Rick Obadiah, Jill Glasband, Mark Smith, Paul Rahill, Bob Inman, Susan Kinney, Betty Adair, George Praether, and Jim Draper.

Finally...

Thank you, Gwen Kubasak (Mesquite, NV)

My loving wife and most cherished confidant of 38 years and mother to our two daughters. In writing this book, no one has endured more or been asked to put up with more, than you. No one understands me more than you. No one loves me more than you. No one loves you more than I do. As always, *AMTBTY*.

Thank you, all.

*"Wisdom is meaningless
until your own experience
has given it meaning."*

BERGEN EVANS
American Educator & Professor

CHAPTER 1

The First Call – Initial Notification

When it comes to something as sensitive as being notified of a death, first impressions are always important. A strong initial show of compassion, attention and respect can buy a lot of leeway should problems arise down the line; but mishandle that first-call and families might prove merciless toward everything that follows. In this chapter, you will discover why initial calls are so delicate for families and how to employ best practices to train your staff to handle them more adeptly. You will also find out why a solid First-Call Form is crucial and how to design one that gathers all the necessary information for your firm.

Case Example – The First-Call Without Communication

The first-call personnel arrived at the residence and were confronted by irate family members. "Where have you been? We called you over one hour ago!" they said curtly. Taken aback, the personnel re-read the written instructions on the first-call sheet which said: Delay making transfer for one hour – clergy to anoint deceased at residence – family will notify us. Showing the family the instructions, they became even more irritated, saying that while the instructions were initially correct, they called the funeral home over an hour ago informing them about the change of plans. The deceased would be anointed "later" at the funeral home. The personnel made the transfer, taking the deceased person to the central care and receiving center, not the funeral home. Two hours later, the family arrived at the funeral home unannounced with their clergyperson to anoint their family member. They were informed that their loved one was not at the funeral home, but at the care center, approximately 10 miles away. No one had explained to the family that the deceased person would be taken to a "care center" instead of the funeral home. Learning this, the client family became infuriated.

It is difficult to imagine anything going wrong when you receive a "first-call." Experience, however, tells us differently. In most instances, you probably do not know the person who is calling to inform you of a death. For the caller, it may be the first time they have ever called a funeral home. Most likely, they are experiencing strong emotions and do not know what to expect.

People begin forming their opinions, making judgments and assessing your competency as they speak with you. You will also begin forming your own opinions about the caller. A lot of things can take place during the initial call and many questions can be asked. You will be offering assurance, putting the caller at ease, and obtaining basic information.

Communication experts say that the person who makes the first contact with the family is the "company gatekeeper" and sets the tone for all that follows. The first-call serves as the foundation of the relationship that will evolve between you and the client family and is the initial step by which the funeral director enters a formal, helping relationship. All employees who answer the telephone need to be trained to properly handle the important first call. During depositions and court testimony, it is not unusual to hear from plaintiffs that they felt their initial call to the funeral-cremation provider was not handled well.

Best Practice for Handling First-Calls Professionally and Effectively

- **Be focused** yet sensitive; be pleasant and helpful.
- **Introduce** yourself and, if appropriate, give your title.

- **Find out** who you are talking with and their relationship to the deceased person.
- **Offer** sincere condolences ("I can't even imagine how difficult this must be for you and your family," or "Is there anyone who is especially in need of assistance right now?").
- **Avoid** trite expressions and slang ("I know exactly how you feel," or "In time, you'll get over this." Say "yes" not OK, etc.).
- **Offer** to answer any questions.
- **Eliminate** any distraction or background noise from your work space.
- **Document** the date and time of the call.
- **Explain** that you need to obtain some information in order to help them.
- **Ask** for clarification about anything you do not understand.
- **Be especially clear** about the correct spelling of the name of the deceased as well as the name and relationship of the caller and the person(s) with authority.
- **Obtain** telephone numbers of all appropriate family members or person(s) with authority.
- **Recognize** "red flag" circumstances that may necessitate special handling, such as suicides, violent deaths, deaths of prominent persons, persons with limited English, and so forth.
- **Only make promises** that can be kept. Be especially careful about promises concerning the time of your arrival, or the date or time of viewing or funeral.
- **Confirm** where the deceased person will be taken. If the location is other than the funeral home, inform the family.

The telephone remains the predominant means of obtaining business. The manner in which the call is handled profoundly affects the sequence of events that follows as well as opinions formed by client families or persons notifying you on behalf of the family. This often includes hospice workers, police personnel, nurses, clergy and others.

The time immediately following a death can be disorienting for the client family. They are suddenly confronted with a myriad of details that, for most people, can be overwhelming. All personnel must be trained to realize that the risk of misinformation is elevated at this time. The caller might be anxious. Other than notifying the funeral home of the death, the caller may not know what else needs to be done. Sometimes friends volunteer to make the initial call. They might be able to provide the name of the deceased person, but are often unable to provide additional information or answer routine questions. Frequently, other family members who need to be informed have not yet been notified.

Your role as "funeral director" and "caregiver" comes into play during the first call. You can help put the caller at ease with your calm assurance that things will be taken care of; you can deal with their immediate concerns and questions and help the family establish priorities; you can begin to develop a timeline and assure the caller that your personnel will follow through on the details.

The best funeral-cremation companies understand the importance of communication during the first call. Employees such as part-time aides, maintenance persons or other workers should *not* be authorized to answer company telephones unless they have been trained or it is an emergency. Training specific employees to answer the telephone ensures that incoming calls, especially first calls, are handled proficiently and professionally. Some companies monitor incoming calls and inform callers of this. In some cases, owners "test call" their firms or get other people to do so. To the owner, this form of "quality assurance" helps determine that calls are being answered promptly, courteously and that accurate information is provided while he/she is away from the business.

Some families in legal cases alleging funeral malpractice claim the problems started with the initial telephone call being poorly handled. When handled properly, the initial call serves as a foundation of caring and professional service. Some important things to keep in mind when answering the telephone include:

- Answer in a timely, expeditious manner
- Be aware of your tone of voice
- Speak slowly and clearly
- Do not rush the caller
- Focus on the caller; listen carefully and without interrupting
- Respond with appropriate empathy

One funeral home places a small mirror on an adjustable stand by each telephone. The mirror allows the person answering the telephone (the employee) to see their own face and observe their own expressions while talking. Empathy and attention to the caller are transmitted over the telephone, as are curtness or insensitivity.

Basic Information on a First-Call Form

Whether the first-call "interview" takes place on the telephone or face-to-face, it is vital that your personnel gather thorough and accurate information on the first-call form. The first-call record is more than a piece of paper with random data on it. It is a standard form used throughout funeral-cremation service and contains vital information that is **the basis upon which everything else develops.** The first-call form should be professionally printed and contain the name of the company on it. In one lawsuit, a funeral home was sued because they wrongfully embalmed a person who, as an Orthodox Jew, was opposed to embalming. The same first-call record sheet contained information on one other deceased person. A receptionist interpreted the conflicting information and erroneously believed that authorization to embalm was received for both persons. As a result, the Orthodox Jewish person was wrongfully embalmed.

While what may be considered essential information varies from company to company, routine first-call information usually includes, but is not limited to:

- The name of the person receiving the call and the date and time it was received
- Name, age and sex of deceased
- Location of deceased-place of death
- Date and time of death
- Name, relationship and telephone number of person calling
- Name, relationship and telephone number of the next of kin or person(s) with authority
- Name of attending physician, including telephone number and address
- Date physician last treated the deceased
- Cause and/or manner of death
- If hospice is involved, name and telephone number of hospice
- If coroner is involved, obtain coroner reference number and name of investigator/deputy
- Special requests or needs of person calling or of the client family
- Name of company personnel dispatched. If an outside first call company is used, document the date and time they were notified

Some first call forms contain a section to document whether or not authorization to embalm was given over the telephone. In addition to checking "yes" or "no" to embalming, this section should also contain the name and relationship of the person granting (or declining) authorization, along with the date and time and name of the funeral-cremation representative.

When receiving a first call, embalming can be a particularly sensitive issue. When seeking permission to embalm, some states require a statement to be read to consumers that clarifies the option of embalming. Others require a basic explanation about embalming to be contained on the Embalming Authorization Form and when seeking authorization over the telephone, that a statement be read to client families explaining embalming. Embalming results are usually more favorable when it takes place sooner, not later. Yet, the word "embalming" and asking for authorization over the telephone during a first call can be offensive to some families, especially with an unexpected death. In some instances, the funeral director may decide to delay asking for embalming authorization until later. Several funeral homes as policy, do not immediately ask for authorization to embalm when receiving a first call. Instead, they call the family shortly after the deceased person arrives at the funeral home to discuss embalming. In face-to-face meetings, such as when a family walks in unannounced to notify the funeral home about a death, the embalming issue can be more easily addressed as a normal part of making arrangements.

Documenting Special Requests

Any special requests, especially those considered unusual, should be documented on the first-call form. These can include such diverse things as anatomical donations to be made, autopsy requests, contagious disease circumstances, the possibility of a wrongful death lawsuit against the physician, shipment of the deceased, arrival of out of town family members, special religious or cultural observances, any sense of disagreement among family members and a request for viewing in a private residence.

Upon concluding the arrangement conference, some families request a copy of all documents. This, in and of itself, should not be reason for alarm. In the event of a lawsuit, all of the contents of the deceased person's file will be subpoenaed and the first-call form and what is written on it will be carefully scrutinized by attorneys and expert witnesses. A first-call form that has been thoroughly and proficiently completed by the funeral-cremation provider will create the foundation for a high standard of care and help the firm in the event of litigation.

On the other hand, an incomplete document or one consisting of several pieces of scratch paper can give a different impression. Most funeral directors who have been in funeral-cremation service a long time have documented a first call under unusual circumstances and outside the office: while attending professional sporting event, while exercising at the gym and even while riding a bicycle on country roads. Due to the nature of the business, we cannot control when a first-call comes in or where we may be at the time. When faced with these and other unusual conditions, the information you obtain should be transferred to a first-call document at the earliest opportunity. *However, saving the original paperwork and scratch notes and retaining them in the decedent's file is a **Best Practice**.*

To ensure accuracy of the information contained on the first-call form and prevent wrong information from being transferred to legal documents, review ALL information on the first-call record with the client family during the first interview. There have been cases where first-call personnel were provided with the wrong social security number from hospital records, or a family member inadvertently transposing one of the numbers. **Best Practice** means double-checking the information so you do not have problems later on.

Some Things You Need to Achieve During the First-Call:

- Obtain accurate information
- Instill confidence in your ability to serve
- Transmit a caring, professional attitude
- Help to develop a timeline for what will happen
- Indicate a willingness to answer questions

Some Things to Avoid During the First-Call:

- An image of uncaring and/or indifference to the caller
- Coming across as an amateur
- Improper, unprofessional language or slang
- Sounding overly solicitous
- A flippant attitude and being in a hurry
- Phony sentimentality
- Inattentiveness to the caller
- Unnecessarily putting the caller on hold
- Random promises or incorrect information
- Inappropriate background music, conversations or noises
- Impatience or irritation in answering questions, especially with those seeking price or general information

Using an Outside or Third-Party Transfer Company

When an outside-transfer company is called to remove the deceased person on behalf of the funeral-cremation provider, document the date and time they were called on the first-call record, as well as the name of the company representative you spoke with. If the first-call form is faxed or sent by e-mail to a transfer-service company, attach the fax or e-mail confirmation to the original document. **Best Practice** means following up on the fax or e-mail with a personal telephone call to make sure the information was received. The use of outside-service providers is discussed in depth in Chapters Two and Ten.

Using an Answering Service

Funeral service is highly personal and when client families call a funeral home, they expect to talk to a real person who is skilled in dealing with loss and death situations. When people cannot get through to a real person, or are forced to listen to annoying voice mail messages, this usually adds to their frustration. A person who is not a licensed funeral director but who is well-trained can impart empathy and understanding on the telephone and handle most calls proficiently and professionally. At times there is a love-hate relationship with the telephone in funeral service. It is the fastest and most reliable communication device for obtaining business, but because our business is 24/7, it also means the addition of well-trained employees to handle calls. Even large companies might not have the means to take incoming calls at all times. Small companies may not be able to pay for a secretary to answer telephones. But, every call to a funeral home is important and can represent income.

Even with advanced telecommunication equipment available today, an answering service that specializes in answering telephone calls for funeral homes can be a lifesaver. This service can be provided by an individual person or a commercial company trained to handle incoming calls and messages. I have had experience using both individuals and commercial companies to answer my company telephones at night, on weekends, holidays or when the staff was working a funeral at a cemetery or church. For many years, the wife of a trade embalmer expertly handled all of our evening and weekend calls. Years ago, funeral homes never considered having anyone other than their employees answer the telephones at night or on weekends. Answering service companies were not available

10

to serve funeral homes. Unlike physician, law and accounting offices, it was a market considered not worth pursuing. When I first employed a commercial company to answer my funeral home's telephones, it was a new experience for both of us. At first, they believed telephone calls to the funeral home would be like the calls coming to other business they served. A substantial amount of my time and energy was required to train their personnel to deal with the special needs and considerations of our callers. The company learned that, regardless of the hour, people must never be told that the funeral home is closed or that no one is available to help them. Also, it should be made clear that incoming calls should not be placed on hold, or told to call back in the morning. In addition to basic answering service skills, personnel had to be taught about dealing with people in grief and in a heightened emotional state.

Among other considerations, the funeral director should ask about the staffing requirements of the company. How many people will be available at any given time to answer incoming calls? The expected call volume of the funeral home, as well as the current call volume at the answering service, is very important. It can mean the difference between your calls being answered in a timely manner (one to three rings) or not answered. It can also mean whether or not incoming calls are put on hold or if callers are rushed. How many other businesses is the answering service handling? If calls are being answered for many different businesses and the company is under-staffed, your funeral home might not be properly represented.

Is there a difference between funeral home staff and answering service staff? The answer is YES. **When necessary,** answering service staff should not hesitate to inform callers about this. As professional as the answering service may be, unless the person has many years of funeral service phone answering experience, they cannot be expected to be as knowledgeable as a funeral director or full-time funeral home employee in handling all questions. For example, laws, terminology and procedures in funeral service are very specific. Admitting to the caller, "This is the answering service, but I can have the funeral director call you back immediately," is usually enough to keep things from getting out of hand. In difficult situations, trying to hide this fact from callers can lead to confusion, misunderstanding or a lost call and serves no one's best interest.

Should a funeral director or funeral home representative be "on call" when using an answering service? YES. **Best Practice** dictates that, regardless of the day or time, all first calls, calls considered to be an emergency, or those beyond the scope of the answering service, should be transferred immediately to the on-call funeral director or funeral home representative. The most experienced answering service should have immediate access to a funeral director or funeral home employee.

Is it better to use an answering service that deals only with funeral homes or one that deals with all types of businesses? The nature of funeral service is unlike that of any other business or profession. In most cases, a funeral home will be better served using an industry-specific answering service than one that serves many different businesses. One important consideration, however, has to do with staff turnover rate. The higher the turnover in staff, the more likely you will have new people answering your phones. Rapid turnover means you will be training new people.

For an answering service inexperienced in handling calls for a funeral home, standard training provided by the service to their employees is rarely sufficient. In most instances, the funeral director will be responsible to see that the answering service staff is trained and represents the funeral home properly. Training, even for the answering service that specializes in serving funeral homes, is not a one-time event, but is ongoing. For example, I provided funeral-specific training to the staff of my answering service every month. Their employees welcomed having their questions answered. Those who worked the late night shift wrote out their questions for me.

The funeral home must provide the answering staff with clear records and basic information (times and dates of funeral activities, requests for donations, directions to the funeral home, churches and cemeteries, etc.). In general, the quality of the information that the funeral home receives on each call is in direct proportion to the information printed on the forms that are to be used to record incoming and outgoing calls. With new technology, many answering services record all telephone calls for possible recall. Most funeral homes require the answering service to fax or e-mail a daily log showing all calls received or made that indicates:

- Name of person answering the call

- Date and time of call

- Name and telephone number of person calling the funeral home

- Nature or description of the call

- Result of the call (transferred to the on-call funeral director, wrong number, will call back, etc.)

The people who perform answering service duties must be highly skilled in communicating, proficient in asking questions to ensure clear information is obtained, empathetic and understanding, patient and courteous even under extreme conditions. They must be taught the importance of keeping information confidential. They must also know their limits in providing assistance and when to ask the funeral director for help. They must know what information can and cannot be shared with callers (never give out phone numbers of family members; do not mention the cause or circumstances of death, etc.). They should be instructed to **never** share their personal beliefs with callers (such as cremation versus burial, open casket versus closed casket, funeral versus no funeral, etc.), but should inform callers that the funeral director will answer all of their questions.

Case Example – A Good Laugh and an Unexpected Party

The answering service received the first call at 8:00 p.m. and notified the on-call funeral director. The death occurred at a residence approximately 15 miles away from the funeral home. When the funeral director arrived at the address, it was a vacant lot. While he was checking his map, another funeral home arrived at the same address. In the next 10 minutes, eight more funeral homes arrived on the scene, all with the same first call information and address. All 10 funeral homes responded to the same crank house call. Good natured, even at this hour, they all laughed at how they were tricked. Taking advantage of being together, they drove to a nearby restaurant and ate dessert.

The first call record becomes the foundation upon which all future work is based. The manner in which the first-call is handled will affect the bottom line and reputation of the firm and the relationship you have with the client family. The first-call record is an important document and should be retained on a permanent basis in the decedent's file.

If, for any reason a lawsuit develops, all documents contained in the decedent's file, including the first-call form, will be subpoenaed and carefully scrutinized by the plaintiff attorney and expert witness. Additionally, the staff member who took the first-call information will likely be deposed. Pay attention to who handles these delicate calls. If a person performs poorly in taking the first-call, they will probably also do poorly in deposition. **Do not let a sloppy appearing or incomplete first-call form or untrained staff member work against you.**

CHAPTER 2

Transfer and Identification
of the Decedent

The transfer of a deceased person from the place of death to the funeral-cremation provider's facility—often referred to as the "first call" or "removal"—is widely considered one of the most routine duties of a funeral home. In fact, transfers can be very risky. They can be fraught with mistakes that can lead to lawsuits and costly jury awards or settlements. It is with the transfer that we first see changes in the "chain of custody" of human remains—and those changes are laden with danger, especially when this important task is entrusted to an outside contractor. This chapter will show how poorly planned and executed transfers have led to litigation. Step-by-step best practices are provided for safe transfers, including identification procedures and receipts.

The deceased person must always be transferred from the place of death before providing further care. You may never need to produce detailed accounting of transferring a decedent. However, if the need arises, there is nothing as valuable as documenting **every** step you take when assuming custody of the deceased.

Basic Responsibilities

Whenever a funeral home or cremation service provider is called to serve, it is the responsibility of the transfer personnel to make certain that only the correct body is transferred, whether from a hospital, long-term care facility, residence, retirement center, scene of an accident, another funeral home, coroner's office, common carrier (airport, railroad station, etc.) or another facility or location.

A body in transit is subject to potential hazards, including but not limited to traffic delays, accidents, detours, mechanical breakdowns, fire, theft and even in some cities, car-jacking. **Best Practice** dictates that unnecessary side trips with the decedent in the transfer vehicle should be avoided. Any stop, other than for traffic lights, introduces an increased element of risk. One funeral director was seen visiting a topless bar on his way out of town to conduct a graveside service. He parked the hearse carrying the casket in the parking lot at the bar. Other patrons in the bar talked about this and eventually the family learned of the incident. A lawsuit followed.

Ideally, no more than one body should be transported at a time in any one vehicle. Multiple decedents in one vehicle increase the potential for misidentification. Since outside commercial first-call companies may transport multiple persons, it is important they use strict recordkeeping and tagging procedures for all deceased persons.

Once the body is placed inside the transfer vehicle, it should **never** be left unattended. Though rare, there have been reports of bodies stolen from funeral vehicles and morgues for the purposes of filing fraudulent insurance claims, harvesting organs and body parts and removing property from deceased persons.

The use of outside service providers (commercial first-call companies) to transport decedents is common practice among funeral-cremation providers. However, this practice introduces an additional level of risk for the funeral home. Outside service providers are discussed in Chapter Ten. The service of transporting decedents carries paramount responsibility. The funeral-cremation provider is obligated to ensure that first-call personnel working for outside contractors are competent in executing their duties. **Best Practice** and procedures should be reviewed and approved by funeral home management before hiring the outside company.

Documenting the Transfer

Whether a transfer is made by the funeral-cremation provider's direct employees or by employees of an outside first-call company, detailed records from the beginning of the *chain of custody* can help in your defense in the event of a lawsuit. As **Best Practice**, items to document during a transfer include:

- **The time of departure from one's office or home base location**

- **Time of arrival at the location of the decedent**

- **The manner in which identification was made (toe tags, wrist band, etc.) and signed by a witness**

- **All valuables and personal effects on or with the decedent. Record them on a "receipt for personal property" inventory form signed by a witness**

- **A receipt for the decedent, signed by a family member, caregiver or other qualified representative at the place of death, and by the person making the transfer**

- **The time of departure with the decedent**

- **The time of arrival at the funeral home, crematory, care center, etc.**

In addition, any deviation, detour or untoward event occurring during the transfer should be documented. This might include such things as a required stop at the coroner's office or physician's office or long delays due to a traffic, weather, etc. To repeat: At no time should the deceased person **ever** be left unattended in a funeral vehicle.

Case Example: Sloppy Procedures Leads to Mix-Up

The funeral home employee taking the call was exhausted from the hard work and long hours of the previous days. He hoped to be able to sleep through the night but it was not to be. The call came in at 2:30 a.m. He got dressed and drove to the funeral home to get the first-call vehicle. The deceased was an 80-year-old Asian woman who died at home of cancer. At the residence, the two sons of the deceased assisted the lone funeral home representative in placing the deceased on the transfer gurney and into the funeral vehicle. The employee then met briefly with the family to gather preliminary information. They requested Catholic services, including two days of visitation and authorized embalming. The family asked to postpone coming to the funeral home to make arrangements until the following day. The employee left the residence at 4:00 a.m. Only a block away from the residence, he received a call on his mobile phone from his office notifying him of another first-call, at a residence just a few blocks away from the first residence. Exasperated, the employee drove directly to the second residence. The second decedent also was an elderly Asian woman and a member of the Buddhist faith. With assistance from family members, the employee made the transfer and placed the second decedent in the funeral vehicle, adjacent to the first decedent. As he did with the first family, he met with the second family to obtain some preliminary information. Embalming was not authorized; the person was to be cremated as soon as possible without any ceremonies. While driving back to the funeral home and dreading the long day ahead, the employee stopped for a cup of coffee at a local 24-hour donut shop. He arrived at the funeral home with both decedents at 5:45 a.m. One by one, he brought both decedents into the preparation room. Returning to the van to retrieve the paperwork on both decedents, he met a neighbor who was taking an early morning walk. Acting neighborly, he chatted for several minutes and then returned to the preparation room with the first-call paperwork. Looking at both decedents on their respective gurneys, he became uncertain as to each person's identity. Both gurneys and cot covers were identical. He wondered which person was which? He could not remember which person he brought in to the preparation room first. He could not recall with any certainty which person he placed in the van first and on which side. He uncovered both decedents and visually inspected them, but found no identifying tags or markings to help him. Both decedents were female and of Asian descent. Both decedents died from cancer and happened to be bald. The employee tried to recall his actions and the events of the early morning. To the best of his ability, he determined who he thought was whom and attached a funeral home identification tag around each decedent's toe. The Buddhist family that requested cremation as soon as possible made arrangements later that morning. Not wanting to make funeral arrangements that same day, the Catholic family came in a day later and arranged for visitation, a vigil and a funeral mass. At the visitation, now the third day following the transfer of the decedents, the Catholic family discovered that the person in the casket was not their mother. The funeral home employee who made both transfers and became confused had incorrectly tagged the decedents at the funeral home. The Catholic who was to be buried was wrongfully cremated and the Buddhist who declined embalming was wrongfully embalmed, dressed, cosmetized and placed in a casket for viewing.

In this case, the funeral home representative committed many errors, starting with his arrival at the first residence, and failed to follow proper procedures when making the transfers. As a result, a sequence of tragic events unfolded. Regrettably, this funeral home learned some hard lessons that proved to be financially costly and extremely damaging to their reputation.

Best Practice Guidelines for Transfers

What steps can be taken to ensure that something like this never happens to you? Employing **Best Practice** reduces the potential for misidentification anytime you take custody of a deceased person or transfer custody. In addition to having policies and procedures written down, **all** staff members who are involved in the transfer of decedents must be trained. That training must be documented in personnel files and training procedures should be reviewed by management at least annually. Training is not only for an apprentice, but for everyone who may be involved in transferring decedents, including employees of outside transfer (first-call) companies who may be hired (even occasionally) to act on your behalf. It should also be on-going, not just a one-time event.

All that takes place during the transfer process should be recorded on a first-call record or similar document, thus providing a written history or "trail of documentation." This trail demonstrates a level of professionalism and will serve as valuable documentation in the event of questions or a lawsuit. The trail begins by recording the time the call was received and the name of the person receiving the call. **Best Practice includes:**

- **Responding personnel should document** the time of departure from the funeral home or other location, the time of arrival at the location of the decedent and the time they return to the funeral-cremation facility with the decedent.

- **If death occurs in a hospital or other institution,** it is important to be on record with the institution. Be sure to sign the institution's release book—a log or record book often kept in the admitting or nursing office and sometimes in the morgue that contains the names of deceased patients. Even though this log remains with the institution, it provides an important timeline that can be referenced in the event of any disparity. If a log or release book is not used in hospitals or nursing homes in your area, suggest to administration that they use one. Recordkeeping of this nature helps protect all parties.

- *Before* **moving the person** onto your transfer cot, always confirm and re-confirm the name that is on your first-call form.

- *Before* **moving the person** onto your transfer cot check ALL tags that may be attached to the deceased. Check for wrist tags, toe tags or adhesive labels or other markings that may be affixed to the exterior of wrappings. ALL names must match and be legible.

- *When there are multiple tags on the deceased person,* double-check to make sure that the same first and last names appear on all tags and that they are spelled the same way. Nothing can be taken for granted. Transfer personnel may need to unwrap the person and inspect the body for other tags before moving it.

- *Before* **moving the person,** the funeral-cremation provider or transfer company should attach their own tag to the deceased person - even when other tags are already attached (such as a hospital wrist band or coroner toe tag). The funeral-cremation provider's tag or transfer company's tag is customarily attached around the person's ankle. Only use tags that cannot slip off or be removed unless they are cut off. The best tags are constructed of a permanent material that is waterproof and resistant to the effects of body fluids and embalming fluids. **Do not use tags made of paper.** A "fastening" or "locking" system that goes around the ankle is preferred to a "tying" system around a toe. Permanent tags are invaluable in preventing misidentification and in providing a long-term form of identification during prolonged sheltering, storage or shipment of the deceased person, and especially in the event of disasters such as floods, earthquake and fire.

- **The tag should remain attached to the body at all times,** whether the person will be cremated, buried, entombed or shipped. When it becomes known that the deceased will be cremated, a second tag, often the color red, should be attached to the deceased. See Chapter Eleven for further details.

- *Before* **moving the person to the transfer cot,** inspect the body for any valuables or personal property. Complete a "Personal Property Receipt" for each transfer. Ask for a witness to be present during your inspection. It is just as critical to document "no property on or with the body" as when there is property. Ask the witness to sign the personal property receipt; keep the receipt in the decedent's file.

- **Only under extreme circumstances** should more than one deceased person be transferred in the same vehicle at the same time. Extreme caution must be exercised to prevent misidentification. **Each person must be individually tagged before being placed in the transfer vehicle** using the tag of the funeral-cremation provider or transfer company in addition to any other tags that may be present. Once the person is inside the transfer vehicle, drive directly to the funeral home, care facility or final destination.

- **Document** the day and time of arrival at the funeral home, care facility or other destination.

- **Record** where the deceased person was placed (on the embalming table, in refrigeration storage, etc).

IMPORTANT NOTE:

Attaching your tag to the deceased *does not* **unmistakably verify or authenticate the identity of the deceased unless it is attached in the presence of the client family or their representative.** There is a significant and all-important difference between attaching a tag for purposes of preventing a "mix up" and formally verifying the identity. Only the next of kin or their designated representative can perform formal identification. Verifying identity is thoroughly covered in Chapter Five.

Learning from Hospitals

As a standard of care, hospitals and other inpatient facilities attach an identification bracelet around the wrist of each patient at the time of admission. The wrist band serves as one form of identification to prevent a mix-up of patients. In addition to asking the patient for his/her name, the wrist band is checked and double-checked by hospital personnel before any procedure is performed, before delivering food or administering medication to a patient.

Funeral-cremation providers cannot ask the deceased for their names, but for identification issues, should copy similar steps of diligence as practiced by hospitals. It is just as important for funeral-cremation providers to be certain about the identity of decedents in their custody to prevent misidentification.

Universal Identification System - A System to Consider

The Universal Identification System (UIS) is the first tagging system especially for funeral-cremation service. Created by Innovative Supply, Inc. of St. Paul, Minnesota, it is much more than another band. It incorporates a permanent ankle bracelet with a (non-repeating) six-digit number embossed into it. Each number is assigned to only one bracelet and will never be duplicated. The band, constructed of high quality stainless steel and titanium, withstands the extreme temperatures of cremation and is not affected by body fluids or the strongest embalming chemicals. The band is designed to prevent mix-up of decedents, reduce the likelihood of misidentification and provide a permanent tagging and number system that can be referenced to ensure identity. The band should be placed around the ankle of the deceased by funeral-first call personnel before the body is moved onto the transfer cot. A self-locking attachment on the bracelet means that once the band is in place, it cannot be removed unless it is cut off. For persons who will be cremated, the specially-numbered tag is collected along with the cremated remains and placed inside the cremated-remains container. (This tag is in addition to the metal disc supplied by the crematory.) In my opinion, the UIS is the best tagging system on the market presently available to funeral-cremation service.

Case Example: A Transfer Done Incorrectly

In a recent lawsuit, both the medical center and funeral home were taken to task. The medical center was accused of releasing the wrong decedent to the funeral home. The funeral home employee who made the transfer from the medical center admitted that he took the word of the morgue supervisor as to the identity of the deceased; he did not check the name of the decedent on the hospital tag before moving the body. As a result, the funeral home transferred the wrong body. Unfortunately, the funeral home did not have a policy requiring verification of identity and cremated the wrong person. The defense for the funeral home was based on the fact that the funeral home did nothing wrong; that the hospital and hospital alone was at fault in that they gave the wrong person to the funeral home. The jury ruled against both the medical center and the funeral home, but placed the majority of the wrongdoing on the funeral home. The court ruled that the funeral home was last in the chain of custody and, as a result, was the last entity that could have corrected the misidentification but failed to do so. By failing to check the tags on the decedent and failing to verify the identity (before cremating the person), the funeral home committed the majority of wrongdoing.

When accepting a deceased person from any source, the funeral-cremation provider cannot take the word of someone else (nurse, physician, coroner, morgue attendant, clergy, etc.) as to the identity of a decedent. Transfer personnel are responsible for checking and double-checking all tags that may be on the body. **Making sure that you transfer only the correct person is too serious a matter to ever be determined by hearsay.** The importance of proper transfer procedures and checking the name on all tags can be **measured in the damages awarded against the funeral home** by a court or jury failure to tag, for mistagging and for failing to verify the identity of the deceased that results in misidentification.

Case Example: A Transfer Done Right

Two patients in the same long-term-care facility and in nearby rooms died within minutes of one another. In the course of preparing them for transfer, a nurse who was already over-burdened and pressured inadvertently attached wrong tags on the toes of the decedents. The funeral home employee, however, followed safe practice policies. Before moving the decedent, he checked the name written on his first-call sheet with the wrist band and toe tag on the body. He immediately noticed that the names on the tags did not match. He called the nursing supervisor and the potentially damaging error was corrected.

In my personal experience at a large medical center, the decedent was the only person at the time in the morgue. The deceased was neatly wrapped in a sheet. On the exterior of the sheet was a piece of adhesive tape with the name of the deceased written on it. Unwrapping the sheet to check the body, there was no hospital wrist band or other tags on the body. I questioned this. The morgue attendant assured me that this was the correct person. "After all," he said, "this is the only person in the morgue." Politely, I told the attendant that without a hospital wrist band or toe tag containing the name of this person, I could not accept custody. At my insistence, this matter was immediately reported to the nursing office. A nurse who personally knew the decedent and had cared for him while he was in the hospital came to the morgue. Witnessed by a supervisor from the nursing office, a hospital wrist band was attached to the deceased person. As added protection, I asked them to document this occurrence on hospital letterhead and to have the paperwork signed by both nurses, the morgue attendant and myself. I was furnished with a copy of the report for the deceased's file. Upon arriving at the funeral home with the deceased person, I called and informed the family of what happened at the hospital. Before proceeding further, I required a family member to come to the funeral home and verify the identity of the person that was in my custody. Following **Best Practice** in this situation prevented a potential serious problem for the medical center and me.

Outside and Third-Party Companies

Whenever you hire a commercial first-call company, you introduce an added level of risk. Just because you use an outside provider does not mean your firm has any less of an obligation to ensure the transfer takes place without incident. The funeral-cremation provider may not always know the person who will make the transfer but is nonetheless responsible that they properly execute their duties.

Good business sense suggests having a written contract between the funeral home and the outside transfer company. Among other things, the contract should outline specific duties and responsibilities, list specific procedures to be followed and outline the expectations of each party. Contracts as well as policy-and-procedure manuals should be reviewed and updated annually.

In my personal experience, many employees of commercial transfer companies view first-calls as a part-time job. They might lack the same level of dedication and training as that of full-time, career-oriented employees at a funeral home. Owners, anxious to hire, can overlook performing background checks or inspecting driving records. Attire and personal grooming habits can be ignored. They might not be as fully trained as they need to be and might be unaware of the sensitive and serious nature of this work.

It is essential that the outside transfer company agree to tag each person they transfer, whether they use the funeral home's provided tag or a generic tag. The tagging system should be reviewed by the funeral-cremation provider to make certain it meets appropriate standards. In cases when the transfer company is hired to provide this service on an on-going basis, the funeral home usually supplies the transfer company with their own tags, to be used whenever they represent that funeral home.

In addition to tagging procedures, the funeral-cremation company should not hesitate to establish appropriate attire standards for the outside provider's employees when representing that firm.

When choosing a transfer-service company, price is often a determining factor. In the long run, choosing the lowest priced company or service to represent you does not always represent the best value. Additional information concerning outside contractors is discussed in Chapter Ten.

Today, fewer American deaths occur in residences than in decades past; more take place in medical institutions. Hospitals continue to grow in size and struggle with budgeting, staff turnover, non-English-speaking or-reading employees, training issues and other human-resources issues. These challenges (and deficiencies) can also affect funeral service. The funeral-cremation provider cannot take anything for granted when making a transfer, even from the most prestigious institution. The demands made upon medical and convalescent centers can mean that several different staff persons become involved when a death occurs and in handling decedents. As some funeral-cremation providers have experienced, this results in improper tagging of decedents and misidentification before the funeral home becomes involved. This alone is reason enough to cause the funeral-cremation provider and transfer company to employ **Best Practices** and be diligent in adopting strict tagging procedures each and every time a removal is made.

Deaths Involving Hospice

The number of deaths among patients under hospice care continues to increase. According to the National Hospice & Palliative Care Organization, in 2005 more than 800,000 Americans died under the care of hospice. Seventy-six percent of these deaths occurred at a private residence. According to the NHPCO, there were 586,000 residential deaths in the United States in 2004.

There is a special relationship between funeral service and hospice. Many funeral directors serve on the boards of directors or advisory staff of local hospice organizations and provide training and education to the professional and volunteer staff. In my experience, family members whose loved ones are under hospice care want to participate during the transfer process. It is not unusual for family members to remove medical devices from their loved one, offer to help wrap the deceased person, help lift and place the person onto the transfer cot and even escort the transfer vehicle to the funeral home. Some families can be concerned with details that funeral-transfer personnel might not consider, such as covering the face of the deceased person during a transfer from the residence.

It is important that transfer personnel not act hurriedly. Avoid quickly moving the deceased person onto the gurney and/or placing the person in a pouch and zipping it up. Meet with the client family and inform them as to how you make the transfer before performing it.

The local hospice organizations I was involved with appreciated learning about the tagging methods and **Best Practice** steps we employed. It provided assurance that their patients would not be misidentified. It served as another means of differentiating my services from other companies. In all of my years, I cannot recall one instance when a family member or hospice personnel refused to sign my funeral home's form confirming that an ankle tag was attached to the deceased person. The high standards of care we exercised contributed to a stronger working relationship between my funeral home and the local hospice organizations and provided added peace of mind to the client family.

Transfer and Decedent Receipt

Every step in the chain of custody while handling decedents must be documented. Just as a first-call form is used to gather initial information when you are notified of a death, **Best Practice** requires a receipt for the deceased person be obtained by the funeral-cremation provider when custody is assumed and the transfer is about to be made.

A Decedent Receipt Form should contain the following information:

- Name of the deceased person

- Name and address of the funeral-cremation provider or crematory

- Name of funeral-cremation provider's first-call representative(s) making the transfer

- Name of facility or location from which the deceased person is being removed

- Date and time of the transfer

- A statement indicating the location as to where the deceased person will be taken (funeral home, crematory, care center, etc.)

- Signature of witness (next of kin or family representative, nurse, morgue attendant or other qualified person)

- Signature of funeral-cremation provider's first-call representative(s)

Once a deceased person is in your custody and any subsequent transfers are required, (even on a temporary basis to the coroner's office, medical institution for an autopsy, tissue procurement, embalming or refrigeration center, etc.) **Best Practice** means the transfer must be documented with **another** receipt, in each case, signed by the person relinquishing and the party accepting control of the deceased person. It is important to maintain an historical record of every change in the chain of custody.

At some funeral homes, the task of transferring a deceased person is often delegated to the employee with the least amount of experience and often without adequate training or supervision. This is just asking for trouble. It can be an injustice to the inexperienced or new employee, also. The best employees once started at the "bottom of the rung" and at one time, all of us were inexperienced. Like a seed planted in the ground, inexperienced employees need nurturing, watering and feeding. They must be **instructed** as to what procedures to follow and **trained** to know the mechanics of the job. Their actions must also be **monitored.** As early as my pre-teen years I assisted my father with transfers. He taught me this was serious business and a solemn occasion, never to be taken casually. To him, each first-call was an opportunity to further build his business and another way to differentiate his service from that of others. His lessons are as true today as they were decades ago.

Transferring a decedent is much more than just a reflexive exercise of moving a deceased person from Point A to Point B, performed in a casual manner by just anyone and without documentation. **When Best Practice procedures are in place and all personnel are instructed and trained in following them, everyone's best interests are served. Every time.**

CHAPTER 3

Arrival of Deceased
at the Funeral Home

The arrival of the deceased person at the funeral home or cremation facility is another seemingly routine event; in fact, it is one of the most critical changes in the "custody of care" of deceased persons, and one that significantly affects a timeline for all that follows. When that arrival is accompanied by a timely, well-documented "in-processing" regimen, the provider can do much to bolster the quality of care and defend criticisms and queries that might later arise. But delays and poorly documented processes at the arrival stage can lead to costly mishaps for the funeral-cremation provider. In this chapter, you will discover best practices and how to avoid such problems, ensuring that every deceased person is treated with respect and appropriate oversight from the moment he/she arrives at your facility.

The simple but important act of documenting the arrival of a decedent at the funeral home, crematory facility or care center can easily be treated as routine. But, when you understand the full nature of being entrusted with and accountable for a loved one in your care, you realize there is nothing routine about it to the client family. For them, the death and all that follows are emotional, extraordinary events. They expect your firm to be deliberate, proficient and accountable in the care you provide. Being accountable means documenting **every** step you take, including the time of arrival at the funeral home, cremation facility or care center. It is the next crucial step in the chain of custody after the properly performed (and documented) transfer of the deceased person from the place of death.

When questions arise or a problem develops, the sequence and timing of events and checklists are always important. The more complete and thorough the records are, including timelines, the better it is for everyone. While seemingly unimportant to some people, timelines are important in litigation. Attorneys are trained to carefully scrutinize timeline records concerning all contact between the deceased and the funeral-cremation provider. The more detail contained in the file, the better the chance for a strong defense. Less detail generally means more vulnerability and can begin a series of other potentially damaging questions. Inadequate or incomplete records will be used to demonstrate such things as sloppiness, casual attitude, impersonal treatment, inattentiveness or other claims of poor care.

Case Example: Unhelpful Attendant Leads to Six-Figure Verdict

The owner of the funeral home was testifying on the witness stand. He was charged with negligent care by unnecessarily delaying embalming for two days, which led to the body purging during visitation and soiling the decedent's clothing and casket interior. The lawsuit alleged that during visitation, flies hovered around the face and hands of the deceased person and a foul odor emanated from the body. When informed by the family, the visitation attendant told the family that he was not an embalmer, did not know what could be done and that he was the only one on duty. The attendant made no attempt to notify the owner or the embalmer of the funeral home. The family took it upon themselves to purchase deodorizing spray, insect repellant and cotton and plastic from a local grocery store which they used on the deceased person. During cross examination, plaintiff's attorney asked the funeral home owner to provide a step-by-step timeline of events, from the time of the first-call, to the transfer from the hospital, arrival at the funeral home, the start of embalming, and the start of viewing - three days after the death occurred. The funeral director could not recall the timing of these events, and no such details were contained in the file. To emphasize his point, plaintiff's attorney asked the funeral director a series of questions to which the funeral director could only (embarrassingly) answer, "I do not recall":

- What was the exact time you were notified about the death?

- What time did you leave the funeral home to make the transfer?

- What time did you arrive at the hospital to make the transfer?

- What time did you arrive back at your funeral home with the decedent?

- What was the condition of the body upon its arrival at your funeral home?

- Where did you place the decedent upon arrival at your funeral home?

- What day and exact time did you call the embalmer?

- You received verbal authorization to embalm during the first call but you testified that the decedent was not embalmed until two days after arriving at your facility. Why was embalming delayed?

- What care did you render to the body before it was embalmed?

- Under what conditions did you store the deceased person?

- Describe the embalming procedure that was performed on this person.

- Where is the embalming-care report?

To the dismay of the funeral home owner and the defense attorney, plaintiff's attorney succeeded in turning these seemingly minor details into major points of contention. The jury interpreted the lack of documentation and delayed embalming as unprofessional and negligent treatment of the decedent. Routine and simple questions could not be answered with any detail by the funeral director-owner. With every, "I do not recall," the jury's sympathy toward the bereaved family increased. The verdict found against the funeral home and the family was awarded damages in the high six figures. The judge also made a point of telling the funeral director that the lack of documentation by anyone who considers himself/herself a professional is abhorrent and inexcusable behavior.

Steps to Take Upon Arrival

When the body of a decedent arrives at the funeral home, crematory or care center, **Best Practice** dictates that first call personnel should document the following information on a "Decedent Arrival" Form:

- **The time and date of arrival** at the funeral-cremation or care facility

- **The name(s) of the person(s) making the delivery** and name of their employer, if an outside firm handled the transfer

- **Valuables and personal items on or with the body.** (These must be inventoried and kept in a secure place)

- **Where the decedent was placed,** such as on an embalming table, in refrigeration storage, etc.

- **If embalming is to be performed, the name of the person notifying the embalmer,** along with the day and time of the call to the embalmer

My experiences as an expert witness inspecting a decedent's file too often confirms inadequate documentation as to how the deceased was handled. Funeral service is a proud profession and most practitioners take pride in rendering a high level of professional care. However, when each step along the way is not documented, it becomes one person's word against another. Adding to one's vulnerability, most lawsuits occur several months after serving a family. Without facts written down, it can be impossible to remember the details months later.

Some people in funeral-cremation service resist and object to detailed record-keeping. Granted, it is a learned skill; when employed, it becomes your ally in the event of questions or if a problem arises. A file lacking in such documentation increases your vulnerability and undermines your defense.

Contrary to the popular book, *Don't Sweat the Small Stuff*, written by Richard Carlson, Ph.D. in 1997, funeral-cremation providers must concentrate even on the small details. There is no small stuff when serving bereaved people and having custody of their loved one. For sure, there is no such thing as small stuff during litigation. The **Best Practice** conforms with using documentation. The peace of mind of the client is best preserved when how their family member was treated is proven by documentary evidence.

CHAPTER 4

The Arrangement Conference

There is nothing routine about the arrangement conference, even when the family making arrangements is known to the funeral arranger. Every arrangement conference is different, unique and tests the ability of the arranger and the client to communicate clearly across a wide range of subjects. The atmosphere might be charged or relaxed, but at no time can the arranger presume to know what the client family wants or understands. One of the common complicating factors in the conference is the reluctance of the survivor to admit that he or she does not understand what is meant by certain words, terms and phrases. Therefore, the arranger must be especially skilled and sensitive in not assuming that he/ she has communicated effectively just because the survivor nods or says, "Yes." The heart of a successful arrangement conference is communication, and the onus for excellence is on the funeral arranger, not on the bereaved client. Among the other important issues to be resolved are: Determining the person or persons with authority, establishing informed consent procedures and services to be provided, how much information is considered adequate, as well as dealing with common-law relationships and multiple disagreeing parties. A number of forms concerning disclosure, authorization, release and receipt are highlighted that enable the reader to gain a sense of what it takes to develop Best Practice procedures during the arrangement conference.

Why the Arrangement Conference Must be Professionally Conducted

Along with possibly meeting the family at the time of transferring the deceased, the arrangement conference is the first in-depth, face-to-face meeting between the arranger and the client family. During the arrangement conference, the client family receives information about funeral-burial-cremation planning and obtains answers to their questions and concerns.

In a short period of time, many decisions will be made, much planning will occur and much information will be shared. Few people are aware of the many details that must be dealt with. Also, the family might be under the impression that whatever needs to be done is uncomplicated and should not take much time. Even when only minimum service is requested, the arrangement conference can be filled with apprehension on the part of the client family, which in turn complicates the communication and planning process for the most experienced arranger. All staff members who come in contact with client families should acquaint themselves with the guidelines and recommendations contained in this chapter.

While a poorly conducted arrangement conference by itself may not be reason alone for a lawsuit, it can set the stage for dissatisfaction that can contribute to anger and confrontation. **Best Practice** requires effective communication. The model for attaining the best possible results depends on a two-way method of ensuring that communication was *sent, received, and understood.* The sender of the message (the funeral arranger in this instance) communicates to the receiver (the client family) information important for the receiver to know to make informed decisions. But unless the arranger employs an active method of verifying that the message was received and understood, it cannot be established that the client family heard the message.

For example, if the arranger tells the client that it is important for him to establish which person has authority to decide the manner and means of how to dispose of the deceased person, and is told by the client that he/she is the one, does that complete all that is necessary for the arranger? **Best Practice** dictates communication has not actually occurred, as there was no verification of the receipt of what was communicated, nor recognition of understanding of the message. The arrangement conference is often charged with emotions of client families who might not have heard important information due to their own emotional turmoil; issues they had with the deceased person; issues created by the deceased person who may have had specific verbal instructions to the client about the deceased person's own arrangements being strictly complied with, and more. The situation is not always ideal for communication. But it is the obligation of the arranger to ensure that the client understood what the options were to select from when the final choice was made and the agreement signed. The standard of care is for the arranger to use care and discretion discerning the needs of the client family.

The best arrangers take pride in being good communicators, skilled listeners who know the value of building rapport and making sure the conference starts off right. They know that dealing with people who have experienced a loss demands clear communication. They must use unambiguous language and allow adequate time for people to express their views and opinions. At the same time, they must provide direction for all that will take place.

A few years ago, a research study conducted by a medical-specialty group pointed to a lesson that should be learned by funeral-cremation providers. The medical study found that, on the first visit with a patient, the physician, within 15 seconds of asking what the problem is, interrupted the patient, not allowing him/her to even finish the thought. One can only wonder just what specific complaints and conditions were not diagnosed by the physician, only because the opportunity to listen was terminated by the interjection of the physician's own comments.

Best Practice to help the conference proceed smoothly includes:

- **Take time** to become acquainted with the client family. Learn about their relationship to the deceased person. (Do not jump right in with the business aspects)

- **Take a leadership role** and be an active participant who helps the family uncover needs and wants. (Be more than just an order-taker)

- **Be forthcoming** about all services, choices, alternatives and costs, especially complying with General Price List requirements

- **Share an outline** of the items to be covered early in the conference

The Value of Sharing an Agenda

It is safe to assume that most people are inexperienced in making funeral, burial or cremation arrangements. Other than disposition of the body, most people are oblivious to all that must be discussed and decided.

After becoming familiar with the client family, the arranger should share an agenda early on. It is an important step that helps the arrangement conference flow smoothly. For the client family, knowing what will take place helps relieve anxiety, demonstrates you are organized, and maximizes the opportunity for the client to "hear" and understand the message. The benefit for the arranger is that having complied with best practices lessens the chance for misunderstanding and potential complaints or claims.

You might say to the client family, "Thank you for sharing personal information with me. I want to begin making the arrangements you want. In the time we are together we will discuss:

- The legal documents, including the death certificate

- The services that we make available

- How you would like to say goodbye and the ceremonies you want

- The casket (or container), that you will select, for your (father, mother, uncle, aunt, etc.)

• Details at the cemetery (or crematory) or other plans you may have for disposition."

Successful professionals, especially those who provide personal services, know the importance of sharing an agenda with their clients. Everyone likes to know what will happen and what will take place. When dealing with loss situations, if people are kept in the dark or information is not forthcoming, they will often feel more stressed. **Do not assume that client families know what will take place.** People respond more favorably when they know what will happen. Some funeral homes provide client families with a pre-printed agenda that covers major items of discussion. For a personal service professional, not sharing an agenda can be viewed as amateurish.

The arrangement conference can be emotionally charged and families might be hypersensitive. Any mistake, no matter how innocent, can begin distorting and confounding communication. It will be difficult to recover from even the slightest hint of incompetence. Referring to the deceased by the wrong name, pronunciation errors, referring to the sister of the deceased as the daughter, discussing burial when cremation is selected and allowing outside distractions to interfere with the conference are all things that can negatively affect the atmosphere.

This can progress into what is known as the cascade effect, wherein dissatisfaction mounts on the part of the client family at the apparent incompetence of the arranger. Soon, nothing is going smoothly and frustrations build. When there is no bond between arranger and client family, the arrangement conference degenerates into an ordeal to get through instead of a positive, relationship-building experience.

The funeral director wears several hats during the course of serving a family. During the arrangement conference, he or she is both a businessperson and a professional caregiver and must balance both roles. As business people, you must exchange information concerning the General Price List, discuss financial matters and obtain legally required information. The professional side means being sensitive to feelings, listening carefully, treating all information (cause of death, finances, etc.) confidentially and creating an environment for the expression of emotions. The funeral arranger cannot act merely as a passive, disinterested gatherer of information. The arrangement conference is a time for becoming acquainted, for putting people at ease, as well as for answering questions and presenting choices and alternatives. Moreover, a skilled arranger asks about the expectations of their client and does not hesitate to disclose potential complications or problems that he/she may see ahead of time.

Best Practice in Determining the Person(s) with Authority

Due to the importance of this subject, determining the next of kin is also discussed in Chapter Eleven.

In all cases, it is vital that the arranger identify the person(s) who has the legal right to control disposition.

As this book was written, many state legislatures were in the process of redefining their laws concerning primacy and who has authority to control disposition. Because we see many relationships that can only be defined as entangled, determining who the next of kin is or who has the authority to act can be difficult. To underscore this point, there are two such cases prominently featured in the news that have resulted in lengthy court battles: James Brown, the singer, and model Anna Nicole Smith. Of possible benefit is that the general public is now more aware of the complexities in determining who can control disposition.

In some cases, the next of kin might not be the person who has the legal right to control disposition. It is not uncommon to deal with decedents who have a history of multiple marriages and divorces. Also, there may be extended family members, "significant other" partners, alternative living situations and some people may not know what the words, "next of kin" mean. Well-intentioned friends may want to step in, oblivious to legal requirements and the (personal) decisions that must be made. If the arranger is passive about this critical requirement and begins making funeral-burial-cremation arrangements only to discover that he/she is not dealing with the person(s) with authority, a difficult situation can develop. Determining who has the authority to make legal decisions regarding embalming, burial and cremation can challenge the court system.

Regardless, **Best Practice** dictates:

During all phases and on all issues, the funeral arranger may act only after receiving authorization to do so from the person(s) with the legal right to control disposition of the deceased.

Approximately 45 of the 50 states, plus the District of Columbia, have written laws establishing an order for determining the next of kin and/or primacy. Some states have defined funeral-cremation or disposition laws that define this order. Primacy can also be contained in statutes governing wills, probate codes or laws of descent and distribution.

Best Practice requires that:

Each funeral/cremation provider and arranger be knowledgeable of the law in his/her state for determining next of kin.

Confrontation and ill feelings can develop when members of the family who are not the next of kin or well-meaning friends step in. Unaware of any order, they believe they or any family member can make funeral decisions. When informed otherwise, they can become offended and accuse the arranger of making things more difficult for the bereaved family. It can be helpful to have a copy of the state statute in every arrangement office and when questions come up, review them with everyone present.

Each state determines their order and may vary from the general order that follows in establishing next of kin:

- Self, through a legally completed preneed directive, where recognized by law

- The deceased person's representative in a legally prepared Health Care or Advanced Health Care Directive, where recognized by law

- Surviving spouse of the deceased or registered domestic partner (where permitted by law)

- Surviving children of the deceased

- Surviving parents of the deceased

- Surviving siblings of the deceased

- Adult person in next degree of kinship in order named by law

With more frequency, arrangers are being presented with a Power of Attorney by a client, representing they have the authority to make the decisions concerning disposition of the deceased person.

Power of Attorney

When making arrangements for disposition with a person who is named Power of Attorney (POA) or Durable Power of Attorney (DPOA), the arranger must act legally and exercise diligence and care.

It is critical to know if your state law has a mechanism for an **individual to appoint an agent to make disposition arrangements and what form the instrument for appointment must be.**

Three key considerations include:

1. Does your state recognize Power of Attorney authorization?

2. Does the Power of Attorney document include disposition rights?

3. What instructions by the deceased person are contained in the document for disposition?

What is a Power of Attorney?

Power of Attorney is a legal document by which one person (called the "principal") gives legal authority to another person (called the "agent" or "attorney-in-fact") to act on behalf of the principal.

Adding the word, "Durable" to Power of Attorney (Durable Power of Attorney) means that the authority to act on behalf of the principal continues to be in effect in the event the principal becomes incapacitated, but usually ends upon death unless the state allows it to continue with limited purposes that may include handling disposition of the body. Many states have specific statutory forms and witnessing requirements that must be used as a part of the Durable Power of Attorney in order for it to include disposition of the body.

At present, 23 states allow an individual (principal) to appoint an agent to carry out the disposition of the body: California, Connecticut, Delaware, District of Columbia, Idaho, Illinois, Iowa, Kansas, Maine, Michigan, Minnesota, Missouri, Nebraska, Nevada, New Hampshire, New Jersey, Ohio, Oklahoma, Rhode Island, South Carolina, Texas, and Utah and Virginia. **Be advised:** Laws continually change and might have changed since publication of this book. You must be familiar with the laws in your state.

In some states where disposition rights are permitted and contained in the Power of Attorney document, it might also give the agent, who might not be the next of kin or a blood relative, the right to control disposition. In all states, except Connecticut, this right even overrides the authority of a surviving next of kin, including a surviving spouse. This means that a surviving spouse does not have the authority or legal right to control disposition but such authority rests with the designated agent **providing that the instrument of appointing the agent complies with state laws.** The funeral arranger should ask to review the original Power of Attorney document to make sure instructions for disposition are contained in the DPOA document and the document complies with state law requirements. Make a copy of the sections of the document that apply.

Best Practice requires that, due to evolving laws, those interested in learning more about Power of Attorney should check with their individual state funeral association or attorney.

Whenever there is doubt as to who has the legal right to control disposition, the funeral-cremation provider must halt further action until the matter is clarified. In instances when you are dealing with a person who has DPOA, you must be aware there may be others with a superior right or claim, and you need to look beyond the DPOA and inquire as to whether or not other blood relatives exist. To help you determine the next of kin or person(s) with authority, there are many resources available such as the courts, an attorney, your state funeral-cremation association, State Board or coroner's offices. A funeral-cremation provider must follow all laws in determining who has the legal right to control disposition in his/her state.

Case Example: What would you do?

1. Prior to his death, the deceased (principal) named a close friend as his agent in his DPOA.

2. Among other instructions contained in the DPOA, it states that the agent designated in the DPOA, shall arrange for disposition and may, at his discretion, authorize an autopsy examination of the remains.

3. The deceased person has other immediate family members who otherwise would be considered the deceased person's next of kin.

4. In the arrangement conference, the DPOA requests that the deceased person be cremated.

5. Cremation is in direct opposition to the wishes of the surviving family members.

How should the funeral arranger proceed? A suggested **Best Practice** to employ would be:

1. Explain to the agent that cremation is final and irreversible, and

2. That while instructions contained in the DPOA allow for disposition, they do not specifically mention cremation.

3. Decline to perform cremation unless the DPOA agent obtains a court order for cremation.

Many arrangers have experienced instances where the person making the arrangements claims to be the spouse but in truth, is not the spouse. They can claim to be the only child, or someone else. Some states have statutes protecting funeral-cremation providers from liability in cases of false representations made by others. During the arrangement conference, alert and experienced arrangers often sense that something is not right. All practitioners must abide by the primacy laws in their state. These laws are explicit and even when you do not have an indication that something is wrong, it is prudent to ask probing, personal questions to ensure you are dealing with the person with the legal right. The following questions might be helpful to ask during the conference:

• How long have you been married? When did you get married?

• How did you celebrate your last wedding anniversary?

• How many children do you have? What are their ages?

• Who are the other family members?

• Who are the other decision makers?

Questions like these are not foolproof. I have asked them myself only to be surprised by the response. I have heard responses like:

- "Well, we are not exactly married but after living together for 30 years, we might as well be"
- "We never officially tied the knot"
- "I am just like a son and the family wants me to take care of everything"

Best Practice requires your full attention and discernment to determine whether to pursue follow-up questions if your inquiries are answered with hesitation or evasively. You must ask for clarification.

Common Law Relationships

Common law relationships do not determine next of kin. Less than one-third of states recognize "common law" relationships. As a result, "surviving partners" or "significant others" are not automatically the next of kin. According to the Legal Information Institute and the book, *Living Together: A Legal Guide for Unmarried Couples,* by Toni Ihara, Ralph Warner and Frederick Hertz, the following states currently recognize common-law relationships:

Alabama	Ohio (if before 1991)
Colorado	Oklahoma (if before 1998)
Georgia *(if created before 1997)*	Pennsylvania (if before 2003)
Idaho *(if created before 1996)*	Rhode Island
Kansas	South Carolina
Montana	Texas
New Hampshire	Utah
(for inheritance purposes only)	Washington, D.C.

Best Practice requires that due to continually changing laws in your given state, those marriage laws of a particular state should be reviewed and verified for the specific situation presented to you at the time, and not rely solely on this information.

Dorian Solot and Marshall Miller of the Alternative to Marriage Project say, "There is a common misperception that if you live together for a certain length of time (seven years is what many people believe), you are common-law married. This is not true anywhere in the United States."

Marriage, in its essence, is usually seen as a voluntary union for life of two people to the exclusion of others. Most states that recognize common-law marriages define it to be when heterosexual couples become **legally** married without license or ceremony. It is not usually recognized to be legal when two people simply live together for a certain number of years. Only when a common-law marriage legally exists and certain requirements have been met are you a legally married couple. Funeral-cremation providers, arrangers and cemetery personnel must be familiar with laws governing marriage and common law relationships in their state. Scott Gilligan, attorney and legal counsel for the National Funeral Directors Association, urges that in performing funeral-burial-cremation services and in determining who has the legal right to control disposition, the funeral practitioner must act with the blessing of law, meaning according to the primacy laws in your state. For more information, check with your state to learn about specific requirements and/or seek the assistance of an attorney.

Best Practice requires:

When questions arise as to who is the person(s) with authority to act, the arranger, funeral-cremation provider or cemeterian must not make the decision as to who has the authority for disposition based only on his/her own interpretation. When necessary, seek clarification from an attorney or seek a ruling from a court.

Case Example: Multiple Spouse Scenario

I was making arrangements in my office with a lady whose husband died at the Veteran's Hospital. My secretary interrupted the conference and told me I had a telephone call. I politely replied, "I cannot be interrupted now, please take a message." Assertively, she told me again, "Mike, you need to take this call, it is important." Excusing myself, I took the call. It was the

Detail Office supervisor at the Veteran's Hospital. She told me, "I am in the office with the wife of the decedent and there are some questions." I replied, "You must be mistaken, I am in my office now with the wife who is making funeral arrangements." The supervisor said, "We have a problem and this is why I am calling you. It appears the decedent has two wives."

As it turned out, the deceased was married to two different women and each one had a legal marriage certificate. Neither wife was aware of the other and they lived in communities about 20 miles apart. The following day I met with both wives who thankfully acted civilly toward one another. However, one wife wanted her husband buried in the veteran's cemetery and the other wanted her husband cremated and the cremated remains buried in the veteran's cemetery. This was a new experience for me. I explained to both wives that due to this unusual circumstance, I could not proceed with any services. The wife who requested cremation would not agree to have her husband buried and a stalemate ensued. After two days, and at my urging, the wives petitioned the court for an order for disposition purposes. Each wife appeared before the judge and was given an opportunity to plead their case. In the court order, the judge ruled that the decedent would not be cremated but would be buried in the veteran's cemetery. The judge further stated to both wives that after this situation was resolved by a higher court, only then could the prevailing wife do whatever she felt compelled to do with the remains.

When the Next of Kin is Unavailable or Hospitalized

What should be done in instances when the person(s) with authority is unreachable and completely unavailable and other family members desire to arrange funeral ceremonies? The arranger must distinguish between funeral ceremonies and disposition of the deceased person. Funeral directors strive to accommodate the wishes of people who seek our services and be sensitive to the needs of people who represent themselves as mourners. Yet, it is most important that they respect the legal rights of the person(s) with authority and/or the written directions made by the deceased person prior to his/her death. None of these can ever be overlooked and the funeral director-arranger must not position himself or herself as an "arbiter of rights" in one's motivation to provide services. Not all family members might be familiar with what the person with authority might want or be knowledgeable as to what instructions the deceased person stipulated in writing or verbally prior to his/her death. In general, anyone can arrange and hold funeral ceremonies but **Best Practice** requires that two critical aspects must also be considered. Without receiving written authorization from the person(s) with authority:

- **Is it permissible to have the body of the deceased person present at the ceremonies?**
- **Can disposition of the deceased person take place?**

Presented with these circumstances, the funeral-cremation provider must act legally, carefully and prudently. All attempts to contact the person(s) with authority must be thoroughly documented including:

- **Record** the name, relationship, date and time of all persons spoken to
- **Identify** the manner of communication (whether in-person, on cell phone or through e-mail or other written confirmation)
- **Maintain** a written record of what was discussed, such that it provides a record of the communication, with the comments and responses of all parties
- **Maintain** copies of all written communications
- **Send** all mail with a minimum of a delivery verification or proof of service or even by return-receipt request
- **Keep** a written record of all discussions and comments with all parties

The funeral-cremation provider cannot proceed with disposition, especially cremation, without written authorization from the person(s) with authority. In some states, there is a statutorily defined period of time, usually within several days from the date of death, in which the person with authority must act. If the person(s) with authority fails to act within this period of time, the right to arrange funeral events and disposition of the body of the deceased person may pass to the next person(s) in line, according to the order of primacy in the state or to a public agency, such as the Public Administrator (or similar agency in your state), who may grant authorization for disposition, or when authorization is received through a court order. **Best Practice** of a funeral director-arranger would be to obtain copies of such court orders, to be maintained with the materials verifying permission and direction of the arrangements and disposition of the deceased person.

To be safe, the body of the deceased person should **not** be publicly viewed or present during any ceremony unless authorization is given by the person(s) with authority or a court order grants this be done. **Best Practice** means that the funeral director must take into consideration the fact that the person with authority would not want the body present or that, prior to death, the deceased person left instructions with the person(s) with authority asking that his/her body not be a part of funeral events.

When the next of kin is hospitalized, and arrangements have been made by other family members on the behalf of the person with authority, family members may be required to carry contracts and documents to the next of kin for signature. At other times the arranger must travel to the person with authority to make arrangements away from the funeral home. I recall several instances when it was necessary for me to make funeral arrangements in a hospital room where the person with authority was a patient. Depending on the funeral activities planned and the wishes of the next of kin, it can also mean discussing sheltering the deceased for an extended period of time until the person with authority is released and able to attend funeral activities. In cases when the person with authority cannot be found and no state agency is authorized to be involved, the funeral-cremation provider will need to obtain a court order for disposition.

Best Practice requires that under no circumstances should disposition take place until it is authorized in writing by the person(s) with the legal right to control disposition.

Fax Authorizations

Receiving authorization through facsimile transmission (fax) is generally acceptable in most areas of the country. Exceptions might include faxed authorizations for cremation. You must check your local laws, with your attorney or with your local court to make sure fax authorizations are acceptable for the reasons you seek. However, fax authorizations should be followed up with signatures provided on a hard (original) copy of the document(s), and notarized. Having the faxed documents notarized means that proper identification was presented to the notary person by the signing-authorizing person(s). **Authorizations through e-mail transmission should not be accepted.**

Indemnity Agreement

An **indemnity agreement**, sometimes called a hold harmless agreement, is a written contract between two or more parties for the purpose of one party agreeing to protect another party against future lawsuits, losses and claims for something another party did, or neglected to do. According to funeral-service attorney Harvey Lapin and plaintiff attorney David Overstreet, **indemnity agreements are inadequate to resolve these types of issues and provide poor protection.** Some funeral-cremation providers and arrangers believe they can protect themselves from a lawsuit over violating another person's right by obtaining an indemnity agreement or hold-harmless agreement from those persons making arrangements who are not the person(s) with authority. This is simply not true.

One can recognize the limitations of such efforts by noting that others who have not signed the indemnity agreement will not be bound in most situations to the signature of another person who was not authorized. A provision of this type only provides a false sense of security for the funeral-cremation provider if it is not properly drafted, does not comply with the state laws and is executed by the legally authorized person(s). The indemnity clause might provide rights to the funeral director and/or funeral home, and remedies against the client signing the paper, but if they do not have assets available to defend and indemnify the funeral director and/or funeral home, it is not worth the paper it is written on.

Being Alert to Family Dynamics

During the arrangement conference, the arranger must listen and read the client family and observe the dynamics going on. Many factors cause people to act differently. Within the same family there might be no uniformity and relationships can be different than from what they appear to be. **Best Practice** means being alert to:

- **The relationship of those present to the deceased**
- **Agreement or disagreement among those present**
- **Is anyone absent who should be present?**
- **The manner of death (violent versus anticipated)**
- **Is anyone sedated, tranquilized or is the odor of alcohol present?**
- **Is there a language barrier or a culture barrier?**
- **Do they appear rushed, impatient or overly demanding?**
- **Is anyone confrontational or threatening?**
- **What prior experiences have they had with planning a funeral?**
- **Do they seem withdrawn and immobilized by what's happening?**

- **Is anyone present exhibiting perfectionist tendencies?**
- **Are there disabilities such as hearing, sight or age-related factors?**

Dealing with Perfectionists

Dealing with people with expectations unable to be satisfied or those considered to be perfectionists – or learning that the deceased was a perfectionist – could be especially challenging clients. While we all might have some tendency to manifest perfectionist impulses, the perfectionist client can be relentless in a vain attempt to control situations or issues that are just not subject to the control of anyone. They can be highly critical of the slightest deviation from their often unexpressed expectations. The funeral-cremation provider or cemetery can easily become the focus of their anger and frustration. It is important that the arranger recognizes this early on during the planning stages. As accommodating as you might be, it can be impossible to satisfy people who are perfectionists. Your best efforts could still lead to anger, dissatisfaction and a lawsuit.

Case Example: The Client Unable to be Satisfied

Several years ago, I served a family that I suspected was going to be difficult to satisfy from the moment we first met. Arrangements were being made by the deceased's two surviving daughters. From the moment they entered my building, the daughters found fault with practically everything. The parking lot was too small. The outside smoking area did not have enough seating. The color of the carpeting was too bold. They did not like the fact that my funeral vehicles were silver in color as they preferred white vehicles.

The new state-of-the-art sound system we installed was not adequate. They did not like the fact that the funeral home was on a major boulevard, and more. These red flags made me question whether I should serve this family or not. Throughout the arrangement conference, it was necessary for me to provide detailed explanations of every item that was discussed. I documented their comments and, not to leave any stone unturned, required the signatures of both daughters on all authorization, consent, release and disclosure forms. Pointedly, I asked them to tell me about their expectations for my services before proceeding. Up front, I told them what I could do and could not do, and what they might expect. At the end of the conference, I asked both of them to recap for me, in their own words, what was discussed and what would take place. (Note the use of verification by the sender of what the receivers understood). By the time we concluded more than four hours later, everyone confirmed they understood what would happen. I like to think that under these circumstances in dealing with two daughters who expected perfection, I proceeded carefully to ensure a positive outcome.

Reaching Informed Consent

Some clients who become plaintiffs look at the funeral-cremation provider's failure to reach informed consent as another basis for a lawsuit in which the client family believes they have been wronged or deceived. Statements such as, "No one told me this would happen," "The arranger promised me something else," or "This is not what I expected" can be reason for disappointment leading to a lawsuit.

Informed consent is the principal that permits people to agree (consent to, and authorize) something to happen after all the relevant facts have been disclosed to that person. It originates from the legal and ethical right that the person(s) with authority has the right to decide what can and cannot be done pertaining to the preparation of the body of a deceased person, funeral-burial-cremation activities or "end of life services, ceremonies and celebrations" and the manner and location of disposition. **Informed consent is much more than a signature on a form.**

Informed consent is an extension of the client family – provider relationship, not a long checklist of things to accomplish during the arrangement conference. It encompasses focusing on disclosing the necessary and legal information, giving the best personal service, increasing client family satisfaction and reaching a mutual understanding among all parties as to what will take place. Reaching informed consent strengthens your defense in the event of a lawsuit.

Requirements for informed consent vary from state to state but in general, the person(s) with authority must be given specific information concerning procedures that will occur, their risks, likely outcomes, options and choices and costs. It means the person(s) with authority comprehends what they are authorizing, participates in making decisions and:

1. Has the actual authority to control disposition

2. Has been fully informed about options and choices

3. Has been informed about relevant risks and specific issues which are uncertainties

4. Has been assessed as to his/her level of understanding

5. Has affirmed understanding of options, choices, risks and specific uncertainties

6. Has had all costs disclosed

7. Acknowledges they agree, consent to, and authorize the specific services identified (which must be in writing in the funeral-cremation business, as well as many other kinds of business or professional relationships)

To help reach informed consent with a client family, some things the arranger should discuss are:

- **Legal requirements**

- **Treatment recommended** (like embalming or, if declined, controlled temperature storage)

- **Potential outcomes and risks** of certain services (like airline shipment, restorative arts procedures, delayed embalming)

- **Alternative courses of action** (air shipment versus vehicle shipment, choice of cemeteries, choice of crematories, etc.)

- **Recommended procedures and policies** (cremation, identification viewing, minimum care, witnessing, etc)

- **Answers to any questions** the client family might have

Ascertaining How Much Information is Considered Adequate?

Reaching informed consent does not mean that every conceivable detail must be discussed, but the person(s) authorizing the services must comprehend what he/she is authorizing. The authorizing party must be competent and consent must be voluntary. Some people can feel vulnerable and powerless during the arrangement process. The authorizing party must be an active participant in making decisions, not merely asked to sign forms. The arranger must act reasonably and prudently, in a manner in which other funeral-cremation providers would act under the same or similar circumstances. Explanations contained on various forms should be written using layperson's terms, not technical jargon.

What is adequate involves what a reasonable person would want to know about the issue involved. While some people desire little information, others demand to know all of the intimate, exact details. Reason and discretion are to be your guide. You might be best served by effective communication upon the issues, and in the process confirm for yourself that the client has *heard*, *understood* and *verified* to you their understanding of the issue. Often we deal with people who do not know what to expect. Some feel vulnerable because they do not know what questions to ask. It may be necessary to provide persons with information that is new to them. Attorney Harvey Lapin says, "It is better to over disclose, than to not to disclose."

There are three basic approaches to keep in mind in ascertaining how much information may be required:

1. **What would a typical arranger explain to a client family about a particular procedure or service?** This approach allows the arranger to determine what information is

appropriate to disclose. Unfortunately, this approach typically means that little information is provided and in most circumstances, informed consent is not achieved. In this approach, the focus is arranger-focused rather than on what the client family needs to know.

2. **What would the average client family need to know in order to be an informed participant in the decision?**
   This approach focuses on the client family and what they would need to know in order to understand the decision at hand.

3. **What would this client family need to know and understand in order to make an informed decision?**
   This can be the most time-consuming and demanding approach, since it requires tailoring information to each client family.

For the funeral arranger who asks, "How much information is enough?" the answer must take into account:

- Providing sufficient information described in terms a layperson can understand
- A discussion of alternative treatments or procedures
- Disclosure of risks, including those that might be unforeseen
- Disclosure of costs and timing
- Disclosure of limitations and downside risks
- Disclosure of who will perform services

The **Best Practice** to the question of how much information is enough is one that meets both your professional obligation to provide the best care and respects the client family by allowing them to have a voice in making all decisions. In general, it is always better when you provide more, not less information.

As an example, most funeral homes provide a consumer-oriented brochure about cremation that contains an explanation of the process. Review this information (as well as the disclosures contained in the Cremation Authorization Form) with the client and answer any questions they might have. The arranger is responsible to ensure the client family understands what will take place.

No matter how you feel about informed consent here is the **Best Practice** rule of thumb: **Inform before you perform.**

The General Price List

For the funeral-cremation provider, in a manner of speaking, informed consent begins with the General Price List (GPL). The Federal Trade Commission Funeral Rule that went in to effect in 1984 requires all funeral providers to comply with the Rule. This means that you must give the General Price List to anyone who asks, in person, about funeral goods, funeral services, or the prices of such goods and services. The List must be theirs to keep. When a client family walks into your business, you may offer condolences, but the General Price List should be provided as soon as possible.

However, you must offer the price list when you begin discussing any of the following:

- The type of funeral or disposition that you can arrange;
- The specific goods and services you offer; or,
- The prices of your goods and services.

The Rule states, "The triggering event for giving out the General Price List is a *face-to-face* meeting. This meeting can occur *anywhere*, not just at your business office. When the discussion of prices or arrangements takes place in the family's residence or while transferring the deceased person from a hospital, the General Price List must be handed to the family." All funeral personnel who may come in contact with funeral consumers must be familiar with the requirements of the Funeral

Rule. For complete details, go to www.ftc.gov/funeralrule.com or check with your state or national association.

Use of Forms

Printed forms comprised of authorizations, consents, releases and disclosures covering relevant areas are aids in reaching informed consent and should be a normal part of the arrangement conference. Verbal explanation without written acknowledgement is rarely sufficient. Clearly written descriptions of procedures and services facilitate the process of safe practice and confirm that discussions took place. Once again, the arranger must act legally, carefully and prudently.

Some funeral-cremation providers avoid using all the necessary authorization, consent, release and disclosure forms that they should, arguing that they are time-consuming. Others do not feel it is necessary to explain services in writing; some feel that presenting more than one or two forms is burdensome or confusing to the client family. Lapin states that these funeral-cremation providers are usually the defendants in lawsuits.

Obtaining signed authorization, consent, release and disclosure forms is an **essential** part of the arrangement-planning process. The signed forms should be maintained in the decedent's file. They are central to risk management and serve to confirm that details were openly disclosed and discussed ahead of time. Above all, the use of forms should deliver excellence in professional service. **In the event of a lawsuit, these forms can serve as the basis of your defense.**

Practically all aspects of the care and services performed by funeral-cremation providers require informed consent. Limitations, risks, potential problems and costs are some areas that must be discussed and agreed upon. Before any form is signed, it should be reviewed with the client family to make sure they understand it. They should be given ample time to read the form and ask questions.

Merely getting a signature on a document does not constitute informed consent. If the informed consent is called

into question, it will be your burden of proving the client family understood what they signed.

Professionals like physicians, attorneys, accountants, investment advisors, insurance agents and others, proceed only after they have explained the details, made full disclosure, answered the patient or client's questions and received written acknowledgement and authorization from them. Consumer purchases such as homes, appliances and automobiles involve extensive processes of disclosure, release and consent.

Exercising **Best Practice** and legal procedures is not burdensome, a waste of time or an inconvenience to the professional or to their clients. It is an essential part of providing personal service. Funeral-cremation providers and cemeterians should view their services the same way and proceed only after full explanation, disclosure and written authorization is received. Even though embalming may be performed after receiving verbal authorization, it nonetheless requires that you document the date, time, name and relationship of the person granting the verbal authorization and the name of the person receiving the authorization. That permission should be acknowledged in writing during the arrangement conference.

Does it make sense to use authorization, disclosure, consent and release forms during the arrangement conference? Yes.

Does it help to achieve informed consent? Yes.

Does it provide a degree of protection to the provider? Yes.

Can they be used in your defense in the event of a lawsuit? Yes.

Does the rule of thumb, "inform before you perform" make sense? Yes, always.

The use of printed forms that outline your services reinforces the fact that you are:

- **Client-focused** and open to explaining your services

- **Frank** about limitations and clear about what can and cannot be done

- **Willing to acquaint** the client family to your role as a professional and as a practitioner in treating the body
- **Willing to commit** to what service you can, and cannot deliver
- **Eager** to answer questions
- **Committed to avoiding** misunderstanding by putting important facts and details in writing
- **Documenting facts** in the event of questions or problems

Funeral planning is a serious matter with legal, social, financial and psychological ramifications. It is worth repeating: **Reaching informed consent involves much more than obtaining a signature on a form.** Asking a client family to just "sign" without going over the contents of each form can destroy trust. Reviewing each document and its contents with the client family builds trust and enhances communication and adds value to your service.

The best forms in the world will not prevent you from being sued, but having them demonstrates that you acted prudently and suggests that you explained things. Properly executed documentation reduces the risk of litigation and, if you are sued, improves your credibility in front of a jury.

By **Best Practice**, each form should be presented one at a time to the client family. Review critical sections on the form with them. Would you expect anything less from your physician in recommending a procedure to be performed? Would you question the trustworthiness of the automobile dealer who said, "Oh, you don't have to read all of this, just sign here." How would you react if your financial planner told you, "Don't worry, this investment will make a lot of money. Just sign here." If we desire to be seen as professionals providing a valuable personal service, open discussion about every aspect of our services, care to the deceased person and products must become a routine that strengthens the bond between client and provider. Contrary to what some arrangers believe, families appreciate having information. It adds to their peace of mind.

Avoiding full disclosure and failing to reach informed consent shortchanges the client family and jeopardizes the reputation of the funeral-cremation provider. It increases your vulnerability to being sued.

In addition to county, state or federally mandated forms, other customary forms to consider for use in your own **Best Practice** in the arrangement conference include:

- First-call death notification
- Verification of identity of deceased
- Casket rental acknowledgement
- Cemetery-grave space disclosure
- Mausoleum-crypt space disclosure
- Authorization for removal and disposal of medical devices and prosthesis
- Authorization to photograph deceased
- Authorization to scatter cremated remains
- Authorization for shipment of deceased
- Authorization for temporary release of custody for autopsy or medical-legal examination
- Urn-capacity disclosure
- Request to witness cremation process
- Wood casket disclaimer or metal casket disclaimer
- Confirmation of delivery of deceased to funeral home
- Confirmation of delivery of deceased to crematory
- Authorization for disposition of cremated remains - other than scattering
- Acknowledgement when merchandise is not provided by the funeral home
- Minimum-care authorization when embalming is declined

- Outer-burial container disclaimer
- Receipt for personal property after funeral activities
- Directive for release of cremated remains
- Release of liability for personal property used during funeral activities
- Receipt from cemetery for burial-entombment
- Order for release of the deceased person to your custody
- Witness of transfer of deceased from place of death
- Authorization for overnight stay of deceased in other than the funeral home
- Authorization for shipment of cremated remains
- General receipt of decedent from funeral home
- Embalming-care report
- Decedent service record
- Disclosure when interns or apprentices will perform duties, and that they will be under supervision
- Disclosure when the deceased person will be taken to an off-premises embalming or care facility for embalming or sheltering
- Disclosure that certain duties might be performed by sub-contractors

CB Legal Publishing Corporation provides specialized legal forms for funeral and cremation businesses. Their contact information may be found in the Reference section in this book.

During a lawsuit, plaintiffs always question what was discussed and said by the arranger during the arrangement conference. For the arranger who has conducted hundreds of arrangements, he/she can feel that what was discussed or agreed upon is obvious. The attorney, however, will ask for detailed information as to what you said and what you discussed. When questioned during a deposition or during examination on the witness stand, the arranger often responds by saying, "I explain everything to every family, "I've always done it this way" or "I always explain this to every family." The word, "always" can be problematic. While it might be obvious to the experienced arranger, it is not necessarily obvious to the client family. The client family can have their own interpretation as to what they were told or thought would happen. Not having details in writing does not help your image in front of a jury.

The author Jack Carew defines communication as the transmission and reception of meaningful messages. The death of a loved one can contribute to misunderstandings, mistaken assumptions and misinterpretations on the part of the bereaved. Language barriers, use of translators, emotional distress or sorrow, mental instability, attention deficit disorders, intoxication and duress behind the scenes all complicate the situation. A simple question like, "Would you please tell me in your own words what I have just said?" is a great help to the arranger in making his/her own assessment of the level of the client's understanding and whether communication is effective. While our verbally expressed words must be carefully chosen and delivered with the correct emotion, clearly written forms, documents and electronic media are **essential** aids in helping us avoid misunderstandings and achieve informed consent. Such devices provide tools for the arranger to use to help the client navigate through what is expected to be a difficult emotional time for the client with well thought out, effective communication materials. Signed and dated documents that can be referred to in the event of questions help confirm what was agreed upon. On the other hand, the absence of documentation makes the funeral-cremation provider vulnerable.

I know of arrangers that have audio-recorded some arrangement conferences as a way of developing accurate records of what was said. Done by other professionals, it might be an approach to consider, especially when serving a client family with a litigious history. Always **inform before you perform.** Obtain written permission from the person(s) with authority before audio-recording the conference. Check with an attorney regarding what would constitute proper authorization for recording the arrangement conference.

Even if we practiced under ideal circumstances in an ideal society free from any threat of lawsuits, funeral-cremation professionals and cemeterians need to make sure that client families understand and acknowledge what they are arranging and purchasing.

Most arrangers take pride in being good communicators. Using documents is another form of communication that helps ensure clear understanding of what you provide. It makes good sense. It is **Best Practice**.

CHAPTER 5

Verifying Identity of a Deceased Person

*Even in today's highly litigious society, there are some families who will understand, forgive or tolerate minor mishaps that occur during the complicated, time-sensitive course of funeral and cremation services. Families may question the appearance of the hair or clothing of the deceased person and might accept apologies for a minor delay in the course of events. This chapter discusses the one area in which there is no room for error, no reasonable excuse and often no forgiveness. Misidentification of the deceased person does occur. Since the consequences of misidentification are so severe, it is essential to know what circumstances predispose to misidentification and what **Best Practices** can be used to lessen the chance of it occurring at your firm.*

The best way to ensure against misidentification and wrongful disposition or transfer is to develop a policy at your funeral home or crematory requiring verification of identity of the deceased person **before** any form of disposition or transfer takes place. Whether the person will be buried, entombed or shipped, a verification policy benefits the funeral-cremation provider and client family in the following ways:

- **It stipulates** that the deceased person in custody is the same as that identified in writing on the documents that pertain to that decedent

- **It underscores** your professional responsibilities in providing cremation services

- **It stresses** the irreversible nature of cremation
- **It helps facilitate** grief and be an aid to survivors in accepting the reality of the death

Means of Verifying Identity

The general methods to identify deceased human remains are:

- Visual recognition
- Using a photograph supplied by the authorizing agent to compare the image of the person when he/she was alive to the appearance of the dead person
- Matching physical characteristics (scars, tattoos, deformities, etc.)
- Fingerprint comparison
- DNA analysis
- Medical-dental comparison

Visual identification is the most accurate, fool-proof and simple method for the funeral-cremation provider. While viewing a deceased family member can be difficult and we can relate to persons who are reluctant to do so, knowing beyond a doubt that you have the correct person in your custody is **central** to all of the services you make available. Once identity has been confirmed, it adds to everyone's peace of mind. As an analogy, just as a physician treats his/her patient and knows that in order to accomplish a beneficial outcome, the patient may have to endure some discomfort, we can empathize with a family, knowing that seeing the person dead can be distressing even while the confirmation provides reassurance.

I am reminded of a story of a funeral director friend of mine who was making arrangements with a physician whose son was killed in an automobile accident. The physician refused to view his son's body. Several years later, the same funeral director served the same physician again for another son who died. This time, in a tragic sequence of events, the physician accidentally backed the car over his son, killing him in the driveway at their home. Refusing to view again, the funeral director said, "It will be helpful for you to you to see your son. If you would like, I will be with you." With that, he escorted the physician into the viewing room where the physician saw his son. The physician and funeral director became good friends because of this. Through their long friendship, the physician could not thank the funeral director enough for encouraging him to view his son.

Forced viewing, on the other hand must be avoided. Even well-intentioned words by the funeral director could be misconstrued as an exertion of force on someone to view the body. This can be risky for the funeral director. For example, had the funeral director said to the physician, words to the effect, "Come with me. You need to see your son," and taken his hand and walked him into the viewing room, a different scenario might have developed. Forced viewing could become intentional infliction of emotional distress, possibly even assault, battery and even false imprisonment, in some circumstances.

Viewing – A Way to Assure Other Family Members

Risk reduction aside, it is psychologically beneficial for at least one family member to view the deceased person. This person can then provide assurance to other family members. Funeral directors must be advocates for the value of viewing the body of a deceased person, even if it is for just a moment. This is based on the psychological fact that most of our memories are visual memories; denying or avoiding the opportunity to view the person "not breathing" or "dead" can make it more difficult for survivors to accept the reality of death. I have experienced instances in which the bereaved spouse was administered sedatives and tranquilizers to "ease their grief." Weeks later, after exhausting the supply of medication, he or she would ask, "What happened to my husband?"

The funeral director is responsible even when errors of

identification are made before he/she assumes custody of the person's body. The funeral director, as the **last** person in the chain of custody, has the (last) opportunity through verification of identity, to correct misidentification and prevent wrongful cremation, burial, entombment or shipment. Just as a surgeon must abide by the standard of care and be certain of the patient's identity before a procedure occurs, it is a standard of care for funeral-cremation providers to be certain of the identity of the deceased person before disposition. When dealing with litigation concerning misidentification or wrongful cremation, it is difficult for any expert witness or industry authority to testify and say that it is unnecessary for a funeral-cremation provider to see to it that the identity of the deceased is verified.

Verifying a person's identity must not be treated with indifference or avoidance. It is the foundation of all risk-reduction methods and the best way to ensure you will never cremate, bury, entomb or ship the wrong person. If you take exception to this, it means you practice outside the range of accepted professional standards. It means you operate on the basis of assumption or conjecture.

Case Example: Same Last Names

Two male patients died on the same day at the same hospital within hours of one another. One patient occupied a room on the second floor, the other on the fifth floor. Unrelated to one another, they shared the same common last name. Hospital personnel on the two respective floors were unaware of this unique situation. Following hospital policy, the in-charge nurse on each floor checked and double-checked the wrist tag of her deceased patient, completed a "decedent toe tag" and attached it to the correct person's body before having the patient moved to the morgue. When the funeral director and morgue attendant entered the morgue to transfer one of the decedents, they only looked for the last name of the deceased. The funeral provider mistakenly transferred the wrong decedent to the funeral home. This serious error was not discovered until the next day when the grandson of the deceased came to the funeral home to see his grandfather and place a handwritten letter in his hand before he was cremated. The grandson informed the funeral home that the person they had was not his grandfather. At the time, this funeral home did not have a policy that requires verification of identity but further problems were averted by the grandson's observation.

Policy Contents for Verifying Identity

The following **Best Practice** guidelines should be used in developing a policy for verifying the identity of decedents:

1. That verification of identity is company **policy** and is performed for each decedent that comes in to the custody of the funeral-cremation provider (regardless of disposition). **It is not an option.**

2. Verification is performed by the person(s) with authority or their **designated-in-writing** representative.

3. Verification must be documented on a form specific for this purpose and contain the name of the deceased, the date and place of death, the date and time the verification took place and the printed name, signature and relationship of the person(s) performing it.

4. Verification should take place in an appropriate room such as a slumber or visitation room. It should **never** take place in a preparation room, garage, flower room, storage room, and carport area or refrigeration room.

5. In instances when verification is performed at the crematory, it should take place in an appropriate location away from the cremation chamber. Verification of identity (seeing the person) is separate and different than witnessing cremation (observing the container being placed into the chamber).

6. Whenever possible, verification should take place with the person's body in the container that will be used for disposition or the cremation.

7. For cremation, once verification has been completed, the container should be closed and the name of the deceased person prominently written on the outside of the container in permanent ink.

8. To reduce misunderstanding about the purpose of "verification of identity" and how it differs from formal, public viewing, inform the client family during the arrangement conference that it is a private, time-limited act, taking seconds to several minutes in order to ensure the identity of the decedent.

9. Prepare the person(s) who will do the verification ahead of time. Sit with them in an office before escorting them to the person's body. Let them know what they will see, how the deceased is covered or clothed and where it will occur. Offer to be present with them. The manner in which you conduct verification of identity is a direct reflection on how you see yourself professionally and the level of sensitivity you offer to your clients.

10. When completed, invite the person(s) to sit in your office. Answer any questions they may have. **Before he/she leaves,** have them sign, date and time the Verification of Identity Form.

Identification of Decomposed or Other Difficult Cases

Respectfully, I do not completely agree with what is written in the embalming textbook, *Embalming – History, Theory, and Practice* (Fourth Edition, Page 38) that says, "There can be circumstances when it is unwise for the body to be identified or viewed by the family or family representative. Such conditions can be death was due to fire, extreme trauma, or if the body is in a state of advanced decomposition." I believe the author has innocently confused "verification" with "viewing" and desires to protect the family from this task. **In all instances, deceased persons must be accurately identified.** This is sometimes performed by visual means (at the funeral home, the crematory, the coroner's facility, disaster management receiving center, the hospital or at the scene of an accident) or by other means outlined earlier in this chapter and discussed further on in this chapter. Simply stated, the funeral director must be certain of the person's identity in his custody. He/she cannot perform services or funeral activities including disposition while saying to a client family, "I am uncertain as to whose remains I have," or "We think this is your husband." Someone, by some means, must provide assurance to the client family and the funeral director.

When identification has been established by another source, such as the coroner, and by another means, such as fingerprints or DNA analysis, ask for written acknowledgement attesting to the identity of the person and the method(s) they used in determining identity. If they refuse to provide this to you, document it with the name and title of the person refusing this request, along with the day and time, and retain this in the deceased person's file.

Identification is primary. Viewing is secondary.

By all means, the funeral director should inform the family as to the condition of the deceased person and when necessary, provide them with reasons for caution regarding viewing. The funeral director should **not** prevent the next of kin, the person with authority or their designated-in-writing representative from viewing the deceased person. In my professional opinion and experience, I have informed many families of the condition of their family member, what to expect if they view the person, and that viewing the person will not be pleasant and may give them memories filled with discomfort. I am a firm believer that the decision to view or not to view is a decision to be made by the family, not unilaterally by the funeral director. For the family that decides to view the person, it is important that the funeral director exhibit a hands-on, participatory role and offer to "be there with them" to lend support and answer any questions.

After informing the family and providing cautionary advice, and the family insists on viewing, the family should sign a Release-Disclosure Form **before viewing the person.** The form should be prepared on the funeral home's letterhead and state that the funeral home has duly informed the family as to the condition of the deceased person, has informed them as to what they can be expected to see when viewing the person, that the funeral director provided caution to the family, explaining that this experience can be unpleasant and discomforting. The form should also contain a separate hold-harmless statement releasing the funeral home from any later action or claims that might result from their decision to view their family member. CB Legal Publishing Corporation provides release forms for this and other related purposes. Their contact information can be found in the resource section.

When viewing is declined (but identification is certain), the person(s) with authority should sign a release-disclosure that states he/she has declined to view the person, that the funeral home made the opportunity available, and that the person(s) with authority releases the funeral home from any future actions or claims that might result from not viewing the deceased person.

Even in situations where the physical condition of the person is extreme, the funeral director and/or embalmer should make some preparations to the body. If the deceased person is in a pouch, he/she should be treated with embalming powder or chemicals to help minimize odor. Damaged areas, especially around the head and face can be wrapped in gauze; if possible, place the person in plastic coveralls or unionalls. In some cases, the family might request the deceased person to be dressed. When this is possible, it should be done. When this is not possible, it should be explained to the family.

Case Example – A Father's Need to Know

During the Vietnam War, I had a friend who was killed when he received a direct hit from a mortar in his foxhole. I had a close relationship with his father, who was my baseball coach. My friend's identity was confirmed by two of his friends who shared the same foxhole, but survived the attack with non-life-threatening injuries. The mother and father received a full report as to how their son was killed, as well as confirmation from his two friends in the foxhole as to his identity. After the vigil ceremony, the father remained at the casket until everyone had left the funeral home. As I approached him, he said to me, "Mike, you have to do me a favor. I need to see my son. I want you to open the casket." The Killed in Action Report provided by the Army explained that their son received the full impact of the mortar shell and as a result, only his legs and one arm were recoverable and inside the casket.

Reminding the father of this, he said to me, "I know this, but I need to make sure it is my son." I asked the father, "Knowing what is inside the casket, how will you know this is your son even if you look at him?" He told me that when his son was 10 years old, he had an accident while riding his bicycle and had surgery on his left ankle, leaving a severe scar about six inches long. He explained that if he saw the scar, he would know for certain that this is his son and he could assure the mother, as well. In his presence, I opened the casket and uncovered the body parts. In plain view, we both saw the scar on the left ankle. The father began crying and we hugged one another for several minutes. As he left he said to me, "Sometimes fathers have to do tough things. This was the toughest, but now I am sure this is my son."

Using a Waiver Instead of Viewing the Person's Body

I have dealt with families who have initially declined to "view" the deceased person for the purpose of verifying identity. Some have even refused to designate another person to act on their behalf. When faced with this situation, some funeral-cremation providers resort to using a "waiver." **Using a waiver for this purpose is not recommended.**

A **waiver** is a written statement in which one person gives up a right or a claim and agrees to abandon and/or refrain from making an argument, objection or performing an act. In this case, it means refusing (waiving) the right to view the body to verify identity and in doing so, agrees not to seek any remedy against the funeral-cremation provider or crematory in the event of misidentification/wrongful disposition.

To the client family (and funeral-cremation provider), a waiver is a convenient way out of having to deal with this task and allows them to breathe a sigh of relief. For the provider, a waiver can mean one less contact with the deceased person until the person is taken to the crematory and an additional level of protection from a lawsuit.

In most instances, a waiver provides a false sense of security for all parties, especially the provider. When there are multiple persons who share equal authority to control disposition, one person's signature on a waiver, made on behalf of the other people who share the same authority, does **not** constitute a legal waiver. **Only an individual himself or herself can waive his or her rights.** For a waiver to be legally executed, each individual with legal authority must waive his or her rights in writing.

Even when all persons who possess the legal right agree to this, a waiver is not the "cure all" you want it to be. **A waiver from one family will not protect you from the other family whose loved one has been mistakenly cared for or disposed of.** Further, not all courts necessarily recognize a waiver for this purpose, even one that appears to be properly executed. As an owner, I have declined serving the family rather than risking the potential for a mistake.

Verification by Photograph

Sometimes funeral-cremation providers resort to using a photograph as another method to verify identity of decedents in their custody. It is done to "save" the client family (or their designated-in-writing representative) from viewing the person or make it more convenient for the funeral director. Some funeral-cremation providers make the mistake of automatically taking a photograph of every decedent. Verification using a photograph should be acknowledged in writing on a form entitled, "Verification without Viewing." Anytime a photograph is used for this purpose, caution must be exercised. The photograph must be recent enough and contain enough "clarity" to make the comparison to the decedent valid **beyond any question or doubt.** Placing additional responsibility on the funeral director's shoulders to "make the verification" is not recommended. It adds to your liability in the event of mistaken identity.

Critically, Best Practice means that you do not take photographs of the deceased person for any purpose without receiving express written permission in advance from the person(s) with authority. Infringing on a person's privacy can have serious consequences today. All parties should agree that the photograph is taken for (comparison) verification purposes only and will remain the property of the funeral-cremation provider, retained on a confidential basis in the file. The person providing the comparison should print his/her name on the back of the photograph, and along with the date and time, sign the photograph attesting to the correct identity.

Digital photographs should never be taken by the funeral-cremation provider. Privacy issues and security concerns with digital photography add to extreme liability exposure. Digital photographs can be easily reproduced and manipulated electronically, are difficult to control and with the touch of a button, can be sent worldwide.

Other Means of Verification

It is not recommended that the funeral director take it upon himself or herself to verify the identity of decedents solely by matching scars, tattoos or deformities, as described to you by someone else or from a picture. These means are too ambiguous and leave much room for error. Most funeral-cremation providers do not possess adequate training in this type of verification.

Verification by **fingerprint comparison, DNA analysis and medical-dental comparison** are scientific methods and at present, beyond the knowledge and expertise of most funeral-cremation providers. These forensic methods are used by coroners, laboratories, CIA-FBI-police and other highly trained forensic experts. **Fingerprint records** made or latent prints left before death can be compared to those taken from the person's body. **DNA evidence,** available before death, can be compared to that recovered from post-mortem tissues. **Dental and medical characteristics** discovered visually or through x-rays can be compared to ante-mortem records and films. Dental evidence has long been recognized as a reliable means of positive identification and changes in one's dental structure are very slow after death. Other than visual means, fingerprints, if they are on record, are generally recognized as the best form of identification to establish positive identification.

In cases when the identity of a deceased person was made by an official agency using scientific means, ask its representatives to provide you with a statement of verification and retain it in the decedent's file. Review it with the client family. In cases when identity is not 100% positive, do not cremate.

A funeral-cremation provider who fails to verify the identity of a deceased person in his/her custody prior to disposition or shipment assumes responsibility and liability for any act of misidentification that may result. If the funeral director accepts any items or materials that might be questionable and uses these questionable items as a means of verifying identity, he/she assumes the liability as well. **Importantly, identification is not just a one-time event. It does not end with the verification at the funeral home or crematory facility. It is a continuous process performed throughout the entire sequence of custody, to final disposition.**

CHAPTER 6

Care and Preparation of a Deceased Person

This chapter is not a text on embalming, a subject handled well and at length in a number of excellent resources. This chapter, on the other hand, deals with considerations that involve responsible care of a deceased person once it enters custody of the funeral director. The funeral director cannot be passive in attending to the deceased person, even when the client family requests no embalming or professional care. The funeral director has an enduring responsibility to ensure that all deceased persons receive excellent care and that adequate, accurate records of such care are maintained. Further, the need for care must be properly explained to the family. A request for no care or minimal care must never be equated with neglectful care.

No matter what form of disposition is selected, the body of the deceased person is the focus of funeral activities. For relatives wishing to view the deceased person, there is no one element of our services that has more effect on overall satisfaction than a well-presented person. Ron Hast, the publisher of *Mortuary Management* says, "Embalming is the best way of keeping the deceased during the memorial event." For most client families, this marks a starting point where they can begin to deal with the reality of the death.

Similarly, no other element of service carries greater potential for liability than having custody of and being responsible for the body and property of a deceased person. The responsibilities and duties are interrelated, complex and carry with them obvious potential liability. It may very well be that more lawsuits are filed against funeral homes by clients who claim improper, inadequate and negligent care of the deceased than from any other reasons. Many claims have developed out of little or no communication between the funeral director and staff and the family.

Informing the Family and Receiving Authorization

For the funeral-cremation provider, involvement begins when you are notified about a death. The provider's degree of involvement with the body of a deceased person varies from minimal (sheltering and/or refrigeration) to extensive (embalming, restorative arts, cosmetic application, casketing, etc.). In all cases, local, state and/or federal regulations regarding embalming or other care must be followed. Regardless of the degree of care agreed upon or that may be required, it is critical that you **"inform before you perform,"** even when only minimal care, such as basic refrigeration storage will be provided.

Regarding embalming, the Federal Trade Commission Rule requires the following disclosure to consumers: "Except in certain special cases, embalming is not required by law. Embalming may be necessary, however, if you select certain funeral arrangements, such as a funeral with viewing. If you do not want embalming, you usually have the right to choose an arrangement that does not require you to pay for it, such as direct cremation or immediate burial."

Some states require that additional disclosures concerning embalming be made and even govern how authorization or the refusal for embalming be documented. When embalming is not authorized, some states govern what care and treatment should be rendered to a deceased person. California, for instance requires every funeral establishment and funeral director who holds unembalmed human remains for a period longer than 24 hours to place the deceased person in refrigeration at a temperature of 50 degrees Fahrenheit or less. Funeral-cremation providers and embalmers must be knowledgeable of the FTC

Funeral Rule and the laws in their respective state pertaining to the care and treatment of deceased persons.

Embalming without authorization or without acting under the laws of your state means the funeral home and embalmer can be accused of mutilation. In the book, *Mortuary Law,* attorney Scott Gilligan points out that, mutilation, although slight and necessary, is involved in embalming a deceased person. He goes on to say, "Generally, a funeral director has the right to do this as the mutilation is implicitly sanctioned by the permission given to embalm the body. If, however, the embalming is done without permission, the tort of mutilation of the body occurs."

Case Example: The Coroner Advises Embalming

A funeral director received an unidentified person from a coroner who advised him to embalm the body. The funeral director followed that advice and embalmed the person before the next of kin could be located. When the next of kin learned of the embalming, he sued the funeral director for mutilation of the body. Because the embalming had not been authorized by the next of kin, the court permitted the action and held that it was not a defense for the funeral director to claim that the embalming was beneficial.

Opening Discussions with a Client Family

Best Practice means documenting **all** discussions with a client family concerning care of the deceased person on a form specific for this purpose and maintaining a record of these discussions in the decedent's file. Care that is accepted (such as bathing or dressing) as well as care that is rejected (embalming or cosmetic application) should be documented. Such a form should contain:

- The name of the deceased person and date of death

- The name and relationship of person authorizing or rejecting elements of care, including the date and time

- An itemized list of treatment authorized or rejected (embalming, refrigeration only, sheltering only, bathing only, etc.)

- The name and signature of the funeral home representative

Most people do not know what must be done with a dead person's body, what laws govern care and treatment of deceased persons and might not be aware of options available, such as refrigeration, minimum care instead of embalming, anatomical donation or means of lawful disposition. Cremation is discussed in Chapter Eleven, but it should be noted that cremation is not technically a *method* of disposition, but actually a step *toward* final disposition (scattering, earth burial, entombment, placement into a niche, etc.). The funeral director's responsibilities include outlining all options and recommended professional care that is available. In some circumstances, special care or handling is necessary, such as when burial will be delayed, when shipment will occur, for morbidly obese persons, for those with disfigurement, persons in various stages of decomposition, when death was due to certain infectious diseases, highly edematous bodies, deaths due to violence and when anatomical donations have been made, and more.

Case Example: Getting Started on the "Right Foot"

The deceased person weighed more than 600 pounds and died in a small room in the back of his residence. Responding to the scene, the funeral director informed the family that because of the size of the deceased person, a sliding glass sectional door and adjacent window and section of a wall needed to be removed before their family member could be transferred. Because of the configuration of the room, the funeral director suggested that using a forklift would make carrying the deceased person easier. The funeral director also explained to the family that it would be necessary to transport their loved one in a flat bed truck, not a traditional funeral hearse. Further, the deceased person would not be taken to the funeral home but instead to an off-site embalming center capable of accommodating his size. The family appreciated knowing this and agreed to all of the funeral director's recommendations. The funeral director agreed to assist a family member who worked in construction with the dismantling. On funeral home letterhead, the funeral director listed all of his recommendations and obtained the written authorization of the next of kin and homeowner before proceeding with the transfer.

Custody Factor

A physician once said, "The secret to care **of** the patient consists in caring **for** the patient." The same is true for the funeral-cremation provider and the embalmer. No matter the circumstances or the physical condition of the deceased person, the bottom line is that every person must receive respectful and adequate care during the entire period of custody, even when embalming will not be performed. The formal training embalmers receive impresses upon them that, in all cases, deceased persons should be cared for as if they were a member of their own family.

The lawful rights of the funeral director undertaking a funeral and disposition are primarily derived from two sources:

1. **Rights which are granted and imposed by state statute**

2. **Rights arising from the contract entered into between the funeral-cremation provider and the person with the right to control disposition**

Custody imposes a claim of accountability and liability that continues up to the point of disposition or until custody is dutifully transferred to another responsible party or agent.

Respectful treatment includes at least three important parts:

1. Sheltering the deceased person in a safe, private environment

2. Providing sanitary conditions under which the deceased person is held

3. Careful documentation of the care during the period of custody and of any treatment rendered

Sheltering means a safe environment or room where privacy and security are assured. Access must be restricted to authorized personnel only and safeguarded against any accidental entry or viewing by the public including but not limited to unauthorized employees of the funeral home, visitors, outside delivery personnel, client families and others. Over the years, there have been instances when deranged individuals have harmed deceased persons inside funeral homes. In one such case, a person entered the funeral home through an unlocked side door and assaulted a body in a visitation room. The court ruled that the funeral home violated the duty of care it has with the client family. While rare, the funeral-cremation provider might be liable for such occurrences if it does not take reasonable precautions to protect the deceased person. Some states are very specific as to persons who are allowed in embalming or preparation rooms and require the applicable statute to be posted on the door leading into this area.

Sanitary conditions means freedom from contamination from such things as vermin, potentially harmful substances or filth while sheltering the deceased person. There is also a public health component to sanitary conditions, meaning the funeral director is charged with promoting the general health of the public and employees. While some persons debate the benefits of embalming and how it should be represented to the public, many other duties and responsibilities of funeral service are involved in promoting public health. In endeavoring to obtain authorization for embalming, it is misleading to contend or tell consumers that the reason for embalming is to protect the public health. It is also a violation of the Federal Trade Commission Funeral Rule and many state laws to represent that embalming is legally required when that is not the case. Although the public health aspect of funeral service is not always apparent, funeral directors function in public health duties distinct from embalming. Some of these include:

- Accepting appointments as local coroners and deputy coroners
- Reporting suspected criminal activity observed on deceased persons
- Reporting suspected child abuse or spousal abuse on deceased persons
- Reporting the possibility of an unreported communicable disease
- Participating in relief efforts during disasters (hurricanes, earthquakes, floods, etc.) with recovery, tagging, sheltering, refrigeration, transporting and disposition efforts
- Providing education following episodes of school or community violence
- Completing death certificates and providing statistical data used by government and private agencies

Documentation means developing paperwork to record all aspects of care and treatment throughout the period of custody. It includes preserving notes of discussions regarding special requests, documenting the condition of the deceased person during the period of custody and obtaining written authorization for agreed-upon procedures as well as procedures not agreed upon.

Sheltering Guidelines

When care involves only sheltering the deceased person, often in refrigeration storage, some **Best Practice** guidelines to follow before placing the deceased person in refrigeration include:

- **Unwrap, and if necessary, undress the deceased person.** Inspect the remains, describing the general appearance and condition on the embalming-care report. Record the presence of medical devices, surgical incisions, trauma, and skin color. Inventory clothing and valuables on the deceased person as well as any personal property given to the funeral personnel by the family. Any suspicious conditions such as marks or bruises on the body should be documented and reported by the embalmer or funeral director to authorities.

- ***Do not remove* any identification** tags that might be on the deceased person. Do compare the name on **all** tags and ensure first and last names match.

- **Attach your own identification tag to the deceased person,** preferably around the person's ankle.

- **Place a gown or other suitable cover on the deceased person** and wrap in a plastic or cloth sheet or place the remains in a pouch.

- **Attach additional identification** with the name of the deceased person to the exterior of the wrapping or pouch.

- **Record the date and time the deceased person was placed in refrigeration** on the embalming-care report and refrigeration log.

- **Do not stack deceased persons** on top of one another.

- **Elevate the head and shoulders** to decrease postmortem lividity in facial tissues if there is a chance that the deceased person will be embalmed later.

- **Record the temperature of the refrigeration unit** in a "refrigeration log" book.

- **Check both the refrigeration temperature and condition of the deceased** at least daily and record this activity in the log book.

Special Note: regardless of the condition of the remains or form of disposition, **Best Practice** means the name of the deceased should **never** be written on any part of the body. Writing the name or marking the body of a deceased person in any way, such as with a permanent marking pen, is unprofessional and constitutes disrespect. Considered a form of defacing the body, it significantly increases liability in the following ways:

- If this is the wrong person or the wrong name is written, misidentification is compounded and can mislead anyone else who observes the misidentification.

- If someone wants to inspect the deceased person, such as the coroner, next of kin, police, transfer agent or foreign consulate office (in the event of shipment), this practice will be viewed as being unprofessional.

- Writing or marking on the body of a deceased person is **not** a standard of care. In addition to being the basis for a possible lawsuit by the family, defacing the body is a cause for disciplinary action by most state licensing boards.

Embalming-Care Report

As the standard of care and further recommended by the American Board of Funeral Service Education, embalmers must dutifully record all forms of care and treatment on a form commonly known as an embalming report or, as preferred to be known by this author, an embalming-care report (as not all deceased persons will be embalmed but receive some element of care). This document should be permanently maintained in the deceased person's file.

An **embalming-care report** is a written report completed by the funeral director, and/or embalmer or technician that substantiates the condition of the body of a deceased person and any physical manifestations from the time of assuming custody to disposition and/or legal release-transfer. It describes all forms of treatment and procedures rendered by the embalmer as well as results, irregularities or complications during treatment.

In the textbook, *Embalming: History, Theory & Practice*, Robert G. Mayer writes:

> "An embalming case report should be completed for each body. This should be done for each body brought into the embalming room or embalming facility. Applicable portions of the report should be completed if the body is not embalmed or minimum preparation was performed for identification, if the body is embalmed for local disposition, or shipped to another funeral facility."

Mayer goes on to emphatically state:

> "Case reports should be filled out in detail and kept as a permanent record. The report should be complete enough that accurate descriptions could be given of (1) the body before preparation, (2) manner and methods of the preparation, and (3) any post embalming treatments."

Best Practice means:

An embalming-care report must be completed by the funeral-cremation provider, embalmer or embalming-refrigeration center for each decedent that comes into their custody, whether it will or will not be embalmed, when the deceased person has already been embalmed and regardless of what services will be arranged.

In reviewing records as an expert witness during litigation involving questions of professional care, it is surprising how often the case file contains no report or information indicating how the body was cared for or what procedures were performed. No record or an incomplete report raises serious concerns about the level of care and can be the "Achilles heel" in a lawsuit. Some defense attorneys estimate that as much as 85% of the defense can rest on documentation. For any embalmer holding himself/

herself to high standards of accepted mortuary practices, failing to document is inexcusable. **It means you practice below the standard of care.** It can be compared to a physician failing to document the care he/she rendered to a patient.

In the event of a lawsuit, the absence of documentation can be construed as the absence of care. Without documentation, it is difficult to convince anyone that proper care was administered. Lawsuits rarely occur immediately after the completion of service, but generally months later. This makes recall of particular procedures or treatments extremely difficult and questionable. Basing a defense on the premise that, "I always do what needs to be done," and having no written documentation of what you did is no defense at all. In fact, such a comment may be an admission, exposing you to further liability claims.

On the other hand, in the event of questions concerning professional care rendered, or when there are questions when you have received a deceased person that was embalmed by another firm, an embalming-care report completed in detail not only makes accurate recall possible, it becomes a strong element in your defense.

Some firms photograph the deceased person before and after embalming. **A deceased person should never be photographed without first receiving the written authorization of the next of kin or person with authority.** As noted on page 77, digital photography should not be used as it is impossible to guarantee security and privacy. With the push of a button, a photograph can be sent worldwide over the Internet.

Contents of an Embalming-Care Report

Most reports usually consist of several sections. Not all sections apply to all deceased persons, but those sections that do apply must be completed, even for persons that will not be embalmed or those persons embalmed and shipped from another funeral facility. The report should contain the name of the funeral-cremation provider, embalming center, or in the case of a third party (trade) embalmer, have his/her name printed on the report. Adequate space must be provided to record details of what was performed and the results. Most embalming supply companies provide embalming care reports at little or no cost to funeral homes and embalming centers.

To be considered adequate, the following **Best Practice** sections should be contained in an embalming-care report:

1. **Statistical Data Section** that records such things as the name, age, sex, height, weight; distinguishing features or marks, like beards, tattoos or body piercing; scars, place, date and time of death, time the deceased arrived at the facility; and any personal effects. Also, record the name of the person who prepared and attached the identification tags to the deceased person. Especially note instances when there are no tags attached.

2. **Pre-Embalming Section** that records the condition of the deceased person; the presence or absence of rigor mortis, purge, needle marks, discoloration, edema, trauma; whether or not an autopsy was conducted, and if so, if viscera was returned; organ or tissue donations; and the presence of any medical devices on the body.

3. **Embalming-Preparation Section** that records name and license number of the embalmer; starting and ending time of embalming; grooming performed, such as shaving and shampooing; mouth and eye closure methods; vessels raised for injection and drainage; types and quantities of arterial and cavity fluids and mixtures; overall response of the body during embalming; surface and/or supplemental embalming treatments; cavity aspiration or hypodermic treatments performed; treatment and disposition of viscera after an autopsy.

4. **Post-Embalming Section** that records restorative and/or cosmetic treatments; re-aspiration or hypodermic treatment; use of plastic protective garments; where

the deceased was placed following embalming; recommendations for further treatment; and overall condition of the body.

5. **Certification Section** to be completed and signed by the embalmer, technician or person in charge of refrigeration.

In addition to being a lasting record that can be referred to in the event of questions, the embalming-care report also:

- Records changes in the physical condition of the body during custody

- Can be used during legal proceedings, especially in cases of trauma

- Provides valuable information to a **receiving funeral home** when shipment occurs

- Provides a chronological list of care

Vernie Fountain, the founder of the Fountain Academy of Professional Embalming Skills makes available to embalmers the finest embalming-care report currently available. His contact information is listed in the Resource section of this book.

Minimum Care When There is No Embalming

As more people choose less formal elements of service and ceremony, and as "natural" viewings and funerals become more frequently requested, fewer deceased persons are being arterially embalmed. This poses some challenges:

- Everything a funeral director does in caring for a deceased person while the body is in custody, and in serving a client family has legal implications and carries liability.

- Funeral directors cannot treat requests for even minimum service casually.

- Funeral directors perform certain public health functions and must ensure a clean environment for employees and the public. They must see to sanitation and temporary preservation of deceased persons in their custody until disposition, even when embalming is not performed.

- Funeral directors must always treat the deceased person respectfully, caring for it as if it was a member of your own family.

When a funeral director assumes custody, he/she takes on an added degree of responsibility; in all instances, minimum levels of sanitary care must be provided to every decedent. Members of the public do not know what needs to be done or what care should be provided but expect that there will be an appropriate level of care. When embalming is not authorized, every client family should be made aware of minimum levels of care. As stated earlier, discussions of this nature with client families should be documented. Some states, such as California and Massachusetts have laws governing what care must be administered to a deceased person by a funeral home when there will be no embalming.

In discussions of minimum care with funeral directors and embalmers when embalming did not occur, they have said, "We did not provide any care." This is not true. **Some** care was provided, even if only involved safely transporting the deceased person in one of your vehicles and providing shelter and refrigeration at your facility. The real question is what level of care did you provide? Ask yourself these two questions: Would the attention you gave to the deceased person and the care you administered be considered "adequate" by your peers, by a client family and by a jury? Is it the same level of attention and care that you would provide to a member of your immediate family?

Viewing when the Deceased Person is Not Embalmed

Surprisingly, some funeral directors and embalmers are under the impression that only deceased persons that have been arterially embalmed can or should be publicly viewed. I do not disagree that an owner of a funeral home has the right, subject to any legal restriction, to establish protocol and viewing standards for his/her own funeral home. This includes the right to withhold public viewing of the deceased person that has not been embalmed.

It is unfortunate, that given the growing number of requests for no embalming, little or no training is provided to embalmers as to how a deceased person can be prepared for public viewing using means other than arterial embalming. The book, *Funeral Customs the World Over* (Robert Habenstein and William Lamers, Sr., Bulfin Printers, 1974), describes many cultures that do not embalm deceased persons but whose rituals nonetheless incorporate public viewing (of unembalmed deceased persons). For generations, these practices have endured in countries in South America, Eastern Europe and even hot climate countries in Asia and Japan. It includes Muslim, Catholic and Jewish communities. They wash and dress the body, and use refrigeration, ice packs and other means available to retard decomposition during formal ceremonies and presentation of deceased persons. In some cultures, the deceased person remains on view until the odors of decomposition signal the time for burial or cremation.

All steps taken during the usual embalming process, except for arterially injecting the body and performing cavity embalming, should be performed when preparing an unembalmed deceased person for public viewing.

Case Example – The Concerned Nurse

One afternoon, I was asked to present an in-service training session to emergency room and hospice nurses at a medical center. During the discussion, one nurse asked what is done to a deceased person when a funeral home assumes custody and what is done when there will be no embalming. I explained the minimum care procedures in place at our funeral home. When I was done, she responded by saying, "I'm glad to know you provide dignified, professional care even when there will not be a funeral and that you carry on after death with care just as we do while patients are alive." Establishing minimum care standards helps to develop a bond that exists among all caregivers.

Minimum care can be defined as a level of attention administered to the body of a deceased person by a funeral director, embalmer or refrigeration-care center that maintains the safest possible levels of sanitation and hygiene to the decedent, employees and general public while ensuring that privacy, respect and the wishes of the client family are not compromised. At its most basic, minimum care is sheltering the deceased person and allowing for the verification of the identity of the deceased person. Minimum care is provided when embalming or other treatment or procedures will not be performed.

Many funeral-cremation providers and embalming-care-refrigeration centers across the country have adopted minimum care standards of varying degrees.

Best Practice dictates that minimum care should include at least the following:

- **Attaching the funeral home's identification tag** to the deceased person and checking that the first and last name on all other tags match

- **Unwrapping and undressing** the deceased person

- **Inspecting the deceased person** for valuables, medical devices and overall physical condition

- **Topical cleansing,** sanitizing and deodorizing

- **Closing the eyes, positioning the body** as straight as possible and covering it with a gown

- **A non-invasive method of closing the mouth** includes using the "dental tie" process

- **Rewrapping the deceased person** in a plastic or cotton sheet and/or placing it in a body pouch. If a pouch is used, a separate name tag should be attached to the exterior of the pouch

- **Placing the deceased person in refrigeration or other hygienic care that does no harm.** When using refrigeration, the condition of the body must be checked and documented on a daily basis

Note: In some states, closing the mouth of the deceased person using accepted mortuary practices (needle injector and/or suturing, etc.) is considered to be an invasive procedure - and as such, prohibited unless authorization is first obtained from the person(s) with authority. Considered non-invasive, the dental-tie procedure is one option. Funeral directors and embalmers must be familiar with their state regulations concerning this and any minimum care restrictions that may exist. In all cases, however, **Best Practice** means **informing** the client family about your minimum care procedures **before performing** them.

Some funeral-cremation providers argue that minimum care is not necessary, that it is time consuming, adding to operational expenses. As they do with embalming, families have the right to refuse minimum care. Some funeral homes list minimum care as a (declinable) option on their General Price List. Some benefits in providing minimum care are:

- The deceased person is more presentable for verification of identity

- It double-checks that all forms of identification are attached and that all names match

- It acquaints the provider with the physical condition of the body

- It shows respect to the deceased and to the client family

- It helps ensure a safer, more hygienic workplace for employees

Case Example: A Hard Lesson

At my former funeral home in southern California, up until 1973 it was standard procedure to place deceased persons who were to be cremated directly or who were not to be embalmed, into refrigeration storage **without** checking the body. For instance, if the deceased person was transferred from a nursing facility and was wrapped in five sheets and the mattress, my personnel placed the deceased person into refrigeration this way. One particular occurrence, however, changed all of this.

The deceased person died at a convalescent home and was to be cremated as soon as possible without any ceremony. She arrived at the funeral home wrapped in numerous sheets and was immediately placed into refrigeration storage until the disposition permit was obtained. Two days later, she was delivered to the third-party crematory and was cremated. When the family came to the funeral home several days later to retrieve her cremated remains, they asked me, "Where is my mother's diamond ring? She never took it off, even while she was in the convalescent home."

Because our procedures did not include checking for valuables or other property, we did not know about the diamond ring until now. Checking the paperwork from the convalescent center, the diamond ring was plainly listed on the receipt. The receipt was signed by one of my employees. In talking to my employee about the fact he said nothing to any one about the ring, he admitted he did not read the receipt that the convalescent home had prepared before signing it and was unaware of the ring being on the deceased person. After settling on a value, I compensated the family for the value of the ring. I learned a tough, expensive lesson. From this point forward, I instituted new minimum care procedures that included unwrapping deceased persons, checking for personal property and valuables, straightening the person, topical cleansing and rewrapping the person in a new sheet, all of which served the funeral home and client families well.

Embalming

Embalming is one of the most purposeful services; yet it is among the most misunderstood of all of the services provided by funeral directors. Most client families are not knowledgeable about modern embalming practices. Claims of negligent, improper or "poor" embalming may well be one of the leading causes for lawsuits involving funeral service and continue to increase across the country. It is quite likely that there is more litigation brought on when deceased persons are embalmed than when they are not embalmed. Dissatisfaction with the presentation of the deceased at viewing can cause the family to question your competence and professionalism. Being unhappy with the "way mother looks" can lead to anger and lawsuits, with claims including emotional distress, deception, public humiliation, breach of contract and more. No one ever wants to hear dreadful comments such as:

- "Dad looks terrible; what did you do to him?"
- "I'm not happy with the way she looks."
- "Why is he so swollen? He wasn't like that in the hospital."
- "Why is the blouse wet and stained?"
- "Why is there a foul odor coming from the body?"
- "You told me that you would make him look good."
- "Why are there flies on his face and around the casket?"

Complaints often arise from:
- Purging of fluids from the mouth and/or nasal cavities
- Foul odors
- Discoloration of the face and hands

- Distention-swelling of the face, neck and hands
- The presence of flies and / or maggots around or on the body
- Soiled clothing or casket interior
- Fluids leaking from the casket

While not a cure all, many lawsuits can be avoided by documenting the pre-embalming condition of the decedent and discussing it with the client family as soon as possible. Often, the arranger who will meet with the family is not familiar with the physical condition of the deceased person. In an attempt to be assuring to the client family, arrangers can "speak out of school" and offer assurance when they should not. Making unqualified, random statements like, "Your mother will look fine" can be misleading, raising the expectations of the client family and setting the stage for disappointment and a lawsuit. To avoid this, the arranger should view the deceased person and / or confer with the embalmer and obtain his / her assessment prior to making any promises to the family or statements concerning appearances. Making statements as to how the deceased might look should not be left to chance or happenstance.

The arranger should never avoid frank discussions with the client family concerning the condition of the deceased person's body during the arrangement conference. Arrangers should also ensure that embalmers are given ample time to do the work that is necessary, especially when restorative or corrective procedures are required.

Communicating with the Client Family

Any concerns that may be raised by the family or the embalmer should be addressed immediately. Good communication among the arranger, the embalmer and client family is vital. **Best Practice** means the funeral director-arranger should discuss such important things as:

- **The general physical condition of the deceased,**
  especially if edema or jaundice are present, an autopsy

was or will be performed, bone or tissue donation has or will occur, the deceased person is obese or disfigured, or death was due to violence, etc.

- **Any special procedures required or recommended** by the embalmer, especially additional time that may be required

- **Any special requests by the family,** such as hair coloring, trimming of beards, sideburns or moustaches, etc.

- **The expectations of the client family** regarding the appearance of the deceased person

- **Any conditions that may restrict or limit** the embalmer in meeting both the appearance and time expectations of the family

Important: Make sure you document the content of discussions you have with the client family.

When the deceased person is not at the funeral home and the arrangement conference is underway, it is all right to ask questions to begin assessing the condition of the deceased person. I taught my staff to say, "I have not seen your father and have not received any information from the hospital about his physical condition. Please tell me:

- "What was your father treated for?"
- "What happened to your mother?"
- "What are some treatments he/she received?"
- "More about her physical condition."

Such questions help uncover potential problems ahead of time. Learning about the medical history, effects of chemotherapy, trauma, accidental death or work-related diseases, disfigurement, obesity, recent surgery, autopsy, anatomical donations and other conditions, alerts the arranger, who in turn can alert the embalmer to conditions that might require special attention. These questions also alert the administrative staff ahead of time to potential medical certification problems or possible coroner involvement that may not otherwise be discovered until funeral services have already been scheduled.

Whenever in doubt, ask the family and view the deceased yourself. If you are not qualified or able to assess a situation, ask for help. Do not assume or guess. Obtain clarification from the client family or investigate more fully when you are asked such things as:

- Will you be able to straighten dad's body out?"
- "Can you get rid of the swelling?"
- "Will you be able to hide the marks on his face?"
- "Would a photograph help you in repairing the damage?"
- "When he arrives from Mexico, will he look like he used to?"
- "We want grandma to look perfect and wear her wedding dress from 45 years ago!"
- "We want dad to wear his uniform from World War II."
- "Can you get rid of the yellow color?"
- "Will the recent surgery cause any problems?"
- "All of these caskets look small. Will dad fit in any of them?"

Offering assurance without having the facts is careless behavior. Well-intentioned words can be misinterpreted and cause disappointment, leading to a lawsuit. The client family can have expectations that may not be possible even with the most talented embalmer and restorative artist. Some people believe that embalmers are magicians and can correct any physical problems and re-create the appearance of the deceased person from years ago. Words of assurance by the arranger must be clear. Promises that cannot be met must not be made.

Using an Off-Premises Refrigeration-Embalming Facility

Not all funeral homes and crematories have on-site refrigeration facilities and some do not have embalming facilities on their premises. Some firms use a centralized facility for refrigeration and/or embalming, meaning that all decedents are brought to this facility, embalmed or otherwise prepared and then delivered to the funeral home at a designated time. Other funeral homes with a large refrigeration storage area rent space on an at-need basis to other funeral homes.

Under most circumstances, the client family assumes that the deceased will be brought directly to the funeral home they call for service, not to an off-premises facility. **Inform before you perform** is the rule and when a deceased person will be taken to an off-premises location for any reason, it should be disclosed to the family ahead of time. Not informing them can be disconcerting and misleading.

Remember! Best Practice means that whenever actual custody is transferred to someone else, including a transfer for a temporary period of time (such as to a refrigeration facility) and the deceased is no longer in your immediate control, the client family must be informed.

Performing Due Diligence of the Off-Premises Facility

Performing due diligence ensures the off-premises embalming or care facility is properly staffed, licensed and adequately maintained even if the funeral director is the owner of the off-premises facility. Inspections should be conducted on an unannounced basis and documented. Proof of inspection should be maintained in a permanent file at the funeral home. **Best Practice** means you are certain that:

- **The facility meets all legal and regulatory requirements** of federal, state and local governments, including standards of OSHA, EPA and other applicable agencies.

- **The security and privacy of deceased persons** are maintained at all times with entry to authorized persons only

- **Proper tagging and identification** of deceased persons are in place at all times.

- **A log book records** the receiving and discharge of all deceased persons.

- **A log book records** the temperature of the refrigeration area.

- **Licenses** for applicable employees are current and on file.

- **The facility carries separate and adequate amounts of professional liability insurance** and your company is listed as an additional insured.

- **A receipt is issued and recorded** in the log book in every instance of receiving or discharging a deceased person.

Federal Trade Commission Funeral Rule and Embalming

Embalming, and in particular, the legal necessity of embalming, is one of the specific areas in which the FTC prohibits misrepresentation. All embalmers must be fully aware of the Funeral Rule regarding embalming, as well as the statutes and rules of the state in which they are practicing. Furthermore, it is a violation of the Funeral Rule if the funeral director fails to inform the consumer that embalming is not required by law, except in special circumstances. The mandatory disclosure regarding embalming must be placed on the funeral-cremation provider's General Price List and doing so meets the obligation of informing the consumer about embalming. Scott Gilligan succinctly explains it is a violation of the Funeral Rule to inform consumers that embalming is required as a practical necessity in the following cases:

1. When the consumer wishes to have direct cremation;

2. When the consumer wishes to have immediate burial; or,

3. If refrigeration is available and there is to be a funeral with no viewing and there is to be a closed casket.

According to the FTC Funeral Rule, it is a deceptive act or practice for a funeral provider to:

1. Represent that state or local law requires that a deceased person be embalmed when such is not the case

2. Fail to disclose that embalming is not required by law except in certain special cases

The Funeral Rule does not prohibit funeral directors from explaining that embalming provides a temporary preservation to the body. It does prohibit any claims that embalming (or any other goods or services) will preserve the body for a long or indefinite period of time.

It can be argued that how a funeral-cremation provider cares and treats a deceased person in his/her custody is a strong statement that mirrors how he/she cares for the living. All forms of care and treatment, including minimum care when there will be no embalming, should be documented for each decedent and maintained in the decedent's file. The information in all files must be secured to prevent unwarranted release of information.

CHAPTER 7

Visitation – Wake – Funeral Ceremony

If there is one characteristic about funeral customs, it is their propensity for change and their ability to adapt to new circumstances. One immutable element in funeral customs around the world, among all cultures and all religions, is the common need for the family and community to gather to acknowledge the fact that someone has died. Most often, there is some sort of ceremony and farewell, formal or informal, which helps to synchronize the expression of feelings of grief over the significance of the loss as well as hopefulness of transcendence of the loss. Prayers and musical expressions are common elements of these ceremonies. In some religions, a priest, minister or rabbi is automatically seen as the leader; in other religions, the eldest son takes the lead. In military funerals, the senior officer or chaplain presides. Celebrant funerals can be led by the funeral director, family members or friends. In all instances, the funeral director assists in the planning and coordination by stressing the importance and appropriateness of such events and by directing their dignified conduct. Is there liability inherent in the conduct of visitation and wake ceremonies? In a word, Yes. Yet, careful planning and supervision can reduce the potential for litigation in this important area of public participation in funeral ceremonies.

In several ways, one might compare the visitation and funeral ceremony, even at a church, to that of show business: It is a live, on-stage performance without opportunity for a re-take.

Just as a conductor leads a symphony orchestra and is closely observed by the audience, the actions and mannerisms of the funeral director and his/her staff are closely observed by those attending a visitation or funeral ceremony. The way in which funeral professionals conduct themselves can convey confidence or appear to be "out of place;" they can act calmly, instilling peace, or appear to be rushed, adding to everyone's anxiety. The actions and behavior of funeral directors have a profound effect on their client families' perceptions of the service they receive. Actions and mannerisms causing negative perceptions are not grounds for a lawsuit. However, they can contribute to the development of claims.

Case Example – Unfulfilled Promises

In one case, the deceased person had a large family and was prominent in the community. At the time of making arrangements, the arranger admitted to the client family that the funeral home was not busy. The family requested the main viewing and celebration room, explaining that visitation and the funeral ceremony would be highly attended. Private family-only viewing was scheduled two days later from noon to 12:30 p.m. with public viewing to follow. The arranger promised the large room to the family. Two days later, the funeral home had become busy, serving several families. When the family arrived for their private viewing, the receptionist directed them to a viewing room that was not the large room in the main building they were promised but another room across a walkway from the main building. Surprised at not being in the main room, the receptionist assured them that this room would comfortably accommodate more than 100 people. Without any escort, the family was directed to the other building. All the doors were locked. The family walked back to the main building and asked to speak with the receptionist they initially met. Another receptionist informed the family that, "She is on lunch break for one hour. Can I help you?" After explaining what just transpired, the second receptionist informed the family that her schedule indicated family-only viewing at 1:00 p.m., not noon, that it would take place inside the main funeral home building but in a smaller room. Another family was using the large viewing room. Upset at hearing this, the family asked to see the arranger they met two days ago. They became further frustrated on learning it was his day off. They asked to see the manager and waited more than 15 minutes for him to arrive. By this time, more than 60 friends had arrived for the viewing and along with the family members, were kept waiting in the busy reception area. The manager explained that the large room was currently being used by another family and that a smaller room was the only other room available. In fact, and unknown to the first receptionist, their family member was lying in state and had been ready to view since the family first arrived. This further upset the family. The manager escorted the immediate family into the viewing room. It measured 15 x 15 feet. With flowers, there was seating for only five people and no room to visit with friends. Because of this major mistake by the funeral home, and other serious mishaps that occurred throughout the course of the funeral, the family sued the funeral home.

Educating the Staff and the First Viewing

When dining at an upscale restaurant, the burden for an outstanding experience does not fall entirely on the shoulders of just one person. The duties of the entire restaurant staff are interrelated. The person taking the reservation, parking attendant, receptionist, maitre d', the wine steward, head waiter, assistant waiter, chef and other kitchen staff each contribute to creating a memorable evening. A miscue by any one of them can tarnish the experience. Likewise, the duties of people at a funeral home, crematory and cemetery are also interrelated. Even at the smallest operation, serving a client family is a team effort.

Preparations for the first viewing require going beyond the routine mechanics of setting the casket, arranging flowers and memorials, and preparing seating. Success of the viewing depends upon the proper physical setting and the involvement of and communication among staff about the client family. This becomes even more critical when special circumstances are present, such as when death is due to violence or suicide, the death of a child, the death of a high-profile public person and other types of deaths that require greater awareness on the part of the entire funeral-visitation staff.

Learning about the client family begins when the funeral director is informed about a death and meets the family. Trust develops initially during a properly conducted arrangement conference. The arranger begins by becoming acquainted with the client family, observing their behavior and demeanor and noting how they interact with one another. The best arrangers also know how important it is to share some personal information about themselves with the client family. The arranger should make notes concerning observations about the client family and any special needs discussed, especially noting any peculiarities or red-flag issues. This information should be exchanged with the staff, especially with those who will have direct contact with the family in the future. The more acquainted staff is with a bereaved family, the better the synergy in providing excellent service.

For most bereaved persons, the first viewing is an anxious and uncertain time even if it is only for the purpose of verifying the identity of the deceased. They can be in a heightened state of psychological and physiological arousal that can make people hypercritical and intolerable of the slightest imperfection. Seemingly unimportant, minor actions, words, gestures, or facial expressions can be exaggerated or misinterpreted by the client family.

Case Example – The Ignored Family

My father-in-law died in 1998. My wife and her two sisters still recall with disappointment and heartache the first viewing of their father at my former funeral home. When all of the immediate family arrived at the funeral home at the designated time, no one met them. While waiting in the foyer area, they could hear talking coming from the business office upstairs where the family assumed the staff was. After opening and closing the front door a second time to trigger the doorbell, the family continued to stand alone in the reception area, becoming irritated and wondering if any staff member would greet them and escort them to the viewing room. When no one arrived after waiting five minutes and ringing the doorbell two more times, the family escorted themselves to the viewing room.

It wasn't until 15 minutes later that a staff member entered the viewing room. He offered no apology or explanation and only casually inquired if everything was acceptable.

This type of behavior is never acceptable. This is a critical time for those experiencing the reality of death. What appears to an employee to be a slight mishap or oversight can be indelibly marked in a family's memory, setting off a series of negative events that can cause anger, frustration and feelings of being ignored, disrespected and uncared for.

Timing is an important element of behavior. Unanticipated delays can bring out a number of negative responses in people, especially among those who have recently experienced a death. Timing can bring out immature responses that would not be seen under ordinary, non death-related circumstances. Failure to be prompt can be misinterpreted as lack of care, arrogance, carelessness or as an indication of prejudice.

Case Example – Disbelieving Wife

An Army veteran was to leave for his second tour of duty to Vietnam the next day. Out drinking with his buddies, he returned home intoxicated. His wife was very angry. She shouted at him that while he was out drinking, the baby became ill and she was unable to get the necessary medicine at the pharmacy. In his intoxicated condition, he immediately ran to the car to drive to the pharmacy. At the first intersection, his car was broadsided by another car and he was thrown through the windshield. The wife saw him torn to pieces at the scene and again in the emergency room where he died. At the funeral home for the first viewing, she looked at the open casket and said, "This is not my husband." The rest of the family assured her that this was her husband. The wife entered into a state of mind in which she believed her husband was still alive and that the funeral home had someone else's body.

She felt responsible for her husband's death and while she had anticipated that he might die in Vietnam, she was unprepared to deal with his accidental, un-anticipated, violent death that followed her angry outburst. Funeral directors and visitation attendants must be prepared for totally unanticipated emotional reactions prompted by circumstances unknown to the funeral director.

The Funeral Ceremony

As opposed to more frequent and standardized traditional services of just a few decades ago, funeral services today vary widely, often incorporating nontraditional, less formal components that resemble social, life-centered events and casual gatherings. As customs, cultures and traditions change within communities, funeral observances have evolved as well, and include more secular-based and customized elements. Traditional funerals of the last generation are gradually yielding to more personalized events. Arranging a funeral can require the funeral arranger and staff to deal with much more than the sensitivities of the mourners but also with such things as outside food and beverage service, props and personal memorabilia, live musicians and other forms of entertainment, greater involvement of friends, just to name a few.

Among other duties, the funeral director must focus on promptness, ushering the family and guests and seeing to their comfort, attending to the guest register book, properly displaying floral tributes and personal memorabilia, setting up audio-visual and other equipment, instructing pallbearers, coordinating with clergy, speakers and musicians, and parking automobiles.

Case Example: A Scary Funeral

In some cities in America, funeral directors can be especially challenged at times in arranging funerals. In particular, funerals involving victims of gang-related deaths present a whole new area of risk management for the funeral director to deal with, for participants and funeral home staff alike. In these situations, the funeral home staff will work closely with local law enforcement officials. Because of the potential for danger, police might even advise the family against holding a public funeral. When the family insists on a funeral mass or church service, police often recommend that funerals occur at off-hours of the day (1:00 a.m. to 4:00 a.m.), that obituary notices do not contain the location, day or time of the event, that guests be limited to immediate family only, that the funeral home not give out information to the public, and more. Having experienced dealing with these tragic deaths several times at my former funeral home, on this particular occasion, police informed the family of threats of retribution during the funeral by rival gang members. Special arrangements were made with the clergy, church and cemetery. The funeral mass was secretly scheduled for a weekday at 4:00 a.m., with burial to follow. I explained everything to my staff, including the possibility of violence during the funeral, while driving to the cemetery and during the committal service. I did not order anyone to work the funeral but asked for volunteers to work along with me. I also notified my insurance company about this potentially dangerous situation. The funeral directing staff and priest were provided with bullet-proof vests from the police department. As everyone drove to the cemetery, the hearse and three family cars were escorted by police vehicles and a police helicopter flew overhead. The police and helicopter remained at the cemetery during the committal and escorted everyone back home.

Most funeral ceremonies involve using pallbearers. When dealing with pallbearers, the funeral director is more of an instructor or teacher than director. At times, this routine duty can become complicated. With some funerals, pallbearers can involve a sizeable number of people, and present challenges and additional vulnerability to the funeral home. Lawsuits have been filed against funeral homes when pallbearers dropped the casket, when it was alleged that the casket was not attended by the funeral directing staff or that the casket was irreverently handled. There can be both active pallbearers who carry the casket, and honorary pallbearers who do not carry the casket but form an honor guard through which the casket and family proceed.

Some ethnic groups, as a custom, do not carry the casket by its handles, but lift the casket and carry it on their shoulders. Carrying a casket without using the casket handles over uneven cemetery ground that usually contains hazards (hidden holes, sprinkler heads, uneven marker tablets, etc.) is risky. If one pallbearer stumbles, the casket can be dropped. In all cases, it is important that the funeral director instruct all pallbearers as to how to grip and carry the casket, as well as pointing out the route, any steps or hazards along the way. At the gravesite, the funeral director should inspect the route to the grave before bringing the casket out of the hearse. Unless it is absolutely necessary that a particular pallbearer carry a particular part of the casket (for instance, the son requests to be at the head end), the funeral director should endeavor to have elderly pallbearers, or any person who appears to have a limited carrying ability, positioned toward the center of the casket where the weight is more distributed. If a pallbearer is a child or a handicapped person, the funeral director should not hesitate to make suggestions about positioning this person among the group. For safety, no matter how many active pallbearers may be present, one member of the funeral directing staff should hold the casket at the head end to control forward movement and another staff member should hold the casket at the foot end. With some families, the pallbearers may not speak or understand English. In my area of practice in southern California, it was not unusual to need an interpreter in order to instruct the pallbearers. At the Syrian Orthodox Church, for instance, many of their members did not speak English. Further, when it came to carrying the casket, they did not believe in having only six or eight pallbearers, but as many people as possible to carry the casket to the grave. As a part of their custom, it was an honor to just touch any part of the casket. Try as I would to do otherwise, it was nothing short of organized chaos when the casket was brought out of the hearse. Fifteen or twenty men would step over one another in a rush to grab and lift the casket. To deal with this risk, our insurance company prepared a release form that was discussed with the family during the arrangement conference that they signed. Among other things, the form explained that the funeral home recognized their custom of having many people carry the casket; acknowledged that the casket would be carried on or above the shoulders of pallbearers, as opposed to carrying it by the casket handles; and that the pallbearers would receive instructions from the funeral director. The release also contained a hold harmless agreement in which the family agreed not to hold the funeral home responsible in the event the casket was dropped by the pallbearers.

No matter how the client family chooses to say goodbye, the demeanor of the entire funeral directing staff must continue to reflect respect and concern while exhibiting confidence and being prepared for practically any contingency. In the book, *The Funeral Director's Practice Management Handbook*, Howard Raether wrote, "The funeral director should not assume a negative position unless a request is impossible, impractical or cumbersome to fill. The staff should be alert to anyone becoming hysterical or faint."

Case Example – Leaky Casket

The deceased person suffered from obesity and kidney and liver diseases and died shortly after surgery. In spite of his poor physical condition, the family requested visitation with an open casket. During the visitation, the family noticed that the deceased's clothing was wet and the casket interior was soiled. After talking with the funeral director about the deceased's deteriorating physical condition, the family decided to close the casket. At the funeral mass the following day, family and friends were shocked as they watched fluid drip from the bottom of the casket to the floor of the church. The amount of fluid became so profuse that the priest cautioned those who were to receive communion to be careful walking around the casket.

Not knowing what to do, the funeral staff did nothing. After communion, the priest walked into the sacristy and returned with a towel, which he placed under the casket to soak up the moisture. As the people followed behind the casket making their exit, the casket continued to leak fluid on the floor. When the pallbearers lifted the casket to carry it down the church steps to the hearse, fluid gushed forward and spilled out of the end and side of the casket, soiling the clothing and shoes of some of the pallbearers. During the ensuing lawsuit, many people, including the priest, testified to fluid leaking from the casket and the fact that the funeral home staff merely stood by, without taking any action to help remedy the situation. The funeral home and casket manufacturer were sued for alleged faulty merchandise, breach of contract, negligent embalming and emotional distress.

Handling Personal Property During the Visitation and Funeral Ceremony

For the visitation period, funeral ceremony or related activities, client families often ask that personal property be placed on the deceased person or displayed inside the casket. Personal property can vary widely, ranging from expensive jewelry, photographs, hand-written notes and religious items to tools, sports equipment, liquor, cell phones, cremated remains of a pet and more.

Whenever receiving personal property, the funeral-cremation staff must exercise extreme care. Visitations and funeral ceremonies usually involve many people and there can be a lot of activity. The experienced funeral-cremation provider knows this and when handling personal property of decedents, makes sure safeguards are in place. Claims of missing and/

or stolen personal property are serious and often damage the funeral home's reputation and cause financial loss. The funeral director should not assume his/her insurance company will make good on these types of claims. Some insurance companies have strict procedures as to how valuables must be handled. High deductibles for such claims are not unusual. In many cases, the funeral-cremation provider will pay for lost, stolen or misplaced personal property out of his or her own pocket.

Handling someone else's personal property must not be left to chance or to an individual's discretion.

Best Practice means developing a clear written policy that addresses the accepting, storing, placing and returning of personal property used during funeral activities. It means that all staff members who **might** be involved or who **may** come in contact with personal property are trained and understand the policy. **Best Practice** when handling personal property includes:

- **The arranger discusses issues concerning personal property with the client family** during the arrangement conference. Property should only be accepted with the knowledge and written permission of the next of kin or person(s) with authority.
- **Property received should be accompanied by written instructions** stipulating how it will be used or displayed (placed on the body, placed in a pocket of clothing, placed at the foot end of the casket, placed next to the casket, etc.).
- **Each item must be recorded on a "personal property inventory" form** or similar document that is signed by the funeral home representative accepting the property and the next of kin. The personal property form should contain the name of the funeral-cremation provider printed on it along with the name of the deceased and the date and time the property was received.
- **There must be adequate space on the personal property inventory form to properly describe the property.**

Describing Personal Property

Care must be taken when describing all forms of property on the property form, especially when the property is composed of metal or appears to be a gem stone. **Best Practice** means, for example, that when an item is represented by the family as being solid gold, it should be described as "yellow colored metal;" an item represented as being solid silver or platinum should be described as "white colored metal." Gem stones should be described by color only, such as a red-colored, green-colored or clear-colored stone, not as a ruby, an emerald or diamond. Care must also be exercised when describing such things as wrist watches and time pieces. **Do not** describe a watch by using the brand name imprinted on the face of the watch. Today, knock off versions of many famous brands are on the market and only an experienced jeweler or watchmaker can denote the difference between a "real" Rolex and a fake one. Avoid using words such as "antique," "expensive" or "one-of-a-kind" when describing property. As an added precaution, some funeral homes photograph personal property that is given to them and write an additional description on the back of the photo.

Disposition of Personal Property

Best Practice also means that instructions concerning the disposition of personal property must be clearly written out and understood. Disposition of property must be authorized in writing by the next of kin or person(s) with authority. When the funeral director is instructed to remove the personal property and return it to the family, the name and relationship of the person(s) designated to receive the property must be listed in the written instructions.

In all instances, the funeral director must only return property to the person(s) with authority or to the designated in writing recipient(s) listed on the personal property directive.

Experience tells us that misunderstandings, hard feelings, confusion and disputes among family members and well-intentioned friends (with the funeral director sometimes innocently caught in the middle) can happen with personal property. A clearly defined policy - communicated effectively and understood by all parties - goes a long way in alleviating the potential for misunderstanding and claims.

Under all circumstances, when property is being returned to the designated recipient, a receipt **must** accompany the exchange of property. If the next of kin or person with authority is not present to witness the exchange, **the funeral representative is responsible for verifying the identity of the recipient before it is released. Best Practice** includes requiring photo identification of the recipient, making a photocopy of the identification and retaining it in the file. The legible signature of the recipient and the date and time the property was released should be recorded on the receipt.

Is the Funeral Director Always Responsible for Personal Property?

It is debatable as to whether or not the funeral director is solely responsible for personal property under all circumstances. When it is received, common sense dictates that personal property must be described, accompanied by signed receipts and held in a secure manner, with access to the property limited to specific people only. Under these circumstances, the funeral-cremation provider would be responsible.

However, when personal property will be placed on the deceased person, displayed inside the casket or placed on a table next to the casket in a public setting, the funeral director should discuss security of the property with the client family. Most funeral homes do not do this. Some funeral directors have never experienced an instance of stolen property; some operate with the belief that there is no other choice but to accept total responsibility under all circumstances.

However, security and/or liability concerns involving personal property need to be discussed openly and frankly with the client family. Any agreement must be in writing. When security for personal property will be assumed by the client family it should be clearly stated on the Personal Property Form. Some circumstances in which the family should assume responsibility includes:

- When large amounts of jewelry or what appears to be expensive jewelry will be placed on the deceased person
- When it is known that funeral activities will be highly attended
- When funeral activities are scheduled at a location other than at the funeral home
- When it is evident that disharmony exists among family members, especially concerning personal property
- When the deceased person will remain overnight in another facility (such as a church)

Under these and other circumstances, **Best Practice** means having the agreement in writing, and clearly stating that the family members will provide their own security for the property and be responsible for it; that the funeral home is released from any loss, breakage, theft or other unauthorized removal of the property, except in those instances where a funeral home employee, agent or other representative has been proven to be directly responsible for the property's disappearance or destruction.

Case Example – The Missing Gold Watch

The first viewing was private, for family only. During the viewing, the family asked the funeral director to place the decedent's favorite watch on his wrist, a special edition gold watch with diamonds surrounding the face. As the family looked on, he did so. After one hour, the family informed the visitation attendant that they were leaving to have dinner and that in their absence, public visitation could continue. They promised to return to the funeral home in one hour.

Several people arrived to pay respects and sign the register book. The attendant escorted the visitors into the visitation room. After one hour, the family returned. Standing at the casket, they noticed the watch was missing. Panic set in for the family and visitation attendant as they unsuccessfully tried to locate the watch inside the casket and elsewhere. The names in the register book were checked and only some of the names of the visitors were recognizable to the family. Upset, the family called the police, who responded to the funeral home just as many friends were also arriving for the evening prayer service. In a state of commotion, the police took statements from family members and the visitation attendant and the owner who returned to the funeral home. The friends wondered why police were present and what was going on. The funeral director tried his best to deal with the situation but the family became angrier and blamed the funeral home for the missing watch.

The next morning, the funeral director reported the missing watch to his insurance company. Because it was claimed to be an expensive watch, the insurance company declined making a replacement until they conducted their own investigation. As more time went on and no replacement or financial remuneration came, the family sued the funeral home. The lawsuit claimed breech of contract, an unspecified amount of damages, lack of adequate security, negligence and emotional distress. Unfortunately, this funeral director acted on faith and was irresponsible once he accepted the watch. He failed to inventory the watch, had no accurate description of it, did not issue a receipt to the family and did not discuss security concerns when he accepted it. The funeral director was held liable and eventually reimbursed the family for the value the family reputed it to be. However, in addition to the financial loss for the funeral home, a tremendous amount of negative publicity surrounded this case.

How might the funeral director have prevented this from occurring? During private viewing, when only family members are present, security concerns for personal property are minimal. During public visitation, especially when no one from the family (or their designated representative) is present, security can be a major concern. Some options include:

- Stop public visitation until the family or their representative is present

- Remove the pieces of personal property and store them in a safe or giving them to the family to hold

- Require the family to hire its own security to be present during the hours of public viewing

- Have a staff member present to watch the property and observe all visitors while the family is absent

In some communities, there are people who make it a point to show up at a funeral home when visitation is scheduled, even for deceased persons they do not know. For some of these people, it is a curiosity factor; and for others, it can be with less-than-noble intentions in mind, even with the intent to steal personal property from the body when no one is around. While this is a sad commentary on society and is probably more prevalent in larger, metropolitan areas, no community is completely safe from these occurrences. The funeral-cremation provider, however, must be careful when accepting personal property. In addition to exercising **Best Practice,** the funeral director must be proactive and forthcoming about all issues concerning personal property.

Removing Personal Property

Best Practice must also be exercised when property is removed from the deceased person. Sometimes, property must be removed at inopportune times, such as immediately following a final viewing in the vestibule of a church or in the funeral home chapel with only the minister present after everyone has left. **Best Practice** guidelines include:

- **Use** a "Return of Personal Property" form that serves as a receipt and acknowledgement that property was returned

- **Describe** all property removed including the date and time

- **Remove** property in the presence of a witness,

119

whenever possible and have the witness sign the acknowledgement form

- **Return** the property only to the designated-in-writing recipient

- **Ensure** the funeral-cremation provider representative signs the form

Handling Personal Property for Shipment

Other than clothing, **Best Practice** means that personal property should **not** be left on the deceased person or placed inside the casket during shipment or when any other transfer of custody will occur. In these circumstances, the personal property should be removed from the deceased person and given to the family. The family should deliver the property to the new destination where it can be placed on the deceased person.

The Procession to the Place of Disposition

A funeral procession to the cemetery, mausoleum or crematory is a highly visible, important, integral part of the funeral ritual. Thomas Lynch states, "We process our grief by processing our dead." In the early days of America, great symbolism was attached to the "process" of taking the body from the home to the church and then to the graveyard that often surrounded the church. It was customary to involve many people in the community and several men took turns in carrying the casket. The modern funeral procession of today derives from this custom.

The funeral director is frequently asked to lead the funeral procession by the residence, place of business or other place of significance to the deceased person or the family before reaching the place of final disposition. Somewhat comparable to a parade, a procession for the person with a large family or for the person who is well known, can involve hundreds of cars following the hearse. Even in processions involving one or two cars, there is extreme exposure to risk for the funeral-cremation provider, especially in urban areas. Most lawsuits arising from the procession involve automobile accidents and allegations of negligent planning by the funeral home. Lawsuits usually involve answering the question: To what degree do participants rely upon the funeral home for safe transit while in a procession?

Funeral processions are not as highly regarded in every part of the country and they are not as respected by other people as they once were. Depending on a number of factors, funeral processions can be difficult to coordinate and be a logistical nightmare for funeral directors, funeral escorts and police. In crowded metropolitan areas they can be viewed as a nuisance and a hazard that adds to traffic congestion. As population and traffic on roads has increased, some counties and cities prohibit formal funeral processions. Nearly one-half of the states have laws regulating and defining various aspects of funeral processions, including how they must be conducted. Funeral directors must be aware of local and state laws in his/ her jurisdiction.

Many things add to the difficulty of coordinating a safe funeral procession, such as:

- Cars within the procession can become separated from the main procession.

- Some people in the procession may not know where the cemetery is located and if they become separated, feel they must speed to catch up.

- Other cars on the road may nudge their way into a procession, causing disruption.

- Especially when approaching or driving through an intersection, other drivers not in the procession might be unaware there is a funeral procession and fail to yield.

- Emergency vehicles might need the right of way.

- Persons not in the procession may want to get around it; some will drive unsafely and at excessive speed.

- The customary practice of driving with lights on as a means to identify a procession is no longer effective, as most cars now have their lights on while moving.

- There is no universal sign that identifies a funeral procession. Flags, emergency flashers and windshield funeral stickers are not always seen or understood by other drivers or pedestrians.

- It is difficult to accurately estimate ahead of time the number of cars that will participate.

- Some communities are experiencing an influx of people new to our country who are unfamiliar with this custom and might fail to yield to cars in a procession.

In some areas of the country, processional escorting is a community service provided by local police departments, while other areas permit the use of an outside (third-party) escort service. Some states and local jurisdictions have enacted regulations governing vehicles in a procession as well as addressing issues of liability and rights of funeral directors and funeral escorts. While unusual, some of these regulations give funeral directors widespread authority to do, among other things, stop oncoming traffic to allow the procession through an intersection and to direct other cars that are not in the procession. While this might seem like a good idea at first, I am not convinced that regulations like this are the panacea they are meant to be; they can provide a false sense of security to the funeral director, client family and drivers in a procession. For the funeral director, it possibly adds to his/her vulnerability and responsibility. One can opine that, in essence, the funeral director now assumes the role of ground traffic controller. Two questions come to mind:

1. What provisions for traffic control training or certification are included in these regulations to the funeral directing staff?

2. Even when all provisions are followed, what back-up is provided to the funeral director in the event of an accident or other dispute?

Only a few states (Florida, Idaho, Montana, Ohio) provide immunity provisions that protect funeral homes from certain acts **over which they have no control** that develop from funeral processions.

Even processions escorted by uniformed police and motor escorts are susceptible to accidents from drivers who might not be observant of cars ahead of them or the traffic around them. My former funeral home was sued by a driver who was not a part of the procession and was considered to be in the wrong by the police. Among other things, he was driving with an expired license. He sued nonetheless, mistakenly believing that by suing, he had nothing to lose and would force a financial settlement with the insurance company. I also recall hearing of instances in which hired funeral escorts were hit by other cars, suffering serious injury, even death.

For most people attending a funeral, driving in a procession can be a new experience for them. They might not be as watchful and alert of traffic, of other cars in front of them, or cars behind them or next to them. They might be unaware of how suddenly a car in front of them can come to a stop. Some falsely assume that being in a procession means carefree driving with special rights to drive through stop signs or red lights. Some also presume they do not have to be watchful of crossing pedestrians. In addition, even funeral hearses and limousines are subject to breakdown. I once had a flat tire on the hearse on the freeway while in a procession. **Best Practice** means being sure that all members of the funeral directing staff are trained as to what to do in the event of an accident, emergency or breakdown in a procession and how to document it. You should also check with your insurance agent for additional information. Some things to do include:

- Check the operating condition of all funeral home vehicles prior to leaving the funeral home

- Make sure that all processional equipment (rotating or flashing lights, flags, etc.) that may be required to be on funeral lead cars (hearse, lead car, clergy car, family limousine, etc.) are properly installed and working

- Review the route ahead of time with the funeral directing staff and escort, including any special drive-by locations (residence, favorite golf course, etc.) or possible traffic or construction problem areas or dangerous intersections to be encountered

- Always have an alternate route in the event of detours or other problems

- Coordinate with escorts how lane changes will be performed

- Provide the drivers of the funeral hearse and family limousine with cells phones for any emergencies that might arise

- Provide walkie-talkies or radio communications between the funeral director, driver of the hearse and the escorts

- Discuss the route or special considerations to be taken ahead of time with the family

- Provide printed instructions to all drivers in the procession with directions to the place of disposition and any special notices (do not drive through red lights or stop signs unless instructed to do so by the escort, maintain a safe driving distance with the car in front of you, watch the vehicle in front of you at all times, obey the escort, do not speed, etc.)

- After disposition has been made, the funeral directing staff should document the results of the procession, indicating whether or not an incident occurred

- In the event of an incident, it must be thoroughly documented, including the date, time, names of witnesses, and exact details of what occurred

- Any breakdown of funeral vehicles (hearse, limousine, clergy, and lead cars) requires that the procession must pull over to a safe parking area. The breakdown should be documented by the funeral home on an incident report

- For any accident in the procession, the procession should stop in a safe area, unless directed otherwise by the funeral escort or police. A detailed incident report must be obtained by the funeral home

- When necessary, notify local police and / or emergency services

- Report accidents or unusual occurrences to your insurance company as soon as possible

Funeral homes that conduct processions should check with their insurance provider and make sure that adequate amounts of insurance coverage are in place and that processions are not excluded from coverage in the insurance policies. Even in rural areas, adequate coverage today involves having more than just minimum amounts of insurance. Judgments in the millions of dollars are not unusual when several plaintiffs are involved or for when serious injuries have been sustained in automobile accidents while driving in a funeral procession.

In communities where funeral processions are prohibited or impractical, people should be instructed to drive on their own to the cemetery or place of final disposition. In these circumstances, funeral homes usually provide courtesy maps with directions to guests attending. **Best Practice** also includes reminding all drivers in the procession that there is no formal procession; that drivers are on their own and must follow all rules of the road.

In most lawsuits, plaintiffs' attorneys exercise the "deep pockets" approach. When a lawsuit involving a procession develops, they will name everyone who participated as a defendant. In most cases, however, the funeral-cremation provider is often the primary target. **Best Practice** when conducting processions include:

- **Inform your insurance carrier** that you conduct funeral processions. Make sure this coverage is in place and that processions are not excluded from coverage

- **Be familiar with the people who drive your automobiles** and those who represent your company. Perform background checks on all persons who drive company vehicles; maintain a photocopy of their driver's license in their personnel file

- **Get written assurance** from outside livery-automotive rental companies that their drivers have clean driving records and maintain current licenses

- *Before* **hiring an outside livery-escort company,** require proof of professional liability and automobile insurance coverage. Require the company to name your firm as an "additional insured" on their policy

- **Check with your insurance professional or attorney** to ensure that amounts of coverage are adequate for your area.

- **Provide on-going training** for funeral home employees that is documented and maintained in personnel files

- **Check the condition of your equipment** and obtain a status report of the equipment from any outside livery company

Be aware that a number of other people can be involved in a funeral procession, all of whom may add to the liability for the funeral-cremation provider:

- Clergy
- Family and friends attending funeral activities
- Processional escorts
- Livery-automotive company drivers
- Other traffic and pedestrians who unwittingly enter the procession

The funeral director must provide ongoing training to his/ her staff and have all training documented and maintained in personnel files. The funeral director should be assertive in informing participants in a funeral procession as to their driving behavior and responsibilities while in the procession and be provided with instructions for processions and directions to the final destination. Planning and organizing a funeral procession cannot be treated lightly.

Case Example – The Large Procession

The deceased person was well known in the community. Several congressional representatives, state senators and judges were among those driving in the procession. Along the way, a car that was not a part of the procession failed to heed the instructions of one of the escorts and hit one of the cars in the procession. Several people in the procession were injured including an escort. Many of the dignitaries were witnesses. The ensuing lawsuit involved people suing one another, and all of them suing the funeral home, the funeral escort company and the driver of the car who ran into the car in the procession. In the ruling, the funeral home was found to be at fault and primarily responsible. The funeral home was found liable for not ordering enough funeral escorts for the number of cars in the procession.

CHAPTER 8

Disposition by Earth Burial and Entombment

Anthropologists inform us that the earliest indication of funerals dates from thousands of years ago in central Asia. In North America, earth burial has been the most common form of final disposition with entombment seen among selected populations because of their religious heritage or because of geographic considerations (e.g., the potential for flooding). In areas where winters are severe and the earth is frozen for months, deceased persons may be stored above ground in anticipation of earth burial once the ground is thawed. Although it would seem that earth burial and entombment would present less liability than some other forms of final disposition, it is surprising to consider all the ways in which the funeral-cremation provider can be liable for what many consider to be everyday routine. This chapter also discusses the importance of good relations between funeral homes and local cemeteries. It suggests some ways of finding common ground and working together seamlessly for the benefit of all concerned parties, especially those of the client family.

In the book, *The Funeral Director's Practice Management Handbook*, the late Fred Hunter, a well-known funeral home and cemetery owner states, "The common point between funeral homes and cemeteries as separate entities is their client base. However, the involvement with this base is different." Funeral directors are involved from the time they are notified about the death, through the funeral to the time the body is delivered to the cemetery or mausoleum. Some funeral homes extend their involvement to survivors long after the disposition through various post-funeral (aftercare) programs. Cemeteries, on the other hand, are involved with the deceased person and survivors from the time they purchase property through many generations of family members who may visit the grave or crypt.

In serving the needs of the bereaved, there is overlapping involvement between a cemetery and a funeral home. The cemetery maintains and/or provides (in perpetuity) the burial site and supporting infrastructure: graves, crypts, walls, roads, monuments, gates, lawns, irrigation systems, among other things. The funeral home provides professional resources to help people deal with the loss: safe custody for the deceased, embalming and/or other care, transportation of the deceased person and survivors, specialized facilities and knowledge in other phases of professional care or in administering to the needs of the client family.

Usually, funeral homes and cemeteries are under separate ownership and operation, either by statute or design. There are circumstances when a funeral home and cemetery might share common ground but not ownership or management. In some states, however, funeral home-cemetery combinations exist and are under the same ownership.

For the funeral home not affiliated with a cemetery, the only time the two businesses are in contact is after a death, to assist the client family in making arrangements and usually, then not again until the day of disposition. Many consumers do not see the cemetery and funeral home as being separate. They see the entities as one.

When a grave or crypt needs to be purchased, **Best Practice** dictates that the client family, not the funeral home, select and purchase the property. When the family is not familiar with cemeteries in the area, the funeral director generally makes recommendations and acquaints their clients with various cemeteries in the area. When the family already owns a grave or crypt, the funeral home will typically do several things to be helpful to the family and coordinate funeral activities, including final disposition. Among them:

- Call the cemetery and notify them about the death

- When required, set an appointment for the family to meet the cemetery representative

- On behalf of the family, inquire about any outstanding fees to be paid

- Check and verify the location of the grave or crypt

- Inform the cemetery about the day and time of disposition and any ceremonies to take place

- Inform the cemetery as to graveside equipment that might be necessary, such as chairs and a tent

- Inform the cemetery about the outer burial container

- Serve as the agent of the family and act as the middleman with the cemetery, seeing to any special requests or needs of the client family

When cemetery property has been pre-purchased, some cemeteries fax an interment order to the funeral home and allow the arranger to complete the interment order and obtain the required signatures of the person(s) with authority. As a courtesy to all parties, funeral homes sometimes even collect payment for outstanding cemetery expenses. While convenient for the cemetery and client family (and to a degree, for the funeral home), this can also mean that no one from the family will see the burial site until the day and time of disposition. As a courtesy, some funeral homes make cash advances on behalf of the family to the cemetery for all of the cemetery expenses. When this is done, cemetery expenses are itemized under the cash-advance section on the Statement of Funeral Goods and Services required by the Federal Trade Commission's Funeral Rule.

Benevolent, kindhearted acts like these can expose the funeral home to additional liability. It is not practical for the funeral director never to make cash advances. I have done them myself. However, is it possible that the client family misinterprets the funeral director's intentions and believes the funeral director is in charge of the cemetery? Is the family under the impression that no involvement is required on their part with regard to cemetery matters? Is the family even given the option to go to the cemetery and take care of matters themselves, or does the arranger say, "You do not have to go, I'll take care of everything." Among cemeteries, even those located in the same city, there can be substantial differences as to how each of them conducts their business. I dealt with 15 different cemeteries in my area. Each one had their own operating procedures and requirements. Dealing with such a variety can lead to confusion. Who is responsible if the wrong grave or crypt is prepared, the burial or entombment is made and the mistake is not discovered until later? What if, upon arrival at the cemetery, the family disputes the location of the grave? Does the funeral home want to be involved in cemetery matters if the family is highly particular?

Funeral directors are trusting people. They trust that cemeteries will not make mistakes, and may think, "What could possibly go wrong?" As it turns out, quite a bit. Things change over time, especially if cemetery space was purchased decades earlier. Management and ground crews can change. New areas can be developed and new features, trees and roads can be added to sections within a cemetery that can cause a client family to question if this is the right grave.

These circumstances may not be cause for a funeral home or cemetery to be sued, but they can damage a relationship, hurt one's reputation and disrupt the graveside ceremonies or disposition. How might the funeral home proceed safely and at the same time continue to assist the client family in dealing with the cemetery? Funeral homes that have (innocently) become embroiled in misunderstandings between the cemetery and the client family have learned the value of informing (a client family) before performing. Out of their own due-diligence concerns, some cemeteries no longer allow funeral homes to handle interment orders, refusing to fax them to the funeral home for the family to sign. Many cemeteries require the family to come to the cemetery office to complete the interment order and pay for the final expenses. Years ago, practically all cemeteries allowed funeral homes to complete interment orders that were faxed to them. Many funeral homes take exception to a cemetery that requires the family to go to the cemetery to complete the interment order and verify the grave or crypt, seeing this as being an inconvenience for the family and an uncaring attitude on the part of the cemetery.

How to Set Appropriate Boundaries

To avoid becoming embroiled in misunderstandings about cemetery matters, the funeral director must provide a clear understanding as to the roles of the funeral home and cemetery. In the eyes of the consumer, and sometimes to everyone's detriment, the cemetery and the funeral home are often seen as one. Among other suggestions, the funeral director should inform the family that both entities are separate when this is the case. The best time to clearly define one's role is during the arrangement conference.

Best Practice means using a Cemetery Disclosure Form that helps all parties understand the funeral home-cemetery relationship and confirms that these disclosures were discussed. Some typical disclosures are:

- That the funeral home is not affiliated with the cemetery

- That the funeral home did not select the grave or crypt space and is not responsible for the correct grave being prepared

- That the funeral home only made an initial, courtesy notification to the cemetery of the person's death

- That the funeral home is not responsible for ordering or seeing to the opening or the closing of the grave

- That the funeral home is not responsible for the construction or maintenance of the grave or crypt

- That the funeral home has not been asked to inspect the grave or crypt on behalf of the family

- That the client family is solely responsible for verifying the location of the grave or crypt and paying all expenses to the cemetery in advance of interment or entombment, unless they make other arrangements

- That the family holds the funeral home harmless from all matters concerning the cemetery in connection with the interment/entombment of the deceased person

When working as an expert witness in lawsuits involving both cemeteries and funeral homes, I am often asked by attorneys representing both entities to render an opinion on two questions: "What responsibility does the funeral home have at the cemetery when a burial-entombment is being made?" and "When is the funeral home relieved of its responsibilities?"

What is a Funeral Director's Role at a Cemetery?

A funeral director is a person who engages in the vocation and profession of providing facilities and personnel for the care of dead human bodies, who provides services and conducts ceremonies and who sees to the disposition of the deceased. The work of the funeral director begins when he/she is notified of a death and continues until final disposition or until custody of the deceased person is legally transferred. The funeral director is the agent of the person who hires him/her to perform various services. Through contract, the client family purchases goods and services and the funeral director agrees to furnish them. In agreeing to provide services that result in earth burial or entombment, the funeral director must be familiar with the procedures and requirements of the cemeteries that will be used. Likewise, when hired to perform cremation services, the funeral director must also be familiar with procedures and requirements at the crematory.

The funeral director must make sure that his/her professional liability insurance includes coverage for performing duties at cemeteries, mausoleums and other locations. While generally included in most policies, it is critical that a funeral director be aware of any exclusions or limitations contained in his/her insurance policy. A **Best Practice** would be to have the funeral home listed as an additional insured on the cemetery's insurance policy and for the funeral home to list the cemetery as additional insured on their policy.

Responsibilities at a Cemetery

In answer to what responsibility does a funeral director have at the cemetery, he/she must be familiar with basic procedures at cemeteries and all locations where final disposition will be made. In the book *Mortuary Law*, Scott Gilligan and Thomas Stueve point out that lawful rights of the funeral director undertaking a funeral derive primarily from two sources:

1. Rights defined and provided by the statutes, ordinances and regulations of the jurisdiction where the funeral director practices; and,

2. The contract entered into between the funeral director and the person(s) with the right to control disposition.

Generally, the rights from statute empower the funeral director to take those actions which are incident to the funeral, i.e., transporting the dead, embalming, conducting funeral services, and arranging dispositions in cemeteries and crematories.

In her book, *Grief, Dying and Death: Clinical Intervention for Caregivers,* (1984, Research Press) Dr. Therese A. Rando says, "Today's funeral director must assume a multitude of roles and be trained in a variety of disciplines. How effectively does he or she discharge the responsibilities of caring for the dead and helping the survivors will determine in a large part the funeral director's success."

Client families expect the funeral director to be knowledgeable and proficient in his/her duties and obligations. Client families cannot be expected to know about procedures at cemeteries or crematories. Being familiar with cemeteries means, among other things, having basic knowledge about which entrance to use, whether to wait at the entrance for a cemetery escort, if the funeral director should deliver the burial permit and documents to the cemetery office or hand them to the cemetery escort, the route inside the cemetery to the grave or mausoleum, whether the committal service is performed at the grave or crypt or at a general staging area inside the cemetery, ingress and egress of automobiles in the procession, parking procedures, and more. Under most circumstances, it is not necessary for funeral home personnel to know how to operate heavy cemetery equipment, but they should know enough to determine if things are being done safely and correctly.

When I was a young funeral director, I was taught to anticipate that things might not always go smoothly or as expected at the grave or the crypt. People may faint or become ill, pallbearers can stumble while carrying the casket, the area surrounding the grave can be muddy, cemetery chairs can collapse when people sit in them, another ceremony might take place at an adjoining grave or crypt, and more. In one case, the young grandchildren of the deceased person were running around during the committal service. One of them pushed his younger brother into an open grave that was nearby. The minister had to stop and cemetery attendants had to remove the boy using a ladder. The cemetery was sued for negligent protection of an open excavation. Being a good teacher, my father encouraged me to anticipate unexpected events and to be prepared to manage any (developing) adverse situations.

While there is a fine line between the funeral home's authority and responsibility and that of the cemetery, the funeral director must ensure that the burial or entombment is safely and properly staged and orchestrated in a respectful manner by the cemetery. The funeral director must remain alert to situations that may not be safe: for the transport of the casket to the grave, the placement of the casket on the lowering device, the procession and dismissal of people to and from the grave or crypt, seating areas for the bereaved, and so forth. **The funeral director must remain alert to any actions that could violate the sensibilities of the bereaved and the visitors attending the committal ceremonies.**

Case Example: The Funeral by Invitation Only

The courts have made clear that the right to exclude others from the funeral also carries on to ceremonies conducted at the grave or crypt at cemeteries. In the landmark 1984 case, *Ross v. Forest Lawn Memorial Park*, the mother of the deceased person made it clear to the mortuary-cemetery that the funeral and committal ceremony was to be restricted to invited guests only. The mother was especially concerned that friends of her 17 year old daughter would disrupt the funeral and cause trouble. The cemetery orally agreed to take all reasonable steps to ensure the ceremonies would be private, as she requested. Unruly friends showed up for the funeral ceremony and the committal ceremony wearing clothing that the court described as "not in accord with traditional funeral attire." They began drinking liquor and using cocaine; they verbally and physically abused other guests. Police were called to settle the disturbance. The mother sued the mortuary-cemetery alleging negligence and breach of contract and claiming damages for mental and emotional distress. The California Court of Appeals upheld the mother's complaint, declaring that the mother, as next of kin, had the right of disposition and the right to select the manner and place of burial. Further, the court concluded that the right to determine the "manner" of burial gave the mother the right to exclude others from the funeral. Since the cemetery agreed to take steps to honor the mother's wishes, failure to do so constituted breach of contract. Additionally, because the cemetery was aware that failure to exclude the uninvited guests would cause emotional injury to the mother, she could collect damages for her mental suffering.

When is the Funeral Director Relieved of Responsibility?

Some funeral directors believe that once the deceased person is inside the cemetery and has been delivered to the cemetery, the funeral home is relieved of duty and contractual responsibilities. Some believe that what takes place next is now under total control and direction of the cemetery. While funeral directors do not have the same control at a cemetery that they do at the funeral home, they are still agents of the family.

There is an obligation to explain duties with the client family ahead of time. During the arrangement conference, questions about the cemetery should be solicited, welcomed and answered completely. The funeral director's primary concern must be for the client family.

I do not entirely agree that the funeral home is fully relieved of responsibility once inside the grounds of the cemetery. At the cemetery the funeral director oversees the committal ceremony. He or she are the eyes and ears of the client family, observing the actions of the cemetery to ensure that final disposition is performed correctly and respectfully. It is generally accepted practice for the funeral director or his representative to remain at the grave or crypt until the casket has been lowered into the grave or placed into the crypt. In Pennsylvania for instance, funeral directors are required by regulations to remain. Duties and responsibilities extend beyond typical services listed on the General Price List. It also includes seeing to the burial and entombment of the body.

Case Example: Funeral Director or Bystander?

It was to be a routine committal service held at the crypt. When the family made arrangements with the cemetery three days earlier, they made it clear that they would remain at the crypt to witness the placement of the casket into the crypt. On the morning of the entombment, the funeral home called the cemetery and reminded them of this fact. Arriving at the property, a cemetery escort met the funeral procession and took them to the mausoleum. After directing the parking of cars and escorting the family and friends to the crypt, the cemetery escort left. The funeral director and the pallbearers brought the casket to the crypt. The family was seated in front of the crypt and upon completion of the committal prayers, the funeral director cleared the immediate area around the crypt. The pallbearers helped the lone cemetery attendant place the casket on a hydraulic lift that would raise the casket to the crypt. Only one cemetery attendant was present to perform the entombment. Standing on one corner of the lift, he raised the casket to the crypt opening at the fourth tier. The funeral director, family and friends stood below observing the lone attendant. The worker stopped the lift at the opening of the crypt, but failed to notice that the casket was positioned several inches too high to go in to the crypt. As he pushed the casket from the lift into the crypt, the casket banged the lip of the crypt, making a loud noise that stunned the family and visitors below. Seemingly oblivious to what was happening, the lone cemetery attendant jerked the casket back on to the lift to try again. Without making any adjustments, he pushed the casket again, banging the top of the casket into the lip of the crypt for the second time. The family became visibly upset and implored the funeral director to intercede. Idly standing by, the funeral director told the attendant that the lift was positioned too high and that he needed to lower it. The funeral director then turned to the family and said, "I want you to know, now that we are inside the cemetery, I am not in charge and things like this are beyond my control." The cemetery attendant lowered the lift and began pushing the casket inside the crypt. However, only pushing it from one side, the casket did not go in straight and rubbed against the side of the crypt. The more the attendant pushed the casket, the more it made a loud screeching noise of metal against concrete. Unable to push it completely inside the crypt for the third time, the cemetery attendant jerked the casket back toward himself far enough so he could push it in straight. Finally, on the fourth attempt, and after causing much damage to the top and side of the casket, he succeeded in getting the casket completely inside the crypt. Watching in disbelief, the family was visibly shaken and angry at the cemetery attendant and funeral director. They could not believe that their funeral director did nothing and, in their words, was only a bystander until they demanded he intercede. The family sued both the cemetery and the funeral home claiming breach of contract, negligent and disrespectful care of their loved one. They further claimed the actions of the cemetery caused them emotional distress and public embarrassment. The lawsuit also claimed that the funeral home failed to perform its professional responsibilities and did not take appropriate action to minimize damage to the casket or prevent the family from suffering emotional distress.

In the example above, the conduct of the funeral director was abysmal. He should not have merely been a bystander. I am not saying that he should have climbed on the hydraulic lift with the cemetery attendant and put himself at risk of injury. He could have called a time out, explained his concerns to the family and asked the cemetery attendant to get additional help.

Attorneys who deal with liability issues generally agree that, prior to the funeral director entering the cemetery, most of the liability is with the funeral home. But in the timeline of events, at the other end is the issue of when the cemetery becomes liable. To illustrate, if you had a yardstick, assume that each half inch notch constituted the measure of responsibility for a specific duty. In this illustration, assume that the client family has hired you to bury their family member at a local cemetery. You perform all of the customary and contracted services, (transfer, embalming, dressing, cosmetic application, viewing, church ceremony, procession to cemetery). As you complete each duty, a notch is marked off on the yardstick: One notch on the yardstick signifies the funeral hearse carrying the deceased entering the cemetery; another notch signifies handing the burial permit papers to the cemetery attendant and having him/her sign your receipt; another notch signifies the casket placed on the grave. You continue marking the notches and completing your customary duties until the family and friends leave the graveside or crypt and make their way home. As the agent of the family, you remain to observe the placement of the casket into the vault, the lowering of it into the grave or placement of the casket into the crypt. Attorney Lapin points out, however, that plaintiff's attorney will usually sue both the funeral director and cemetery when an incident occurs.

Receipt for Deceased from Cemetery

When a funeral-cremation provider assumes custody of a deceased person and then transfers custody, even when authorized in writing to do so and as a normal, expected part of his/her responsibilities, a receipt must be obtained documenting the transfer. **Best Practice** requires that, when a deceased person is delivered to a cemetery or mausoleum, the funeral director should obtain a receipt signifying the transfer of custody of the deceased person to the cemetery.

A receipt documenting the transfer of custody is standard procedure when custody is transferred to others, such as:

- A hospital or other institution for an autopsy or anatomical donation
- A coroner or county morgue
- An airline or other common carrier
- The US Coast Guard or Navy for burial at sea
- Another funeral home
- A facility for "winter sheltering"
- An outside embalming-care-refrigeration facility
- An outside crematory
- A cemetery

Is a Burial Permit the Same as a Receipt?

Some funeral directors argue that a receipt from the cemetery is unnecessary and that the burial permit serves the same purpose as a receipt. I disagree. Each component of funeral-cremation service is important, especially to the client family and will be magnified in the event of a lawsuit. Operating a business is becoming increasingly complex. There is more accountability today, especially from those who provide personal services. For businesses and consumers alike, receipts are customary. If I get a receipt from the dry cleaners indicating I brought them a shirt to launder, surely a receipt from the cemetery indicating a transfer of custody of a deceased person to them is **Best Practice** and good business practice. A permit for disposition is only a legal form issued from a county or state office documenting proper filing of the death. Handing the permit to the cemetery attendant does not document the day and time custody was transferred. The permit does not require the signature of the person accepting it. A receipt, on the other hand, documents the day and time custody was transferred along with the name of the funeral director and the cemetery attendant. A receipt at the cemetery completes the "chain of custody" for the funeral home and is an important component of professional service.

A receipt from the cemetery for burial or entombment should contain:

- Name of the deceased person and date of death
- Statement of the funeral home attesting to the fact that the casket contains only the remains of the decedent listed on the form
- Description of the casket (brown-colored steel, dark hardwood, etc.)
- Statement that the casket is delivered in acceptable condition
- Date and time of delivery
- Names and signatures of cemetery and funeral representatives

Disinterment

Disinterment or its synonym, **exhumation**, describes the process of removing human remains from the ground or crypt. Most people and courts do not favor disinterment, based on the public policy that sanctity of the grave should be preserved and the deceased person should not be disturbed.

However, disinterment is done for various reasons:

- When burial or entombment took place in the wrong grave

- To allow people who were together during life to be buried together, either in the same cemetery or another cemetery

- For burial in a family plot, either in the same cemetery or another cemetery

- When a cemetery or section of the cemetery has been abandoned

- In legal action, to promote truth and justice, and to perform an inspection or autopsy

- When a developer obtains the legal right to build on a known burial ground

- When people decide to have their family member cremated

In states that have statutes regulating the exhumation or removal of deceased persons from graves or crypts, such statutes are controlling to all parties. In most states, disinterment is allowed by public officials attempting to determine whether a crime has been committed. Similarly, laws permit cemeteries to change the place of burial or entombment within their grounds, when required and authorized to do so. Laws also permit people who have the right to control disposition, and acting under necessary permits, to remove the body of a person for burial or entombment elsewhere, or to inspect the deceased person during civil action.

In one such case, the funeral home made claims in writing to the client family that embalming would preserve their loved one for a long time. After a period of time, the plaintiff had the deceased person exhumed. The body had greatly deteriorated and was infested with insects. The funeral home was sued for breach of contract for failing to have the deceased person embalmed in such a manner that it would be preserved for a reasonably long time.

State laws vary as to whether a licensed funeral director must be present during a disinterment and reinterment. When a disinterment and reinterment occurs within the cemetery by cemetery officials, they generally have the right to perform this task without a funeral director present. When the deceased person who has been disinterred requires storage or additional handling; when it is necessary to remove the deceased from the cemetery; or when reinterment will be delayed, a licensed funeral director is usually required to be present and provide shelter to the remains.

Guidelines for the Disinterment Process

Under all circumstances, **Best Practice** means **informing before performing.** A cemetery authority and/or funeral home should only proceed with disinterment after all persons with the right to control disposition have been notified, all authorizations have been signed and all required legal permits and releases have been obtained. Except when acting under authorization from a court order, the statutory order of priority as to who controls disposition should apply to disinterment.

The International Cemetery, Cremation and Funeral Association make several recommendations to protect the health, safety and welfare of those involved in the disinterment process. Although they are primarily written for the cemetery, these **Best Practice** recommendations are just as applicable for funeral homes. They are:

1. **The person(s) requesting and authorizing the disinterment** should assume financial responsibility for

any fees charged by the cemetery and for any resulting repair or replacement of merchandise damaged during the process.

2. **The cemetery authority and funeral home should be held harmless** against subsequent claims for decomposition of interred human remains or deterioration of the casket, outer burial container, or other merchandise.

3. **The cemetery authority and funeral home should be held harmless** when acting in good faith in connection with the authorized disinterment, relying upon the disclosures and instructions provided by the interment right owner and the authorizing agent.

4. **Where a dispute exists among interested parties,** a cemetery authority or funeral home should not be held liable for refusing to disinter the remains until it receives a court order or other formal notification signed by each of the disputing parties that the dispute has been resolved.

5. **If consent to disinter cannot be obtained,** the remains may be disinterred by order of the court having jurisdiction where the cemetery is located.

6. **A cemetery authority, or person designated by the cemetery authority,** should be responsible for performing any disinterment or reinterment in the cemetery it owns due to the cemetery's care and maintenance obligations.

7. **The cemetery authority should be allowed to adopt reasonable rules and regulations** for procedures relating to disinterment and reinterment providing that such rules and regulations conform to relevant statutes.

8. **Consent for disinterment is not always required** when disinterment and reinterment are done within the cemetery to correct an error; relocate a deceased person from temporary storage within a cemetery to a place of permanent interment within the cemetery; or reposition an outer burial container that encroaches an adjoining grave. However, these circumstances should be disclosed in writing ahead of time to the family by the cemetery. When these modifications are necessary, the cemetery should notify the client family or person(s) with authority in advance of performing them.

In most states, unauthorized disturbance of a grave or crypt is a violation of law and considered contrary to acceptable community conduct. The unauthorized disinterment of a deceased person is a criminal offense and makes a person subject to prosecution and fines.

Cemetery Inspections and Funeral Home – Cemetery Relations

There exists an on-going potential for flare-ups between cemeteries and funeral homes. Both entities are highly competitive and at times, assert themselves as being superior to the other. Some funeral directors assume they are of primary importance. Their feeling is "this is my family," and as such, have the right to "call the shots." The cemetery, on the other hand, does not like being considered second in line nor looked at by some funeral directors as having only a minor level of involvement. Despite this dynamic, there must be a good working relationship between both entities. Both the cemetery and funeral home serve the consumer; as previously mentioned in this chapter, regardless of the efforts to differentiate both services, rightfully or wrongfully, the consumer generally views cemeteries and funeral homes to be one. Both entities are under the scrutiny of plaintiff attorneys, client families, the media and even Wall Street. When wrongful practice allegations are made against one, both can be considered guilty and both will get sued.

For funeral directors to function in their role and cemeteries to do their work, it is important that both be familiar with the operations, procedures and protocol of each other. Formal inspections need not be performed at each facility; but just as unfamiliarity can lead to distrust and finger-pointing, familiarity can lead to harmony.

I suggest that funeral directors take the lead in establishing good working relationships among local cemeteries. Why? I always considered myself to be a visitor to the cemetery, even when I was performing my professional duties. As the owner of a funeral home in southern California, I contacted management at the cemeteries where we performed burial and entombment services, some among the largest in the country. I invited them to my funeral home for a tour and opportunity to get acquainted. Most of them took me up on the offer. Others asked me to come to their facility.

I asked management a key question that often served as the catalyst to enhancing our relationship, opening the doors for good communication and setting the stage for a positive discussion of any problems we were experiencing: "What sort of things would **you** like **my** staff to know when they make the initial call to the cemetery office, when they arrange for a family to come to the cemetery office and when we arrive at the cemetery gate with the casket?"

When this question is asked, it usually becomes evident that there is a common goal: To serve client families better. It opens the door to explore other areas of common interest:

- If the funeral runs late, what would be helpful to you?

- If there will be a large crowd, would you want to be notified?

- If there are special needs associated with the family, are you willing to accommodate them?

- If a family wishes to have the casket lowered in their presence, is your staff willing and able to do this in a timely and respectful manner?

- When something goes wrong, what procedure would you like the funeral home to follow?
- In the event of an emergency, who should be contacted?
- May we exchange cell phone numbers?
- What is your policy for meeting the funeral procession?
- What is your policy for parking cars in the procession and who should do this?
- How can we work together to make the cemetery-committal experience more memorable for the client family?
- Is there value in having my staff attend some of your training sessions?
- Is there value in having your staff attend some of the training I provide my employees?
- Because we both sell vaults, how can we reach agreement to avoid conflict?
- What should we both do to serve the growing cremation market?

Unless the cemetery manager-superintendent has had personal experience in arranging a funeral, he/she is most likely unaware of the dynamics and procedures associated with planning a funeral from the funeral home's point of view. A funeral director's intention to become familiar with the cemetery should not focus on being critical, but rather to augment the good work performed by them with that of your service.

The funeral director might also consider familiarizing the cemetery with the funeral home operation. Explain to the cemetery your procedures for setting appointments with families and how you work closely with religious and civic leaders and organizations and ethnic groups in the community. Share your challenges with them, as well as the steps you take to train the mortuary staff. Let the cemetery know about the value of performing background checks. If they have not performed this on their employees, suggest that they do. Inform the cemetery about your recordkeeping and the steps you take to maintain positive identification of deceased persons. From this communication, much good will develop.

When necessary, remind the cemetery of your role and the responsibilities that you have when performing burial and entombment services at the cemetery. Some may only see you as a delivery person. Remind them that you serve the client family as their agent and that you are responsible for making sure that cemetery procedures are properly done. Share your policy and procedure manual with the cemetery and ask them to share their manual with you. If they lack such a manual, reinforce the value of them creating one.

The funeral home is not responsible for the actions or operations at a cemetery, but is responsible for alerting the client family to any known deficiencies or existing problems at the cemetery. Just as a funeral director must be knowledgeable as to what to look for when conducting an inspection of a third-party crematory or other outside service provider, so must the funeral director know what to look for to become familiar with a cemetery.

Case Example – Arlington National Cemetery's High Standards

Our country is fortunate to have Arlington National Cemetery, the best-operated and maintained cemetery in the world. It serves as a model cemetery and is under the jurisdiction of the United States Army. What many people, including funeral directors and cemeterians do not know, is that the Director of Personal Affairs performs inspections of the cemetery. Adopted here, their guidelines serve as a model when you want to know what to look for at any cemetery.

The Administrative area covers:

1. Promptly reporting and registering interments

2. Records maintenance of correspondence and historical data

3. Prompt inspection for damage to headstones and other features

4. Training of personnel in cemetery policies, methods and procedures with follow-up by supervisors to ensure optimum efficiency

5. Qualifications and effectiveness of superintendent in performing duties, with attention to appearance, personality and public interaction

6. Satisfactory communication to and from the cemetery

7. Knowledge of cemetery management by superintendents and other cemetery personnel in relation to their positions

8. Estimated number of visitors to the cemetery annually and the basis for these estimates

The Operations area includes:

1. The nature of working relationships between cemetery personnel and funeral directors, visitors, others who transact business or have an inherent interest in the cemetery

2. Determination that the superintendent and other concerned personnel understand and comply with regulations and procedures relating to scheduling, arranging and burying individuals; method of opening, laying out and filling graves; preparing and erecting markers and headstones

3. The adequacy and condition of casket-lowering devices, grass greens, and funeral tents; grave

excavating and filling equipment; feasibility of using other safety-enhancing or labor-saving device

4. Existence of unusual conditions requiring special consideration, such as rock or hard grounds, high water tables, soft soil, slippery slopes, extreme cold, or other adverse condition

5. Depth of graves for single and multiple burials

The Maintenance area includes:

1. The condition of buildings and structures, including monuments, foundations, floors, roofs, exterior and interior painting, water, plumbing, heating, cooling, electricity, sewers and drainage, fire and safety precautions

2. The adequacy of roads, walls, curbs, drains and any soil or erosion problems

3. The condition of lawns, trees, shrubs; insect and pest-control needs

4. The effectiveness of trash and dead-flower removal

5. The alignment and cleanliness of headstones, markers and monuments; legibility of inscriptions; necessity for repairs or replacements

Cemeteries and funeral homes are usually seen as the same entity among consumers. Ambrose Bierce (1842-1914), an American journalist and author of humorous and sometimes bitter and macabre stories, described a cemetery as "an isolated suburban spot where mourners match lies, poets write at a target and stone-cutters spell for a wager." No matter how you may see it, a cemetery contains the remains of human beings. In serving the living, funeral directors and cemeterians have the same objectives: respectful care to the living and providing dignified care for the dead.

CHAPTER 9

Shipment of a Deceased Person

From time to time the funeral director is asked to ship the body or cremated remains of a deceased person to another location or receive a deceased person sent to him/her. This involves a new set of challenges, each of which must be carried out in proper sequence. Performing these responsibilities resembles the coordinated actions of a relay team. Though each person is an individual, they must nonetheless function as a team. Each one has a specialty and is expected to perform at the highest level. Passing the baton to the next runner must be done safely and in a seamless manner. No one wants to drop the baton. If all goes well, the entire team celebrates together. Unlike running as an individual, the potential for error increases as soon as others are involved. For the funeral-cremation provider, dropping the baton can result in a lawsuit. There is little leeway for any mistake. The potential for misunderstanding, disappointment, confusion, stress and confrontation are heightened. Clear communication at ALL levels is essential and everyone must be aware of the crucial role he or she plays. This chapter outlines the roles and responsibilities of all persons involved in shipping and shows what must take place in order to keep complication at a minimum and avoid lawsuits.

The terms *shipment of remains, shipping, ship-out* or *ship-in* are commonly used to indicate the transportation of the body of a deceased person from one location to another. Shipping generally refers to a long-distance transfer. It is common to ship the body of a deceased person or cremated remains from the place where death occurred to the place of final disposition. Commercial and private air carriers, all-terrain vehicles and other modern conveniences make possible the transport of deceased persons, even from remote areas of the world. Shipment services are provided by practically all funeral-cremation providers.

Except when a member of the active military dies, shipment is generally done at the request of the family of the deceased. In most instances, the family is notified of the death of a family member who is away from home. In some cases, an immediate family member may be with the deceased person. The family either contacts a local funeral home in their hometown, who in turn contacts a local shipping service or a nearby funeral home on behalf of the family. Sometimes the family takes it upon themselves to contact a funeral home near the place of death to handle the shipment. At other times, a referral is made by police, hospital personnel or the coroner. In yet other instances, a shipping service may be called to arrange for shipment.

What is a Shipping Service?

A shipping service is not a funeral home but a company that specializes in the preparation and long-distance transportation of human remains and is usually hired by the funeral home representing the family. In some cities, the shipping service has a contractual agreement with a local funeral home to use their facilities and have them perform the work of preparing and transporting the deceased person. The shipping service and the funeral home representing the family work together to expedite what needs to be done. Companies that provide these highly specialized services can be found in most funeral-service publications and many directories, including *The Red Book, Yellow Book* and *Blue Book.*

As an additional resource when shipping human remains, in some major cities in the United States, there are freight-forwarding companies that specialize in sending and receiving freight (human remains) from advertised destinations in foreign countries. Especially useful with international shipment, they can also arrange for domestic shipment. These companies can be found in the Yellow Pages of most telephone directories.

Where recognized by state law, the request and authorization for shipment of one's body can also be (contained) in a prearrangement contract, will, trust or other legal document. When an authorization for shipment is contained in a prearranged contract, the Federal Trade Commission Funeral Rule must be complied with after the death of the individual who made his/her own pre-planned arrangements. Most funeral-cremation providers are notified of a death through a telephone call; the process of shipment is often initiated with verbal authorization from the client family. However, as soon as practical, shipment of human remains should be authorized **in writing** by the next of kin or person(s) with authority to the funeral home hired by the family or shipping service performing the work.

Increased mobility among Americans with worldwide business, educational and pleasure travel, especially among the Boomer and X Generations, means more deaths occurring away from home. This affects funeral-cremation service and can also help determine where and if funeral ceremonies will take place and the manner of disposition. Shipment of deceased persons is a specialized service and is fraught with many potential landmines. Often, Murphy's Law seems to apply: "Whatever can go wrong will go wrong, and at the worst possible time." For the arranger, shipment requires a particular working knowledge, attention to details and understanding. He/she must work with other people who might be outside the control of the funeral home or shipping service. Of key importance is being sensitive to the needs of survivors; careful coordination with those persons concerned with the body, such as coroner officials and other authorities; communicating with the embalmer to ensure the deceased person is prepared in a timely manner; with health officials in the preparation of documents; with airlines, carriers or other transporters for scheduling, just to name a few.

Methods of Shipping Deceased Persons

Shipment of human remains is accomplished using:

- Common carriers, such as commercial airlines or trains
- For-hire carriers, such as long distance funeral transport companies and livery companies serving funeral homes
- The funeral home's hearse or van
- The family's own vehicle
- Charter air or sea craft

Classifications of Shipment

Shipment is classified as being:

- Intrastate, between cities in the same state
- Interstate, between cities in two or more states
- International, between countries
- Local, between two providers in the same area

International, federal, state and local laws regulate commerce, including the shipment of human remains. Airlines also establish certain criteria for shipping human remains. The funeral-cremation provider must be familiar with these regulations as well as preparation requirements of the body, legal permits and certifications, casket or container requirements (including those for cremated remains), outside shipping container requirements, and the policies of airline companies, and more.

Areas for Concern

Deaths occurring away from home require that the "shipping" and "receiving" funeral-cremation providers be more understanding, cooperative, patient, diligent and cognizant of cost, personnel and time factors. Deaths occurring in foreign countries or people wishing to be returned to their (foreign) country demand far greater attention, knowledge and planning.

Areas of particular concern when performing domestic or international shipment are:

- **Releasing custody** of the deceased person to someone else (third party carrier, etc.) or assuming custody from another person (coroner, another funeral home, etc.)

- **Scheduling, timing, distance and cost considerations**

- **Preparation of the body** that goes beyond just routine embalming, disinfection, restorative arts and/or cosmetic application

- **Coordination among several people and/or companies,** many of whom are usually outside control of the funeral home

- **Being aware of climatic and security conditions,** especially if an overnight stay of the remains is necessary

- **Shipping requirements** of states, foreign countries and commercial carriers

- **Legal documentation**

- **Emotional needs** of the client family

International shipment adds to the complexity of the process and requires knowledge of **international** laws involving shipping, container-packaging, certification-documentation and body preparation requirements of individual foreign countries plus the policies and procedures of the common carrier. There is little international agreement on standard requirements for shipping a deceased person. This includes what constitutes an acceptable casket or shipping container.

Foreign Consulate Offices

Dealing with the nuances of foreign consulate offices can be time-consuming and frustrating. They must be notified at the earliest possibility and you need to be informed of their regulations and procedures.

When shipping a person to a foreign country, American funeral directors can view entrance regulations of some foreign countries as being unnecessarily stringent and obsolete. **The most accurate information for each country comes from speaking with that nation's consulate office and having staff there fax the regulations to you.** Preliminary information can be found in funeral service publications such as the *International Blue Book of Funeral Service*, the *National Yellow Book of Funeral Directors*, the *Red Book Funeral Home Directory*, and through the National Funeral Directors Association. Many countries have not updated their regulations for decades. Certain causes of death and diseases may require particular preparations for shipment. In some instances, foreign countries can deny entrance to deceased persons. Some countries, such as Israel, permit the entrance of deceased persons that are not embalmed. Nonetheless, in all cases, funeral directors must recognize that every country is a sovereign nation and as such, reserves the right to develop regulations regarding the transport of dead human remains into its country. Even though you might find certain regulations and shipping requirements of a foreign country to be outmoded, each country develops guidelines that it believes serves the needs of its citizens and visitors. In all cases, **all** regulations must be complied with. Often, dealing with foreign countries can mean language difficulties. It might be necessary to employ the services of an interpreter as well as a person to translate legal documents. It is also advisable to make triplicate copies of documents so a spare copy is always available.

Important note: The requirements for international shipment of human remains, including cremated remains, far exceed domestic requirements. In **all** cases, and regardless of the foreign country, check directly with that nation's consulate office to obtain its exact exit or entrance requirements. Practically all foreign countries must grant documented permission before the deceased can leave or enter their country. Failure to meet requirements can mean that the body will not be allowed to leave or, upon arrival in the country, it will not be accepted but sent back to the sender at the sender's expense. Most foreign countries require inspection of human remains by a consular representative prior to shipment. Additionally, they will band or seal the casket and/or (outer) shipping container.

Contact information for most foreign country embassies located in the United States can be found on the Internet through www.embassy.org or through the State Department at www.state.gov.

Basic Requirements for International Shipment

In general, the basic requirements for shipment of human remains to a foreign country include:

- **A certified copy** of the death certificate.

- **Transit permit** from local authority.

- **Embalmer's affidavit,** typed on funeral-cremation provider's letterhead that states the deceased person was embalmed according to the laws of the state in which the person died and/or in accordance with the requirements of the foreign country. Provide embalmer's state license number.

- **Non-contraband affidavit,** typed on funeral-cremation provider's letterhead that states that only the body of the deceased person and necessary clothing for burial is contained within the casket-shipping container.

- **Non-contagious affidavit,** provided by and typed on letterhead of local health authority or coroner-medical examiner, that the deceased person did not die as a result of a contagious disease and further, that there are no contagious diseases at present in the city and county where the death occurred.

- **United States or foreign country passport.**

International shipment of remains can also be delayed. As expert as you might be in arranging the technicalities for shipment to foreign countries, many factors, including unanticipated circumstances (political, climatic, economic, etc.) can cause protracted delays for the shipping and receiving funeral home or shipping service. When this occurs, the client family must be informed immediately. It can also mean that additional attention and care might be necessary to the body. My former funeral home served many different ethnic groups and shipment to foreign countries was common. When sending human remains to Italy, for instance, having to wait for several weeks for permission from their Consular Office for the deceased person to enter their country was not unusual.

A useful, quick reference resource for shipping and receiving of human remains from abroad is the *International Blue Book of Funeral Service*, published by Kates-Boylston Publications which also publishes *American Funeral Director* and *American Cemetery Magazines*. The chapters, titled *Shipping of Human Remains to Foreign Countries* and *Receiving Remains from Abroad*, are written by Melissa Johnson Williams, a specialist in embalming and shipping/receiving of human remains. The articles provide extensive information about both scenarios. In addition to a country-by-country outline of regulations (subject to change without notice), it contains phone numbers and addresses of many foreign embassies in the United States. Melissa Johnson Williams states, **"the regulations published here are to be used as a guide ONLY."** The rules and regulations furnished by individual governments are subject to modification and revision without notice.

Receiving a Deceased Person from a Foreign Country

In most cases, a funeral director will be contacted by local family informing them of the death of their family member in a foreign country; however, notification can also come from a person working for a United States governmental agency. In either case, the family should contact the US Embassy officials in the foreign country.

Important Note: In their May 16, 2007 *NFDA Bulletin*, the National Funeral Directors Association alerted member funeral homes that recent electronic scams have targeted funeral homes, reporting false notification of deaths of American citizens abroad. The bulletin advised, that when an American citizen dies overseas and the person is to be returned to the United States, the nearest Embassy or Consulate will issue a certificate to accompany the casket. Unless you have been contacted by someone from the American Citizen Services Unit of the Embassy or Consulate, the funeral home should not advance funds. As additional protection, money for repatriation can be sent to funeral homes overseas via the State Department in Washington D.C. **If you wish to verify the legitimacy of a death overseas with the intent to repatriate the deceased person, contact the Overseas Services Office at the State Department by calling 888-407-4747.**

In addition to usual information obtained on the first call record sheet, the following **additional** information should be obtained:

- The exact location of the deceased person, including address and telephone numbers

- Name, phone number and relationship or title of person who notified family of the death

- Name, telephone number and relationship of person with or having custody of the decedent

- Contact name, title and telephone number of US Embassy official in the country where the death occurred

- Location of the decedent's passport (as this is usually needed for entry into the United States and ultimately surrendered to US officials)

As there can be delays when shipping a deceased person to a foreign country, you should also expect delays in receiving a deceased person. In my experience, it is not unusual to receive the decedent more than 24 hours **after** it was originally scheduled to arrive. During the arrangement conference, inquire as to the purpose of the deceased visiting another country. Client families may not be aware that, in some cases, travel to foreign countries can mean that costs of expatriation might be covered through travel insurance; through an individual's company if travel was business-or-education related; or if the trip was booked using a major credit card. In most instances, the funeral director will deal with a representative from the State Department or U.S. Embassy in the foreign country. In the unlikely event you are contacted from a foreign funeral home, you should contact the US Embassy in that foreign country.

Embalming as practiced in the United States might not be available. The condition of remains received from a foreign country can range from satisfactory to abysmal. This fact should be openly discussed with the client family during the arrangement conference. **Do not make promises about scheduling funeral activities or to the physical appearance of the deceased person until you have received the remains and have performed an inspection.**

A certificate of death may or may not accompany the body as some countries do not issue one. Ask the U.S. Consular to issue a "Consular Report of Death Abroad" which is customarily accepted as a similar document by U.S. health departments and insurance companies. **Note:** For funeral-cremation providers inexperienced in dealing with international receiving of human remains, check with shipping services or consultants within funeral service for advice.

Dealing With the Client Family

Performing shipment services, even domestically, means using **Best Practice** while exercising common sense. **Best Practice** means **informing before performing.**

Professionally speaking, **Best Practice** means being mindful and attentive to the sensitivities of your client. Client families cannot be expected to know the intricacies, legalities and procedures for shipping or receiving deceased persons. Your "know how" in these situations is something few other people have. It is the responsibility of the funeral director to anticipate all the things that can possibly go wrong and work to minimize them.

Best Practice includes informing the client family of the risks during the arrangement conference, especially those beyond your control or that of the shipping agent. Some funeral directors, especially inexperienced ones, may take exception to this, mistakenly believing that families do not need or want to know. They refrain from discussing sensitive or potentially negative events that can occur (even those considered to be remote). These arrangers assume that in avoiding discussions of this nature, they are protecting the family and not adding to their grief. I strongly disagree.

Only after the client family has been adequately informed about the complexities of shipment, after procedures have been explained, all requirements have been disclosed, all questions have been answered, and understanding is reached, should the provider proceed with arrangements for shipment. Doing so helps prevent misunderstandings that can lead to lawsuits.

Best Practice also includes providing specific disclosures concerning the shipment of human remains. The disclosures should be contained on a form developed for this purpose, often referred to as an "Authorization to Perform Shipment Services" Form. As confirmation that these discussions took place and understanding is reached among the parties, it should be signed and dated by the authorizing agent(s) and the funeral home representative and retained in the decedent's file.

Case Example: Unexpected Snowstorm

My grandfather, who emigrated to Chicago in 1910 from Czechoslovakia, lived with my mother and father in Southern California for the remaining five years of his life after his wife died. It was his wish to be buried next to his wife in Chicago. My grandfather died in the month of January. My mother and I accompanied his body on the same airplane to Chicago where the funeral and burial would take place. When we left Los

Angeles it was a typical day filled with sunshine and pleasant temperatures. However, a snowstorm blew into Chicago before we arrived, shutting down O'Hare Airport and Midway Airport. Our plane was diverted to St. Louis. As a result, the funeral events that were planned before we left Los Angeles had to be postponed and rescheduled for three days later. Travel plans and work schedules for several other family members were affected as well. I recall my mother saying to me that while this was unfortunate and caused inconvenience for many family members, at least it happened to us and not to a client family.

When making arrangements to ship a deceased person, the following **Best Practice** guidelines are helpful to prevent misunderstandings:

1. **Obtain written permission** from the person(s) with the authority to control disposition of the deceased person or cremated remains.

2. **Disclose all requirements that apply,** such as, but not limited to, scheduling, routing, additional preparation of the deceased, shipping container and/or casket requirements, permits, legal documents, health certifications that may be necessary, consular fees and security regulations. Inform the client family about the additional time that may be necessary to fulfill the requirements.

3. **Both the shipping and receiving funeral home** should refrain from making time guarantees to the family. The shipping and receiving funeral home must work in concert, not against one another. The receiving funeral home must recognize that jurisdictions in other states have their own procedures for releasing a deceased person; that there can be delays in obtaining the body from medical centers, especially those in large cities; coroner procedures can vary substantially across the country, causing delays for several days until their investigation is complete and the deceased

person is released to the funeral home; and that obtaining the physician's signature and certification on a death certificate and meeting local health department requirements can be frustrating in some jurisdictions.

4. **Keep the client family informed** of delays or unforeseen circumstances.

5. **Make it clear to the client family that shipment involves** the funeral home releasing custody of their family member to other people and/or companies. As their provider, you are their agent only.

6. **Document all disclosures** concerning shipment on a form developed expressly for this purpose and have the authorizing person(s) sign it.

7. **Be forthcoming if you are unsure about any procedure or requirement,** but assure the family you will find the answer (inform before you perform once again).

8. **Once travel for the deceased person has been arranged,** provide the family with the itinerary, along with emergency contact numbers for added peace of mind.

9. **Notify the receiving funeral home** and provide them with complete details. Document the name of the person with whom you spoke.

Disclosures on an "Authorization for Shipment" Form

The following disclosures and information should be reviewed with a client family during the arrangement conference:

• Name and address of the shipping funeral home and that you are the agent only

• Name of deceased and date of death

- Name, address and telephone number of person/company authorized to receive the deceased at final destination

- Specific method of shipment (via ground, air, train, van, etc.) or combination, thereof

- The name of carrier or transport service, and when available, the flight or train number, etc.

- Date and time shipment is scheduled or desired

- That delays (beyond your control) due to weather, acts of God, airline-carrier mechanical breakdowns, are possible

- That during shipment, the physical appearance or condition of the deceased may be (adversely) affected

- A release from the authorizing agent, discharging, indemnifying and holding the funeral home harmless from liability, loss, damage, inconvenience or additional expense arising from the decision to ship the deceased person

- Signature and relationship of the authorizing person(s)

- Signature of funeral home-shipping representative; date and time

Type of Shipping Containers

Various containers are used in shipping-transporting deceased persons depending on the geographic location of the deceased person, travel schedule and routing, laws and regulations, requirements of the common carrier, physical condition of the deceased person and availability. Shipping containers are primarily utilitarian – a simple container to encase a casket or deceased person before burial or entombment that facilitates transporting the deceased person in a safe and respectful manner, while, at the same time, making it inoffensive to the people handling the person. The most common shipping containers include:

1. **Air Tray**. This is the most commonly used container and meets the minimum requirements for domestic shipment by air or rail. Designed to hold a casket, it is composed of a 1" X 4" wood frame with a one-piece, 3/8 "wood base. Some air trays use a heavy cardboard base. The casket is lifted over the four-inch frame and placed on the wood base. Heavy cardboard pieces (sides and top) are creased to fit over the top and sides of the casket. The casket is secured to the tray using straps made of nylon. The Casket Airtray was designed by funeral director and *Mortuary Management* publisher Ron Hast in 1960. It replaced a sleeping bag-like padded unit called PADAT.

2. **Combination air tray**. Meeting the needs of the common carrier while providing respectful care to the deceased person, it is primarily used when the casket is not purchased at the point of shipment, but at the point of destination. Almost identical to the air tray, the combination tray often has an inner tray of plastic to prevent leakage; six belt-strap handles; metal protective corners; a head rest for the deceased person; and a foam or shredded paper mattress.

3. **Wood box**. This is also referred to as a "rough" box or a "railroad" box. Constructed of unfinished wood and in two pieces, it is unlined and large enough to hold most average-size caskets or coffins. Handles are attached to the sides of the box. The standard container used for years when shipment was mostly done by rail and wood was plentiful and inexpensive; it is often used for international shipment today. Once the casket is placed inside the box, the top is screwed or nailed closed.

4. **Metal lined wood box**. Almost identical to the wood box, it meets the additional requirements of those foreign countries and common carriers who insist on having a casket encased inside a metal liner that is sealed closed by soldering.

5. **Ziegler case**. Fabricated of heavy sheet metal, this container has a gasket and screw down lid. The Ziegler is used when the deceased person is decomposed, when there is no embalming, or there is the likelihood that bodily fluids might escape. Once the person is placed inside, the cover is compressively latched over the top and against the gasket to form an air tight seal. In some cases, it might be possible to place a Ziegler case inside a casket.

NOTE: Airlines and other carriers discourage funeral homes or shipping services from using any shipping container more than once. This is done to ensure that the container does not deteriorate during handling and to prevent confusion or the possibility of misidentification due to multiple shipping labels that might be attached to the exterior of the container.

Ms. Williams recommends the following **Best Practice:**

• **When using any shipping container that has a wood top, it must be nailed closed** to avoid becoming loose during handling and to prevent any wood chips, splinters or the top itself from causing damage to the face of the deceased person.

• **Use the correct size container.** If an oversize container is necessary, be sure to use one. Placing an oversize person in a standard size combination shipping container puts stress on the container and securing straps can cause disfigurement to the body. Common carriers frequently refuse to accept human remains that are not properly prepared for shipment.

- **Be prepared to answer questions from the shipping agent,** such as the type of casket being shipped and whether or not the deceased person is embalmed.

- **Most domestic airlines today are sensitive to religious and ethnic practices** of consumers and do not prohibit the shipment of deceased persons that are not embalmed. You must, however, adhere to your state laws.

Ms. Williams offers some **Best Practice** guidelines when the deceased person is not embalmed:

1. **Place the deceased person in refrigeration,** at a temperature below 32 degrees Fahrenheit, 24 hours prior to shipment.

2. **Dress the deceased person in plastic or rubber protective plastic garments.**

3. **Place large freezer packs inside the protective garments,** especially around the abdomen, under the shoulders and the back. If the deceased person is in a disaster pouch, place the freezer packs **inside** the disaster pouch. Freezer packs can usually be purchased at a commercial food supply company and at most grocery stores.

4. **Wrap the deceased person in a sheet.**

5. **Refrain from using dry ice,** which is now considered a hazardous material.

Viewing Prior to Shipment

In exercising **Best Practice**, the most experienced funeral-cremation providers arrange for the client family or their designated representative to view and verify the identity of the deceased **before** shipment. Verifying identity is thoroughly discussed in Chapter Five. When the casket will be selected at the receiving funeral home or purchased elsewhere, viewing can take place on an appropriately prepared table or in the combination shipping container. When dressing will take place at the receiving funeral home, the deceased person must be adequately clothed by the shipping funeral home. In addition to wrapping the person in a sheet, a gown or disposable pajamas should be placed on the deceased person. Some funeral homes ask the family to provide "temporary" clothing for the shipment that can be easily removed by the receiving funeral home. Viewing should take place in an appropriate room within the funeral home, such as a chapel or a small slumber or visitation room. Viewing should **never** take place in a garage, flower room, hallway, preparation room or parking lot.

Viewing prior to shipment accomplishes at least three important things:

1. It confirms the identity of the deceased person.

2. The client family sees for themselves the physical condition of the deceased person prior to shipment.

3. If any changes are necessary or requested, they can be performed at the starting point.

Preparation of the Deceased for Shipment

Regardless of the means to transport the deceased, certain professional practices apply in preparing a deceased person for shipment. As pointed out by Edward, Gail and Melissa Williams in the chapter, *The Origin and History of Embalming* in the textbook, *Embalming: History, Theory & Practice* (Fourth Edition, Pages 476-477, McGraw-Hill), shipment of a deceased person and to a great extent, the practice of embalming in this country, originated from the request of relatives of Civil War dead to have their loved ones returned for local burial. Some families personally went to hospitals and battlefields to search for their dead. Embalming surgeons made their services available and the press did much to promote this service and familiarize the previously uninformed public with embalming. Embalming made possible the hygienic transport of bodies.

Documenting Care to the Deceased

Care and preparation of deceased persons is also discussed in Chapter Six of this book. Documenting all aspects of care is a standard of practice. As is written in the textbook, *Embalming: History, Theory & Practice* (Fourth Edition), Robert G. Mayer states on page 10, "The embalming procedures used should be documented on an embalming report for possible future reference." Documenting embalming procedures is referred to as one of the Ethical Performance Standards in the textbook. It is especially important when providing shipment services. A detailed report is an important permanent record for both shipping and receiving funeral providers in the event anything goes wrong. Providing a copy to the receiving funeral home is more than a professional courtesy. It is a helpful record in the event further care is necessary. It is also an important document that can be used in your defense in the event of questions or lawsuit. Without such documentation, you are vulnerable.

While the condition of the remains is of primary concern to the receiving funeral home and, from an ethical standpoint, it must be prepared by the shipping funeral home as if it were being prepared for a local family.

The condition of the remains must also be of primary concern to the funeral home preparing the body and performing the shipping.

For instance, if the body is in poor condition **prior** to embalming, the condition should be thoroughly documented on the embalming-care report and the receiving funeral home (and client family) informed immediately. **Caution:** Some funeral homes take a photograph of every deceased person. This should only be done after receiving written permission from the person(s) with authority. Photographing the deceased person is also covered in Chapter Five of this book. The shipping funeral director or shipping service must take all measures to guard against further deterioration of the body while he/she has custody of it. From embalming to the time the deceased person is released to the shipping agent, critical duties of the shipping funeral home or person having custody of the body includes ongoing monitoring of the condition of the body. Post-embalming problems such as dehydration, purge, leakage, skin slip, foul odors, gas formation, discoloration of tissues, formation of mold and other problems must be guarded against. The embalmer must do all he/she can to prevent these conditions from occurring and if they develop, rectify them before shipment takes place.

For shipment, additional embalming preparations are **standard,** not an exception. Mayer provides a detailed outline of **Best Practices** and the responsibilities of the shipping funeral home. They are:

- **Notify the embalmer** as soon as possible that the deceased person will be shipped.

- **Before embalming, inspect the deceased person,** noting the condition and any problem areas on an embalming-care report.

- **Treat *all* areas of the body thoroughly.**

- **Pay particular attention to external orifices;** pack them with absorbent materials to prevent leakage.

- **Discuss restorative and cosmetic treatments** that may be necessary or other special circumstances with the family and receiving funeral home and whether these treatments should be done by the shipping or receiving funeral home.

- **Place the person in plastic garments** after embalming and before dressing the deceased person in clothing.

- **Maintain respect** by placing a disposable gown or other garments over the plastic garments and wrap the person in a sheet when the person will not be dressed at the point of shipment.

- **Place a liner of plastic inside the interior of the casket or container** to contain any fluids and prevent soiling the casket interior; reverse the pillow or cover it in plastic to prevent soiling.

- **Place absorbent material around the neck, head and facial areas of the deceased person** to contain fluids and prevent soiling clothing or the casket interior.

- **Before shipping, inform the receiving funeral home** about the physical condition of the deceased person. Document and retain in the decedent's file the name of the receiving person spoken to along with the date, time and remarks.

- **Give all details to the receiving funeral home,** including name of carrier, flight number if applicable, date, time, air bill number or other means of tracking, the type of shipping container used and whether or not the deceased person will arrive in a casket. When shipment is done by vehicle, provide the receiving funeral home with the cell phone number of the driver. All fax and email transmissions between funeral homes should be followed up with telephone calls to make sure the information was received.

- **Keep the family informed** about the scheduling and important developments, documenting the day, time and person with whom you spoke.

- **Fax a copy of the embalming care report to the receiving funeral home** and enclose another copy inside the casket/container.

To this list, I add the following **Best Practices:**

- **Ensure that a permanent form of identification is attached to the body,** such as around the ankle, in such a fashion that it cannot be removed unless it is cut off. First and last names must match on all forms of identification.

- **Perform additional aspiration** of abdominal, thoracic, buccal and nasal cavities prior to shipping.

171

- **Secure the deceased in the casket or container** in such a manner that it will not slip down or bounce during transport. If shipment is done in a casket with an adjustable interior bed, lower the bed to its lowest level.

- **Do not ship jewelry or valuable personal property inside the casket or container.** Clothing to be shipped in the casket-container should be wrapped in protective material to prevent soiling.

- **Prominently write the name of the deceased person on the outside of the shipping container** along with the name, address and telephone number of the receiving funeral home.

- **Obtain a receipt** that records the date, time and name of representative accepting remains and any other pertinent information when custody is transferred.

In return, the receiving funeral home should:

- **Cooperate** with shipping provider.

- **Refrain** from committing to scheduled ceremonies or disposition until it is safe to do so.

- **Be forthcoming** with the client family about the potential for delays.

- **Notify** the client family when the deceased person arrives at your facility.

- **Obtain** a receipt that records the date, time and signatures of all representatives and any other pertinent details in **all** cases, when you assume custody.

- **Inspect** the deceased person upon arrival at the funeral home or care center. On your embalming-care report, document the physical condition of the deceased person, noting if re-aspiration is necessary; if restorative work needs to be performed; any areas requiring further treatment; and any cosmetic application to be performed. Many times, the deceased person is shipped with the mutual understanding that restorative and/or cosmetic application will be performed by the receiving funeral home. Document the work you perform on your embalming-care report. Retain the shipping funeral home's embalming-care report in the deceased person's file.

- **Inform** the family about any adjustments or additional treatment that may be necessary.

A funeral director friend once told me of a time when he went to the train station to receive a deceased person. When he arrived at the station with the hearse, he expected to receive the deceased person in a wooden shipping container, commonly used at that time. Instead, the shipping funeral home transported the deceased in a casket which was encased inside a burial vault. Never informed by the receiving funeral home that the vault would also be shipped, the funeral home had to rent a heavy-duty open-bed truck capable of handling the heavy, oversize vault.

When shipment services are requested, both the shipping and receiving funeral homes serve the client family. Anxiety on the part of the client family is usually heightened, especially when something as unfamiliar as transporting their family member is involved. Both funeral homes must be sensitive to the needs of the family and to the work each funeral home is performing. Professional cooperation, due diligence and especially good communication among all parties helps ensure a successful outcome for the client family and the shipping and receiving funeral homes.

Case Example: Left Alone at the Airport

After local ceremonies, the Washington funeral director was to ship the deceased person to Puerto Rico, where additional ceremonies and burial would take place. The deceased person was taken to the airport and consigned to the airlines. Three days later, he received a call from the family. Angry and in tears, they told him that the funeral home in Puerto Rico did not meet their loved one at the airport and was never informed of the shipment. As a result, the deceased person was left unattended, and for two days sat inside a shipping hangar at the airport where temperatures reached over 105 degrees. Not receiving proper care or treatment, the person began decomposing, making viewing for family and friends in Puerto Rico impossible. The Washington funeral director admitted to the family that he never called the funeral home in Puerto Rico; that when he made the arrangements with the airlines, they promised to notify the receiving funeral home. The airline never did. The family sued both the airline and the funeral home, claiming breach of contract, that their right to a funeral and viewing was denied them and for infliction of emotional distress. The family reached a six-figure settlement.

Local Shipment or Transfer of Remains

Local shipment - transferring custody of the body from one (local) provider to another (local) provider - might be necessary. Local transfer-shipment can occur for several reasons. In emergency situations, one funeral home might ask another funeral home to help them as a courtesy. As an example, when my entire staff was working a long-distance funeral and I was at the office with a back problem, I received a residence call. I called a competitor, who agreed to meet me at the residence and help me. There can also be circumstances when a family engages one funeral home and, for whatever reason, changes its mind and selects another funeral home to serve them. In these circumstances, the funeral home that will serve the family should supply the other funeral home with an executed release authorization signed by the person(s) with authority ordering the change of custody. Both funeral homes should cooperate in sharing information and providing any legal documents that may have been obtained to this point. Courtesy should be extended regarding the timing and scheduling of making the transfer. Even transfers among local funeral homes must be documented with a receipt.

Shipment of Cremated Remains

As requests for cremation increase, so too will requests for shipment of cremated remains increase. For our purpose in this section, shipment of cremated remains also includes the release or delivery of cremated remains by the crematory to the funeral-cremation provider, as well as shipment of cremated remains using a mailing-delivery service. There have been many lawsuits throughout the country due to cremated remains being misidentified, misplaced or lost during shipment. For the funeral-cremation provider who is asked to ship cremated remains, proper identification, packaging, labeling and storing is critical, as is the means of shipment. It is vital to have a foolproof system in place ensuring, among other considerations:

- Proper storage, respectful care and safekeeping of cremated remains until they are shipped from the funeral home or crematory or otherwise properly released

- Proper identification of the cremated remains container to ensure that only the correct cremated remains are shipped

- That cremated remains are shipped using accepted carriers

- That cremated remains are shipped in a cremated remains container that meets minimum requirements of safety, durability and respect

All persons who become involved in the chain of custody with the cremated remains must exercise extreme care to prevent any mix-up of identity, misplacement or loss of the cremated remains: from the first call and assuming custody of the body at the place of death; through arrival at the funeral home; storage of the deceased person; transportation to the crematory; the incineration process; removal of the person's cremated body from the chamber; the processing-packaging of the person's cremated remains; the labeling of the container and subsequent return of the person's cremated remains to the funeral home or care-center.

Best Practice Guidelines for Receiving Cremated Remains at the Funeral Home from the Crematory

Most funeral homes do not own their own crematory but use the services of an outside crematory. Lawsuits have developed when funeral homes have misidentified, mishandled and misplaced cremated remains they received from the crematory. Specific procedures must be in place and followed by persons at the funeral home who are designated to retrieve, receive and place them in temporary storage. Guidelines include:

- Cremated remains should only be brought to a **specific location within the funeral home.** Funeral home staff should not leave cremated remains in an area of public activity, such as the reception area, in an arrangement office, employee lounge or the flower receiving room.

- Anyone delivering cremated remains to the funeral home, especially outside service employees or crematory personnel, should be instructed as to the proper location within the funeral home where they are to be received.

- Cremated remains should only be accepted by persons **designated and trained** to receive them (not the cleaning lady, a grounds keeper or temporary workers, for instance).

- Upon receiving them, **inspect** the cremated remains container. Confirm that all labels and legal documents-permits are attached and that the name of the deceased person matches on all paperwork and labels.

- In a log book or other permanent record, list the name of the deceased person, date of death, the date and time of arrival at the funeral home and a description of the container along with the name of the delivery person and person who accepted them, regardless of whether delivery has been made by an employee of the funeral home or a third party.

- In all instances of delivery by a third-party, a receipt for the acceptance of the cremated remains must be issued. The receipt should contain the name of the deceased person, the date and time of delivery, the name of the delivery person, name of the person accepting the cremated remains and a description of the cremated remains container.

- Review the decedent's file and check the instructions for shipping and/or disposition. Check that all paperwork and authorizations are complete. If there is any doubt or question concerning identity of the cremated remains or disposition, **do not** proceed with any further release of the cremated remains, disposition or shipment until the matter has been cleared up.

- If cremated remains will be held at the funeral home even for a temporary period of time, for instance, until they are taken to the post office, place the cremated remains and appropriate paperwork that accompanies the cremated remains in a **locked** cabinet or room. Each container should be placed in its own storage space and externally identified in a predominate manner so identity (name and method of disposition) can be easily discerned by personnel with access to this room.

- Record the date and time cremated remains are placed in storage and its location. Confirm with your signature or initials.

- Most funeral homes have a "daily activity" board in the business or arranger's office that informs employees as to decedents in custody and what will take place.

Write the name of the person whose cremated remains were placed in storage, along with disposition on the activity board. Consider automating this process with scheduling software to ensure tighter coordination among employees and a way to preserve your process in a lasting document.

• When cremated remains are removed from storage and prepared for shipment (or disposition), the reverse order including completing the log records and receipts should be completed. The log book should record every step of custody, including the names and signatures of funeral home personnel who handle the cremated remains.

In my experiences working in litigation involving wrongful shipment or disposal of cremated remains, or when a person's cremated remains have been lost, problems usually arise because the funeral-cremation provider has no procedures or incomplete procedures in place; permits untrained personnel to handle them; treats the handling and temporary storage of cremated remains casually; and does not provide adequate supervision or training to employees.

Case Example: An Unexpected Trip to Hawaii

The funeral director returned to his office from the crematory carrying the cremated remains of two deceased persons. Both persons happened to be in identical urns. He placed both containers on the desk in the business office and carefully reviewed the instructions in each file. Both deceased person's cremated remains were to be mailed to their respective family members - one to the daughter in Minnesota; the other to the son in Hawaii. Transit and disposition permits were attached to each container. He placed each container in a separate shipping container and taped each box closed. He typed out two separate mailing labels.

Before he was about to affix the mailing labels to each box, the front door bell rang. He set the labels down and went to the front door. When he finished with the visitor, the telephone rang and he took the call. While he was on the phone, a florist walked in the front door and delivered two flower arrangements. Returning to the business office ten minutes later, the funeral director became confused over the two shipping boxes. Failing to double-check the contents of both shipping boxes, he mistakenly placed the wrong shipping labels on the containers and took them to the Post Office.

When the packages containing the cremated remains were received by both families – one in Minnesota and one in Hawaii – neither party opened them but placed them in a closet. Three months after receiving his father's cremated remains, the son in Hawaii decided to open the shipping box containing his father's cremated remains. He noticed the name on the paperwork and urn was not the name of his father, but that of someone else. He called the funeral home and reported this. The funeral director checked the decedent's file and confirmed that the urn was sent to Hawaii. In checking the file on the other person, he noticed the urn was sent to Minnesota. He asked the son to hold the urn and that he would call him back.

In a panic the funeral director called the crematory and asked them to check their cremation log book and receipt book. The crematory informed the funeral director that three months ago two cremations were performed for his funeral home, within 24 hours of each other. The log indicated that the cremated remains of both persons were placed in identical urns and that the funeral director picked up both urns on the same day. The funeral director now surmised that he misidentified and mislabeled the shipping boxes. The funeral director called the daughter in Minnesota and explained his error. He asked, "Do you still have the container holding your father's cremated remains that I mailed to you three months ago?" She replied that she did. He asked her to open the shipping box and check the name that appeared on the paperwork and the cremated remains container. Indeed, the funeral director mislabeled the containers. Fortunately, neither client had disposed of them. The daughter in Minnesota was grateful that the error was discovered as the family planned to scatter the cremated remains at a lake in two weeks. In this case, both families were understanding and only wanted the cremated remains of their loved one. In fact, the daughter in Minnesota exhibited a sense of humor telling the funeral director, "Well, my mother always wanted to go to Hawaii and you made it possible." But think of how badly this mistake could have turned out if either family had decided to scatter the cremated remains. The funeral home dodged a potentially costly landmine...this time.

Shipping Cremated Remains

Even in states that do not designate human cremated remains as being the body of an individual, **our training and education impresses upon us that any form or quantity of human remains represents someone's family member.** Funeral-cremation providers must treat each deceased person or a person's cremated remains as if they are a member of his/her family.

The same care and diligence that one would exercise in shipping or transporting a non-cremated human body must also be exercised when shipping or transporting human cremated remains.

The standard method in funeral-cremation service for shipping cremated remains domestically (other than by personally delivering them) is using the mailing services of the **United States Postal Service (USPS).**

At present, Federal Express, UPS and DHL Express (knowingly) do not accept human cremated remains. All shipping companies require being informed of the contents of the package.

USPS delivers to all 50 states and is accustomed to handling human cremated remains. Unlike other services, USPS provides funeral directors and client families with a means of permanently tracking the package anywhere along the shipment process as well as a high-level of security by keeping them under lock and key at all times. U.S. Postal Service employees have been trained to accept a person's cremated remains and, according to Postal Bulletin 22018, they are to **"be sent as registered mail with return receipt services."**

The bulletin goes on to say, **"Employees who do not enforce this regulation risk putting the Postal Service in the uncomfortable position of losing or delaying these items, possibly at the great emotional distress to families of deceased persons. Cremated remains are not to be sent by overnight express mail, regular mail or certified mail."**

According to the USPS, **registered mail** service means that every postal employee who touches the package (of cremated remains) throughout the chain of custody signs their name on a confirmation slip. Further, once they are handed to the USPS, packages containing a person's cremated remains are kept under lock and key at all times, even in mail bags during transport. Return-receipt service means the shipping person receives a receipt confirmation of delivery. These regulations and safe practice policies are important to all funeral-cremation providers and consumers.

Local USPS offices require the person's cremated remains to be in a container and shipping box that prevents any leakage or spilling of contents; that the outer package be wrapped in brown paper and the total weight of the package not exceed 70 pounds. The identity of the contents must be marked on the address side. To ensure the integrity of the cremated remains during shipment, a cardboard urn is not recommended for shipment.

International Shipment of Cremated Remains

It is not advisable for the funeral-cremation provider to mail cremated remains out of the country using the USPS or any other mail or delivery service. Once the package leaves the continental United States, it also leaves the USPS system. It becomes impossible to track or account for the whereabouts of the package. When families request cremated remains sent to a foreign country, the funeral home should recommend that the cremated remains not be mailed but transported by a family member or a friend, carried on board in a container that will pass x-ray screening or placed in checked luggage.

Just as a funeral director must check the entry requirements of a foreign country when shipping a non-cremated person, **the funeral director must ascertain the entry requirements for cremated remains** of the country in question prior to advising the family. You are encouraged to check directly with that foreign country's consulate office for this information.

Carry-On Cremated Remains and TSA Requirements

Since the events of 9/11, the Department of Homeland Security through the Transportation Security Administration (TSA), has implemented new procedures affecting those passengers attempting to transport a container holding cremated remains on airplanes as carry-on luggage. As a result, funeral-cremation service has been affected. Whereas our predecessors never had to deal with these issues, arrangers today must take the new TSA directive into consideration during the arrangement conference.

To avoid potential problems when the family expresses a desire to handle disposition, arrangers can no longer be passive and must ask them in what way disposition will take place. If they will be moved by commercial airlines, **Best Practice** means the arranger must inform the client family about the TSA security directives and assist them in complying with these regulations. Failing to do so can mean that you may be liable for damages.

I know of situations in which family members have arrived at the airport carrying cremated remains and were not allowed through security because the urn did not pass the security checkpoint. In some of these cases, flight and hotel reservations for several family members had to be changed at great expense and funeral ceremonies rescheduled – all because the arranger did not ask the family what they planned to do with the cremated remains. These types of unfortunate situations fuel anger and resentment toward the funeral-cremation provider.

Passengers are still allowed to carry-on an urn, but it must pass through the x-ray machine. Urns that pass through x-ray do not generate an opaque image but allow the security screener to clearly view the contents of the urn-container. **If these criteria are not met, the container will not be allowed through the security checkpoint.** TSA points out that under no circumstances will the screener open the container, even when the passenger insists it be done. If the x-rayed image is opaque, the next option is to transport the container in checked luggage, providing it passes testing for explosive materials or devices.

TSA Cremated Remains Container Requirements

Cremated-remains containers constructed of wood, plastic and unlined lead generally pose no problem for TSA security screeners. If a metal or lead-lined urn will be used, it should be in checked luggage, empty and unsealed. Upon reaching the destination, the person's cremated remains can be transferred into the metal urn. A cardboard urn is never recommended for shipment purposes. Cardboard presents obvious strength and durability concerns and adds to liability for the funeral-cremation provider. A person's cremated remains should **never** be shipped in a cardboard container. A minimum cremated remains container is constructed of a sturdy material like plastic or wood.

Cremated remains may be shipped internationally as "cargo" via scheduled aircraft. The funeral director should check directly with the airlines to ascertain their exact requirements **in addition** to the requirements of the foreign country. In all cases, the package should be identified as containing human cremated remains and be issued its own, separate air way bill. This allows the package to be tracked at all times during shipment. Cremated remains should not be shipped internationally with other items, but by themselves.

Proportioning Cremated Remains

In the early 1990s, "Options" by Batesville advanced the concept of marketing small-sized urns to the industry and referred to them as "keepsake urns." Keepsake urns are designed to hold small amounts of a person's cremated remains that are separated from the main body of the cremated remains. Keepsake urns have quickly become common and are available at most funeral homes. Popular with some client families who choose cremation, they provide an opportunity for memorialization in multiple sites and/or permit multiple individuals to retain a portion of their loved one. I am aware of one funeral home that divided the cremated remains of one person into 17 sections and placed them in 17 keepsake urn. Especially when cremated remains will be scattered, keepsake urns make possible retention of a portion of the body. There are three major sizes of keepsake urns:

1. Regular keepsake

2. Miniature keepsake

3. Jewelry keepsake

Unlike full size urns that have a capacity of 180 to 400 cubic inches, keepsake-size urns hold small amounts of cremated remains, ranging from minute amounts (jewelry size) to 1 cubic inch (miniature size) to between 9 to 40 cubic inches (regular size). Jewelry keepsake-size urns that hold minute amounts of cremated remains are available in necklaces, rings, bracelets and earrings.

It is critical that cremated remains not be proportioned or divided without first receiving written authorization from the next of kin or person(s) with authority to control disposition and a confirmation that the cremated remains will be used for proper and respectful purposes. When dividing cremated remains, **Best Practice** dictates that your documentation should include:

- The date, time and name of the funeral home representative dividing the cremated remains

- An indication as to the amount of cremated remains separated from the original volume

- A description of the keepsake urn(s)

- Disposition of the keepsake urn(s)

At all times, the identity of the deceased person must be preserved. A permanent form of identification containing the name of the deceased person must be attached to the keepsake urn and/or placed inside the urn.

For the client family, shipment of a family member can be a trying experience. The bereaved family has neither the training or knowledge in determining what needs to be done and cannot be expected to know of the many corollary duties and responsibilities associated with this process. Experience and the ability to communicate qualify the funeral director to be of immense value when asked to perform this service. In all cases, the utmost discretion must be exercised and misrepresentation avoided. This service should only be rendered with the same care and attention to detail as when serving one's own client family.

CHAPTER 10

Outside Service Providers
Duty of Care and Negligence

The philosopher Alfred North Whitehead once observed something that pertains to many enterprises: "Progress brings complexity, and complexity brings decay." In other words, enterprises like funeral service tend to accumulate problems as they grow and mature. To provide an increasingly broad array of services to client families, funeral directors routinely contract for a spectrum of services, ranging from those who clean the building to those who cremate deceased persons. The "undertaker" of old is the "director" of today. Like the general with part of his army out of sight, the funeral director must be circumspect, continually informed and aware of all that is going on. Like the good general, he must practice as though the unexpected could occur at any time. The reader will gain understanding of best practices that must be performed with internal staff and outside contractors in order to operate satisfactorily, even in the absence of immediate, direct oversight.

As an occupation in America, funeral directing evolved by adding to it various tasks that were previously performed by other people and occupations. As detailed in the book, *The History of American Funeral Directing*, a variety of persons or groups within the community participated in caring for the dead and the bereaved in early America. This was done not as a business venture but as a personal service. Friends and neighbors were usually the first people to respond and render aid. As populations increased and tasks involved in caring for the dead increased in number and complexity, a business evolved around persons willing to "undertake" particular tasks and who involved other tradesmen and craftsmen to provide certain goods and services. Among others, it included: People who helped prepare the body, often adult women or a nurse-governess that lived in the area; local neighbors, a sexton or church caretaker who dug the grave; the proprietor of coaches and carts who provided transportation including bearers and under bearers to carry the coffin; and the woodworker-carpenter-furniture maker who made the coffin.

As the undertaking role continued to evolve, these and more tasks became assimilated under the title "funeral undertaker," operating as a service occupation that included preparing the deceased for the wake and putting the person in a coffin and proceeding to the grave. In time, other services and conveniences also were undertaken that supplemented the basic duties, offering burial clothing, emblems, equipment, printed goods and other funeral paraphernalia to the bereaved. In addition to being a furnisher of goods, the undertaker evolved into a provider of personal services to client families.

Today, the care, preparation and disposal of the dead are entrusted to licensed professionals including funeral directors, embalmers, cemeterians and crematory owners and operators who involve other support personnel.

Duties to a client family vary widely based on needs of the survivors, legal requirements in different jurisdictions, manner of death, timing, geographical elements, type of disposition, ethnicity, customs, religious beliefs and practices, to name a few factors. It is safe to say that no two families have the exact same needs and wishes. The funeral director must be prepared to serve an increasingly wide spectrum of consumers.

As was the custom years ago with undertakers, modern-day funeral-cremation providers find it necessary to hire people to perform certain duties who are not employees of the funeral home but who work outside the direct employment of the funeral home, crematory or cemetery. Known as outside-service providers and more legally identified as independent contractors, they can also be referred to as "tradespersons" by people within the profession and industry.

Independent contractors provide valuable assistance to funeral-cremation service and depending on their specialty, make themselves available 24 hours a day. They are frequently hired for both short and long-term projects. Some companies hire independent contractors/outside service providers as replacements for full-time employees. At some point, practically all funeral homes, crematories and cemeteries use outside providers, even large operations or corporate-owned entities.

In the funeral-cremation and cemetery businesses, independent contractors/outside service providers include, but are not limited to, first-call services, part-time funeral directors, trade embalmers, crematory services, cosmeticians, hairdressers, processional escorts, security personnel, livery-automobile rental, pallbearers, parking and door attendants, receptionists, visitation attendants, flower delivery services, long distance transfer services, cemetery grounds attendants, heavy equipment operators, grave diggers, landscape maintenance personnel and others.

Classification of Workers: Contractor or Employee?

Over the years, the use of independent contractors (self-employed workers who make their services available to perform a specific task) has increased dramatically. While some companies use independent contractors/outside service providers for financial advantages, such as avoiding unemployment taxes, Social Security withholding, employee benefits, workers' compensation, 24-hour availability, and more, others use these workers for the convenience factor, that is, to perform a particular job only when help is needed or when it is convenient to hire them. This can help turn some of a funeral home's high **fixed** cost of personnel into a **variable** cost.

However, employers can also assume significant risks by hiring these workers. One major concern is how workers are classified. Employers who misclassify workers as independent contractors can be liable for back taxes, penalties to the IRS, personal injury damages of the worker (that may or may not be covered by worker's compensation), and for the acts or omissions of the worker.

Employment law varies among states. In addition, the Internal Revenue Service differentiates between independent contractors and employees and applies a variety of control factors when determining whether a worker is an independent contractor or an employee. The average business owner may not know how employment determinations are made and he/she may believe a worker is independent when he/she is not, risking mis-classification of people. **Best Practice** includes discussing all working relationships, especially those you consider to be outside contractors, with your attorney and accountant. The IRS is known for often challenging contractor relationships. A business that fails to properly classify workers is vulnerable to investigation and possible taxes and penalties.

The Internal Revenue Service has established criteria to determine whether a worker is an employee or an independent contractor. Check with your lawyer, accountant and/or local IRS office for complete information. An adverse ruling against true independent-contractor status will hold the funeral-cremation provider and/or cemetery responsible to pay all back taxes, possibly with interest and penalties.

Generally, according to the IRS, as of the date this book was published, a person classifying himself/herself as an independent contractor:

1. Decides by themselves how to perform the job; establishes his/her own procedures and is without supervision during the completion of the job. The entity (funeral home, crematory, cemetery) engaging the service is only interested in an end result.

2. Sets his/her own hours and work schedule.

3. Hires his/her own assistants, supervises them and pays them.

4. Provides his/her own instruments, tools, equipment and materials.

5. Is usually paid a flat fee for the job.

6. Is free to work for more than one entity and is allowed to seek additional opportunities with others.

7. Makes a profit or loss as a result of the service provided.

8. Pays his/her own incidental expenses.

9. Receives no training from the engaging entity.

10. Concludes the relationship when the job is completed.

11. Agrees to perform specific duties for prices agreed upon in advance.

12. Does not receive insurance, pension, retirement, vacation or sick leave benefits from the engaging entity.

13. Presents a bill for services upon completion of the job.

14. Has a written contract describing the services, the cost of services and payment expectations.

One broad standard for determining if the worker is an "employee" is if the hirer of the worker has the right to control the details of their work performed. If so, the worker is an employee. By this broad standard, without specific legal protection, many workers thought to be "independent contractors" might actually be determined to be "employees."

All working relationships with persons you consider to be independent contractors should be discussed with your attorney or accountant to ensure they are truly independent.

Another area of potential liability stems from the fact outside service providers/independent contractors are not under the direct employment of the funeral home. This can affect liability and the level of duty of care for the funeral-cremation provider and cemetery who engages these workers.

Examining the "Special Relationship" Factor

The relationship between funeral-cremation provider and client family is often recognized by courts as a *special relationship*. **The basis of liability often rests on the duty owed to those with whom there is a special relationship.** During the arrangement conference, discussions of a highly personal nature occur, placing the arranger in a position of special trust. The bereaved family tells their story and in their own words, expresses their concerns. In return, the arranger shows respect, empathy and understanding and ensures confidentiality of information and feelings shared. In addition, the provider is entrusted with custody of the body of a deceased person. Tom Frankovich, plaintiff's attorney in *Bealmer v. SCI,* is most notable in interpreting the special relationship as meaning that once the deceased is in the custody of the funeral-cremation provider, a level of care will be performed without requiring further supervision by the family or person(s) with authority to control disposition.

To some degree, comparisons of this special relationship can be made to relationships between physician and patient and attorney and client. For the funeral director, crematory operator and cemetery who are entrusted with the body, it means the professional is expected to exercise a higher duty (of care) in protecting the decedent, sheltering the decedent in a private, secure location, treating the person with utmost of respect and guarding against any harm. During formal mortuary education, students are admonished to "treat each deceased person as if it was a family member." In the book, *Embalming History, Theory & Practice,* Robert Mayer reminds all members of the profession of the key ethical performance standard that is contained in Section

One: "The supreme ethic for the funeral service profession has come to be known as reverence for the dead."

When hired by a client family, the funeral-cremation provider, as the agent of the person(s) hiring him/her, has rights delegated to him/her by the next of kin or person(s) with authority to control disposition. In carrying out the preparation of the deceased person and the direction of the funeral services and disposition, the funeral-cremation provider is under various legal and contractual duties: Statutory laws of the state, the funeral contract, and case law or decisions by courts. If the funeral director violates these duties, he/she will incur liability to the state and/or the client family. Among other things, you become liable for damages resulting from any allegedly harmful, improper or negligent care or acts of employees as well as harmful, improper or negligent care or acts from persons you hired who are outside your direct employment (independent contractors/outside service providers).

Best Practice means that you must perform due diligence when hiring outside service workers, placing yourself in the best possible position before something goes wrong. It is too late to begin risk management after something goes wrong. The performance of outside service providers is considered as if the work was performed by you.

Case Example: What You Don't Know Can Hurt You

The family arranged with the funeral director to have their father embalmed and dressed. No formal funeral was planned, but the family requested 30 minutes of private viewing before burial. Three days later, the family came to the funeral home to see their father. When the casket was opened, the family immediately smelled a foul odor. Their father was in a decomposed state, discolored and purging fluid from the mouth and nose. His clothing was wet and soiled, and the casket interior fabric was stained. In the ensuing lawsuit, it was discovered that the trade embalmer was providing embalming services without having a current embalmer's license. The embalmer retired three years earlier but continued working "on the side" with three local funeral homes. Because the local funeral homes knew him, the embalmer decided he could save money by not renewing his license. The court awarded the family substantial damages to compensate them for the personal injuries they experienced when they viewed their father in a decomposed state. The state board brought disciplinary action against the funeral home and the embalmer was denied a license.

Due Care - Negligence

The terms "duty of care" or "duty to act with care" describe the performance of duties in such a manner that ordinarily prudent and diligent persons would exercise under the same or similar circumstances. It means not acting negligently. Negligence is also discussed in Chapter Fourteen.

The concept of negligence came to America in the early 18th century from common law as practiced in Great Britain. The word "negligence" is defined in the Columbia Electronic Encyclopedia (Sixth Edition, 2003) as "a breach of an obligation (duty) to act with care, or the failure to act as reasonable and prudent persons would under similar circumstances." Most acts of negligence are inadvertent, however in a formal complaint attorneys use words such as **willful, wanton, reckless or deliberate** to describe various degrees of negligent conduct that are not considered to be inadvertent.

Negligence is also the name of a legal theory, called a cause of action. A **tort** is a civil wrong (as compared to a criminal act) causing damage or injury. A tort may be such an act, or failure to act, done willfully, negligently, or in some circumstances may involve strict liability. While a tort is not a breach of contract, violation of contract terms may provide another legal theory to aggrieved parties. To establish negligence, a plaintiff (a client family, for example) must prove that the defendant (the funeral-cremation provider):

- Had a duty to the plaintiff (client family)
- Breached that duty (by failing to act as a reasonable funeral-cremation provider)
- Caused loss or damage by their particular acts or omissions
- Could foresee the nature and extent of the loss or damage to plaintiffs from the breach of duty

While the description of negligence has changed over the years, the basic concept has remained the same. Today it encompasses virtually all unintentional and intentional, wrongful conduct that injures others. The Thomson Corporation, the leading research and database publisher, cites claims of negligence as being the chief source of modern civil litigation in America.

What is the Reasonable Person Concept?

One of the important aspects in considering whether or not negligence occurred is the reasonable person concept. A person is considered to have acted negligently if he/she has departed from the conduct expected of a reasonably prudent person acting under similar circumstances. If a person engages in an activity requiring special skills, education, training or experience, such as an embalmer or a crematory operator, the standard by which his/her conduct is measured is the conduct of a reasonably skilled, competent and experienced person who is a qualified member of the group authorized to engage in that activity. Anyone who performs these special skills, whether qualified or not, is held to the same standards of conduct as those properly qualified to do so because the public relies on the special expertise of those who engage in such activities.

For example, at some family-operated funeral homes, the person who dresses the hair of a decedent can be the owner's wife or another person who, while skilled in hairdressing, is not a licensed hairdresser. This person works on an "as needed" basis only. This person, however, is held to the same standards of conduct as that of an experienced, licensed hairdresser.

In determining whether a person has acted as a "reasonable person" would have acted in a similar situation, some factors considered are: Knowledge, experience, the perception of the person, the activity the person is engaged in and the circumstances surrounding the person's actions. Primarily, the "reasonable person" is the standard set forth by expert testimony on a given procedure or method of handling the situation at issue in the particular situation. Experts are commonly asked to provide information beyond common knowledge of jurors, such as scientific theories, data, tests and in cases involving professionals, informing the jury as to the standard of care and what was to be expected of the professional.

Funeral and cremation providers, like some other professionals (lifeguards, fire and police personnel and emergency medical technicians) have an additional, **special duty of care.** If for example, a person who is swimming calls for help and a person who is a lifeguard hears the call and fails to respond, this person can be held liable for breaching the special duty of care as a lifeguard, even if off duty.

Entrusted with the custody of a deceased person, the special duty of care requires proper care when the person is moved from the place of death, during the period of transportation, ensuring correct identification throughout the entire period of custody, documenting the physical condition of the person and all forms of treatment, providing shelter in a sanitary and safe location, protecting the person from harm, treating it with respect and ensuring its privacy. The same duty of care applies to independent contractors-outside service providers who may be hired by the funeral home, crematory or cemetery.

Being Familiar with Outside Contractors

If, for example, the services of a hairdresser are needed, meeting the duty of care means the funeral-cremation provider should do more than look through the Yellow Pages Directory and hire the first hairdresser listed or first one willing to work on a deceased person. It includes protecting the deceased person from careless or reckless behavior, or unqualified workers.

When exercising duty of care, **Best Practice** means that you are familiar with independent contractors before you hire them and know that they share the same work ethic, value, philosophy and concern for deceased persons that you do.

The reasonable person concept means even foreseeing the potential for unlawful or negligent conduct of others if the situation warrants. For instance, a funeral provider may be found negligent if the independent contractor failed to lock the doors after a late night embalming, and jewelry was removed from the deceased. **The duty owed by the funeral provider to the client(s) was not eliminated by the hiring of an independent contractor.**

Qualifying Independent Contractors

Learning about the independent contractors means more than asking questions about price. It means asking tough, probing questions, demonstrating due diligence, such as those pertaining to whether or not professional liability insurance coverage is in effect, the policy limits, references of work performed for other persons, history of lawsuits or complaints, and other qualifying information about the level of experience of the independent contractor to ascertain their competency. It means conducting an interview before hiring the independent contractor, even if he or she is known by your colleagues. Notes on your conversations, interviews and research should be kept as part of your permanent files. Just as consumers ask you tough questions, so must you ask tough questions of independent contractors to assess their qualifications, experiences and abilities.

When using independent contractors, **Best Practice** recommendations include:

- **Maintain a confidential file** on the independent contractor.

- **Require references before hiring the person** and place all references in the file.

- **Check the references and document that you did this.** Faulty or negligent checking of references can increase your liability. Document telephone calls and/or letters sent to the references with names of persons spoken to including their comments. A paper trail can be important if anything goes wrong.

- **Refrain from making price the main criterion for hiring someone.** Check reliability, work ethic, character and so forth. If the worker has a history of problems, it is better to discover it before they do any work for you.

- **Mutually agree upon a probationary-trial work period** to ensure each party is comfortable with the work arrangement and quality of work.

- **Develop an itemized list of services to be rendered** along with the cost for each service.

- **Draw up a contract listing job expectations, costs, payment and so forth.** For example, if it's funeral home policy that all embalmed decedents be placed in plastic garments, write it down. If the limousine company is expected to provide soft drinks and bottled water, write it down. If the processional escort is expected to assist in parking vehicles, write it down.

- **Review the independent contractor's policy and procedures manual.** Make sure that his/her method of doing business corresponds with yours. If it does not, evaluate whether to insist on your standard being complied with by the contractor.

- **Sign a contract** that clearly sets out the duty and obligations of each party.

- **List one another as an additional insured** on each others insurance policies.

197

It is worth repeating: **In nearly all cases, the funeral-cremation provider and cemetery assumes the liability of all independent contractors they hire for the actions, negligence, recklessness, harm or loss as if you did the work yourself.** Checking references and hiring only reputable professionals that perform their duties according to the standards of the industry and profession is **Best Practice** and helps mitigate your exposure.

If a lesser-known independent contractor under consideration does not have the same long-term track record and reputation that another contractor does, your duty of care to investigate this person increases. For example, in some areas of the country, there are companies that cater to funeral homes by supplying limousines, hearses, flower vans and additional (funeral) personnel. The duty of care to investigate an established, well-known company whose work is familiar to the industry may be less than that for a newcomer providing similar service. An independent contractor whose work is known to be of lesser quality increases your liability from the "knew or should have known" premise. Perform screening checks thoroughly and document them. Your business can be at stake.

Case Example – The Unprepared Funeral Director

The defendant funeral director was being crossed examined by plaintiff's attorney. With the skill of a surgeon, the attorney questioned the funeral director about his knowledge of the facts of the case. The funeral director felt confident and believed his defense attorney adequately prepared him for testimony. Before the funeral director took the stand, the defense attorney instructed his funeral director client to answer honestly and not guess at any answers – that if a question was asked by plaintiff's attorney that he did not know the answer to or was unsure of the answer, he would answer by saying, "I don't know."

Plaintiff's attorney was also prepared and purposely planned to ask the defendant funeral director some questions that he believed he would not be able to answer.

"How many decedents are cremated on a yearly basis by the outside crematory you regularly engage?" "I don't know," answered the funeral director.

"Describe how the body was held at the crematory before it was cremated?" "I don't know."

"What are the qualifications of the crematory operator?" "I don't know."

"Describe the process as to how the crematory operator removes the cremated remains from the cremation chamber?" "I don't know."

"What type of processing machine does the crematory use to reduce the bones?" "I don't know."

"What is the crematory's procedure for packaging and labeling the cremated remains?" "I don't know."

By this point, the funeral director was noticeably uncomfortable at not being able to answer so many questions, but the plaintiff attorney kept on.

"In what manner does the crematory dispose of metal or foreign objects extracted from the cremated remains?" Again, he answered, "I don't know."

"Who manufactured the cremation chambers at the crematory?" "I don't know."

"When was the last time you or a regulatory agency inspected the crematory?" "I don't know."

Plaintiff's attorney finally backed away. The funeral director silently breathed a sigh of relief. He followed his attorney's advice, but felt uneasy.

After putting the defendant funeral director through this series of tough questions, he asked one more question that he knew the funeral director could answer: "How many years have you been a funeral director?" With pride and a sense of confidence, the funeral director sat up in his chair, adjusted his suit coat and with conviction said, "I have been a licensed funeral director and embalmer serving my community for 25 years!"

The attorney nodded his head at the answer and smiled at the funeral director. He then turned away and walked to the jury box. Looking at the jurors he paused for a moment and slowly said, "Ladies and gentlemen of the jury, I ask you, after 25 years of being a licensed funeral director and providing cremation services to his community, shouldn't he know?" From the expressions on the juror's faces and the nodding of their heads, it was obvious that a convincing point was made. This type of interrogation often takes place during a lawsuit, and I believe that funeral-cremation providers must know about the various aspects of services they provide (both those provided by funeral home staff and those contracted to outside providers) and the merchandise they sell.

Liability Insurance Coverage

Insurance is discussed in depth in Chapter Fourteen. But it is important to mention insurance when using an independent contractor. **Best Practice** means that all independent contractors, as well as suppliers and vendors you do business with, must carry *professional liability-errors and omissions* insurance for themselves.

To err is human. Yet, like a tight-wire performer in a circus, you practice without a net. If you do not have the safety net of insurance standing ready to defend you and indemnify you, it can be disastrous. The challenges and liabilities your business faces everyday increase whenever you rely on people outside your direct employment or supervision, including the products and equipment you use and/or sell. Professional liability insurance provides protection against claims that the policy holder (independent contractor, etc.) becomes legally obligated to pay as a result of an error or omission in his/ her professional work.

Before engaging an outside contractor or tradesperson, **Best Practice** means taking the following insurance items into consideration:

1. **Require evidence of insurance coverage.** A Certificate of Insurance, available upon request from their insurance company, proves a current policy is in force. It contains such things as the name of the insurance company, type of insurance, limits, name of carrier, name of insured and policy effective dates.

2. **Only hire those outside service providers who have current professional liability insurance or errors and omissions insurance for the type of work they do.** A vendor, for instance, commonly has products liability insurance. It is essential that you are aware that acts of professional negligence or errors are **not** covered by a commercial general liability policy.

3. **Require that the independent contractor or vendor has his/her insurance company name you as an additional insured on their company's policy and recognized as a certificate holder** and provide you with a copy of the additional insured endorsement. This also means the insurance company will notify you when and if the policy cancels prior to its stated date. As an additional insured, the insurance company providing coverage to the independent contractor / vendor / supplier acknowledges that the insured performs duties or supplies merchandise to you and that coverage will be provided for mistakes, negligence, recklessness or harm committed by their insured party. If, for example, the funeral home is sued as a result of work done by the independent contractor, the funeral home may be defended under the policy of the independent contractor just as the independent contractor is defended. Being named as an additional

insured provides you with an additional level of coverage. **Note:** There are over 50 types of additional insured endorsements. Choosing the correct form of endorsement for your firm requires assistance of legal and insurance professionals.

4. **Check the limits of coverage.** Geographic location, type of business and services offered can affect what would be considered to be appropriate and adequate. In most instances, a limit less than $1,000,000 for professional liability insurance for professional service providers could be considered inadequate today. Some states may have minimum insurance statutes for certain classes of professionals. When this is the case, at least statutory limits must be carried. **Note:** Umbrella or excess insurance coverage beyond the primary policy limits may be an economical method of obtaining sufficient coverage limits. If the contractor has excess coverage, be sure your firm is named on all policies of the contractor.

5. **Determine how the insurance premium is paid and whether it is paid by the individual contractor or through a group,** such as an association-sponsored insurance plan. Premiums paid on a monthly basis raise a warning, as these policies can easily be cancelled, leaving you exposed.

6. **Ask about their history of claims and lawsuits.** Document in writing what you are told.

7. **Treat history of many policy cancellations or expiration notices as a red flag.** It can mean inconsistent coverage and/or some form of legal and/or financial trouble.

8. **Provide your insurance company with the names of all independent contractors, vendors and suppliers you hire** and a description of services and merchandise.

202

With all insurance matters, seek the advice and assistance of your insurance agent and attorney. Most will gladly review insurance policies and Certificates of Insurance submitted by outside service providers, suppliers and vendors.

Off-Premises Facilities

At times, it can become necessary for the funeral-cremation provider to use off-premises facilities for various purposes: A crematory, an embalming center, a refrigeration-storage facility, just to name a few. Using an outside crematory is discussed in Chapter Twelve. As the agent of the client family, the funeral-cremation provider is responsible to make sure that any facility used for the storage, care or preparation of human remains operates lawfully, in a proper manner and is duly licensed. Some important **Best Practice** considerations to be sure of include:

- **Licensing requirements**, if any, for the facility and activities of the facility. (For instance, is the crematory duly licensed with all applicable permits and licenses?). Are licenses and permits current and posted in view?

- **Security**. Especially if the facility is used to hold human remains, the absence of a building security system can add dramatically to your liability. Is the building protected by an alarm system and who is contacted in the event it is activated? Are all outside doors able to be locked? Who are the persons with keys and who has access? Is the building structurally sound and protected from floods, fire and so forth?

- **Controlled access**. Is the facility away from public sight? Are doors kept closed at all times? Is access restricted or is the public allowed to enter unescorted? Is there a waiting area for visitors?

- **Procedures to maintain identity of the deceased**. When decedents are brought to the facility and when they are removed, is it recorded in a log book? Are receipts issued? How is the decedent tagged? How are decedents stored? When in a container, is the name of the decedent marked on the exterior?

- **Minimum-care standards.** To meet standards of care, each decedent must be inspected and monitored on a daily basis. Is refrigeration available? What is the temperature of the refrigeration unit and is it checked throughout the day and the temperature recorded in a log book? Is the deceased person checked at least once a day and the condition recorded in the decedent's file? Is the facility kept clean and sanitary?

- **Personnel at the facility.** If a license is required to perform certain duties, are licenses up-to-date and posted in plain view? Have background checks been performed on all employees? Is there a dress standard?

Transferring a Deceased Person to an Off-Premises Facility

Best Practice means **informing before performing.** In particular, it means informing the client family if the decedent will be brought to an outside facility for any reason. Some funeral homes do not perform embalming on their premises but use an off-premises facility for this and other forms of care. When this is the case, it should be disclosed to the family at the time of receiving the first-call or as soon as it is practical. Even if a lawsuit does not develop, a relationship can be harmed and your reputation damaged by not informing the client family and obtaining their permission before for this. Being a professional means being sensitive to your clients and knowing that for some of them, there can be personal, cultural, symbolic, religious, spiritual and ethnic considerations that may make the use of an outside facility unsatisfactory for them.

Any transfer of the decedent to a facility other than yours should only be done after receiving proper authorization to do so. I know a funeral home that is no longer recommended by members of a local church. This developed when the members felt the funeral home deceived them by not disclosing that loved ones are not brought to the funeral home but to a facility located 15 miles away. When verbal authorization is received during the first-call or written authorization is granted, the name of the authorizing person and their relationship must be recorded along with the date and time it was granted.

Inspecting Off-Premises Facilities

Due diligence also means inspecting the off-premises facility on a regular basis. **Best Practice** guidelines include the following:

- All inspections must be documented with proof of the inspection retained in a permanent file. **An inspection that is not documented is the same as "no inspection."**

- Inspections should be unannounced. If, at any time you are denied the opportunity to perform an inspection, consider this to be a red flag and investigate it further.

- Conduct inspections at various dates and hours throughout the year.

- If you notice something wrong during the inspection, document it thoroughly. Notify the owner/manager of the facility. Only resume using the off-premises facility after being assured that the matter has been corrected. If it is a serious offense, stop using the outside service provider and report your findings to appropriate authorities.

- Provide the owner/manager with a copy of the inspection.

For most funeral homes, crematories and cemeteries, using the services of outside contractors and tradespersons are an important ingredient in fulfilling the needs and wishes of a client family. However, to reduce the risks associated with tapping this workforce, you must employ **Best Practice.** Among other things, this means performing due diligence and being familiar with all aspects of work to be performed by them.

CHAPTER 11

Cremating a Person's Remains

The length of this chapter reflects both the importance and complexity of the subject: Cremation. *What the careful reader might interpret as repetition is an indication that the attention to detail exercised by the funeral-cremation provider must also be repeated by the crematory operator. This chapter encompasses two related, yet separate perspectives: Cremation as viewed by the funeral director and cremation as viewed by the crematory. The potential for problems associated with cremation — authorization to cremate; identification of the human body and maintaining identification throughout the cremation process; delivery of the deceased person to the crematory; and the subsequent release of the person's cremated remains, security, safety, packaging of a person's cremated remains and storage — **all** must be carried out in detail and carefully documented. The process of cremating a person's remains is, in itself, a simple matter. Yet the entire process is a minefield of potential liability for the funeral director and the crematory owner and operator.*

Cremation from the Funeral Director's Point of View

Six Reasons Why Cremation Represents a Top Liability for Your Firm

Assuming responsibility for the cremation of the mortal remains of a person is among the most important activities rendered by anyone in death care services. More than any other area of practice, cremating the body of a human being presents the most exposure to liability, especially for the funeral home that uses an outside crematory. A number of factors contribute to the increased liability of cremation. It is vital to be aware of these factors.

1. Cremation is an irreversible process. If the wrong person is cremated, or is cremated without obtaining proper authorization or is improperly cremated, the consequences can be extreme compared to mistakes in other aspects of funeral service. If the wrong person is buried, entombed or shipped, these mistakes, while still serious, can usually be resolved.

2. In the United States, cremation is, for the most part, a non-participatory event. In most instances, it takes place behind closed doors. In stark contrast to earth burial or entombment, family members rarely view cremation. The more responsible and consumer- focused funeral homes are encouraging greater participation by client families, suggesting processions to the crematory and attendance during cremation. Many funeral homes still resist encouraging such participation and alarmingly, some crematories discourage it all they can in an attempt to keep outsiders from attending.

Unlike the United States, cremation is performed with great ceremony in most countries, even those considered third-world nations. Depending on local custom and ritual, the cremation process begins with the family and friends accompanying the body in a procession to the crematory or the location where the cremation will take place. A family member may light the funeral pyre and as the person is consumed by flame, religious ceremonies, story-telling or other life celebrations take place. Afterwards, the family may even collect the skeletal framework from the chamber or pyre, place the bones in sacred containers or distribute some bones or fragments to other family members.

Additionally, burial/entombment takes place in real time, on a prearranged day and hour, at a familiar location (cemetery) and attended by familiar people (family, friends, clergy, funeral director, etc.). By contrast, cremation remains a mystery to many people: Most people do not know where the crematory is located, what the building looks like and can only guess who performs it. Mistakenly, some funeral directors believe that client families do not need to know this information. Unless specific arrangements are made in advance, the family may not know when it will take place. Cremation is often done at the convenience of the funeral home or the crematory operator.

3. Even though the number of cremations continues to increase across the country, many people remain uninformed about cremation, viewing it as something new and a recent way to handle the dead. Surprisingly, I have sat with people during arrangements who did not know that cremation involves burning the person's body. Yet for others, cremation is a means to quickly remove the person's body from the living and a way to circumvent having a traditional funeral that has no appeal to them. Funeral directors must not assume that when people choose cremation that they understand all that cremation means. Especially because cremation is irreversible, it is necessary to explain most aspects of the process to reach informed consent. Failing to adequately explain cremation not only relegates it to a mere commodity but increases the chance for misunderstanding that can lead to a lawsuit. Some funeral directors and arrangers are equally uninformed and unfamiliar with cremation. Many are not aware of the history of cremation and its role in contemporary funeral practices. What takes place at a crematory is only hearsay for them.

Case Example: "Poof"

I greeted the elderly gentleman as he entered the lobby of my funeral home. He appeared to be disoriented and his facial expressions told me he was in pain. He told me that his wife of 55 years just died. The nurse told him he needed to make arrangements. I informed the man that he had time to do this, that he need not rush to make arrangements. I suggested that we postpone the arrangements and if he would like, I would meet him later at his home with other family or friends at his side. As I spoke, he would not look directly at me, but gazed upward toward the ceiling behind me. I could tell he was in grief and hurting inside. Even when I asked him simple questions, he would hesitate several moments before answering, thinking hard for the answer. His answers were brief and he spoke softly so that I had to strain to hear him.

I asked him, "What are your thoughts about burial or cremation for your wife?" After what seemed like a long time, he said, "I think I will just have her cremated." This man was in no frame of mind to make final arrangements or decisions at this time, but needed support. I asked, "How familiar are you with cremation?" About 20 seconds went by while he pondered this question, all the while looking at the ceiling behind me with a pained expression on his face. Finally, he said, "When you cremate her body..." and did not finish the sentence. I sat in silence. Seconds later, he looked at me again and said, "I don't really know what happens... the body goes...poof." His answer astounded me. I replied, "Poof? What do you mean by this?" He said, "Cremation makes the person disappear and it's done with."

From a professional and safe practice perspective, I could not proceed in good conscience with this man at this time. I told him that we had to postpone our discussion. I offered to contact his daughter and have her assist him until we could meet another day. While an extreme occurrence, given this man's state of mind, any decisions he might have made could have jeopardized my business and reputation. It was obvious he was in extreme grief and could not concentrate. We met two days later and he was joined by his daughter. They thanked me for being patient and understanding. The man arranged for his wife to be buried, not cremated. He admitted he was not familiar with cremation but that some of his friends had been cremated.

4. The vast majority of cremations are performed at crematories not owned, operated or affiliated with the funeral home serving the client family and decedent. In the United States, less than 2,000 crematories serve 20,000 funeral homes and cremation businesses. This means that the funeral home hired by the client family – the firm entrusted with the responsibility to care for the person's remains - transfers custody of the body to a crematory operated by personnel not under the direct or immediate control of the funeral home, often without informing the family or receiving authorization. The funeral home is responsible to the client family to ensure that the cremation is performed in a dignified, respectful manner. Some colleagues may not want to hear this: even the most dedicated crematory operator does not share the degree of personal connection with the deceased person or client family that the funeral director/arranger does; in most cases, the crematory operator has no real person attachment to the deceased person. Rather, cremating a person is merely a task to be completed.

A physician friend of mine told me that during his first year of medical school, he was scheduled to dissect one of several cadavers. It would be just another nameless, faceless cadaver. Pulling back the sheet that covered the cadaver, he looked in stunned silence at the body. He recognized the cadaver as someone he worked with during a summer job at a country club. Suddenly, this cadaver was no longer nameless or faceless to him. It was a person. Like the gravedigger who digs a grave, buries one body after another and refills the grave, cremating a human body is an impersonal task for the crematory operator unless a personal connection is made. An impersonal relationship is more likely to allow for decisions by the crematory operator based on expediency rather than on a personal commitment to the client family.

Outside Crematory Agreement

Additionally, when an outside crematory is used, there should be a Crematory Agreement between the funeral-cremation provider and crematory. The agreement should acknowledge, among other things, that: cremations are performed in a timely, respectful manner; that unannounced inspections are welcome; that the crematory complies with state, county and local laws; that appropriate licenses are maintained and cremations are performed according to local and industry standards. The agreement should also establish the price, state that the crematory maintains professional liability insurance and list the limits, agree to name the funeral-cremation provider as additional insured on the crematory's liability insurance policy and provide indemnification among parties. Like any agreement of importance, a Crematory Agreement should be reviewed by legal counsel.

5. The client family usually assumes that the funeral home they call for service will actually perform the cremation. You must disclose that the funeral home will not perform the cremation itself - and that a representative of the funeral home might not be present during the cremation process must be revealed – if either or both of these statements are true. You must also reveal that cremation will be performed at a third-party crematory, off the premises of the funeral home when this is the case. Failure to reveal these important details can be construed as misleading. **Inform before you perform** reduces the risk you will be charged with failing to disclose these facts, whether the crematory is located down the street or in another state. One only needs to look at the Bayview Crematory scandal in Seabrook, New Hampshire, to learn a valuable lesson regarding these and other issues. As an expert witness, I have heard the ire of family members who were not informed about such details.

5. Using a non-owned, off-premises crematory means the deceased must be transferred. Additional travel exposes the decedent to mishaps that, while remote, can range from theft or car-jacking, traffic accident, or other risks not present when the crematory is located on the grounds of the funeral home. Additionally, when using an outside crematory that happens to be located in another county or state, the funeral home needs to consider that it might need to obtain a transit-transfer permit before transporting the deceased person to a crematory in another county or state.

Some states classify cremation as final disposition. However, most states consider cremation a process that prepares the body for final disposition. Irrespective of how cremation is classified, once the person has been cremated, final disposition can take place. As per the needs and requests of the family, final disposition does not always occur right away and can be delayed.

Best Practice for reducing liability exposure when providing cremation services include:

- **Obtain** authorization from the person(s) with authority to cremate.

- **Use** a Cremation Authorization Form that discloses critical elements of cremation.

- **Reach** informed consent as to the cremation process.

- **Cremate** the correct person.

- **Ensure** the identity of the decedent throughout the process of cremation.

- **Remove** medical devices, jewelry and personal items prior to cremation.

- **Ensure** that a decision concerning final disposition is agreed upon.

- **Have** in place procedures for the handling and storage of unclaimed cremated remains.

- **Take** extra precautions when using a non-company owned, outside crematory.

Authority to Cremate

The Cremation Authorization Form is an important legal document. Obtaining the signature of the person(s) legally entitled to control disposition can be arduous for the provider and confusing to the client family. Among family members there can be discord as to who shall control funeral decisions, including the nature, location, timing, and even with who is welcome to attend. From what colleagues across the country tell me, these issues are becoming increasingly commonplace.

In my career, I have dealt with many people who were willing to sign the cremation authorization documents when, in fact, they did not possess the legal right to do so. I have also encountered some who were less than honest about their true relationship to the deceased and some who, while rightfully the next of kin, were surprised to learn that the right to control disposition had been legally assigned to someone else. I have also been threatened with a lawsuit by children of the deceased if I did not follow their opposing funeral wishes. Mishandling these and other sensitive situations can result in negative publicity, a loss of a client-family relationship and perhaps a lawsuit. More than once I had to decline performing cremation because the person making arrangements, for one reason or another, did not possess the legal right to authorize cremation.

In some cultures, a friend is chosen based on previous experience and savvy to serve as the person who is called when a death occurs. He or she is asked to make all decisions and funeral arrangements on behalf of the immediate family. Unaware of modern funeral arrangement protocol and legal technicalities, the term, "next of kin" and primacy issues can be seen as irrelevant. Without any legal documentation to support their position, but acting only as a helper to the family, these friends can mistakenly assume they have the authority to arrange for disposition, including cremation. Presented with such a predicament, you must try not to alienate anyone, nor position yourself as being confrontational or dispassionate, or viewed as a problem person. **You must only act after receiving authority to proceed from the person(s) with legitimate authority.** I approach these situations with respect for the law and emphasize that by everyone working together, the end result can be mutually satisfying. At times, to resolve these predicaments, it became necessary for me to travel to the residence of the person(s) with authority to make arrangements. On several occasions arrangements were made in a hospital room where the next of kin was a patient. ("Determining the Next of Kin" is discussed in Chapter Four.)

Faxed Authorizations or Authorizations at a Distance

There might be times when the person(s) with authority is unable to appear in person to provide authorization, such as when living in a distant city. Under these circumstances, signatures on all **original** authorization forms and legal documents should be notarized, especially authorization for cremation.

Faxed authorizations for cremation can only be received if the crematory accepts this as a means of authorization and when it is backed up by receiving the original authorization form that has been notarized. You must also ensure that local courts approve of faxed authorizations for this purpose. **Best Practice dictates that e-mail transmissions should never be accepted as authorization to cremate.**

In broadest terms, the possession and control of the body of a deceased person for the purposes of the funeral and disposition is a fundamental legal right of survivors. Their rights include, but are not limited to, the form, type and location of disposition, including invited guests, except where law gives one or more of these rights to the decedent and such rights have been previously exercised in writing.

Even for the experienced funeral-cremation provider, determining the next of kin and/or correctly interpreting state law concerning rights of survivorship in some circumstances can be difficult, complicating the arrangement-planning process. Failing to adhere to the legally established hierarchy of next of kin according to your state laws can place your business in serious jeopardy. It requires that you fully understand the laws of survivorship in your state. When necessary, seek counsel from an attorney who is familiar with funeral-cremation laws, the rights of survivorship and probate-estate matters in your state. Today, the funeral-cremation provider must know the "rights of survivorship" as they pertain in his/her state.

As this book is being written, next of kin and primacy issues are under review by both federal and state lawmakers. Existing laws and proposed modifications to them are being debated.

The outcome will profoundly affect funeral-cremation practices in determining the order as to who has the right and authority to control what happens to a deceased person. Every funeral director and arranger must be aware of what changes, if any, are taking place in their state laws. **In some cases, the next of kin might not be the person who has the legal right to control disposition.**

Important: When there is any uncertainty as to who has the legal right, the funeral-cremation provider must not make a decision based on his/her own interpretation of law or circumstances but must act with the blessing of law.

Harvey Lapin, Esq., former legal counsel for the Cremation Association of North America, states, "It is better to be sued for not performing a cremation than to perform a cremation without proper authorization." **When in doubt or things do not seem just right during the arrangement conference, disposition of the body, especially when cremation is selected, must not take place until the issue of who has the legal right has been clarified beyond any doubt.**

Case Example: Favorite Son and Disowned Daughters

The person making arrangements identified himself as the son to the deceased and the only surviving next of kin. The decedent's wife died years ago and was buried in a local cemetery. The son wanted his father cremated and the cremated remains buried in the same grave with his mother. During the arrangement conference, the arranger rightly asked if there were other surviving children, to which the son replied, "No, not really. I am the only one. I am in charge and will pay the expenses." Alertly, the arranger asked what was meant by the words, "No, not really." The son explained that several years ago his mother had a serious disagreement with her (still surviving) two daughters and disowned them both. The son, who was unemployed, lived with his mother in her home and provided care to her. His mother designated him as the executor of her estate and with the exception of a $100,000 life insurance policy that listed the daughters as equal beneficiaries, he was named as the beneficiary of the remainder of his mother's estate. No other rights were assigned to him.

The arranger informed the son about the nature of cremation and pointed out that state law (in this particular state) requires written authorization from **all** persons who have the authority to cremate. In this case, all three surviving children would need to sign the cremation authorization. The son refused to contact his sisters and asked the arranger to contact them. Both daughters refused to sign the cremation authorization documents as they wanted their mother buried with her husband. The son was adamant about having his mother cremated and sought counsel from an attorney. The attorney informed his client that being named executor, living with his mother and being her caregiver did **not** give him power over his sisters or make him entitled to have sole control of the funeral and disposition. The attorney informed the son that, if he wished to pursue matters, he could seek a court order. If granted, the order would provide him with the authority he desired. The decedent was not cremated but buried with her husband. The arranger exercised safe practice, explained the laws regarding next of kin to the best of his ability and, without alienating himself from either party, suggested that the son seek legal counsel. Doing so more than likely prevented a lawsuit.

Funeral Director's Ace-in-the-Hole

At times, final arrangements could only be done after a court order was obtained. A **court order** is an official proclamation by a judge that defines the legal relationships between the parties before the court and requires or authorizes the carrying out of certain steps by one or more parties to a case. I consider a court order to be the funeral director's ace-in-the-hole. By this I mean, that when presented with situations in which parties cannot or will not agree, or the funeral arranger does not know what he or she should do with a deceased person in custody, a court order is an option. Following the order as mandated by a court means that you perform your duties with the blessing of law.

Most state laws address the rights of survivors when it comes to the manner, type and location of the funeral and final disposition. Except in the approximately 30 states where the law allows a person to legally name another person as being in charge of disposition of his/her remains, rights of survivorship generally pass to a surviving spouse who may dictate the type and location of disposition. Where laws allow, a surviving spouse can waive his/her rights to control disposition - but to be legal, this must be done in writing. If a man and woman are married but are not living together, the surviving spouse generally retains the authority to control disposition. Unless otherwise provided for through **legal documentation**, a divorced partner has no right to control disposition.

Unless otherwise provided for through **legal documentation,** if there are adult children surviving and the husband and wife are divorced or one spouse has died, the adult children have the right to control disposition. To be an adult, the child must be 18 years or older. If there is more than one surviving adult child, they all are presumed to have equal rights with regard to disposition arrangements. Still, some states' laws provide that in the event of a conflict among the surviving children, authority is granted to a majority of the surviving children.

When no spouse or children survive, statutes of descent and distribution contained in probate codes in the state of residence for the deceased generally determine the person(s) with legal authority. The order of the person with authority usually varies from state to state; you should seek counsel from an attorney familiar with the order of primacy in your state.

Additionally, some states permit disposition subject entirely to the written directions of the deceased regardless of who survives, including a spouse. An example is when the deceased has made prearrangements, has signed all authorizations and has prepaid the expenses. Where state laws provide for this, even a surviving spouse may not make any "material" or "substantive" alterations to the prearranged funeral instructions, including the decedent's wish to be cremated. Yet other states allow the person(s) with the legal authority to alter the disposition instructions contained in a prearrangement directive. Some states permit advanced directives through a Durable Power of Attorney for Health Care. This directive allows an individual to designate another individual who has the legal right to control the disposition of the body that supersedes the rights of a surviving spouse.

Primacy and rights of survivorship can be major issues when arranging for cremation. Safe practice means not performing cremation until all doubts and questions have been settled.

The words of Harvey Lapin, Esq., are worth repeating: "It is better to be sued for not performing a cremation than performing a cremation without proper authority."

Some states, like Pennsylvania, permit a Document of Contrary Content which assigns authority to a party or parties other than a next of kin. Check with an attorney to see if such a document is applicable in your state.

Cremation Authorization Form

The Cremation Authorization Form is a **specific** written permission from the person(s) who is legally authorized to control disposition that authorizes the contracting funeral-cremation provider to cremate a person's body. As a means to formalize the agreement, it serves two purposes:

1. It contains the signature(s) of the person(s) with authority to control disposition, and,

2. It discloses important details pertaining to all aspects of the cremation process

It is the responsibility of the contracting funeral-cremation provider to obtain a legally signed and executed Cremation Authorization Form.

In providing risk assessments to funeral-cremation providers and reviewing hundreds of cremation authorization forms, I am stunned to note how many authorization forms are incomplete and lack important disclosures that need to be shared and understood by the authorizing party. Some authorization forms are so inadequate they may not be defensible in a lawsuit, and worse, may be evidence against you in a lawsuit. Among others, an authorization form should address the *what, where, who, when and how* of cremation. Failing to include these facts and assuming the authorizing person(s) does not want to know these facts or understands the crucial aspects of cremation, has a way of becoming momentous, especially during litigation.

There is more to accomplish than merely getting a signature on an authorization form. No part of cremation can be left to chance, assumption or a person's imagination.

The past decade can be described as the decade of consumer rights. Courts of law support informed consent doctrine and the consumer's right to know what services they are buying and what they are authorizing.

Full disclosure of details is now the standard, especially when purchasing/authorizing personal services. Expected outcomes must be defined and risks should be acknowledged, not left to conjecture or one's own interpretation. At times, it might be necessary for the arranger to assess a client family's level of understanding about cremation. Even with the popularity of cremation, I still meet people who are not aware that cremation means incinerating a person's body using flame and intense heat.

Best Practice means, that when you are in doubt, ask some probing questions of clients:

- Now that I have explained cremation to you, describe for me, in your own words, what you would like me to do.

- Just so I am sure you understand, explain to me what will take place.

- What additional information would be helpful to you?

Avoid asking the following questions as the answers do not always indicate sufficient understanding on the part of the client:

- Do you understand?

- Do you have any questions?

- Do you need anything else?

- Have I explained it all to you?

You have a responsibility to inform and ensure understanding on the part of your client. Given today's legal climate, and the irreversible nature of cremation, rarely is a one-page authorization form sufficient. Failure to adequately inform can lead to liability.

Because the cremation authorization form must contain considerable information, disclosures pertaining to the process can be contained on individual pages, stapled together and considered as one document in its entirety.

Some crematories require contracting funeral homes to use their Cremation Authorization Form. When this is the case, it does **not** prevent the funeral home from using its own Cremation Authorization Form **in addition** to the (required) crematory's Authorization Form.

When this is the case, the funeral home's authorization form should be retained in the deceased person's file. This is especially critical if the crematory's form does not thoroughly describe the cremation process and omits vital disclosures.

Formatting the Cremation Authorization Form

A Cremation Authorization Form is a consumer legal document and as such, some states may have requirements governing font or type size as well as requiring certain terms to be printed in **bold typeface** or conspicuously printed. The following **Best Practice** formatting recommendations for a Cremation Authorization Form should be reviewed with legal counsel to make sure they meet requirements in your state:

- **Use a type size that it is legible** to the average person.

- **Print the title of the form** (Cremation Authorization Form) on the front and at the top of the page.

- **Number each page in order,** such as "page 1 of 4," "page 2 of 4," "page 3 of 4," and so forth, if separate pages are used.

- **Place the name, address and telephone number of the funeral-cremation provider** prominently on the front page.

- **Use words such as** the "funeral home" or the "provider" and "you," "I," and "authorizing party" to designate parties and relationships.

- **Avoid strikeouts on the form.** Any write-ins or special instructions added to the form should be initialed by the authorizing person(s).

- **Use a separate paragraph or heading for each key disclosure.** Allow space for the authorizing person's initials next to each disclosure.

- **Use "plain" language;** avoid technical terminology that can be confusing. A rule of thumb: Ask a friend who is not in funeral-cremation service to read the authorization form. If he or she understands it, it will likely be understood by client families.

Disclosures to Contain in the Cremation Authorization Form

In 1999, a Model Cremation Law was written and published by Harvey Lapin, Esq., who was then General Counsel to the Cremation Association of North America (CANA), and reviewed by the Cremation Code of Ethics Committee of the International Cemetery, Cremation and Funeral Association (ICCFA). The model law recommends minimum disclosures that should be contained in a Cremation Authorization Form and acknowledged in writing by the authorizing person(s). Funeral-cremation providers who have adopted full disclosure criteria in their authorization form remark how client families appreciate being educated and knowing what is involved when cremation is chosen. Many cremation-related problems can be avoided altogether by using an authorization form that contains complete disclosure about the cremation process.

The Cremation Authorization Form serves two purposes: First, it contains the affirmation and signature of the person(s) with authority to control disposition, and second, it discloses important details of the cremation process.

Best Practice dictates that these disclosures appear on your Cremation Authorization Form to ensure that no part of cremation is left to chance or misinterpretation and that the interests of ALL parties are served:

1. Using a third-party crematory that is not owned by the funeral home, if that is the case.

2. The name and address of the third-party crematory.

3. That the contracted funeral home **will** or **will not** have a representative present during the entire cremation process.

4. That the funeral home is instructed to deliver the person's remains to the crematory.

5. That the crematory is instructed to cremate the person's remains.

6. Name of the deceased person and the date and time of death.

7. Date and time the cremation may be scheduled, subject to any special requests as set out in Item 16.

8. Any special custom, tradition, ritual or witnessing that will accompany this cremation. (Note: Not all cremations are necessarily done the same way).

9. The name, address, telephone number and signature(s) of the authorizing person(s) and their relationship to the deceased.

10. The authorizing person(s) has the legal right to authorize cremation and control disposition of the deceased and further, is not aware of any living person(s) who has an equal or superseding right to the authorizing person(s).

11. That the crematory will not accept custody of unidentified remains. The authorizing person(s) or their designated-in-writing representative has verified the identity of the deceased (how and where this was done, date and time, name and relationship of person verifying identity).

12. A statement that the deceased did or did not die from an infectious, contagious, communicable or potentially hazardous cause of death or one that has been reported to public health authorities.

13. Acknowledge the presence or absence of medical devices, including, but not limited to: pacemakers, radioactive devices, prostheses or other materials or devices that may be potentially hazardous or cause injury to funeral or crematory personnel or crematory equipment.

14. Authorization for the funeral home to remove or arrange for the removal of any such devices, when necessary. Any cost associated with this must be listed on the funeral home's General Price List and/or agreed to in advance.

15. The manner in which removed devices will be disposed.

16. Any special handling or time requirements for the cremation (a particular day, a rush or immediate release, obese, use of more than one urn, etc.).

17. That during the cremation process, it might be necessary for the operator to reposition the deceased person to ensure complete cremation.

18. Authorization for the processing of bone particles and skeletal fragments through mechanical pulverization-crushing that renders them unidentifiable.

19. The name, address, telephone number and relationship of the person authorized to receive the cremated remains from the crematory. (Note: this information must be provided even when the contracting funeral home will receive the person's cremated remains.)

20. The name, address, telephone number and relationship of the person(s) authorized to receive the cremated remains from the contracted funeral home.

21. Details describing the disposition of the cremated remains (where, when, how, by whom, etc.).

22. If cremated remains will be stored or held by the funeral home for disposition at a future time or released at a future time, full disclosure of time limits, related costs and penalties, if agreed-to time limits are not honored. If disposition or retrieval of cremated remains does not occur within agreed time limits, or they become unclaimed, full disclosure as to how and where the person's remains will be disposed of, per your state laws.

23. Acknowledgement that all viewing of the deceased and/or funeral ceremonies have occurred or will occur prior to cremating the body.

24. Minimum container requirements for the person's remains for acceptance by the crematory and prior to the cremation process.

25. Description of the container holding the deceased person prior to cremation.

26. That 100% of the recovered cremated remains will be placed in a cremated remains container (urn or vessel) and a description of the urn or vessel to be used.

27. In the event the recovered cremated remains do not fit into the (original) vessel, a larger vessel will be provided, or the excess remains will be placed into a secondary vessel and kept with the original container in a manner so as not to be easily detached through incidental contact. The second vessel will be properly labeled with the name of the deceased person, date of death and date of cremation.

28. In the event the person's remains are to be proportioned and placed in multiple vessels (keepsake urns, etc.) and/or released to multiple persons, this must be authorized in writing with approximate amounts of proportioned cremated remains listed for each container or designated recipient.

29. In instances when a person's cremated remains will be shipped by the funeral home, list the date of shipment, place of shipment, that a suitable urn must be used and the manner of shipment (U.S. Postal Service, hand- carry, etc.) In cases when the person's remains will be placed in carry-on or checked luggage, the authorizing person(s) should be provided with a copy of the guidelines for shipment of cremated remains by the Transportation Safety Administration.

30. A statement from the authorizing person(s) attesting to the accuracy and authenticity of representations made in the Cremation Authorization Form and confirmation that the cremated remains will be treated with proper respect and in a legal manner.

31. That the authorizing person(s) has been given ample time to read the form and ask questions and that he, she or them understand the authorizations and representations made.

32. A statement of indemnification, releasing and holding harmless the funeral home, its officers, employees and agents and the crematory from any loss, damage, liability or causes of actions in connection with the cremation.

33. Signature of funeral director or representative of the funeral home and date.

34. Full explanation of the cremation process.

Explaining the Cremation Process

Best Practice means that a description of the cremation process should be a part of the Cremation Authorization Form. It may be contained on a separate sheet of paper or in a brochure. The person(s) with authority should sign the description of the cremation process as confirmation of their understanding.

The description should include, but not be limited to: the person's body will be cremated by the crematory in the container selected by the authorizing person(s); cremation is utterly final and the person's body will be consumed and irreversibly reduced by heat and flame; only bone-skeletal fragments will remain; the person's body may be repositioned within the cremation chamber to facilitate complete incineration; microscopic, unintentional commingling of cremated remains will occur from previous cremations; microscopic particles of cremated remains will remain in cracks and crevices within the cremation chamber but that every human and mechanical effort will be made to retrieve and return 100% of the recovered cremated remains (see special note below); personal items on or in the body (bridgework, dentures, eyeglasses, dental fillings, prostheses, jewelry, notes-letters, rosary beads, prayer books, and garments other than the clothing the deceased person might be wearing at the time of cremation) will only be removed with the express written permission of the authorizing person(s); personal items remaining on or in the body will be destroyed during the cremation process and/or made unrecoverable; non-bone fragment foreign material (such as prostheses, hinges, latches and screws) will be separated from the cremated remains prior to processing and may be joined with other like materials and disposed of by burial in a cemetery; if the recovered cremated remains do not fit into the (primary) urn-vessel selected by the authorizing person(s), the excess will be placed into a secondary urn-vessel and kept with the primary urn-vessel.

SPECIAL NOTES:

Vacuuming of the Chamber

Most cremation experts and this author strongly believe that every human and mechanical means must be used to collect 100% of the recoverable cremated remains from inside the cremation chamber. This means that, in addition to brushing and sweeping the interior of the cremation chamber, the interior of the cremation chamber should be vacuumed using industry-specific, specialized equipment after each and every cremation. The residue recovered in that process must be returned to the authorizing agent(s).

Cremation of Possessions

In their *Cremation Guidelines*, the International Cemetery, Crematory and Funeral Association (ICCFA) recommend a disclosure statement that this author endorses: "Prior to cremation, possessions of the deceased shall not be removed or disposed of without the express written permission of the authorizing agent. Possessions include, but are not limited to: dental work, prostheses, pacemakers, jewelry and clothing, other than clothing that the deceased may be wearing at the time of cremation."

Foreign Material

In addition, the ICCFA makes a disclosure concerning foreign material that this author endorses: "Subsequent to cremation, non-bone fragment foreign material such as prostheses, shall be removed from the cremated remains prior to processing and may be commingled with other like material and shall be disposed of by burial in a cemetery."

Having full disclosure on your Cremation Authorization Form and having them acknowledged in writing will be helpful in your defense in the event of questions or litigation. Signatures or initials of the authorizing person(s) at designated points in the document make it difficult to claim that omissions occurred or that anyone was misled or misinformed.

Identification and Cremating the Right Person

The reader may wonder why the authors place such emphasis on the topic of **identification,** as it is discussed in several areas, most notably in Chapters Two and Five.

For the funeral-cremation provider and cemeterian, identification is *central* to all duties and responsibilities. It is the cornerstone of professional care. It is critical when cremation is selected, as this is an irreversible process.

When a person's identity is left to chance or hearsay, many things can go wrong. When questions concerning identity are raised, it results in great apprehension for everyone involved in the chain of custody. Identity can be difficult to recover if continuity is ever lost. In our experience, we have seen again and again the major problems that can arise even if there is the slightest question of identity.

Whether cremation, earth burial, entombment or shipment services are requested, the burden to maintain the integrity of a decedent's identity is on the funeral-cremation provider and on those to whom he/she entrusts the person's body.

Requests for cremation, especially for direct cremation or immediate cremation, pose several additional challenges for the funeral-cremation provider:

1. Regardless of services requested, you must perform certain legal functions and perform all duties in an ethical, professional manner.

2. Everything done in caring for a deceased person and in serving a client family has legal implications and entails liability.

3. Requests for minimal service cannot be treated casually. Do not make the mistaken assumption that requests for "minimal service" mean minimal caring by survivors.

4. Abbreviated services of any type carry a higher risk of misidentification that can have disastrous effects.

As pointed out in previous chapters, it is critical that identification is maintained beginning with the "first-call" and through disposition. **The deceased person is always someone's loved one.**

Before moving the body to a transfer cot, **Best Practice** includes:

- **Check for other tags or other forms of identification** attached to the person's body.

- **Confirm the name on your first-call sheet** to the name appearing on any tags. If multiple tags are attached, all names on all tags must match.

- **Attach your own identification tag** to the person's body, preferably around an ankle. Write the name of the deceased person on the tag using permanent ink and/ or identify with an individual, non-repeating number. Avoid using tags made of paper.

- **Have a witness attest in writing** that an identification tag was attached to the person's body at the time of the transfer

- **Move the deceased person** onto the transfer cot

It is important to note: **Attaching a tag does not unmistakably verify the identity of the deceased person unless it is attached in the presence of the person(s) with authority, a member of** the family or their representative and acknowledged in writing by this person. There is a significant and all-important difference between attaching a tag for purposes of preventing a mix-up (as is customarily done at a hospital, nursing facility, etc.) and formal verification of identity (which is customarily done at the funeral home).

Attaching a funeral home tag to a decedent at the time of transfer is a means of preventing mix-up of human remains. Formal verification of identity on the other hand, is accomplished by viewing the deceased person and having it confirmed in writing. The only possible exception to having the person with authority or their designated representative verify the identity **might** be when the death occurred in the presence of the family or their designated representative and with the family present as a witness, the funeral home personnel attached an identification tag on the deceased person.

Care must also be exercised to ensure that identity is maintained when the person's body arrives at the funeral home or care center. Arrival should be recorded in a log book, listing the name of first call personnel, day and time of arrival and where the body was placed.

Under all circumstances, **Best Practice** means the funeral-cremation provider must never assume responsibility for identification of the deceased. The deceased must not be delivered to the crematory until the identity has been verified.

Attaching the Cremation Tag

As soon as it is determined that the person's body will be cremated, a second tag, referred to as a cremation tag, must be attached to the ankle of the deceased. The cremation tag should be easily distinguishable from all other tags. Most funeral homes use a brightly colored tag, approximately two inches wide and four inches in length that is easily noticed.

This tag alerts the staff to the fact that the decedent will be cremated. The name of the deceased should be written on the cremation tag using a marker containing permanent ink.

Removal of Medical Devices and Property

It is the responsibility of the funeral-cremation provider to train personnel to inspect the person's body for the presence of implants, pacemakers, radioactive devices, artificial limbs, braces and other medical devices/equipment that can present a potential hazard to crematory personnel or equipment, as well as valuables/personal property that may be on the person's body. The person(s) with authority should acknowledge the **presence or absence** of devices in writing on the Cremation Authorization Form. Personal property on the deceased requires completing a Personal Property receipt that describes the items found.

Further, the funeral-cremation provider should remove (or arrange for removal) of devices and property before the person's body is brought to the crematory. Pacemakers and defibrillators are some common medical devices that are considered potential hazards to be removed prior to cremation. These are sealed devices containing batteries and other hardware that, when subjected to the intense heat of cremation, can rupture and possibly explode. Embalmers often remove pacemakers, but defibrillators are usually removed by medical personnel trained in handling them. There is an increased use of implanted mechanical pumps and electronic devices that are used to control pain in patients. Physicians surgically construct a pouch located in the abdominal wall to hold these devices and should be removed prior to cremation.

Radioactive materials that might be implanted require further investigation by the funeral-cremation provider prior to cremation. Used as a treatment for cancer, radioactive seeds are implanted near or on cancerous tumors. Some common radioactive materials include Iodine 125, Palladium 103, Gold 198, Cobalt 60, Radium 226, Iridium 192, Pantalum 182 and Strontium 89. Some might emit gamma radiation that is harmful to unprotected persons. The Nuclear Regulatory Commission recommends that if a person has died within two weeks of having some of these seeds implanted, they should be removed **only** by qualified medical personnel. According to Matthews

Cremation Division, a leading manufacturer of cremation equipment, **Best Practice** requires all radioactive materials to be removed prior to cremation regardless of the type of seeds used or when they were implanted. Contact the physician and / or nuclear medicine department at the medical center before proceeding with cremation.

In general, prostheses (artificial parts) such as screws, plates, short and long bone replacements implanted in the body do not need to be removed prior to cremation. They will be removed from the cremated remains as part of the processing process. Artificial limbs or medical attachments should not be cremated with the person's body.

Removal of Body Piercing

As a testament to changing times, funeral-cremation providers must be reminded that valuables on bodies might no longer only include ordinary items such as rings, watches, earrings, necklaces, bracelets, anklets and toe rings nor be confined to ears, toes, fingers, necks or wrists. Body piercing is common. Diligence now requires thoroughly inspecting other parts of the body that may contain valuables. The tongue, chest, navel, pubic areas and nasal cavity must be inspected.

Final Verification at Funeral Home

In medicine, it is a standard of practice that, prior to beginning a surgical procedure on a patient, the surgeon and medical team perform what is referred to as **time out.** It is a final verification of the patient's identity and review of medical notes pertaining to the planned procedure to ensure everything is correct before proceeding. Funeral-cremation providers would do well to copy this and take a time out before cremating a deceased person.

Best Practice means that prior to placing the deceased person in the funeral vehicle, perform a final identification confirmation. In the presence of the driver or other funeral home witness, open the container.

- **Check all tags** on the person's body.

- **Check that the name of the person on the Cremation Authorization Form** matches the name that appears on each tag that is attached to the person's body.

- **Check that the name on the exterior of the container** matches the name on all tags and the Cremation Authorization Form.

- **Remove the different colored cremation tag** used to designate that this person will be cremated, and place it in a clear envelope or Ziploc bag. Tape or staple the tag to the exterior of the container.

All necessary paperwork must accompany the deceased, including the Cremation Authorization Form, state and county cremation permits, applicable coroner releases plus any other relevant paperwork. The decedent may now be placed into the funeral vehicle and transferred to the crematory.

Best Practice when Transporting to the Crematory

Recent class-action lawsuits across the country involving funeral-cremation providers and outside crematories have brought to the forefront cases where deceased persons have been transferred to the crematory by crematory personnel, not by the funeral home hired by the client family.

In serving the client family, it is the responsibility of the funeral home to deliver the deceased person to the crematory using its own funeral vehicle and personnel, as is customarily done when delivering a decedent to a cemetery for burial or entombment. Doing so provides assurance to the client family that the person's body was transferred safely and respectfully. In documenting the on-going chain of custody, a receipt for the person's body must be obtained upon delivery to the crematory. In addition to a receipt that might be issued by the crematory upon receiving a person's body, the funeral-cremation provider can use its own receipt, as well. A "crematory receipt" is discussed in more detail later in this chapter.

Once the person has been delivered to the crematory, few funeral homes have a policy requiring their driver to remain present during the cremation process. This can be referred to as "drop and run." This is in contrast to **Best Practice** considered customary, normal, expected and professional when delivering decedents to a cemetery for earth burial or entombment. Most funeral homes do not "drop and run" when performing burials but remain to witness the placement of the casket into the grave or crypt on behalf of the client family and to ensure it is done correctly. I do not know of a funeral home that would deliver a decedent to a cemetery, place the casket on the lowering device over the grave, and then leave. Yet, this is often done with decedents brought to the crematory. **Best Practice** means remaining at the crematory to at least witness the placement of the person inside the cremation chamber and the start of the process. This might mean the funeral home delivers the deceased person at the time the crematory is prepared to begin the cremation.

For several years I have reminded audiences at my seminars: "What you do for the burial client you must also do for the cremation client." **There can be no double standard in the respect we pay to the living and the dead, to the burial client or the cremation client.** Therefore, when using an external crematory, a representative from your funeral home should remain with the decedent until the deceased has been placed in the cremation chamber and the process has begun.

Receiving Cremated Remains from the Crematory

In most cases, a person's cremated remains will be picked up by the funeral-cremation provider. In some cases, the person(s) with authority may retrieve them, if these instructions are contained in writing on the Cremation Authorization Form or other written directive and provided to the crematory in advance. **Instructions as to who may receive a person's**

cremated remains must be a part of the paperwork provided to the crematory at the time the deceased is delivered. Yet, in other instances, the crematory will deliver the person's cremated remains to the funeral-cremation provider or person(s) with authority.

When the funeral-cremation provider receives the person's cremated remains from the crematory, the package containing the cremated remains must be carefully inspected and the label read to ensure it is the correct person. The *Permit for Disposition* or *Transfer Permit* must be attached (taped) to the package and contain the same name that appears on the crematory label. As in all instances of transferring custody of remains, a receipt must be issued. The receipt must contain:

- The name of the deceased

- The date and time of transfer

- Signature and printed name of the crematory representative releasing the person's cremated remains

- Signature, printed name and relationship of the person receiving the person's cremated remains

- A copy of the receipt must be provided to the person receiving the person's cremated remains. The receipt should be retained in the decedent's file

When the cremated remains are released directly to the person designated on the Cremation Authorization Form, in addition to a receipt, photo identification (such as a driver's license or passport) must be furnished and a photocopy of the identity must be made and retained in the crematory file. The funeral home should also receive a copy of the receipt and photocopied documents for the decedent's file.

Cremating The Person's Body

Cremation from the Crematory's Point of View

Receiving Decedents at the Crematory and Maintaining Identity

The on-going process of identification **must** also continue at the crematory facility and be maintained throughout the entire sequence of cremation, up to the release of the person's cremated remains and/or final disposition.

Crematory personnel are charged to maintain the identity of the deceased through **all** phases of the cremation process. Accepting the deceased person from the funeral-cremation provider, sheltering and handling the person's body up to cremation, removing the person's remains from inside the chamber, processing, packaging and labeling and releasing the remains are all critical steps that must be carefully performed one at a time and documented.

The International Cemetery, Cremation and Funeral Association through their College of Cremation Services, and to a lesser degree, the Cremation Association of North America, through CANA University, provide on-going education for funeral practitioners, crematory owners and operators. Subject to change and modification, ICCFA offers a certification program that means a person has been trained in cremation procedures and is certified in most aspects of the cremation process and operation of a crematory. More and more state governing agencies are adopting this program as a prerequisite for obtaining a crematory operators certificate. With the permission of both organizations, some information has been extracted from their course of instruction as a guide.

Best Practice for Accepting and Storage of the Deceased at the Crematory

Before bringing the decedent inside the crematory facility, the person making the delivery should present all documents and related paperwork to the responsible person at the crematory (for simplicity's sake, we will refer to this person as the "operator"). The delivery person should remain at the crematory while the operator checks all paperwork and tags.

The crematory must provide appropriate storage-holding space until the decedent is placed into the cremation chamber. Both the funeral-cremation provider and crematory are responsible for the privacy of decedents. The storage area must not be in public view and must be large enough to accommodate a container holding human remains. Storage facilities must comply with existing public laws. Respect for the deceased person and client family means that human remains awaiting cremation must **never** be placed on the floor, stacked one on top of one another or placed side-by-side on the same shelf.

Not all states require crematories to make available refrigeration for deceased persons. Some states require separate refrigeration units in their facility and regulate the conditions under which human remains must be refrigerated, including the maximum allowable temperature of refrigeration units. In general, temperature for adequate refrigeration of human remains requires a temperature of between 36 to 42 degrees Fahrenheit. Some states, like California, permit refrigeration temperatures for human remains awaiting cremation at a crematory to be as high as 50 degrees Fahrenheit. Check with your state laws to ensure you are in compliance.

Refrigeration is a standard of care. If your outside crematory does not provide refrigeration and the cremation will be delayed, schedule delivery of the person's body near the time the cremation will occur. All refrigeration units holding human remains must be locked at all times.

When refrigeration is available, a **"refrigeration log"** should be maintained on a daily basis. The log should record the name of decedents in refrigeration storage, date of death, location of the person's body inside the refrigeration unit, a description of the container, plus the date and time the deceased was placed into and removed from storage. Storage spaces within the refrigeration unit should be numbered so that placement of remains can be accurately recorded. Even when not required by regulations, for health considerations of crematory personnel and respectful care to the body, if the decedent cannot be cremated within 24 hours, the deceased person should be refrigerated. The temperature of the refrigeration unit must be monitored on a daily basis and recorded in the log. **If storage facilities are full and decedents cannot be properly stored or cared for, the crematory must not accept additional persons.** For crematories that do not have refrigeration storage facilities, **Best Practice** dictates that the funeral-cremation provider should deliver the deceased only after calling the crematory and checking that space is available. Increasingly, crematories are adopting a policy of performing cremations on an appointment basis to prevent storage of human remains and to ensure timely cremations. This **Best Practice** is one I salute and recommend.

Before accepting the deceased, the operator must inspect all documents and make sure that:

- All required documents (releases, authorizations, verifications, permits, etc.) are furnished and completed. State laws governing required legal documents for cremation must be followed.

- The Cremation Authorization Form is fully completed and contains required signatures listing the person(s) with authority to cremate and funeral home representative.

- Any special requests listed are legible and understood.

- Those instructions stipulating the release and/or disposition of the person's cremated remains are completed.

- That the signature of authorizing agent(s) appears on **all** documents presented.

- That the signature of the authorizing agent(s) is the same on all documents.

- That the first, middle and last name of the deceased appear on **all** documents and matches on **all** paperwork.

- That the container holding the person's body is acceptable for cremation. State laws governing what constitutes an acceptable container for cremation must be followed. In most instances the container must be combustible, closed, rigid and resistant to the leakage of bodily fluids.

- Any discrepancies or incompleteness must be rectified **before** accepting the decedent.

The decedent may now be brought inside the crematory facility. Immediately upon bringing the deceased inside, the operator must check:

- That the name of the deceased written on the exterior of the container holding the person's body matches the name on the documents.

- That the name of the deceased written on the cremation tag attached to the exterior of the container matches the name on the documents.

The crematory operator has the right to refuse accepting custody of the deceased person. When this occurs, the operator should notify the contracting funeral-cremation provider and provide the reasons the decedent was not accepted, such as no available storage space, incomplete or illegible documentation, unacceptable container for the person's body, to name a few possible reasons.

Receipt for decedent

The operator must issue a Receipt of Decedent for Cremation and provide a copy to the person making the delivery. Among other things, this receipt documents the transfer of custody and should be issued even when the crematory is on the premises of the funeral home. The funeral home must permanently retain the receipt in the decedent's file.

The receipt should include:

- The name and address of the crematory facility
- Name of the funeral-cremation provider
- Name of the deceased, as it appears on all documents furnished to the crematory
- Name and signature of operator accepting the decedent, plus date and time of acceptance
- Name and signature of the person delivering the decedent to the crematory
- Description of the container holding the decedent

In exercising **Best Practice**, some crematories require that a copy of the Verification of Identity form signed by the person(s) making the verification be provided and included with the other cremation documents.

Opening Containers at the Crematory

Laws in your state might prohibit crematory operators and their personnel from opening a cremation container. In general, **the crematory should not open the container unless it is done in the presence of a licensed funeral director who is representing the client family.** Other requirements might also exist for a crematory operator to open a container, such as completing OSHA Blood borne Pathogens training.

The crematory operator has ultimate authority (and responsibility) over the entire cremation process and all things that lead from acceptance of the remains at the crematory, through the cremation process, to final release of the person's cremated remains. **The operator must only begin the cremation process after being certain that everything is correct.** When any doubt exists, the cremation should be delayed. The operator should contact the funeral home serving the family and inform them of questions or concerns as to why the cremation is delayed. Check with your local regulatory agency regarding opening containers.

Maintaining Identification at the Crematory

A crematory must not accept human remains whose identity has not been verified prior to it being delivered to the crematory. It is standard practice in the cremation industry that each crematory maintains an identification system that allows identification of each decedent beginning from the time the crematory accepts delivery until the point in time the crematory releases the person's cremated remains to the designated recipient.

For a crematory, one of the key steps to maintaining identification is by the use of a metal disc, about the size of quarter, on which is embossed a non-repeating number that is assigned to each decedent before beginning the cremation process. Using a metal disc is an industry standard. Discs of various sizes can be used by crematories; some are large enough to contain the name of the crematory. Some states require a particular disc to be used. The disc must be capable of withstanding the extreme temperatures of the cremation process. **Once a disc with its own number embossed on it has been assigned to a decedent, it must remain with the deceased before, during and after the cremation process.**

The number on the metal disc is then recorded in the Cremation Log under disc number and ALL related paperwork (Cremation Authorization Form, etc.) associated with the cremation.

Cremation Log Book

Maintaining a log book has been a practice of inventors, scholars, explorers, and others for thousand of years. **All professional organizations involved with cremation and all manufacturers of cremation equipment recommend, as a standard of practice, that crematories maintain a cremation log.** Long recognized as an important record, many states have adopted laws that require crematories to record all cremation activity in a log.

In lawsuits involving cremation, the log book will be subpoenaed and carefully scrutinized. Failing to provide written documentation of cremations performed in a log will work against you. It is very difficult, if not impossible, to find an expert witness or industry consultant to testify that it is not the standard of practice for a crematory to maintain a log book.

A **Crematory Log** is a permanent, multi-purpose record that lists important details of each cremation performed at the crematory in an accurate, chronological method. It is also a method to help maintain the identity of decedents. The log must be kept at the crematory and be available to inspection. Preferably, the log should be contained in a bound, page-numbered book. **The log should not be a computer-generated record, but a hand-written record.**

Best Practice requires that the following items should be recorded in a Crematory Log:

- Current date
- Operator's name
- Number on the metal disk assigned to decedent
- Name of deceased
- Name of funeral-cremation provider
- Date and time decedent was received at crematory
- Description of container holding decedent
- Date and starting time of cremation
- Ending time of cremation
- Description of urn that will hold cremated remains
- Special requests or remarks
- For crematories with more than one cremation chamber, identify the cremation chamber used (This can be

by number or letter, such as unit #1 or unit A or by manufacturer)

In taking additional safeguards, and to show attention to detail, many funeral-cremation providers weigh the cremated remains after processing and record the weight on the log.

Important note: In completing the log, no information should be altered, erased or changed using Liquid Paper or other correction devices. Instead, a line should be drawn through the mistake and the correction written above the line and initialed by the operator.

Performing the Cremation

Before placing the deceased in the cremation chamber, the operator should inspect the chamber to ensure it is clean and free of any foreign material. The ash pan should be cleaned and placed under the clean out area of the cremation chamber.

Best Practice means that the operator takes a "time out" and double-checks all paperwork. Staple or paper-clip all papers together and attach them to the control panel of the cremation chamber. This is done as a step in maintaining the identity of the deceased. The paperwork must not be in an adjacent office or on a workbench near the chamber but **attached** to the cremation chamber in which the decedent is being cremated.

The metal disc must be placed **inside the chamber**, near the front of the chamber, on the right or left side, with the number side facing down.

Place the container holding the decedent inside the cremation chamber and begin the cremation process. **When the cremation chamber is in operation, the operator must be present at all times.** Among other things, the operator needs to prevent a rapid fire (a person's body burning too rapidly, which causes stack emissions or damage to the inside of the chamber).

The operator must also monitor temperatures inside the chamber (and where required by law, ensure that minimum temperatures are in compliance) and conduct periodic visual inspections to ensure that the cremation is proceeding efficiently and safely. Some states mandate minimum temperatures during the cremation process and may require the use of a continuous chart recorder to document temperatures. According to Matthews Cremation Division, the following states require temperature chart recordings: Arizona, California, Florida, Idaho, Illinois, Louisiana, Maine, Massachusetts, Michigan, Missouri, Montana, New Jersey, New York, North Carolina, Ohio, Oregon, Pennsylvania, Tennessee, Virginia and Washington. Check with your state regulatory agency or crematory manufacturer concerning any questions you may have concerning continuous chart recorders.

Removing the Person's Cremated Remains from the Chamber

These steps constitute **Best Practice:**

- **Record the ending time of the cremation in the cremation log**. After allowing a "cooling" time, the blower should be activated (to ensure that dust and heat are drawn away from the operator).

- **Open the cremation chamber door slowly** to avoid rapid changes in temperature inside the chamber but enough to permit the recovery of cremated remains. Lock the chamber door in place using safety devices provided by the manufacturer.

- **Remove the metal disc before the cremated remains are removed**. Some operators place the metal disc in the corner of the cleanout hopper-ash pan and some place the disc in an envelope with the name of the deceased on it on the side of the pan.

- **Retrieve as much of the cremated remains as possible**. Specialty cremation tools, such as stainless steel cleanout brushes and hoes are used to sweep the contents of the chamber (cremated remains) into the cleanout hopper in the front of the chamber. After

245

sweeping by hand, the interior of the chamber should be thoroughly vacuumed using an industry-specific vacuum to recover all possible cremated remains. The contents of the vacuum and vacuum filter must be emptied into the cleanout hopper with the other cremated remains. Only microscopic particles left in crevices and cracks in the chamber after it has been swept and vacuumed are considered unrecoverable.

• **Carefully transfer the person's cremated remains** and metal disc from the cleanout hopper to a cooling tray. The hopper should be brushed and its contents emptied into the cooling tray. Remove the paperwork from the exterior of the cremation chamber and place it next to the cremated remains.

Processing Cremated Remains

Once the person's cremated remains have cooled, they are ready to be processed. **Processing** means reducing the large fragments of bone into a finer and more manageable consistency by mechanical means; making them suitable for placement into a cremated remains container (urn or vessel); and making the bones unidentifiable. During processing, the bones are crushed and ground into particles resembling coarse sand or small gravel, using an industrial-grade grinding machine. State laws may require processing and govern even the consistency of processed cremated remains.

Processing of a person's cremated remains is a key area of disclosure and **Best Practice** requires it to be a part of your Cremation Authorization Form. The funeral-cremation provider and crematory operator must be aware that not all cremations are necessarily done the same way. With the influx of new ethnic groups to the United States, it should not be taken for granted that all cremation consumers want their family member's cremated remains reduced in size and made unidentifiable. Some cultures, especially among the Japanese, have rituals that include the "passing" of bones of cremated family members from person to person. Even when processing might be required by law, the right to observe a ritual should not be denied any person. Doing so can be grounds for a lawsuit. Processing can occur after rituals have been completed. **Inform before you perform.**

The operator must remove all non-ferrous objects that cannot be placed in the processing machine, such as nails, screws and prostheses. Removal is accomplished by passing an industrial-grade magnet over the cremated remains as well as removing objects by hand.

Unless express written instructions are contained on the Cremation Authorization Form, foreign objects should not be included with the processed cremated remains in the urn. Instead, they will be separated from the person's cremated remains, brushed clean of any residue and disposed of by the crematory according to state and local laws. Some crematories dispose of foreign objects as biohazardous waste and some have them buried in a grave designated only for this purpose. These items must not be placed in regular, everyday trash.

Personal effects to be placed with the person's cremated remains should be itemized in writing on the Cremation Authorization Form. When a client family requests this be done, it is usually done by the funeral-cremation provider, not the crematory operator. Whenever possible, the authorizing person(s) should be present to witness the placement of personal effects in the urn.

Most crematories have a special area designated as the processing area. The person's cremated remains should be brought to this area and allowed to cool. The metal disc and paperwork must accompany the person's cremated remains but must be removed before they are placed in the processing machine. After processing, the remains must be carefully emptied into a sturdy, clear plastic bag. All residue must be brushed from the processing machine and included with the other cremated remains.

As another step in the on-going process of maintaining the identity of the deceased, a label must be attached to the outside of the plastic bag that contains:

1. The name of the person whose cremated remains are contained in the plastic bag

2. The number that appears on the metal disc

3. The date of the cremation

4. The name of the crematory

A standard of practice in the cremation industry, the metal identification disc must be placed inside the plastic bag on top of the person's cremated remains. The plastic bag should be closed using a sturdy lock strap or other fastener. In addition to the metal disc, some crematories use a fastener on which the name of the deceased is written.

In some instances, all of the processed cremated remains of the person might not fit into one plastic bag. When this is the case, the remainder of the processed cremated remains of the person must be placed into a second plastic bag and labeled with the identical information listed above. The **primary** plastic bag should be numbered as "1 of 2" and the **secondary** plastic bag should be numbered as "2 of 2." Each container must be identified with identical information and both containers must be attached to one another in a manner so as to not easily become detached through incidental contact. The plastic bag(s) containing the person's cremated remains must be carefully fitted into the urn-vessel to prevent it from being punctured or torn.

Case Example – The Toothless Client

Several months after receiving his father's cremated remains from the funeral home, the son became curious about what was in the urn. Shaking the container, it sounded different than what he imagined. He opened the urn and sifted through the contents. Mixed among the ashes he noticed what looked like teeth. He removed some of these and asked his friend, an oral surgeon, to tell him whether or not these were real teeth. The surgeon confirmed that they were teeth. The son was concerned, because more than 20 years ago his father had all of his teeth surgically removed due to disease. He returned to the funeral home carrying his father's cremated remains. He asked for assurance that the cremated remains in his possession were those of his father and not someone else. The funeral director was unable to provide the son with a clear explanation of identification procedures and the procedures followed by the third-party crematory. At one point during the discussion, the funeral director told the son, "We have been in business for 50 years. Of course these are your father's ashes." Unsatisfied, the son hired an attorney to begin an investigation. The funeral home and crematory were sued claiming misrepresentation, deception, fraud and that the actions caused the son emotional distress.

Placement into the Urn-Vessel and Minimum Container Requirements

The person's cremated remains may now be placed into the cremated remains container (urn or vessel). More and more crematories are weighing the cremated remains and recording the weight in the log book as an added level of accountability before placing them in the urn-vessel. I support this. In some cases, the funeral-cremation provider might supply the crematory with an urn or vessel that has been selected by the client family.

When the crematory provides a container for the person's cremated remains, **Best Practice** means the container should meet the following minimum standards:

- Constructed of sheet metal, wood or rigid plastic, unless the crematory has received instruction to provide an urn or vessel designed to dissolve in water or disintegrate after earth burial, or the family supplies their own urn-vessel.

Cremated-remains containers constructed of cardboard should not be used, even in instances when the person's cremated remains will be picked up or delivered to the funeral home. Cardboard can easily become saturated from fluids and fall apart; if it is accidentally dropped, it can break; it can be punctured and cause cremated remains to leak through. Cardboard containers do not make a visually pleasing or professional presentation.

If you or your crematory uses a cardboard urn, you are urged to reconsider using this product. The cost difference between a cardboard urn and plastic (utility-type) urn is minimal.

A cardboard urn holding a family member's cremated remains should **never** be presented to a client family.

Biodegradable Urns

In recent years, biodegradable urns, referred to as bio-urns in the industry, have been created as a means of disposing cremated remains at sea, in the water and the earth. This urn is designed to break apart and disintegrate over a short period of time when exposed to water and earthly elements. When a biodegradable urn is selected, no plastic bag should be used to hold the person's cremated remains. Instead, a paper identification label is used and placed inside the urn. The metal disc should not be placed inside the urn with the cremated remains but instead, taped to the exterior of the biodegradable urn. The urn should be labeled on the exterior with a paper label. Before the urn is disposed of, the metal disc should be removed and kept with the other paperwork or retained by the person doing the placement.

It is against the standard of care for a funeral-cremation provider or crematory to commingle the cremated remains of two or more persons without receiving the express written permission from the person(s) with authority representing ALL decedents. In most states, knowingly commingling the cremated remains of people is a violation of law.

Labeling the Urn-Vessel

Best Practice guidelines for labeling packages or containers holding cremated human remains are:

- **Each container must be labeled** with an identical copy of the label that was placed on the plastic bag with the cremated remains and contain (1) the name of the decedent, (2) date of cremation, (3) disc number and (4) name of crematory.

- **When there are multiple containers holding the cremated remains** of the same person, the labels should indicate the total number of containers (#1 of 2, #2 of 2, and so forth).

- **Multiple containers** must be securely fastened together to prevent separation.

- Whenever the person's cremated remains container is wrapped, **a duplicate label must be affixed** to the outside wrapping paper.

- **The Permit for Disposition,** if required by state law, must be placed in an envelope and securely attached to the outside of the cremated remains container. The permit is usually attached using clear packaging tape.

Storage of Cremated Remains at the Crematory

Tom Snyder, my friend and fellow cremation authority, says it well: "A crematory is not a storage facility for remains awaiting cremation or for human remains after they have been cremated. A crematory should only maintain custody of the cremated human remains for a brief time." A declaration to this effect, with a timeline, should be contained in the Crematory Agreement between the funeral-cremation provider and crematory facility and understood by all parties.

Unless the crematory also owns a columbarium or has made special arrangements for long-term storage of cremated human remains, they should be retrieved by the funeral-cremation provider in a timely manner after being notified they are ready. It is recommended that contracting parties agree to a provision that the crematory will hold a person's cremated remains for no more than 72 hours after notifying the funeral-cremation provider.

Within this period of time, the deceased person's cremated remains should be retrieved by the funeral-cremation provider, delivered by the crematory to the funeral-cremation provider, cemetery, mausoleum or other contracting company-person, or shipped per instructions contained in the Cremation Authorization Form.

During the (brief) period of custody at the crematory, the person's cremated remains must be stored in a secure and private location, under lock and key. Only authorized personnel should be allowed access to the storage area.

The crematory must maintain an "inventory log" of human remains in storage. To prevent mix-up or loss of containers, a person's cremated remains should be stored in individual areas or bins or otherwise be held so they are separated from one another. Each space should be marked to make locating a container easier. A numbering system is a simplified method to accomplish this, such as "space 1," "space 2," and so forth. The paperwork for each decedent must accompany each container and be taped to it in such a manner that it will not become separated from the container. The inventory log should be kept in the office within the crematory or affixed to the door of the storage area. **Best Practice** means it should contain:

- The name of the deceased and date of death

- The date of cremation

- Date and time the person's cremated remains were placed in storage room

- Name of crematory personnel placing the person's cremated remains in storage

- Date and time the person's cremated remains are removed from storage

- Disposition of the person's cremated remains (given to funeral-cremation provider, shipped, etc.)

Releasing Cremated Remains

The person's cremated remains must only be released to the person(s) designated **in writing** on the Cremation Authorization Form. The Cremation Authorization Form must contain specific, written instructions that designates who may receive the person's cremated remains **even in cases when they will be released to the funeral-cremation provider.** Any changes to the written instructions on the Cremation Authorization Form must be made in writing from the person(s) with authority. Verbal or faxed instructions can be issued by anyone claiming to be the person(s) with authority and must **never** be accepted as a means of valid instruction.

In all cases of releasing a person's cremated remains, a Receipt for Cremated Remains must be issued. The receipt should be signed by the recipient, state his/her relationship to the deceased, list the date and time and include the signature of the crematory representative. When a deceased person's cremated remains are released to the funeral-cremation provider, the same procedure applies. In addition to a signature, the receipt should contain a form of positive identification of the person receiving the cremated remains, such as a driver's license, passport or other photo identification. Photocopy the form of identification and retain it in the crematory file.

When the person's cremated remains are scheduled to be shipped, a receipt for the person's cremated remains must be issued and signed by the shipping agent or carrier accepting the person's cremated remains. The person's cremated remains must only be shipped through a carrier like the United States Postal Service that provides an internal tracking system and the signature of all handlers during the shipment process.

For additional information on shipment of cremated human remains, see Chapter Nine.

Shipment of a person's cremated remains outside the United States using the US Postal System should be avoided. Once a person's cremated remains leave the United States and enter the postal system of foreign countries, the USPS loses control and any means for tracking.

Lawsuits have been filed against crematories and funeral-cremation providers because delivery was delayed or a person's cremated remains became lost. To avoid problems, when a person's cremated remains are to be sent to a foreign country, advise the person(s) with authority to personally carry them to the final destination point by themselves or their designated representative.

Case Example: Wrongful Release

The mother arranged for the cremation of her unmarried, adult son. Her written instructions on the Cremation Authorization Form directed the funeral-cremation provider to release the cremated remains only to her. She planned to take the cremated remains to an out-of-state cemetery for burial in the family plot. The funeral director told her the cremated remains would be ready the following week. The mother informed the director that she would retrieve them in two weeks and asked the funeral home to store them until she arrived for them. The director agreed and wrote the instructions in the decedent's file. One week later a young lady arrived at the funeral home just before closing time and introduced herself as the fiancé to the deceased. She explained the desperate situation: The mother changed her plans and was in a rush packing for her trip. She was unable to come to the funeral home herself and wanted her son's cremated remains now. Considering her like a daughter-in-law, the mother asked the fiancé to get the cremated remains for her, as a favor. The director looked at the instructions in the file and read that the cremated remains were to be given to the mother. Acknowledging this, the fiancé assured the director that he would be doing the mother a big favor by saving her a trip to the funeral home. The director informed the fiancé that the cremated remains were ready but were still at the crematory. The fiancé offered to drive to the crematory to get the cremated remains. She asked the director to call the crematory and inform them she was on her way. The director called the crematory and instructed them to release the cremated remains to the fiancé. At the crematory, the fiancé signed the Receipt of Cremated Remains form and provided them with photo identification. A copy of her photo identification was made and attached to the crematory's paperwork. Days later the mother came to the funeral home expecting to receive her son's cremated remains. The director explained that the fiancé picked them up last week. The mother informed the director that there never was a fiancé. She explained that her son had dated a troublesome woman for a short time. The troubled fiancé hated the mother and blamed her for causing the breakup with her son. As a result, she began stalking her son and causing other problems. The deranged fiancé fled the state and took the cremated remains with her, refusing to return them. Police in the other state arrested the fiancé and after a long battle, the mother finally received her son's cremated remains. The mother sued the funeral home, the funeral director, the crematory and the crematory operator over the wrongful release of her son's cremated remains.

Disposition of Cremated Remains

In recent years, creative ways of disposition of a person's cremated remains have emerged. Some are unconventional. It is safe to say that (new) forms of disposition will continue to be developed and are currently limited only by the creativity of people.

Even in situations when family members might indicate otherwise, the funeral-cremation provider must still act professionally and recognize that the cremated remains have meaning and worth. While cremating the body might be just a job, the cremated remains represent the mortal remains of a human being.

A funeral-cremation provider or crematory must never participate in or promote improper or unlawful disposition of a person's cremated remains. Disposition must be done in accordance with existing federal, state and local laws and in a civilized, respectful manner.

At all times, the Permit for Disposition must accompany the person's cremated remains. Most state laws and the standard of practice require that the permit document be securely attached with tape to the container. When multiple containers are used (such as small "keepsake" size urns), some states require a separate permit document for each container.

Just as when burying a deceased person, the funeral-cremation provider has the same legal and ethical responsibilities to properly handle and dispose of a person's cremated remains. Responsibilities include informing the client family as to what are legal forms of disposition, and when necessary, what methods are not legal. As a best practice and as part of the informed consent process, many funeral homes and crematories provide the client family with printed guidelines based on their states' laws. This helps prevent claims that "the funeral director never told me I couldn't do that."

Disposition of a person's cremated remains can mean freedom from the restrictions of earth burial and using a cemetery. What were customs years and decades ago might not appeal to everyone today. The term one size fits all is a thing of the past when it comes to disposition of cremated remains.

Traditional and conventional means of disposition of a person's cremated remains include:

- Returning them to the client family for safekeeping
- Earth burial in a cemetery
- Earth burial on private land, where permitted by law
- Placement in a crypt in a mausoleum
- Placement in a niche in a columbarium
- Scattering in a cemetery, at sea or over land or where permitted by law

There are some new and creative ways of disposing of a person's cremated remains including:

- Cremation-only cemeteries or newly developed cremation memorialization sections within existing cemeteries, offering such options as garden settings with unique water features and wildlife, cenotaph plaque structures, niches bored into boulders, niche benches, placement of remains inside living trees and high rise-columbaria.

- Proportioning (dividing) a person's cremated remains among several people or locations

- Placement in pieces of jewelry, art or art deco pieces

- Insertion into atmospheric balloons or shotgun shells as a new way to scatter remains

- Placement or scattering on athletic fields or golf courses

- Transforming particles of ashes into graphite, subjecting it to extreme pressure and heat, causing it to grow into a diamond crystal

- Placement inside living human tissue

- Mixing cremated remains in concrete and placing them within undersea structures, such as the replicated City of Atlantis in the Atlantis Memorial Reef Project in Key Biscayne, Florida

Regardless of the disposition choices you might be requested to fulfill, they must be authorized in writing. When disposition involves shipping all or a portion of the person's cremated remains, a signed receipt for the person's cremated remains must be obtained. When only a portion of a person's remains is used for a particular form of disposition, an approximate weight or amount should be contained in the authorization and on the receipt.

Cremated Remains Disposers

As more states adopt stringent cremation laws, more regulation and license requirements will be enacted to include licensure of persons or companies that provide scattering services. Even in states that do not have existing laws or licensing requirements governing scattering services, **Best Practice** dictates that a person who performs this service should keep detailed records of each scattering performed, including the location, method of disposition and the date and time.

For the funeral cremation provider who uses a third-party service (licensed or non-licensed, depending on the laws in your state) to dispose of a person's cremated remains, the same diligence must be exercised as when using other outside service providers. Outside contractors are discussed in Chapter Ten.

In using a third-party disposal service, the funeral director and/or crematory must be certain that they are scattered as promised and in accordance with federal, state and local laws. In the absence of any law, cremated remains must only be scattered in a prudent, respectable fashion, sensitive to the general public. The funeral director, crematory operator and scattering service must be familiar with the laws in his/her state.

Case Example – The Un-Scattered Cremated Remains

In 1989, in one of the largest lawsuits of its kind, more than 3,000 plaintiffs filed a class-action lawsuit alleging that funeral homes located in Northern California mishandled their family member's cremated remains. The defendant funeral homes contracted with a third-party pilot who promised to scatter the cremated remains in a designated area in the High Sierra Nevada mountain range or over the Pacific Ocean. As part of the scattering service, the pilot agreed to pick up the cremated remains from funeral homes and would fly his plane out of the San Jose Airport. As cremation increased throughout California, his business prospered. Funeral homes offered his High Sierra scattering service as an option to client families. Soon, it was a popular choice among the masses. What the funeral directors did not know was that the pilot rarely made it to the High Sierra. Instead, he drove his car packed with cremated remains to his own property, located in the foothills of the Sierra range, not too far from home base in San Jose, where he dumped them on a pile. One day, a group of hikers came across the dump site and noticed what appeared to be bits and pieces of human bones. They called the local Sheriff Department and local news stations, which responded to the site. During the trial, the pilot offered an explanation for not scattering by air as he promised. He became afraid of flying, finding it too dangerous to deal with the up-drafts and down-drafts that occur when flying near mountains. Over 1,000 legal firms represented 3,000 plaintiffs and among other claims, successfully sought for and received damages for emotional distress that reached into the millions. During the trial, one of the chief plaintiff attorneys said, "The funeral industry people are the Darth Vaders of our society."

In offering or recommending scattering-dispersal services, **Best Practice** requires funeral-cremation providers to conduct due diligence and inspections before recommending anyone and ensure that you are familiar with these service providers as you are with all other third-party providers. There are no exceptions. **Inform before you perform** must be included in all discussions with a client family and/or when seeking or receiving authority to dispose of a person's cremated remains.

Commingling of Cremated Remains

Inform before you perform. Commingling is a cause of litigation in the United States. The issue of commingling may not be an issue with some consumers or client families but it has become an issue with plaintiff attorneys.

Commingling should be considered from two distinct viewpoints:

1. During the cremation process, including processing the cremated remains; and,

2. During disposition.

The standard of care throughout the cremation industry is that cremations are performed individually, with only one person at a time in a cremation chamber. It is against the standard of care, and in many states, a violation of law, to cremate more than one person at a time in the same chamber without receiving the express written permission of the person(s) with authority representing both deceased persons. Even with permission, many crematories decline to perform this service.

In many instances the funeral director is involved in performing disposition with or on behalf of the client family. When the funeral director is directly involved and the person's remains will be scattered, the funeral director should perform this on an individual basis, not combine (commingle) the cremated remains of two or more persons. Cremated remains of two or more persons should never be combined without receiving the express written permission from the person(s) with authority representing **all** decedents. In addition to violating the standard of care, in most states it is a violation of law to knowingly commingling human cremated remains.

After each cremation, it is a standard of practice to clean the inside of the cremation chamber, collection trays, processor equipment and all other tools and equipment that comes in contact with a person's cremated remains. Thorough cleaning means removing as much residue of a person's cremated remains as possible by brushing, sweeping and vacuuming and seeing to it that it is included with the person's cremated remains. Thorough cleaning after each cremation reduces commingling from previous cremations to minute proportions.

Be that as it may, commingling of people's cremated remains from previous cremations cannot be avoided. Unless it is the first cremation performed in a new cremation chamber, inadvertent microscopic commingling of cremated remains will occur.

Microscopic particles of cremated remains accumulate in crevices and cracks of the floor and other places inside the chamber. Even when a vacuum is used, it is impossible to collect all of the microscopic particles. However, **Best Practice** means **informing before performing. Best Practice** dictates that this issue is discussed and disclosed to the person(s) with authority at the time of making arrangements and **before** cremation is performed. Commingling is a key disclosure that must be contained on the Cremation Authorization Form and disclosed ahead of performing the cremation and acknowledged in writing by the person(s) with authority.

Infant Cremation

Some funeral directors and crematory operators mistakenly believe that infants or fetuses may be cremated simultaneously with an adult in the same chamber. This is false and can have profound repercussions for the funeral home and crematory. Most client families trust that cremation is an individual, almost intimate procedure; that their family member will be cremated on an individual basis with no surprises as to how it will turn out; and that 100% of the recoverable cremated remains will be returned to them. As Tom Snyder says, "Alone is alone, whether it's an adult or an infant. I think you violate the privacy of both parties when neither party has authorized another person to be in that space." Snyder goes on to say, "It is challenging to perform a solo cremation of an infant (and especially a fetus) in a way that yields cremated remains you can actually give back to the family."

A somewhat widespread, false belief is that it is permissible to cremate an infant with an adult as long as the infant is placed in a special tray, separate from the adult, thereby avoiding commingling. Pans used to cremate infants are about 30 inches in diameter, with a 10-12 inch rim. They are capable of holding about 12 pounds of weight. With the air turbulence that occurs during the cremation process, it is impossible to use a pan like this and expect that there will be no commingling.

Snyder offers the following **Best Practice** guidelines when cremating an infant or a fetus:

- Place the infant in the special infant pan alone.

- Schedule the infant cremation after one or more cremations have been performed.

- Ideally, make the infant cremation the last one of the day. This allows the cremation to be performed using ambient heat within the chamber, a more gentle heat, without the onslaught of burners and blowers that would otherwise dissipate the cremated remains of small infants.

In writing this chapter and discussing the contents with leading authorities in the cremation industry, I question why some funeral-cremation providers place such a low value on their cremation services and perform this important service significantly below their actual cost. Given the tremendous exposure to liability, the attention to detail that is necessary and the unique services and facilities of a funeral-cremation provider and crematory, it seems to this author that the average cremation should cost more than the average burial. Cremation is an irreversible process; the smallest mistake can have a massive impact on one's business and personal life. It is a finely detailed process in which so much can go wrong. If one step is out of place or overlooked, everything can fall apart as if it were a house of cards.

CHAPTER 12

Using an Outside Crematory and Crematory Inspections

Less than 2,000 funeral homes own their own crematory, meaning the majority of funeral homes rely on an outside or third-party crematory to perform that function. The increasing use of cremation exposes the funeral director to liabilities beyond those encountered with traditional earth burial and entombment. When using an external contract crematory, the funeral director is responsible for conducting and maintaining records of regular and thorough inspections to be sure that the handling of deceased persons and the conduct of crematory personnel conforms to the highest level of respectful care. So, too, must the crematory document each cremation. This chapter draws on valuable lessons learned the hard way to identify what funeral directors must do to reduce risks associated with the use of an outside crematory.

As the agent of the client family, you should carefully consider which outside (third-party) crematory you select as your partner. That means being familiar with crematory procedures and crematory personnel. After the grisly findings of the Tri-State Crematory scandal in Georgia were made public and became the top story on the 6:00 News in 2002, funeral homes across the country received inquiries from consumers asking about procedures during the cremation process and how something like this could have happened.

Some people in funeral-cremation-cemetery service mistakenly believe that clients choosing cremation do so out of a lack of care for the deceased person, or, wrongfully assume that, because "it's only a cremation," the same level of care and diligence afforded burial clients is not necessary. This is dangerously wrong thinking. Whether a funeral home or crematory wants to accept this, there is great public interest in cremation and concern as to how a person's body will be treated. How it is done, where it is done and who performs it are only a few concerns voiced by the public.

Having any service performed outside the immediate control and watchfulness of the funeral-cremation provider, **especially when utilizing the services of an outside crematory**, adds a level of complexity to one's professional responsibilities and duties. You may not know the crematory owner or operator and may not be familiar with their procedures. Chapter Ten addresses using outside contractors.

When a funeral home is hired by a client family to provide cremation services and then utilizes the services of an outside crematory, it means the cremation of the deceased person now becomes, in essence, a shared responsibility between the funeral home and the crematory. Some funeral directors will be surprised to read that **the funeral home does not relinquish its responsibilities by merely delivering the deceased person to the crematory or through the act of transferring custody to them.** If you believe that "once the deceased person is at the crematory it is no longer my problem," you are mistaken. Some funeral-home owners have learned hard lessons, becoming concerned only after they are involved in litigation. As the agent of the client family, the funeral director's responsibilities are continuous, throughout the entire process of cremation, including retrieving the person's cremated remains from the crematory and seeing to their proper release or disposition in concert with the written directions on the Cremation Authorization Form. There is no such thing as the funeral home being "off-the-hook" just because the deceased person is now at the crematory.

Disclosures and Due Diligence

The funeral home that uses an outside crematory is like the tightrope walker who performs his/her acts without a safety net. For the funeral director, the only "safety net" is through disclosure of certain facts to the client family before cremation takes place and by performing due diligence of the outside crematory. Funeral directors understand disclosure more easily than they understand the meaning and importance of due diligence.

Disclosure is defined by *Black's Law Dictionary* as, "to bring into view by uncovering, to lay bare, to reveal to knowledge, to free from secrecy or ignorance, or to make known." At its most basic, it is sharing important elements of processes or procedures with the client family. It is important that certain disclosures be contained on the Cremation Authorization Form and revealed to the client family during the arrangement conference. As an added step of protection, many arrangers require the authorizing person(s) to write their initials next to each disclosure as a way to acknowledge that certain facts were both revealed and understood. An extensive list of recommended disclosures are provided for your consideration in Chapter Eleven.

Due Diligence

Black's Law Dictionary defines **due diligence** as "prudence, vigilant activity, attentiveness, or care, of which there are infinite shades, from the slightest momentary thought to the most vigilant anxiety." It goes on to define it further as "a measure of prudence, activity or constant personal attention, as is properly to be expected from, and ordinarily exercised by, a reasonable and prudent person under the particular circumstances."

In using a third-party crematory, "cremation due-diligence" means acting prudently and with constant personal attention. It means that no matter how you personally feel about cremation ("I would never choose cremation for anyone") or how you may view people choosing cremation ("They don't care about their loved one" or "They are second-class compared to burial families") or where cremation stands on your priority list ("Once the deceased person is out my door, it's someone else's problem"), **you are responsible** for the actions of the third-party crematory you hire to perform this service. **It is as if you performed the cremation yourself.** With fewer than 2,000 crematories serving approximately 20,000 funeral homes, the majority of funeral directors place immense trust in their third-party crematory. The funeral homes that placed their trust in the Tri State Crematory in Georgia paid a horrific price.

With cremation, the funeral director must understand that his/her name, reputation and livelihood are on the line. Performing due diligence will help you protect your name and reputation. Ensuring the quality of a local crematory partner is indispensable to success and peace of mind. What you do not know can destroy you. **Due diligence requires activity and personal involvement.** It means that inspections must take place.

Most cremation authorities consider inspections to be the cornerstone of a due diligence program. I agree. In practically all cremation-based lawsuits, the funeral homes using that crematory are always named as defendants. One only needs to be reminded of past cremation scandals: the mass cremations, ghoulish mutilation of deceased persons, illegal removal and sale of body organs and dental gold made public in 1986 in southern California at the Lamb-Sconce Funeral Home and Crematory, written about in the book, *Chop Shop,* by Kathy Draidhill; the on-going investigation of the unlicensed Bayview Crematory in Seabrook, New Hampshire, with potential for thousands of illegal cremations that may have occurred; the Tri-State Crematory in Noble, Georgia, where deceased persons scheduled for cremation were instead buried in makeshift graves or disposed of in a nearby lake; the recent discovery by the State of California and subsequent closure of the long-established Grand View Memorial Park and Crematory in Glendale, Calif., and potential for thousands of improperly conducted cremations. Each of these gross violations could possibly have been avoided if funeral homes had conducted inspections and reported violations to the legal authorities. Many funeral homes were named as defendants in these lawsuits. Those that survive have an uphill battle to stay open. Inspections by funeral directors are not taking place as they should. In a spot survey of 200 funeral homes conducted in May 2005 by *The Cremation Report* (published by Kates-Boylston Publications), only 61% admit to doing inspections. What was inspected was not noted in the report. Worse, respondents admitted that most inspections took less than one hour.

This chapter should not be misconstrued as a blanket indictment against third-party crematories. The majority perform their services properly and lawfully, treating deceased persons respectfully. But, it is worth repeating: **what you don't know can destroy you.** Reasons that some crematories do not adhere to high standards include:

- **Cremation is viewed as only a business activity**; bottom line is all that counts.

- **There is no relationship or attachment to the deceased persons or client family**; deceased persons are viewed as only a cipher.

- **Cremation is performed by the seat of the pants** – some people get into the business without adequate knowledge or skill. Lacking sensitivity, cremating a deceased person is merely burning a body. Training for staff is minimal, focusing more on operating equipment and emissions control, not quality of care.

- **With costs rising and profits declining, operators are instructed to lower costs**. Streamlining usually means cutting corners by reducing staff, dispensing with training and relaxing standards.

- **It is difficult to recruit high-quality personnel.** Low wages contribute to staff turnover and it can be a struggle to get the job done. Hiring the wrong people at any cost is dangerous. Unscrupulous (unsupervised and untrained) employees can be easily tempted. A crematory in California hired workers without performing background checks to run the crematory. They turned out to be recently paroled convicts. Ownership provided little oversight to their actions. Personal property began missing from deceased persons, dental gold was illegally removed and cremated remains were packaged in bags and sold as "kitty litter." These criminal activities have all but caused the business to close its doors.

- **Lack of oversight or supervision by management.** For some crematory owners, an out of sight, out of mind attitude prevails. They view cremation to mean non-care by a family or a second-class option. After providing minimal instruction to their personnel, employees can be left alone. Attention to crematory employees and procedures only comes when the owner learns that something has gone wrong.

- **Lack of unannounced inspections by local funeral homes** using the crematory

Reasons Funeral Directors Hesitate in Performing Inspections

Concern for the customer also means seeing things through the eyes of the customer. Even if a funeral home owns and operates its own crematory, it is wise to conduct inspections as suggested in this chapter. The prudent funeral director recognizes that he/she is the eyes and ears of the client family and is obligated to use only those persons or services who are qualified, licensed, and competent and who share a similar philosophy of serving others. It means being the customer's advocate. It means not taking anything for granted.

Funeral-home owners must be aware that anytime a local crematory becomes involved in any controversy – even those considered minor – it will likely be breaking news in your area. Your friends and client families and media will ask you about any involvement you may have had with the crematory. Even if you had no relationship with the crematory in question, be prepared to hear angry comments. You may even be considered guilty by association among some people. Families that you previously served may call you or come in, seeking assurance that their loved one was not mistreated. It was difficult operating a funeral home and cremation service business during the scandalous 1980s when funeral service in California was rocked by major cremation lawsuits. Like many funeral homes that were recognized as the "community funeral home," we received numerous telephone calls from the public and media inquiring about these scandals and our procedures. Thankfully, my entire staff was well trained and versed in best practices. Fortunately, inspecting our third-party crematory had been standard procedure for us since 1975. My funeral home was never even remotely involved in any scandal. Instead of putting our head in the sand, we opted to become proactive in dealing with this negative situation. We embarked on a community awareness initiative to educate our neighbors and differentiate our service from all other firms. Local newspapers and television stations appreciated our openness and held several interviews at my funeral home and at the crematory we used. Concerned funeral directors worked with the California legislature to establish thorough cremation standards and laws beneficial to the public and practitioner alike.

Case Example: Close Encounter of the Wrong Kind

David Sconce, of the infamous Lamb-Sconce Funeral Home and Crematory of Pasadena, California visited me at my office in an attempt to perform cremations for my firm. Prior to Mr. Sconce taking charge, the Lamb Funeral Home and Crematory was owned and operated by brothers, John and Lawrence Lamb. Both brothers had distinguished careers and reputations, even taking turns serving as the President of the Pasadena Rose Bowl organization. Their funeral home and crematory were among the most respected and successful firms in California. When my father first established his funeral home in 1955, he became personal friends with the Lamb brothers and used their crematory. However, after the immediate family retired in the late 1970s, the operation changed. We began using another crematory. Each deceased person Mr. Sconce could obtain from local funeral homes for cremation represented considerable revenue to him and his accomplices through the illegal harvesting of body parts and dental gold. Like other local funeral homes at the time, I was unaware of any wrongdoing or any illegal side business. However, during a visit to my company, it became apparent that something wrong was going on. He pitched me on doing business with him. In his own vernacular, he described his "funeral director oriented" services…his people would pick up the body anytime, saving the funeral home the trouble of driving to the crematory or holding the body. He promised prompt service…the cremains would be available to us by morning of the next day. He explained that doing business with him meant that I could make a buck with cremation. His service even included "picking up the body" on our behalf directly from the hospital or nursing home, saving us the expense of making the removal or having to be bothered when the "case" was just a simple 'shake and bake' (his words to describe direct cremation). He also agreed to file the death certificate on our behalf with the state registrar's office and obtain the disposition permit if the coroner was not involved. What, might you ask, would all of these services cost me? Including cremating the body the total cost is $55! I could not have been more surprised if he had offered to sell me a new Cadillac for $500. At the time, my outside crematory was charging $50 just to perform a cremation. He concluded by telling me his services and charges "represented a significant savings to my actual costs." Early on I had suspected something foul. By now, my suspicions were confirmed that something was going on that I did not want to be a part of. Without answering Mr. Sconce, I demanded that he leave my premises immediately.

Unfortunately, many funeral homes in southern California did not act as prudently and used the crematory operated by Mr. Sconce. When the scandal became public, some of these funeral homes were caught in the media frenzy and were sued.

Inspections help assure you of the competency, professionalism and commitment to ethical standards of the crematory. Inspections can serve as added insurance and another method of insulating your company from a lawsuit. Yet, many funeral directors procrastinate or totally avoid performing inspections. Some of the more typical excuses for not conducting inspections are:

- **"I have never done one before."** Like learning how to ride a bicycle, swim, or speak in public, performing an inspection is a learned skill. This will be covered in-depth later in this chapter. Learn how to do it.

- **"I've been in business for 40 years and never had to do one before."** Times have changed; the business climate has changed; levels of accountability have also changed. The public is skeptical and the media watches over your shoulder like never before. My father never had to worry about doing a crematory inspection or, for that matter, being sued. While I provided the same services in the same building he did - and like my father, was a licensed funeral director - we practiced in different eras. Be reminded: The good old days are gone. Welcome to a new era.

- **"It's just like snooping."** If you want to look at it this way, go ahead. Being a funeral director today requires much more knowledge than our predecessors: FTC and OSHA compliance, handling the remains of people who died of new diseases, obtaining an insurance salesperson's license are only some "new" things to learn. As unwilling and reluctant as you might have been years ago to deal with these matters, you have learned to comply and benefit from these added duties. Today, you must also learn to be an investigator. Compounding this, inspections are done, in part, to prove a negative – that something is not right. It can be uncomfortable playing investigator with people we know. "What will they think of me," you ask? Funeral directors are relationship-oriented people and can be, to a fault, trusting souls. Because you are trustworthy, you believe in your heart that other people are just as trustworthy. This may be all well and good with some things and some people. When trust is broken, or a question arises, and it has to do with cremation, it can mean losing everything: your business and reputation, your retirement accounts, your private residence and personal investments. Let me help you: **You are not snooping; you are inspecting. It's your name and your business.**

- **"Crematory inspections are the responsibility of the authorities."** Some states have an agency responsible for inspecting crematories. In most cases, inspections are infrequent and when done, generally focus on emissions and smoke-fire standards. State officials do not inspect nor can they be expected to be knowledgeable about the things that matter to you and your client families the most: care and professional standards. Simply stated: **Cremation is too important of a service to be left up to any state inspector.**

- **"I already have enough to do and quite frankly, cremation does not generate enough revenue to deserve any more of my time."** Will you say this to a reporter during a television interview? Will you repeat this statement to a jury? Would you make this statement to your local newspaper? When you make a presentation about pre-need to the local senior citizens center or provide in-service education to your local hospital's nursing staff, do you share this fact with them? If I understand, you are saying: "I'm busy directing funerals and make enough money from performing burial services and selling caskets and vaults." I interpret this attitude to mean that the measure of respect you provide to the bodies of deceased persons, including those you cremate or prepare for shipment and the amount of attention you provide bereaved families is in proportion to the amount of money they spend at your funeral home. Hopefully this attitude has not infiltrated among your employees. Would your attitude be different if cremation revenues more closely mirrored burial revenues? I'd argue that things would not change much, but your choices become clear: Increase your cremation fees to an amount that would make inspections and more professional care a worthy endeavor for you and stop providing low-cost cremation services. Just because a family chooses cremation for a family member does not mean they are any less worthy of your best efforts or are less deserving of your attentiveness. Just because a burial family chooses minimum service and merchandise does not make them any less worthy, either. Put your money where your mindset is.

- **"If I detect something wrong, I don't know what I should do."** There are varying degrees of "wrong." A lapse in filling out a receipt, having a messy work area or employees forgetting to properly secure an outside door can usually be corrected by a conversation and a written report. On the other hand, if you notice a bucket hidden in a corner that is filled with material resembling perhaps commingled cremated remains; see deceased persons awaiting to be cremated lying on the floor of the crematory; discover there is no cremation log book;

notice white-out corrections or erasures in the log book; or see what appears to be more than one deceased person in the same cremation chamber, these are **serious** problems that demand your full attention and **immediate** action. Document your findings, including the date, time and the names of all crematory employees and other witnesses present. If you are an employee of the funeral home, immediately notify the owner of the funeral home or your immediate supervisor. Tell the crematory operator what you have found and if necessary, to stop what is going on. The funeral home owner or supervisor must notify the owner of the crematory and demand that any improper practices stop immediately. Any activity considered to be improper or of a "serious" nature must be documented. It also means you must not use the crematory until proper practices are in place and you have been assured in writing that they are followed by employees. Depending on the severity of wrongdoing – **but always when state laws or standards of care are violated** – notify your personal attorney and insurance company to be "on record" with them, report findings to appropriate state licensing bureaus or state boards, notify the state attorney general's office, and/or notify local law enforcement agencies.

Defining an Inspection

As was mentioned in Chapter Twelve, inspections are not confined only to third-party crematories but should include **all** outside-third party providers, even cemeteries you frequent. Few funeral directors that employ an outside trade embalmer would argue with the common sense of requiring the embalmer to provide a copy of his/her current state license. A funeral director that employs the top-rated livery-limousine rental company should require proof of adequate insurance by the livery company. Yet, some funeral directors resist performing inspections of the outside crematory, believing the inspection will be viewed as an infringement or a challenge to the integrity of the owner and operator. Just as the process of due diligence can be misconstrued, funeral directors may misconstrue what an inspection is. Inspections are performed for several reasons. To cover all elements, there are three ways to define an inspection.

An **inspection** is:

1. A survey, investigation or other procedure necessary to carry out your responsibilities to your client-family customers

2. An evaluation, review, study and/or analysis of activities in order to recommend improvement to policies or procedures and identify corrective actions

3. A process that assures compliance with standards, emphasizes best practices and identifies fraudulent activity and/or abuse

I hope these definitions cause you to see inspections differently, as a way of complimenting your personal service and another way of assuring families of your commitment to them. It also provides you with sleep insurance. Seeing is believing; just as you have seen all the aspects of earth burial and entombment over the years, so must you also see for yourself what goes on at the crematory.

Your inspection is **not** a licensing or audit inspection that might be performed by a state inspector. Your inspection is performed as one of your duties. It reinforces the "special relationship" you have with client families. In particular your inspections are:

• Focused on the **quality of care** rendered to a deceased person

• Performed to enhance **your reputation and credibility** in your community

- Done in the **best interests** of the consumer and your profession
- Another form of risk reduction and way to prevent other people from reaching into your pocket

A contention by the plaintiff's attorney that the funeral home defendant "knew or should have known" is often raised during court proceedings and can be damaging to the defense. An example of how it has been used is offered in a case example in Chapter Ten. The immeasurable value of performing on-going crematory inspections and having records supporting them is proven in the 1997 California case, (*Hansell versus Santos Robinson Funeral Home and Pleasant Hill Cemetery*). The funeral home used a third-party crematory located at the cemetery. Plaintiffs were awarded damages of $20 million from the cemetery and crematory for conducting improper cremations, multiple cremations, commingling of cremated remains and other abuses. The court ruled that the funeral home did "not have vicarious liability" due in part to the documentation they produced that proved they had conducted on-going inspections of the crematory. As a result, the funeral home was not liable for any damages.

Key Attributes in Conducting a Crematory Inspection

1. **Inspections must be unannounced.** The crematory should not be notified in advance. If your current crematory does not allow unannounced inspections, find a different crematory. If you arrive to conduct an inspection and are not allowed entrance into the facility, this is a giant red flag. A common thread in most third-party scandals is that the crematory provided pickup and delivery service to funeral homes to keep people away from the crematory.

2. **Inspections must be documented**. An inspection that is not documented is worthless. It is as if no inspection

took place. As you should with all outside providers, start an Outside Crematory file and keep a copy of the inspection in the file. Do not throw out copies of former inspections but maintain them on a permanent basis. If the crematory ever comes under review or question, your documentation will help your defense.

3. **Inspections must be on-going.** Inspections are not a one-time event but should be performed as long as you use a third-party crematory. It is recommended that you perform more than one inspection each year. Many funeral homes conduct two or three inspections a year. Certain events trigger more frequent inspections such as a change in crematory ownership, when a new crematory operator is hired, you are notified by the crematory's insurance company that the policy will expire or be cancelled, you hear complaints from other colleagues or you feel uncomfortable about something when you visit. Inspections should take place during normal business hours unless you observe something out of the norm (cremations only being performed late at night, for instance). Vary the day and time that you choose to do an inspection.

4. **Inspections must be thorough.** Your inspection is not a social visit nor is it a matter of strolling around chatting about the weather or yesterday's baseball scores. As an inspector, you have a well-defined role: Your inspection is business and you should conduct yourself accordingly. You must be considerate of the crematory personnel and the demands made on them at the time, but they must also be respectful of you doing your duty. It is wrong to expect them to stop what they are doing and act as your "host." The crematory does not revolve around you. If they are busy, do your inspection while staying out of their way. Ideally, you want them to be busy when you inspect so you

can observe their procedures in action and how they handle cremations from other funeral homes. Arrange your schedule to permit enough time to do a proper inspection. A thorough one takes time, usually three to five hours. It involves much more than peeking inside the cremation chamber and checking for debris on the floor. It is a combination of checking the log book and licenses, reading policy and procedure manuals, asking questions about things you don't know about, observing behaviors, noticing the attire and language of personnel, inspecting the exterior of the facility and documenting your findings. It may also involve interviewing some personnel. To help you be complete and provide documentation for the file, take a pre-printed inspection checklist with you.

5. **Inspections should not be performed by the same person.** To ensure the greatest objectivity, if possible, assign this duty to two or three key people in the company. Have them alternate among themselves. This also helps ensure that inspections are scheduled and performed without partisanship. It also encourages comparison of findings from different perspectives.

Performing a Crematory Inspection

I view inspections as a critical component of client family and decedent care. More than many of my colleagues, my experiences from owning and operating a funeral home in California and providing cremation services have made me critically aware of what can go wrong, especially when oversight and accountability is absent and obtaining the lowest cost is primary. Remorsefully, I understand that not everyone subscribes to the same degree of concern for people choosing cremation that I do. But I hope that, with differences aside, we can agree that people ask for our help and guidance at the worst possible time in their lives. In many instances, they blindly place a great deal of trust in us. We must always keep our clients interests paramount.

Two Types of Inspections

There are formal-comprehensive inspections and informal or "mini-inspections." When performed, both types of inspections provide assurance to client families and added "sleep insurance" to the funeral director.

Mini-inspections are inspections performed **in addition** to formal inspections. As added protection, all funeral home employees that transfer deceased persons to the crematory should be trained to perform mini-inspections and made aware of their importance. A practice that originated at my former funeral home, a mini-inspection is done by the funeral home representative **every time** he/she delivers a deceased person to the crematory. They were instituted as a way of keeping everyone alert (funeral home employees and crematory personnel) and to ensure that, as much as possible, management always knew what was going on at the crematory. The mini-inspection form was retained in the deceased person's file. If something was not right, I wanted to know immediately. The mini-inspection form was simple. Contained on company letterhead, it consisted of the name of the deceased person, the date of death, the date and time of delivery, and the name of the funeral home representative. Only two questions were to be answered by the funeral home representative:

1. The name of the crematory representative that greeted you and accepted the paperwork and deceased person, and

2. Did you notice anything out of the ordinary or unusual when delivery was made?

In most cases, nothing unusual was noted on the form. In one instance, an employee noted that he thought he smelled the odor of alcohol on the breath of the owner who received the deceased person. I called the owner and asked if he had been drinking? He told me he had a two-martini lunch. In another instance, I was informed that a cage filled with rabbits was stored in the same room where deceased persons were being held. Calling the crematory, the operator told me that the rabbits belonged to his son. Their home was being remodeled and the rabbits were being held at the crematory temporarily during construction. I complimented the operator on his high standards of performing cremation in the past and asked him, "How would you feel if a film crew from a television network or a reporter and photographer from the local newspaper stopped by unexpectedly to do a story? Would the rabbits enhance or degrade your level of professionalism?" He understood and without argument, promised to remove the rabbits at the end of the day. Over many decades, I know that mini-inspections greatly benefited my company as well as those of other funeral homes that used this crematory.

Formal-Comprehensive Inspections

These inspections are performed by people that have been designated by management to perform this duty. An inspection performed by a funeral home is different from an agency audit or state inspection or an OSHA or environmental compliance inspection. For the funeral director-inspector, key is knowing **what to inspect**. Having a checklist of items to inspect helps ensure it is thorough.

Crematory Checklist

The following items should be noted for comment on the Inspection Form:

- Name of funeral home representative performing the inspection
- Date and time of the inspection
- Name and address of the crematory
- Name of crematory owner
- Name of crematory operator or representative present

- Emergency phone numbers
- List certificate or state required training or licensing programs attended and dates for all crematory operators or managers
- Names of all personnel working at crematory or those with access
- Proof of employee training
- Whether or not background checks have been performed for operators and assistants and dates
- Name of property-casualty insurance company and proof of insurance
- Names of all personnel who are bonded
- Attire of personnel
- Usual days and hours of operation
- Condition of the exterior of the crematory building and surrounding grounds
- Condition of the interior of the crematory building
- Number of cremation chambers and manufacturer of each
- Date(s) of installation; date(s) of last service
- If applicable, date of last regulatory inspection and name of inspecting agency
- All required local, county, state and federal licenses and permits are current and posted in public view for both the facility and personnel
- Refrigeration facility and capacity
- Temperature of refrigeration facility at time of inspection
- Procedures for accepting a deceased person (including receipt form)
- Procedures for maintaining identification of deceased persons

- Presence of metal identification disc with deceased person at all times
- Storage of deceased persons awaiting cremation
- Cremation documents attached to control panel during cremation
- Method of removing deceased person from cremation chamber
- Tools and equipment used to reposition or remove cremated remains
- Condition and location of processing room or area
- Type of processing machine
- Minimum urn provided by crematory for packaging
- Procedures for labeling urn
- Policy and procedures for storing cremated remains
- Policy and procedures for releasing cremated remains
- Type of security for cremated remains in storage
- Describe policy for handling (excess) cremated remains that do not fit into the original urn
- Policy for recovering, handling and disposing of: jewelry, dental gold, prosthetic devices, medical devices, casket hardware
- Policy and procedures (operational) manuals
- Policy on cremating animals (This must not occur in the same chambers used for cremating human remains)
- Policy for witnessing of cremation and facilities available
- Alarm or security system on premises; method of securing exterior doors and windows
- Cremation Log book

Further Suggestions During Inspections

In addition, the person performing the inspection should never hesitate to ask questions about anything he/she is unfamiliar with. For instance, if you see a tool and do not know what it is for, ask for an explanation. If you are unclear about any step of the cremation process that you observe, ask for information. If you wonder why something is done a particular way, ask for an explanation. An inspection also means learning all you can and sharing best practices.

Above all, you want to make sure that crematory operators and personnel working at the crematory are familiar with the policies and procedures (P&P's) listed in their manuals. It is worthless to have policies listed in a manual that operators are unaware of or that are not carried out. As you read the crematories P&P manual, note any conflicts that may exist between company policy, state law and standard practices. In practically every state, a funeral director-crematory operator is subject to disciplinary action for misinterpreting state law.

Important: If you are denied access to any part of the crematory at any time, especially for purposes of conducting an inspection, this should be immediately documented and reported to the management of the crematory and funeral home. Access should never be denied to a user of the crematory or licensed funeral-cremation personnel. In fact, an inspection should be welcomed.

Cremation Log Book

In particular, you must take time to inspect the Cremation Log Book. It is the official record that a crematory is obligated to maintain. It should list each deceased person received (including those in refrigerated storage) and each cremation performed. Even in states that do not require a log, it is a standard of practice in the cremation industry for a crematory to maintain an accurate record of all cremations.

The cremation log book should not contain any white-out entries or erasures. The log should not be an electronic record,

but a handwritten record containing at least the following information:

- Name of deceased person and description of the container
- Name of funeral home or provider and name of the representative making the delivery
- The number on the cremation identification disc assigned to the deceased person
- Date of delivery to crematory
- Date of cremation
- Starting time of cremation; ending time of cremation
- Name of crematory operator
- Date and time of processing of the cremated remains
- Description of urn
- For crematories with more than one chamber, the number or description of the chamber in which the cremation occurred

Some crematories weigh the cremated remains and record the weight in the log book as an added measure of risk management and accountability. It is a practice this author endorses.

It is worth repeating: When a funeral home uses an outside crematory, in essence, the cremation becomes a shared responsibility. Choose your crematory partner carefully. Exercising due diligence makes sense and ensures a win for everyone: the funeral home, the crematory, the client family and the profession.

CHAPTER 13

Unclaimed Cremated Remains

"Out of sight, out of mind," is a type of rationalization that sometimes applies to the handling of a person's cremated remains. Some survivors tend to procrastinate when informed of their responsibility to call for cremated remains of a loved one. Often, this is merely a variant on the common theme of denial. Funeral directors, too, tend to procrastinate, though doing so only increases their potential for liability. Storage areas overcrowded with years of unclaimed cremated remains become a liability. Labels that once identified a person's cremated remains and other related records can be lost. No funeral home is free from natural disasters and employee errors. The best way to reduce liability is to stress the importance of timely retrieval of a person's cremated remains, even if economic sanctions must be added to the contract for cremation care. It is during the arrangement conference that the arranger must impress on the survivors that a person's cremated remains are not just ashes, but the remains of a human being and therefore, deserving of respectful and timely treatment. This chapter addresses the multi-dimensional problem of unclaimed cremated remains and offers concrete suggestions and best practices for reducing this area of liability.

To their chagrin, practically every funeral home and crematory in the country has some cremated remains in their custody that are unclaimed. Although some people might find it difficult to believe, there are people who arrange for the cremation of their loved one and then fail to retrieve that person's cremated remains in a timely manner, even abandoning them entirely at the funeral home or crematory. In the July 2005 issue of *The Director*, Scott Gilligan, Esq., general counsel for the National Funeral Directors Association, wrote, "Without realizing it, many funeral homes have a 'liability time bomb' sitting in a closet, stored in a basement or hidden away in some cabinet: unclaimed cremated remains." I agree.

As cremation's popularity continues to increase nationwide, funeral home owners, directors and crematories are faced with a growing dilemma as to what to do with unclaimed cremated remains in their custody. Of the more than 700,000 cremation performed in the United States in 2006, the Cremation Association of North America (CANA) estimates that nearly 5%, or 35,000 cremated human remains from that year alone, were unclaimed from crematories and/or funeral homes. If CANA's predictions for the future growth of cremation are correct, by 2025 it can mean as many as 70,000 cremated remains of persons will be unclaimed every year.

Having custody of - and being responsible for - unclaimed cremated remains represents a substantial risk for the funeral home or crematory that can lead to liability claims against them.

A Nationwide Dilemma

There are some funeral homes and crematories that have thousands of unclaimed cremated remains dating back 75 years or more. They are not alone in dealing with this dilemma and the "forgotten dead." A state hospital in Oregon holds 3,489 urns containing the cremated remains of patients who died in the facility from the 1880s to the mid-1970s. This situation has prompted Oregon lawmakers to discuss new laws to decide on proper disposition of the urns. Using medical records on hand, the state is making attempts to contact relatives of the former patients. It is quite possible that other institutions across the country are holding comparable numbers of unclaimed cremated remains at their facilities.

Some state lawmakers, licensing boards and professional

associations are waking up to the plight of their licensees and members concerning the associated liability and unnecessary expense of holding unclaimed cremated remains. Working together, they are developing regulations that serve the interests of both the public and practitioners to ensure the timely retrieval and legal disposition of a person's cremated remains.

In my opinion, states that have failed to address cremation issues, including disposition of unclaimed cremated remains, do a disservice to their citizens and to the practitioners licensed to perform cremation services. Licensing boards, professional organizations and state funeral-cremation associations that have failed to petition lawmakers to develop new provisions are poorly serving licensed practitioners and the members of their associations. At the same time, funeral-cremation providers who do not establish policies regarding the timely retrieval or disposition of a person's cremated remains - even in the absence of laws in their state - and do not address the issue with client families during the arrangement conference fail in their professional responsibilities. By default, you set yourself up for needless liability from having unclaimed cremated remains.

It stands to reason: as more and more people choose cremation there will be more cremated remains unclaimed. That is why it is vital for funeral-cremation providers and crematory owners to encourage their state lawmakers to adopt statutes to deal with this important, but overlooked aspect of cremation as thoroughly as they have provided laws governing burial, entombment, and shipment.

In dealing with this dilemma, funeral-cremation providers and crematories ask:

- What safeguards should be taken when storing a person's cremated remains that are considered unclaimed?

- What steps can be taken to prevent the incidence of unclaimed cremated remains?

- How long must cremated remains be kept?

- What is the funeral director's or crematory operator's liability if a person's unclaimed cremated remains are lost, misplaced, wrongfully released and/or disposed of?

- In states without provisions in law, what should be done with a person's unclaimed cremated remains?

- How is the funeral director responsible – and for how long?

The Responsibility Factor

When a person's cremated remains are considered unclaimed, some funeral-cremation providers show no interest or sense of urgency in dealing with them. I have heard funeral directors say, "If the family members don't care, I don't have to care, either." This is false reasoning. The responsibility that accrues to funeral directors and crematories derives from several sources. Among them are:

1. **The nature of the object** (a person's cremated remains) and the likelihood that they are important to the survivors, even when claiming them is delayed.

2. **Above all, funeral directors and crematory operators share a professional responsibility to show respect for the body of a deceased person**, no matter what its condition may be, regardless of the circumstances or the perceptions you may have about the survivors, or the process of cremation.

3. **The nature of the relationship the funeral director has with client families**. It is a special one. They place trust in your service and counsel; they see you as the expert and "master of details" who is there to assist them in making decisions.

4. **The relationship the funeral director may have with the deceased person prior to his/her death** (pre-need) and with survivors claiming the person's cremated

remains and/or concurring with the method of disposition. It is also a special one.

5. **The role of the funeral director as a member of the helping professions not to violate the sacred trust of grieving people**. The funeral director must maintain this trust even when there is little chance of being compensated for going beyond the call of duty.

From a professional standpoint, it can be argued that one's responsibilities are never-ending when it comes to custody and disposition. Without the express written authorization from the person(s) with authority or acting under law, a funeral-cremation provider or crematory is not empowered or may not authorize decisions regarding disposition of unclaimed cremated remains. Conceivably, he/she is responsible for them in perpetuity.

In some states, other laws may also apply in which the funeral-cremation provider or crematory unwittingly becomes the permanent guardian of the deceased person after holding a person's cremated remains for certain period of time. Depending on your state laws, being named the permanent guardian (of a deceased person) places additional responsibility on your shoulders. This means you have the duty to act according to the "best interest" standard, to act as a reasonable person would act in a similar situation and to guard against loss, damage, harm, wrongful release or disposition of the person's cremated remains.

Liability Factor

Some of the more obvious liability problems include:

- Misidentification that could occur over time

- Loss or misplacement

- Theft

- The destruction of your funeral home or storage facility from fire, flood, hurricane, tornado or earthquake that can render identification or recovery impossible

- Denial of insurance claims. Without receiving confirmation in writing from your property-casualty insurance carrier, **do not assume** that your present insurance policy provides coverage for storing (unclaimed) cremated remains at the funeral home, crematory or off-premises storage facility

In addition, holding and being responsible for a person's cremated remains can result in an almost unlimited number of accusations against you if one or more of the above tragedies occur: The client family might claim they have been harmed, denied their right to practice their cultural-ethnic-religious funeral customs and suffered emotional distress. In one such case, the funeral home was unable to locate the cremated remains of a person who was cremated only six months earlier. The family claimed that the person was never cremated but instead the person was sold to a research laboratory. More common accusations include:

- Breach of contract
- Deceptive or unfair business practices and failing to adequately inform the customer
- Treating a person's remains below the standard of care
- Fraud
- Negligence

Why People Fail to Retrieve a Person's Cremated Remains

It is helpful to understand some factors that lead people to abandon cremated remains or procrastinate in claiming them.

- The arranger is passive and does not make the decision of what to do with the cremated remains a priority during the arrangement conference.

- Some consumers incorrectly believe that when they choose cremation, no other decisions need to be made.

- Some people are unaware of options for disposition. Still others, when informed, choose scattering as the simplest, least involved option and as a way to appease the arranger. Many of these people never return to claim the person's cremated remains.

- Psychologically and emotionally the person's cremated remains are merely ashes and viewed as a nuisance by the arranging parties.

- Families are separated geographically, socially, emotionally and culturally.

- People live longer with growing generational gaps. In some situations, family members may not know one another or the deceased person.

- More people live away from their place of birth and origin and make funeral arrangements at a distance.

- The arranging party might be waiting for someone else to die, such as a spouse, so disposition for both person's can occur at the same time.

- Some families are split over arrangements to be made or personal issues.

- Some people just cannot decide, even after all options have been clearly explained to them.

- Some people are angry at the deceased person for causing them further concern and inconvenience, even after death.

In the words of funeral-service attorney Scott Gilligan, "When people walk away, they aren't avoiding a legal obligation, just a moral obligation" in claiming their loved ones cremated remains.

There can be legitimate reasons for someone not claiming cremated remains. I have personally experienced situations such as: the person(s) with authority dies, becomes hospitalized, embarks on a lengthy trip or changes their residence. In one such instance, after cremating his wife, the husband visited his daughter who lived in another state. While there, he unexpectedly became ill, was hospitalized for several months and then died. The daughter had her father cremated by a local funeral home and was unaware that her mother's cremated remains were still at my funeral home waiting to be picked up. Never having met her and not having her name or phone number on file, a year went by before she finally came to retrieve her mother's cremated remains.

Some people arranging for cremation do not know there is anything to deal with. In their mind, they made the decision to cremate and that is the only decision they need to make. They mistakenly assume that cremation is an end to itself. **Arrangers must not assume that consumers know all they need to know**. Just as no arranger would fail to discuss and put in writing details of earth burial or entombment, you must finalize details for retrieval or disposition of a person's cremated remains.

On the other hand, some people will do or say anything to avoid dealing with the person's cremated remains. I have made arrangements with people whom I knew had no intention of ever retrieving the person's cremated remains. Statements like, "I'll come by next week," or "Please hold them for just two weeks," can be empty promises.

Funeral-cremation providers are trusting individuals who want to be helpful and do what they can to make decisions easier for their clients. While admirable, this can be a detriment. No funeral home would consider arrangements for burial to be complete without requiring the family to designate a cemetery, see to it that cemetery details are complete and set a day for the burial. Yet, when it comes to the disposition and/or retrieval of a family member's cremated remains, the funeral arranger can be just the opposite. In wanting to accommodate the family and be the nice guy, for the funeral home, all too often "next week" turns into several weeks; after several unreturned phone calls, it is now months. All of a sudden it becomes years and you are still holding the cremated remains, not knowing what to do.

Unclaimed cremated remains occur more often when:

- The funeral-cremation provider or crematory fails to establish a written policy addressing timely retrieval or disposition of a person's cremated remains

- Arrangers are improperly trained as to how to address the issue during the arrangement conference

- The arrangement conference ends without anything in writing as to who will retrieve the person's cremated remains or how disposition will occur

- Wishes made during the arrangement conference are nothing more than a "whim," leaving the issue undecided or entirely up to the convenience of the client family without any timeline specified. ("Just hold them... I'll pick them up when I return from my business trip.")

Treating the issue of timely retrieval of a person's cremated remains passively or indifferently and failing to obtain written authorization for disposition results in a funeral home or crematory acquiring more unclaimed cremated remains.

If you do not handle this issue assertively, you will surely find yourself with a closet full of unclaimed cremated remains. It becomes next to impossible to play catch-up. Locating family members is time-consuming and frustrating; over time, people tend to care less. You become by default the Public Storage, Inc of unclaimed cremated remains.

How to Prevent Abandoned-Unclaimed Cremated Remains

There are some constructive, **Best Practices** that management and arrangers can follow to help client families recognize the need to make firm plans for the disposition or retrieval of the person's cremated remains.

The key to eliminating the liability associated with unclaimed cremated remains is to avoid having them in the first place. The **Best Practices** listed below are not arbitrary. They have been developed over time out of necessity and through my personal experiences and those of other funeral-cremation providers and crematory operators across the country.

1. **Develop a written policy** that addresses the issue of disposition and/or retrieval of a person's cremated remains.

2. **Share the policy with all arrangers**. They must understand it and be skilled in communicating the policy to client families.

3. **Insist that the arranger be assertive, not passive, in discussing this issue**. It must be mandatory for this issue to be (automatically) covered during every cremation arrangement conference.

4. **Require that arrangements for disposition be decided upon and identified in writing** on the Cremation Authorization Form during the arrangement conference.

5. **As a part of the Cremation Authorization Form, include a section called "Disposition of Cremated Remains."** List various choices, such as: Deliver to (name and address) cemetery; Mail to (name, address, telephone number and relationship of recipient); Release to (name, address, telephone number and relationship of recipient); Scatter by funeral home (or by a third party); other disposition (specify). **A decision must be made during the arrangement conference**, even if the decision is to mail or deliver the cremated remains to a family member. Confirm the choice with the signature or initials of the person(s) with authority.

6. **In boldface type, include key parts of your policy on the Cremation Authorization Form**, such as this statement: Cremation cannot take place until a directive for the disposition of the person's cremated remains are made and contained in writing on this authorization form. In states where laws are established and identify and authorize the funeral home to perform disposition of unclaimed cremated remains, cite appropriate sections of this law on the authorization form. Inform the family how disposition of the cremated remains will occur in the event they do not retrieve them. Confirm understanding with the signature or initials of the person(s) with authority.

7. **Consider implementing a financial incentive associated to your policy** that reinforces a client family making disposition or retrieval decisions during arrangements. This is discussed below.

Financial Incentives

More funeral-cremation providers offer a financial incentive to client families who will not decide upon disposition, and in those states where no statutes are contained for the legal disposition of unclaimed cremated remains. The incentive is a financial one, used as a means of creating an urgency with the family to have them decide upon disposition and/or retrieve the cremated remains in a timely manner (according to the terms listed on the Authorization Form or other contract) and not abandon them. During arrangements, an additional sum of money is required as a good-faith deposit. When the person's cremated remains are retrieved or disposition occurs within a specific period of time, the deposit is refunded to the responsible party. If disposition does not occur within the period of time specified on the Cremation Authorization Form, or within the statutory time limit, the deposit is forfeited and used by the funeral home to offset the expense of placing them in storage or seeing to their lawful disposition. The deposit should be large enough act as an incentive and in cases when the person's cremated remains are abandoned, to help defray your expenses. At this time, I am aware of funeral homes that require deposits varying from $150.00 to $500.00. Higher amounts would naturally create a greater incentive for timely retrieval.

To prevent unclaimed cremated remains at the crematory, some crematories have also instituted a good-faith deposit from their funeral home clients or charge them an additional fee for storage, above and beyond the cremation fee, if the cremated remains are not retrieved by the funeral home within several days.

Safeguards When Storing Cremated Remains

Whether a person's cremated remains will be held for a day, a week, a month or longer, steps must be taken to prevent misplacement, misidentification, wrongful release or disposition, loss, theft, damage as well as protection from other perils such as fire, flood, hurricane, tornado and earthquake.

Important: Management at funeral homes and crematories often designates one employee as the "person in charge" of managing cremated remains. This person is usually left to devise his/her own system for storage, identification and record keeping. Alarmingly, at many firms, no one, including management, is familiar with the system developed by this person. While the person in charge is available, no one pays attention or is concerned about the unclaimed cremated remains or bothers to learn the system in place. Without management oversight or guidance, the "system" can come crashing down when the one person in charge leaves the firm, becomes ill, dies or retires and fails to inform management or another employee about the system. I have witnessed instances when the person in charge died and the secrets to his/her storage system, whereabouts of the record book and key to the storage room were "taken" with him. To make matters worse, this fact is often not discovered until a family member arrives to retrieve his or her loved one's cremated remains and chaos ensues. Compounding the problem, when (and if) the "right" person's cremated remains are (eventually) found and given to the family, it can raise questions by the family as to whether or not these are really the cremated remains of their loved one. A lawsuit can develop. In one such instance, after not receiving a satisfactory answer and being unconvinced as to the identity of the cremated remains they were given, a family decided to tell their story to the local newspaper. Three days later, on the front page of the local newspaper appeared the headline and story: "Local Funeral Home Loses Then Finds Body."

Just as the funeral-cremation provider and crematory must document every step during custody and maintain a system that prevents misidentification of decedents, so must you also maintain an accurate system that documents all persons whose cremated remains are in short-term or long-term storage. All persons designated by management to handle cremated remains must be knowledgeable about all aspects of the system.

Additional, related information regarding storing and receiving cremated remains is in Chapter Nine.

Best Practice guidelines for the storage of cremated remains include:

- Store them in a secure room or fire-proof cabinet, away from public activity, under lock and key. Ideally, the room or cabinet is devoted to this purpose only. Do not hang the key to the lock in public view.

- Restrict access to designated employees *only* who have been trained in handling them.

- Affix a "log" to the exterior of the room or cabinet where the cremated remains are stored. Each time an employee enters and exits the room or cabinet, the name of the employee, date and time should be recorded.

- Maintain a written record of **all** cremated remains in custody. List the name of the deceased person, date of death, date of cremation and the date and name of the employee who placed them in storage. Allocate space to record the date and time of (eventual) release, name and relationship of the person who retrieves the person's remains and the name of the funeral home employee releasing them. Keep this record book in a secure place such as a fireproof safe. A duplicate record book should be kept in a separate location.

- Do not stack containers on top of one another. If they are to be stored vertically, each level should be separated by some means, such as wood planks between the containers or additional tiers of shelving. Containers of person's cremated remains should **never** be placed on the floor.

- Mark each container so that identity can be ascertained at all times and in a manner that ensures identification even if the container is exposed to such things as fire or water. Instead of using tags, permanent methods include *engraving* or *etching* the name of the deceased person and date of death on the container or attaching (with screws) a metal name plate bearing the person's name onto the container.

- Do not store cremated remains that are in cardboard containers. Only use containers constructed of metal, wood, plastic or other durable materials. Cardboard disintegrates when exposed to fire or water and can be punctured from sharp or blunt objects. Any writing on cardboard can smear or fade. As added precaution, after the container is engraved or a nameplate has been affixed, it may be placed in an individual, clear plastic bag and sealed closed.

- Avoid containers wrapped in paper with the name of the deceased person written on them using a marker pen. This is **not** a permanent method of identification. In time, paper crumbles and the writing can become illegible, especially if it becomes wet. In the event of fire, paper wrapping burns and the identity of the person's cremated remains can be lost.

- Do not tie, staple or tape identification tags to the exterior of the container as a means of identification. If they separate from the container, identity can be lost. Over time, tape becomes brittle and disintegrates.

- Store each container in its own bin or its own space and keep separate from other containers. Shelves that hold containers of cremated remains should have spacers that make individual bins or spaces. Using a grid system, individual spaces should be identified by some means, such as Shelf 1, Section A, Space 12. The exact location must be recorded in the record book as well in the decedent's permanent file. A duplicate copy of the grid system should be maintained and kept in a separate location.

- Notify your insurance company and inform them as to the number of unclaimed cremated remains in custody and the manner in which they are stored. A potential liability that they may not be aware of, you must be "on record" as informing the insurance company and, in the event of a disaster, have your insurer in your corner.

- Update the record book and inspect the condition of all containers of unclaimed cremated remains at least once a year.

Disposition of Unclaimed Cremated Remains

Laws governing disposition of cremated remains that may be in place in your state must be carefully followed. At present,

299

only a handful of states have laws addressing disposition of unclaimed cremated remains. The absence of law presents a quandary for the funeral-cremation provider and crematory. No funeral director or crematory welcomes unclaimed cremated remains or being responsible for them. Deciding on the best, most practical, safest, cost efficient and most professional means of disposition can be challenging. No matter how remote the chance might be, best practice means you must also keep in mind that family members may arrive someday to claim them.

Even when permitted by law, a funeral director or crematory should strongly resist scattering unclaimed cremated remains but should consider reserving the option for retrieval should the family want them at a future time.

Before any form of disposition occurs your actions should be guided by asking yourself at least two questions:

1. What do my state laws permit?

2. What is considered prudent and professional?

Acting prudently is always recommended. Even when acting according to law, it is standard practice to attempt to notify the person(s) with authority before disposition occurs. Some state laws and regulations outline how often and in what manner such attempts must be made to contact client families. Some state laws require the funeral home to place notices in the newspaper. **Every attempt that is made must be documented and retained in the deceased person's file.**

Contacting Family Members

A rule of thumb procedure for contacting family members is:

- Make at least three (3) attempts on three (3) different days

- Use the US Postal Service or other mail service that provides return-receipt confirmation

- Send written correspondence on company letterhead

- Keep a copy of all written correspondence in the deceased person's file

- Retain all receipts-confirmation slips from the mailings in the deceased person's file

- Document all telephone calls in a permanent log, even those made to friends of the family or employers

- In the telephone log, document the name and relationship of the person you spoke with and the time, date and result (e.g., no longer living here or employed here, no answer, phone disconnected, etc.)

- Maintain the log in the deceased person's file

The contents of the letter urging people to claim cremated remains will vary from company to company. For best results, it should be brief and friendly but business-like. Do not make any threats and do not be judgmental. Instead, give them the benefit of the doubt, assuming they need reminding and have overlooked this. Personalize the letter; use the deceased person's name as well as their relationship to the deceased person, such as, "The cremated remains of your grandfather, John Doe, are at our funeral home. It is imperative that you contact our office to claim them as soon as possible. If you do not have transportation, we can make arrangements to deliver them to you at your convenience."

You also want to urge the person to act and view claiming their family member's cremated remains as being in their best interest. "We are open 7 days a week, from 8:00AM to 6:00PM. We are unable to hold your grandfather's cremated remains beyond (provide date). If we do not hear from you by (provide date), your grandfather's cremated remains will be taken to the ABC Cemetery (provide city, state, zip code) and placed in a crypt in a mausoleum. If you claim them after (provide date), you will be subject to paying all fees as established by the cemetery for the opening and re-closing the crypt. At present, the opening and re-closing fee is $300.00 and is subject to change. We want to save you this unnecessary expense and offer any assistance to you. Please, may we hear from you?"

Case Example: A Claim after 20 Years

A young woman walked into my office and asked to speak with me. She explained that two years ago she moved to southern California from New York. Twenty years ago, when she was 10 years old, her mother and father were killed in a traffic accident. Her grandparents, who became her legal guardians, believed they were acting in the child's best interest at the time. They did not permit her to see her parents or attend the funeral. Her mother and father were cremated. She had no idea what was done with her parent's cremated remains or what she could do to determine their whereabouts. Visibly upset from telling her story, she told me that even after 20 years, she regrets never seeing her parents after they were killed and not being allowed to attend the funeral. However, her greatest regret was not having a place where she could "visit" her parents. She asked me what she should do. She had several mementos from her parents with her in a small box including a lock of hair from each parent, some pieces of their jewelry, several photographs, a copy of their obituary notice and two memorial folders from the funeral.

I suggested that the first step should be to try to determine what happened to her parent's cremated remains. I called the funeral home in New York that 20 years earlier conducted the funeral and cremation. The funeral home was glad to help but asked for time to research their records. Thirty minutes later the funeral home called me back and verified the information I had. The two people were cremated but the grandparents made no definitive plans for disposition of the cremated remains. According to their records, both the mother and father's cremated remains were being held as "unclaimed" in storage at the crematory. Relieved at this news, the daughter began to cry.

One week later, both containers of cremated remains arrived at my office. One week later the daughter held her own farewell ceremony in our celebration room, attended by a handful of her friends. The ceremony consisted of her sharing the memories she had of her mother and father with her friends and a procession to the cemetery. Her mother and father's cremated remains were placed into a companion niche. As I escorted her to her car, she gave me a hug and with a smile on her face said, "Thanks to you, after 20 long years, I now have a place where I can bring them a flower!"

Placement in a Grave or Crypt

Especially when dealing with a large inventory of unclaimed cremated remains, some funeral-cremation providers and crematories have made arrangements for unclaimed cremated remains to be buried in a grave, placed in a crypt or in a columbarium. Because there is the possibility that retrieval can occur time and time again over a period of many years, placing them in a crypt is generally more practical than earth burial. It is easier to open a crypt, retrieve the container of cremated remains and close the crypt than it is to disinter a burial vault and possibly having to break it open to retrieve the container. **Before doing this, however, you must be certain that your state laws and cemetery regulations permit this.**

Before any container is placed in a crypt, **Best Practice** requires that each one must be **permanently** identified listing the name of the deceased person and the date of death. Diagram the crypt and measure all four sides of the interior, marking the dimensions on the diagram. Using a grid system on the inside of the crypt, record the **exact location** where each container is placed in the crypt.

Best Practice dictates that you **do not stack containers on top of one another** inside the crypt but separate them using metal shelves or another type of permanent divider. In the record book list the name of the deceased person and the exact location of the container. A duplicate record book should be kept in a separate location. Any time the crypt is opened to remove a container or place additional ones inside, record the date, time, name of deceased person and the name of the funeral home representative in the record book. When a family member retrieves their loved one, an employee who is knowledgeable as to the system and who has been trained should accompany the family to the crypt. In all cases, a receipt for the person's cremated remains must be issued, listing the date and contain the signature and relationship of the recipient. Keep the receipt in the decedent's file.

If this is permitted in your state and a cemetery agrees to accept containers of unclaimed cremated remains for burial or entombment, check with your insurance professional as to the need for a separate rider (as additional coverage) to your existing professional liability insurance policy.

Further, disposition should only take place after a written agreement between the funeral-cremation provider and cemetery has been prepared and reviewed by your attorney. The agreement must contain the signatures of the principals of the funeral-cremation provider or crematory and the cemetery. As a reminder, funeral homes and cemeteries are governed by separate licensing agencies in most states. This means both parties must comply with their respective laws and regulations. Both parties must be certain that no laws are violated.

For many people who choose cremation, it is their first experience not only in arranging for cremation but also with death. The manner in which funeral-cremation providers conduct themselves in dealing with the burial family must also serve as the guide in dealing with the cremation family: provide all relevant information to the arranging parties and permit them to make the decisions. There can be no equivocation: **As decisions about burial are made by client families, so must decisions be made concerning the disposition of a person's cremated remains.**

When burial services are planned, no funeral-cremation provider would proceed arranging details if the client family was undecided on the cemetery. Similarly, when arrangements for final disposition of a person's cremated remains are undecided or there is a question as to whether or not the person's cremated remains will be retrieved in a timely fashion, **Best Practice** suggests that cremation should not take place until all parties reach agreement.

CHAPTER 14

Risk Assessment and Insurance

Every thoughtful funeral-cremation provider at some point, usually in the middle of the night, has nagging thoughts about vulnerability to lawsuits, especially after reading sensational headlines about the latest funeral or cremation debacle. Funeral directors recognize their vulnerability, but at the same time, listen to a small voice inside them that whispers, "Yes, you are vulnerable, but you can never afford enough insurance to cover every possibility." This chapter helps you assess your business, your building, and your employees and prepares you for a reasonable discussion with your insurance carrier. It shows how having the right kind of insurance products can provide you with peace of mind. It will help you uncover vulnerable areas that you might not be aware of. It will clarify some of the popular misunderstandings about risk assessment and the proper use of insurance in your business plan.

The subject of insurance may not excite you. But protecting a business you own and your personal assets is vitally important to the ongoing survival and ultimate success of your livelihood. Each funeral-cremation provider's risk exposure is unique and should be reviewed on a personal, in-depth basis while contemplating a variety of factors that might or might not be under your control. Learning that your limousine carrying a client family was involved in a serious accident - or that the cremated remains you mailed to a widow two weeks ago failed to arrive - are two scenarios that will surely get your attention. Unfortunately, too many business owners wait until they experience incidents such as these to conduct this important

306

inventory of their exposure. While many funeral-cremation providers cannot envision the occurrence of such tragic events, they eventually learn that they can take action that might prevent a recurrence of comparable and costly events in the future. **The time to evaluate your exposure is now, and obtaining proper insurance for your business is not a luxury but a necessity.**

Funeral-cremation and cemetery service operates in a changing, often volatile climate. You perform your duties with emotionally distraught and over-tired clients, who might be filled with misconceptions about funerals, cemeteries, cremation, and costs, and who might be unaware of protocol or legal requirements while questioning your motives. It can be overwhelming and fatiguing even for the most experienced arranger.

Funeral directors must continuously adapt to every family and must recognize that, given these and other conditions, **there is no such thing as a risk-free funeral, cremation, burial, entombment, shipment, placement, transfer, scattering or for that matter, arrangement conference.** Even the smallest of errors or oversight on your part can cause a family to seek legal counsel against a funeral-cremation provider.

There was a time in our society when professionals were not a target of lawsuits. The funeral director and other personal-service providers were known personally by their clients and the quality of their services and counsel were never questioned. Even in instances of obvious negligence or error, clients, patients and families would never have considered legal action against any professional.

This leniency is no longer the case. The work you do – and your relationship with client families and decedents – is very different from that done by other professionals. Funeral- service professionals are held to higher levels of accountability. Rarely is there a second opportunity to do things correctly. Fewer clients are willing to accept errors of any kind, especially from professionals; the smallest error or failure can trigger powerful emotions.

Often when a funeral-cremation provider is being sued, there is no advance warning. The lawsuit comes as a complete surprise, sometimes not until many months after serving the family. A client family that feels a particular aspect of service was performed incorrectly or believes they were harmed in the process may not even express their displeasure to the funeral director or cemetery directly. Instead, they seek the advice of an attorney. Your first indication of any discontent is a letter from an attorney demanding money or threatening legal action.

We cannot run from responsibilities nor can we escape from dealing with people's emotions. Reality tells us that both the consumer and the legal profession have learned to shoot modern bullets. **They are called lawsuits.**

Purpose of Insurance

Risk and accountability are an inescapable part of the business world today. Practically any risk that can be quantified quite possibly has a type of insurance to protect it. You might be sued even though you have done nothing wrong. Common forms of insurance include life, health, disability, credit, worker's compensation, among others. For our purpose, however, discussions will center on property, casualty and professional-liability policies, usually known as errors and omissions insurance.

Unfortunately, there is no way to completely avoid the possibility of being sued, regardless of the level of care you employ. Purchasing insurance is one method used by professionals and businesses to protect against risk and resultant loss. The basic purpose of insurance is to anticipate serious losses and provide you with relief from catastrophic events.

While most people associate loss with financial loss - monetary payments covering liability for actions, a loss of an investment, a person's inability to earn income, and more - it can also mean "other" loss beyond monetary payments.

For the community funeral-cremation provider and/or cemetery, other losses can be significant: The loss of goodwill, loss of reputation and loss of time, energy and focus while defending claims. Given such immeasurable exposure, everyone working in or for the organization has a stake in preventing claims or allegations of wrongdoing.

Changing business and professional practices, as well as societal norms, create new types of exposure that previous generations of funeral-cremation providers and cemeterians never had to face. My father, who taught me the business, did not have to be concerned with lawsuits and did not look over his shoulder at governmental agencies, the legal profession and the media. It is unfortunately true that America is a litigious society.

The American Business Development Company states:

- Between 80 and 90 million lawsuits are filed in this country each year.

- With approximately 70% of the world's attorneys in the United States, there are more lawyers per capita in our country than any other country in the world, approximately 1 attorney per 280 citizens.

We live in what has been called a rights-oriented culture and one in which it is becoming acceptable to blame everybody else for our troubles. When something goes wrong, it's time to sue and any negotiations take on the feel of a nuclear disarmament treaty.

The Need for Risk Assessment

Owners and managers of even the smallest companies must assess the impact of potential risks – both known and unknown - and set in place measures that minimize them as best as possible. Assessing means **identifying, evaluating and prioritizing** risks. Once this inventory has been done, resources can then be allocated to handle them.

Risk assessment is a process that systemically **identifies** the risks and hazards inherent in an operation and lists the assets that need to be protected in a business-professional practice.

Assessment is the first step in controlling and mitigating potential risks. It takes into account *external* and *internal* factors.

"Taking a comprehensive inventory of your exposures could make the difference between the survival of your business and closing your doors following a catastrophic loss," states James Metzger, Chairman and CEO of The Whitmore Group, Ltd., a premier insurance broker to funeral homes, crematories and cemeteries located in Garden City, New York. "The best time to perform this process is NOW. Unfortunately, people are often too busy to assess the exposure of their operation. Assessing one's exposures should be a standard operating procedure performed every six months or after any major change to the business, even changes to their building. You can't control everything that can happen, but you can make certain that you protect your company against loss in the areas that you can control."

External factors are those beyond your direct control. Factors such as trends in the industry and business, neighborhood demographics, the international, national and local economies, and competition and legislative actions would be considered areas where an individual funeral director would have very limited control.

Internal factors are those which we can control, including such matters as full and part-time personnel, policies and procedures, maintenance of facilities and equipment and compensation.

Some people view risk as a threat while others see it as an opportunity to improve upon existing services and processes - or create new ones - that will elevate their operation and distinguish it from the competition.

For example, in the late 1970s, most funeral-cremation providers documented only minimal disclosure of services to their client families. As a funeral director during that period of time, my entire staff – along with my attorney and insurance agent – worked as a team in assessing various aspects of our operation. Among others, we developed release, authorization, receipt and disclosure forms for use in the arrangement conference. I was aware of other funeral homes that had been sued due to families claiming they did not receive adequate information before spending thousands of dollars on a funeral, with which they were not satisfied. I also had many people in the arrangement conference ask more and more questions. These forms were designed to more fully inform client families about elements of service and risk.

While forms alone will not prevent a lawsuit, they provided an added level of protection for my business while helping to educate client families. We discovered that using these forms created a new awareness for the entire staff and contributed to a higher level of service. As they helped to educate families, they also helped differentiate my funeral home from other providers who considered such validation of their services to be unnecessary. One benefit of using the forms and educating our client families is that my funeral home was asked to provide this information to the local senior citizens. Every month, the local senior center invited my funeral home to have lunch with their members and answer seniors' questions on funerals and related topics. *An informed consumer is a good consumer.*

When Should a Risk Assessment be done?

- Before using a premise for the first time
- Before a job is first undertaken
- Before new equipment is used
- When new health and safety information becomes available
- Before new procedures or policies are adopted
- Before using off-premises facilities, such as a refrigeration center or crematory
- Before employing independent contractors or outside service providers
- Before selling a new product or service

- Before using hazardous substances or equipment
- As a part of the design and construction of a new facility
- Following an accident
- If you have never performed an assessment before

Risk assessment is not a one-time event but requires monitoring and periodic review. It must also be documented, especially noting the date it was performed, significant findings and revisions. Many companies retain this documentation in their business insurance file. Depending on the risk, the nature of the business and how quickly it changes, it could be done quarterly, semi-annually or annually.

Involving Employees in the Assessment Process

Risk assessment should not be considered only a "management" function. It works best when it involves everyone from all sectors of the organization: ownership, management, technical, body preparation, and other full-time and part-time employees. Often not included by management, employees play an especially critical role in risk identification, as they are generally most knowledgeable about the intricacies of their work and the hazards present in performing it. Sometimes the most valuable contributions to the assessment process comes from the employees themselves who perform the specific tasks. These are the people that see the operation from the inside while performing the everyday functions of the funeral home, crematory and cemetery. The owner or manager might overlook certain details while looking at the big picture only. For instance, my part-time evening attendants first alerted me to valid concerns regarding personal property that was often placed on deceased persons. They were concerned that some deceased persons wore extremely valuable jewelry. As attendants, they wanted to know a best-practice procedure for returning such items to the family and what steps they should take in the event of a robbery or a report of "missing" property. Seen as real concerns by my part-time employees, these property-related

312

concerns caused me to seriously consider these things and take precautions to prevent such events from occurring.

How to Conduct a Risk Assessment

Risk assessments, especially those performed for the first time, can be time-consuming for the persons in charge. As mentioned above, it is best to involve more than one person from the company in a team effort. The entire operation should be studied unless you are performing a regulatory assessment, such as for OSHA. Missing a key area can prove to be a costly oversight. For instance, if you failed to review your automobile insurance and did not take into consideration the new vehicles you purchased - or if you sold your limousine and now rent one as needed - additional assessment or modification to existing coverage might be necessary. Most insurance professionals encourage funeral-home clients to review their vehicle schedules quarterly to maintain accuracy. "Perhaps the most alarming correspondence a funeral director can receive is a letter from his or her insurance company stating that the injuries sustained by the passengers in the new or borrowed vehicle will not be covered because that car wasn't added to the policy when delivery was taken, or that the policy does not allow for coverage of hired and non-owned vehicles," says Metzger.

You should also seek advice from outside sources and need to know as much about the process as possible in order to be thorough. Check with your national or state funeral association, other colleagues and with your friends who might have done a risk assessment in their business.

When I conducted my own risk assessment, I began by separating the operation into categories: facility interior; facility exterior; parking lot; all walkways, entryways and exits; exterior signage and lighting; licenses required for professional staff; licenses and insurance required for all outside service providers; suppliers and vendors; owned automobiles; rented automobiles; areas for public assemblage and use (restrooms, coffee lounge, ceremony rooms, etc.); equipment (church trucks, kneelers, flower racks, etc.); furniture and fixtures (chairs, sofas, candelabras, etc.); and security systems. In addition, background checks were conducted on full-time and part-time employees.

The operation end of the business was categorized in similar fashion: transferring a decedent; body preparation and handling; funeral ceremonies in our facility; funeral ceremonies at an outside facility; funeral processions; outside crematory; and use of common carriers.

My team included my primary funeral director, business-office manager and myself. We endeavored to be methodical and thorough and urge you to do the same. Working together, we began by walking around the interior and exterior of the premises, area by area, with a notebook. Anything that could pose even a small risk was written down and a special note was made as to who it might affect (an employee, a visitor, a bereaved family, handicapped person, the casket delivery person, etc.). For some findings, it was necessary to ask for advice from other people: contractors, my attorney, my insurance professional, city planning department, fire department and security specialists.

Once **identified, evaluated and prioritized,** the business owner has three basic options in dealing with risk:

1. Avoid the risk entirely (by eliminating procedures or certain operations);
2. Assume the risk yourself, either in whole or partially; or,
3. Transfer the risk to insurance.

1. **Avoiding the risk entirely** may not be practical. Risk is always inherent in owning and operating a business. For the most part, avoiding risk entirely for a funeral-cremation provider or cemetery means not being in business. For one, most funerals involve many people. We encourage people to come to the funeral home and visit with the bereaved family. We conduct processions to cemeteries that can involve hundreds of automobiles. We readily assume custody of possibly

the most valuable "property" in the world: someone's own family member. The wise person takes advantage of all resources available and does all he/she can to minimize any likelihood of negative events. Doing nothing and saying to yourself, "We've always done it this way," or "we've never had a problem or been sued before," is not smart business today.

2. **Assuming the risk yourself** can also be extremely difficult and dangerous for most funeral-cremation providers and cemeteries. Except for minor claims, it is impossible to know how much money needs to be extracted from the business and set aside to cover an occurrence. Awards for damages can be staggering today. Also, money set aside for this purpose is generally not tax-deductible as a business expense. Assuming the risk by yourself is a gamble. Acting as if, "I hope it never happens" is flawed reasoning.

3. **Transferring the potential for loss** means purchasing insurance. Insurance is the most logical form of risk protection used by practically all professionals and businesses. By its very nature, insurance is a practical form of risk management. However, you must be certain that the insurance you purchase covers the risk to your business.

History of Insurance

Insurance companies are in the business of assuming risk on behalf of their clients and through the issuance of an insurance policy, these companies promise to pay money in the case of any covered loss. The best insurance companies also work with their clients to help them avoid catastrophic financial events. According to E.J. Vaughn, author of the book, *Fundamentals of Risk & Insurance* (Columbia Press, 1986), the earliest form of insurance began almost 4,500 years ago in Babylonia. Traders used to bear the risk of the caravan trade, loaning money to caravan operators who had to repay the loan with interest when the goods arrived safely at their destination. A more modern form of insurance evolved to help merchants move goods across the oceans in sailing ships, to minimize financial losses from shipwrecks and pirates. Ship owners noticed that while some merchandise was lost to pirates or fires, not all ships were lost. The owners placed money into a pool to cover the losses of shippers whose merchandise and ship was lost, giving each of them a fair chance of not being wiped out by a disaster. They computed the probabilities of losses to determine how much each ship owner needed to pay in order to cover potential losses. Investors, who were original underwriters, received compensation for their financial backing, which they factored into payments now called premiums.

Today, an insurance policy is a legally binding contract between an insurance company (insurer) and the person, business or organization buying the policy (policyholder or insured). The policyholder is often the person insured. In exchange for payment of a specified amount of money (premium), the insurance company promises to provide coverage and pay for certain types of loss and/or damages that are specified in the insurance contract. When loss or damage occurs that meets the terms of the insurance policy, the loss is "covered" by that policy. An insurance company measures loss or damage, or the potential for loss or damage; and provides coverage in purely financial terms, receiving its compensation through the payment of money from the insured.

Most insurance companies have substantial resources, but also transfer or spread a part of their financial risk over a broad financial network involving other insurance companies. This is called "reinsurance." Depending on the risk potential of the business or practice - and/or the amount of coverage desired - several insurance companies could be involved in providing coverage within one policy to one insured party. A reinsurance company provides insurance to an insurance company.

Specially tailored types of insurance policies are available to manage practically all types of risks for practically all types of businesses and professions. Separate policies might be written for a particular risk, such as "professional liability" or "directors and officers liability." Some policies are "packaged" to provide protection in several areas under one policy.

Choosing an Insurance Company

Doing business with an insurance agent or company that is not familiar with the intricacies of a particular profession, industry or profession can be risky. Funeral-cremation and cemetery businesses are very complex operations. **The best insurance professionals understand the nuances of a specific business or profession, are involved in the industry and profession and are acutely aware of the risks involved.**

Prior to placing your coverage with just anyone listed in the telephone directory or with a neighborhood broker who promises an inexpensive package to cover all of your business and professional needs, you have a responsibility to your business to identify an insurance representative that can best demonstrate his or her knowledge of your industry. Failing to perform due diligence can be costly when you are sued by a third party or when you experience a loss. Choosing insurance coverage based solely on how much the annual premium costs can also prove disastrous and a decision you will sooner or later regret. As a funeral-cremation provider with experience in risk management, I have become a firm believer in two old (yet wise) adages:

1. You get what you pay for; and,

2. If it seems too good to be true, then it probably is not true.

Funeral-cremation providers and cemeteries pride themselves on the fact that they are community-based, and, as a result, endeavor to do business with local merchants whenever possible. While I, initially followed this model when purchasing insurance for my funeral home, I learned the greater importance of obtaining the proper coverage at the best price – and updating it – as my business grew, as the public changed and as the profession evolved. Insurance specialists like The Whitmore Group, Ltd., have developed an in-depth knowledge of the funeral, cremation and cemetery businesses: Such companies are involved in the profession, they address our special coverage needs and only place coverage with carriers that demonstrate the ability to afford proper protection.

Dealing with specialists and purchasing specialized insurance coverage often becomes necessary. Too often, the funeral home - as a community-based business - feels pressured to obtain insurance coverage from another local business. Not all local agents always keep abreast of the demands of our practice. "Assuming that the local general insurance broker has sufficient and adequate insight to secure the proper coverage could be a dangerous decision," states James Metzger. Like other high-profile, personal-service businesses, funeral, cremation and cemetery operations are specialized and have massive exposure to risks. Few insurance people know the intricacies of our business and its exact needs.

Additionally, a general-insurance package written years ago to cover "all the business needs," must be carefully examined and evaluated to make sure it meets today's requirements. Having the wrong type of insurance can be worse than having no insurance at all. It can be a serious oversight to have what appears to be adequate insurance coverage, even with substantial limits, but one that contains exclusions for aspects of our work that have become customary and usual. Choosing an insurance company and agent based solely on friendship might feel like a good decision, but it can be damaging to your business if you are sued.

It is common practice for insurance companies to modify their products in response to recent claim experiences. Typically, they lower coverage amounts for areas that produce numerous claims and large awards - and offer instead new insurance packages that provide coverage for areas likely to result in fewer, smaller claims. The standard Insurance Services Office, Inc. (ISO) General Liability policy is a perfect example. As claims related to wrongful termination, discrimination and pollution increased, coverage amounts for such incidents diminished to the point where those areas of exposure were excluded from conventional plans. Special policies that provided coverage in these areas could be purchased separately, but at a higher cost than in earlier policies.

The operation of a funeral-cremation business and the required duties of the professional continue to evolve, becoming more sophisticated and specialized. The same is true for insurance. It is also very diverse and specialized.

This book will not cover every type of insurance that is available but concentrates on an explanation of basic and customary insurance widely used today. There may be other types of insurance that you may need to consider based on the intricacies and size of your operation. Consult your insurance professional for the types of coverage that may be necessary in your business.

Some decisive factors used to determine insurance needs include where the business is located; the nature and full scope of the business; the services and products offered; leases on property and equipment; financial or employment contracts; payroll and numbers of employees; loss and claims history; industry/business trends; and other aspects.

This chapter discusses some major types of insurance critical for today's business and professional climate. Practically all insurance can be classified into three general categories:

1. Property insurance

2. Casualty insurance

3. Employee benefits insurance

1. Property Insurance

This insurance protects real and personal property, providing broad coverage against physical loss or damage.

Funeral-cremation providers and cemeteries face the potential for multiple and unusual risks. A major fire can greatly affect your business and income; your ability to re-open your doors as quickly as possible can also have an impact on your business and income. It is best that property insurance be identified as an "all-risk" policy, covering physical assets such as, but not limited to:

- The physical structure of the building including fixtures, carpeting and glass
- Equipment and machinery
- Office/business furniture, equipment and computers
- Inventory and supplies
- Personal property kept at the business site
- Loss of business income (due to fire, lightning, windstorm, flood, earthquake, etc.)
- Improvements and betterments

While the policy form is called "all-risk," a more thorough review of the complete policy will inform the policyholder of which perils the policy does **not** protect against. Typically, coverage for losses due to earthquake, flood and toxic waste are not provided unless specifically requested by your broker. Even when requested, many carriers will not provide coverage for these perils and your broker or agent will be forced to purchase coverage separately and for additional cost.

With your insurance broker or agent, carefully examine your policy, paying particular attention to coverage, limits, deductibles and exclusions. You must know whether the policy provides coverage for **replacement** cost or **actual cash value** for reimbursement. You must know which types of coverage you have or when coverage is limited. Another important coverage that can be provided under this broad form is called **commercial crime**. This form of insurance protects the policyholder for losses due to employee dishonesty, loss from money orders and counterfeit paper currency and depositor's forgery. Coverage for counterfeit cashier's checks, however, would have to be requested specifically. On one occasion, I agreed to accept payment for 35 individual flower orders. The orders totaled more than $3,000.00 and the agreement was that everyone would pay during visitation and by cash. All 35 individuals paid as promised, however, when the cash was deposited, the bank identified $900 as being counterfeit.

2. Casualty Insurance

This insurance provides liability coverage to third parties for bodily injury or against actions or claims due to negligence or perceived negligence. It will be covered more broadly on subsequent pages. Among other things, it provides coverage for:

- Professional liability (errors and omissions)
- Commercial general liability
- Automobile liability including hired and non-owned vehicles
- Personal and advertising injury liability
- Product liability
- Umbrella liability
- Directors and Officers liability
- Fiduciary liability

3. Employee Benefits Insurance

This insurance provides coverage for employees (workers), including worker's compensation, health, dental, life, long-term care, disability insurance and more. Some of these types of insurance may be required by regulation. For example, worker's compensation is required in most states where an employer has W-2 employees providing protection to employees if they suffer a serious injury on the job.

Special Note: If a funeral home subcontracts certain operations or jobs, workers' compensation laws provide that the principal contractor (funeral home, crematory or cemetery) is responsible for compensation to employees of **uninsured subcontractors,** unless the subcontractor has insured this obligation himself/herself. Before hiring any subcontractor, obtain a **certificate of insurance** from them as evidence that they have the appropriate type of insurance in force and in appropriate limits. Also, notify your insurance carrier that subcontractors are hired by you to perform certain jobs.

Professional Liability Insurance/ Errors-and-Omissions

Without Professional Liability on your Business Owners Policy (BOP) or Package policy, the coverage you purchased might provide the same level of protection purchased by the owner of the candy store down the street from your funeral home or crematory. "In our experience, it's not the frequency of professional liability claims that has been a problem. It's the size of the amounts awarded," says Metzger, whose company insures thousands of funeral homes nationwide. In other words, while professional liability claims do not appear as regularly as slip and fall general liability claims, the dollars awarded to claimants are typically more substantial.

It cannot be said any clearer: **This type of business insurance is critical coverage for the funeral-cremation provider and cemetery.** Like many other insurance products under casualty insurance, errors-and-omissions coverage is a separate type of insurance and usually customized to meet the needs of a specific group. For example, errors-and- omissions coverage for a physician will be different than that for a certified public accountant.

Professional liability/errors-and-omissions insurance is appropriate for anyone in the helping or servicing professions, for people who give advice or represent the needs and interests of others. Among others, physicians, psychologists, lawyers, accountants, financial planners, architects, stockbrokers, teachers, insurance agents, travel agents will have this type of insurance coverage.

Professional liability insurance protects your business from claims alleging negligent acts, errors and omissions that could lead to potentially catastrophic losses arising out of the performance of professional services, even against unknown or unforeseeable claims. A separate policy that covers professional liability is recommended.

What is Professional Negligence?

Negligence is also discussed in Chapter Ten. Professional negligence is the failure to exercise the degree of care, knowledge or skill of an average person in good professional standing under circumstances similar to those in which the injury or damage occurred. The degree of care is the level of caution, prudence or forethought legally required to avoid causing harm or loss to another person. In determining liability, depending on the circumstances and relationship of the persons involved, a professional exercises degrees of care, commonly described as ordinary, due, reasonable, great, or utmost. In funeral service, a special relationship exists between the funeral-cremation provider and the deceased person and the client family and the degree of care is usually described as utmost.

The Need for Professional Liability/ Errors-and-Omissions Insurance

From purely a liability standpoint, formalizing a contract with client families can help limit liability in certain areas. Using the finest disclosure, release and authorization forms with every family does not guarantee you are lawsuit-proof. **Whether a claim has merit or not, the amount of damages sought and mounting a legal defense to prove your innocence can financially overwhelm a business.** In particular, errors-and-omissions insurance covers crucial aspects of our duties and interactions with a client family and the deceased person.

Many of the services provided by funeral homes and crematories are highly specialized and cannot always be performed risk-free or with a guaranteed outcome. Some client families may not fully understand the intricacies involved. Our special relationship, unique facilities, 24/7 availability, plus the need to verify identity, embalming and restorative art and the custody factor, are just a few risks that some people outside the business might not be aware of.

I recall making arrangements with the son of a deceased person who became upset during the arrangement conference when he learned we did not have custody of his father who died just a few hours earlier in a local hospital. The nurse at the hospital told him, "Your father will be moved immediately." He understood this to mean that the hospital would deliver his father to the funeral home and that they would do it immediately. He did not know that hospitals have their own procedures to follow when a death occurs and that the funeral home – not the hospital – performs the transfer.

Some families can have expectations for outcomes beyond our reach. Some can be unreasonable. Sometimes funeral directors and embalming technicians make mistakes. Some examples of allegations by client families that in all likelihood would involve professional liability/errors-and-omissions coverage are:

- Presenting the wrong decedent for viewing
- Unhappiness with the appearance of the decedent, presence of foul odors and fluids purging from the body
- Transferring or shipping the wrong person
- Cremating the wrong person
- Embalming the wrong person or improper storage/ refrigeration/care
- Failure to embalm in a timely manner
- Missing personal effects
- Administrative incompetence causing a delay of disposition

- Inappropriate handling of the deceased person at time of transfer
- Wrongful disposal of a person's cremated remains or personal property
- Losing a person's cremated remains
- Using a non-licensed embalmer or other non-licensed personnel where licensure is required
- Inappropriate or offensive language in presence of a deceased person and client family
- Burying the wrong person
- Burying the correct person but in the wrong grave or crypt
- Failing to reach informed consent before performing duties
- Removing a shade tree over a grave site without notifying the owner
- Fluids leaking from the casket
- Uncaring demeanor by staff members
- Failing to seal a casket or outer burial container according to the manufacturer's standards
- Failure of performance by independent contractors or outside service providers hired by the funeral home, crematory or cemetery

Irrespective of the services that you provide and no matter how well you perform them, customers can claim that you failed to do something correctly on their behalf or that you failed entirely to do something they requested. The customer's perception of your actions or your failure to act without their knowledge or understanding may lead them to the conclusion that this error or omission ultimately cost them money or caused them harm in some way.

The two important benefits of professional liability/errors-and-omissions insurance are:

1. It ensures that funds are available to pay for judgments **up to the limits of coverage** when it has been established that a client family has suffered damages or losses, and

2. It pays expenses for legal representation and court costs **but only up to the limits of coverage.**

Limits of coverage, sometimes referred to as limits of liability, are the stated **maximum dollar amounts** that a policy will pay for a claim on the insured's behalf. Errors-and-omissions policies clearly state a maximum limit for each claim - that is, the most it will pay for a single claim. The policy also states an aggregate, which is the most it will pay for all claims during the policy period.

Inquire as to whether your policy includes defense costs *within* the limit or if defense costs are *in addition* to your limit of liability. When involved in litigation, some funeral directors have been surprised to learn that defense costs (for the services of an attorney, for instance) are **included** within the policy limits. If a funeral director has $1 million of liability insurance, it is conceivable that defense costs could eat up a substantial amount of coverage.

The Professional Liability coverage is offered on either an occurrence policy or a claims-made policy. The policy wording will dictate the manner in which the coverage is afforded but the "occurrence" form is the most recommended policy.

The **occurrence form** affords coverage under the policy that was in effect at the time the alleged incident took place. Even if a claim is filed three years after a policy has expired, any coverage that would be afforded for this claim would be provided by the expired policy. The coverage reverts back to the policy in place at the time of the loss.

The **claims-made form** affords coverage under the policy that is presently in effect regardless of when the incident allegedly took place. Coverage is provided by the policy that is in effect at the time the claim is made to the insurance company. For example, an incident might have taken place three years ago, but the claim was only brought to the insurance company this year. The current policy would then provide the coverage for this incident, even though the actual event took place three years ago. The "claims-made" version is a more high-maintenance policy that might require the policyholder to maintain his or her professional liability coverage even if he or she is no longer in business, due to the fact that all coverage ceases once that policy expires. Failure to renew this policy would leave the insured without future protection for potential claims alleging negligence for past activities.

Also, when changing from a claims-made policy to an occurrence policy, **be sure to request a retroactive date that preferably dates back to the inception of your company.** By selecting this date, your company will be protected against claims that are alleged to have taken place prior to the date of your new occurrence policy. The new occurrence policy will then provide tail coverage in the event that claims arise out of activities predating the effective date of your new policy, even though coverage was previously provided on a claims-made basis.

Importantly, a professional liability policy contains a "declaration page" listing specifics of the policy (name of insured, policy period, limits of coverage, deductibles, and so forth). Policies are usually divided into sections that clearly define specific areas of coverage and conditions. An "endorsement" section lists expanded coverage or gives explicit explanation or wording to describe present coverage; an "exclusion" section lists coverage that is not included in present coverage.

How Much Coverage is Necessary?

This is a very common question. Before attempting to answer, it is important to note:

Having professional liability insurance does not increase

your chance of being sued. It makes you more prepared if a lawsuit is brought against you.

More than ever, professional people are held accountable for what they do or fail to do. Nationwide, lawsuits against funeral-cremation providers alleging negligence are increasing dramatically every year. Ordinary people who would never consider the filing of a lawsuit can be influenced by friends or events they read or hear about through the media. **These outside influences can generate a sense of entitlement in these same people.** In its course on liability insurance, Hays Affinity Solutions, a company that provides risk-management services, reminds their clients - and rightfully so - that, at any time and in any given situation, a person who becomes dissatisfied with your service or product can choose to bring a complaint against you. Regardless of its merits, it can take years for a lawsuit to be dismissed. While you might ultimately be exonerated from liability and wrongdoing, your legal fees can be staggering - and the damage to your reputation irreparable.

Professional liability insurance helps relieve you from the financial burden of defending yourself against lawsuits that might not have anything to do with your direct involvement. If you were even remotely involved in the disputed work or product, you are likely to face a lawsuit regardless of whether or not it is determined that you have done anything wrong. **While the end result vindicates your actions, your defense costs can still be immense.**

Until recently, and for the most part, funeral, cremation and cemetery businesses have stayed under the radar screen of the legal profession, except for major cases that have developed. Especially among plaintiff's attorneys, this is no longer the case. They have received their wake-up call. Headlines in major newspapers and leading media services have brought our business to their attention and into the living rooms of millions of people, reporting some of the immense settlements in recent funeral-crematory-cemetery lawsuits, some involving criminal proceedings. Judges and juries are generally sympathetic to claims of mental anguish and emotional distress. Monetary awards of several millions of dollars are not uncommon.

Assessing How Much Professional Liability Insurance is Needed

Best Practice means that given today's climate, the smallest funeral-cremation provider or cemetery, even those operating in rural America, should **never** consider less than $1,000,000 of professional liability/errors-and-omissions coverage. In most areas of the country, $1,000,000 of coverage is totally inadequate. When assessing your particular needs to determine coverage amounts, there are many **Best Practice** factors to consider. Among them are:

- The geographic location of your business
- The legal environment of your geographic location
- Trends affecting the profession and industry
- Number of employees having direct contact with client families
- Number of families served on an annual basis
- Whether the transfer of remains is performed by staff or contracted out?
- Whether embalming is performed by staff or contracted out?
- Whether refrigeration is available on or off premises?
- Are you performing more cremations?
- Are cremations performed on site or contracted out?
- If cremations are performed at an outside crematory, do you remain at the crematory during the cremation process and monitor what takes place?
- In your area, do more deaths occur at residences or in health facilities?
- Are cultural, religious, ethnic, socio-economic and demographic profiles changing in your area?

- Do you have a written policy/procedure manual for every aspect of your operation? Is it documented that all employees received a copy and that they have read it?

- Do you provide ongoing risk reduction training for all employees - and is training documented? (This is in addition to required units of continuing education.)

- Do you have a tagging policy, accompanied by a foolproof identification system before performing disposition?

- Do you require receipts for delivery-release-acceptance of deceased persons?

- What is your claims history? An amount of insurance coverage in place for several years and once considered sufficient can be grossly inadequate in today's litigious business climate. **Saying that you are a third-generation owner and the funeral home has never been sued may not be valid basis for determining current insurance needs.**

Many funeral-cremation providers and cemeteries that become involved in lawsuits in are surprised to learn of "limiting factors" contained in their professional liability-errors and omissions policy. Many professional liability policies include coverage for $1,000,000 under a standard Business Owners Policy (BOP). This type of coverage might not always be the best and the limit can be insufficient. Also, there can be other limiting factors:

- $1,000,000 usually includes **both** the total of defense and court costs as well as all monetary awards.

- It is an aggregate amount, often for the entire policy period, or life of the policy.

- Coverage specifically excludes coverage for acts of fraud, when fraud is proven. Today, fraud is being affirmed in a number of third-party crematory lawsuits.

• The policy might not provide coverage for acts committed when previous insurance was in force - or might not provide coverage for acts committed after the policy expires.

Stand-Alone Policy

For these and other reasons, more and more funeral homes, crematories, cemeteries and outside providers are obtaining a **stand-alone professional liability insurance policy.** While the premiums for this type of "premium" coverage can be slightly more expensive than the "included" type, this sort of policy provides substantial broad professional liability coverage and limits of coverage. Depending on your exposure, the limits under this stand-alone policy can easily be increased without affecting other parts of your insurance. One way to protect your limits is to have your insurance broker secure a quote that offers a $1,000,000 professional liability limit, which would be separate from the $1,000,000 limit available to address other general-liability claims.

It is worth repeating: The stated limit of coverage in the policy includes both the defense costs and all monetary awards payable as a result of a covered lawsuit.

Today, it is not unusual for defense costs alone to come close to depleting the entire limits of coverage. When this happens, the business or individual becomes personally responsible for paying the monetary award. This is a critical, limiting fact and requires a careful assessment of limits and the limiting factors contained in your policy. **As a Best Practice, a separate professional liability/errors-and-omissions policy is quickly becoming the preferred choice.**

Commercial (comprehensive) General Liability Insurance

This type of insurance is usually the first line of defense and is offered as a package that protects a business against incidents occurring on your premises or at other (covered) locations where business is conducted.

Four basic categories are usually included under commercial general liability insurance:

1. Bodily injury and tangible property liability: property damage caused by you to property owned by someone else

2. Personal injury: libel and slander

3. Advertising injury: misrepresenting a product or service

4. Medical payments: no-fault medical payments for slip-and-fall accidents at your premises or caused by you

Commonly, a standard limit of commercial general liability insurance is $1,000,000 **per occurrence.** This coverage includes the cost of defending lawsuits that claim you are responsible for causing bodily injury or property damage. When higher limits of coverage for this type of insurance are requested, it is provided through an Umbrella Liability policy.

Note: To many people, the term general liability insurance can be a misnomer. Comprehensive general liability insurance does not protect your business against every liability or exposure. In particular, it excludes coverage for claims related to the delivery of professional services. Professional Liability-Errors and Omissions insurance is a separate type of insurance and is not normally included in commercial comprehensive general insurance. Many funeral-cremation providers who carry high limits of general liability insurance ($5 million and above) are under the impression that this includes coverage for professional liability claims. **It does not.**

Commercial General Liability insurance must be carefully reviewed and particular attention paid to exclusions and whether coverage exists for hazards that do not now exist but may develop during the life of the policy.

Umbrella Liability Insurance – Best Practice Recommendation

Most people do not expect a disaster to strike. But every business, large and small, is vulnerable to a major catastrophe or major lawsuit. Think about some of the major litigation you have heard about lately involving funeral, cremation and cemetery services and the huge settlements accompanying them. For most of the providers involved, these losses far exceeded their primary insurance coverage. Umbrella insurance is available to individuals, companies and organizations to protect them from claims **above and beyond** the amount covered by existing policies or for claims that may not be currently covered.

Umbrella insurance is usually inexpensive when compared to the limits being provided and the coverage is unquestionably worthwhile to obtain. It can actually save your business and personal fortune. For instance, if a company has $1,000,000 coverage under a Commercial General policy and there is a claim settlement for damages for $1,500,000, the umbrella policy would cover the additional amount. Without umbrella coverage, the company or individual would be responsible for paying $500,000. Umbrella policies provide additional coverage to general liability, primary auto liability (including hired and non-owned automobile liability), employer's liability, and, in some cases, personal insurance policies.

Umbrella policies do not always apply to professional liability-errors and omissions policies but can be tailored to do so. In fact, most umbrella carriers will find a way to preclude claims arising from all professional services through an exclusion on their policy. Consult an insurance professional for details.

As Metzger explains, "Several years ago, our company realized that, although our clients were purchasing umbrella limits for their operations, most umbrella carriers would attempt to exclude the professional liability, which is, by far, the funeral-cremation provider's most valuable coverage and greatest exposure. We determined that a need existed for funeral directors for an industry-specific umbrella product that was able to provide these higher limits and include coverage for the professional liability exposure."

As a **Best Practice** consideration, The Whitmore Group developed a risk-purchasing group called Funeral Directors Planning Group (FDPG) that provides umbrella limits up to $10 million to the participants in funeral, cremation and cemetery businesses. Metzger goes on to say, "This means that Whitmore is able to offer the $10 million limit of liability at a price that most carriers would charge an insured for a $3 million umbrella limit."

Products Liability Insurance

There are growing numbers of disputes concerning warranties and products associated with funeral-cremation-cemetery goods. In many instances, liability from failure of a manufacturer's product is unclear. While it makes good sense to be named as an "additional insured" on insurance policies from all companies you buy goods from (caskets, vaults, urns, chemicals, fluids and other saleable products), inquire about having this type of insurance contained in your comprehensive general insurance package. Your sale of such goods may expose you to product liability.

Products Liability insurance provides protection for claims arising out of the insured's products or the reliance upon representation of manufacturer's or products warranties.

Questions of liability can also arise when a subcontractor installs your product or performs services on your behalf, such as interring an outer burial container or a monument. One way in which you might avoid such confusion as well as avoid the assumption of unintended liability is by having your suppliers agree to indemnify you or assume the risk on your behalf. **This issue should be included in any contractual wording between your firm and the supplier's firm.**

Best Practice means that you should ensure that all parties from who you buy goods currently carry General Liability,

Product Liability and Workers' Compensation insurance and always require them to name your company as an "Additional Insured" party on their policy.

Employment Practices Insurance

This insurance provides defense and indemnity protection against claims arising from employer-employee relationships. It can include disputes over wrongful termination, claims of sexual harassment, discrimination, failure to promote, infliction of emotional distress, mismanagement of employee benefits, and more. No company, large or small, is immune from these types of lawsuits. This insurance is often added as an endorsement to existing business insurance policies **but policies offering the broadest employment related practices coverage are most often purchased as a stand-alone product.** The insurance industry describes an **endorsement** as an amendment that is written to cover unique items or special circumstances. It can also be a change to an existing policy to modify the terms of the insurance contract.

Commercial Crime Insurance-Fidelity Bonds

This insurance is necessary due to the serious nature of funeral-cremation providers who frequently become the custodian of another person's personal property. This insurance covers acts of employee dishonesty, robbery, theft or disappearance of property inside or outside of the business premises, including property of deceased persons while in the care and custody of the funeral-cremation provider. Some states require this type of insurance for those engaging in pre-need sales.

Dealing with Personal Property

Insurance coverage alone is not sufficient to protect your professional reputation when you are presented with a claim concerning the personal property of others, especially claims involving a deceased person or a bereaved family member.

Internal procedures must be in place when handling or dealing with personal property. **Best Practice** includes doing the following:

- Inspect the deceased persons for personal property with or on them before assuming custody

- Have a witness present during your inspection, whenever possible

- Complete a personal property receipt for **every** deceased person. Even when there is no personal property on the decedent, the receipt should clearly state: No property taken

- Carefully list all property on the receipt, including any items of clothing

- Once the property is in your custody, maintain it in a secure location and with access limited to authorized personnel only

- When releasing property, issue another receipt that is signed, dated and timed by all parties

- Retain all property receipts in the decedent's file on a permanent basis

Choosing an Insurance Company and Agent

Funeral homes, crematories, cemeteries and outside service providers face exposure to risks that most other businesses do not. Few people can compete with the challenges you face on a daily basis: our relationship with the deceased person is special and requires the utmost of professional care; dealing with a bereaved family means that all staff members be respectful, sensitive and understanding; our facilities are highly specialized and our services personal in nature; our products are specialized and for a distinct purpose. Insurance for funeral-cremation providers and cemeteries is also specialized.

Insurance is a commodity that you purchase. A policy is a

promise to provide you with relief from catastrophic events. Choose your insurance professionals carefully. **Best Practice** criteria to keep in mind are:

1. **Choose an insurance company that understands the specifics and nuances of your business** and ideally, is involved in the profession.

2. **Use a broker and company that specialize in coverage** for a particular profession.

3. **Concentrate on the breadth of coverage,** not only the annual premium.

4. **Understand limits, deductibles, co-payments and exclusions of your policies.** I have seen cases where a funeral home owner learned he was not covered for a claim only after being sued.

5. **Determine how the insurance company responds to claims,** how they are handled and paid and how they respond to lawsuits.

6. **Do not rely on verbal statements claiming that "all of your business needs" are covered.** Without exception, all forms of coverage must be in writing and clearly spelled out.

7. **In the event of a lawsuit will the insurance company allow your input with respect to defense counsel?** Some insurance companies do not take into consideration your position in your community. I have seen insurance companies fight needlessly when a claim could have been easily settled and vice-versa, often creating more ill-will and public relations problems for the funeral home.

8. **Ask for the name of the insurance company's panel counsel.** There might be more than one law firm they use. Investigate their experience in funeral cremation-cemetery litigation or similar cases. For instance,

you do not want a team of lawyers representing you if their previous experience has been largely with environmental-law issues.

9. **Especially with professional liability-errors and omissions insurance, make certain the company specializes in this form of coverage.** Ask them how many carriers they represent and how many other funeral-cremation providers or personal service professionals they insure. **Be certain that your broker attempted to secure a quotation with a limit for professional liability claims that is separate from the limit available for the general liability claims.**

10. **Know the claims history of your firm.** What are your exposures? Are they high, low or tolerable? Are they changing? Talk with colleagues about their experience in lawsuits and with claims. Are your limits adequate or too low?

11. **Educate yourself and train your staff.** Understand how your company can prevent claims; ask your insurance carrier to perform or assist you with a risk management audit or hire a third-party who is experienced in funeral-cremation service and litigation to conduct an risk-management assessment of your operation.

12. **Schedule a review of your insurance at least annually** with your insurance professional.

13. **Determine ahead of time how your insurance company will assist you** when a claim is filed and what your responsibilities are.

Successful risk reduction consists not only of learning to avoid practices and/or situations that raise your exposure to risk but in adhering to **Best Practice**, which includes having protection through insurance tailored for your specific needs. Experience tells us that no matter how careful you might be, in all likelihood, at some point in your career, you will be subject to a claim for damages. There is an old saying that has more truth than fiction: **There are two kinds of funeral-cremation providers: those that have been sued and those that will be sued.**

It is not enough to have an insurance policy that only appears to cover your business. You must develop insurance that covers all areas of potential liability, even those that may be unseen at this time. All forms of insurance must be reviewed and, if necessary, modified and updated on a regular basis to ensure it meets changing conditions, trends in the marketplace and attitudes in the workplace.

Insurance coverage, being attentive to the details in your policy, a preventive risk assessment audit, ongoing training of all staff members and analysis of incidents helps reduce the risks in your professional practice. Above all, careful documentation must accompany all steps. There will always be the need for you to study, to review and discuss with staff any incident that places your business in jeopardy, whether due to an oversight, an error, a miscalculation, misstatement or misjudgment.

The way human nature is, there is very little stimulus to evaluate policies and procedures when everything appears to be going smoothly in our practice. When things get bumpy - or when there is an oversight or a mistake - we have a concrete opportunity to learn. Make use of this opportunity and carefully examine what happened and why.

Involve the entire staff and discuss it thoroughly. Ask them for suggestions and help as to how the mishap or oversight could have been avoided or handled differently.

"What could possibly go wrong?" is a worthwhile question to ask. Risk reduction is not just an annual event or a review of business practices done while sipping a cup of coffee and casually strolling through your facility. **In present day funeral-cremation-cemetery operations, risk identification, evaluation, prioritization and reduction are necessary obsessions and Best Practice.**

CHAPTER 15

When You Are Sued: What to Do and What Not to Do

Unless you have been sued, there is no way you can understand what it is like to sense the bottom falling out beneath you as the top caves in and you suddenly feel lost, alone, scared and worthless, all at the same time. You are afraid to tell anyone what has happened. You wonder if you will ever be able to trust again. What can you do? The problem will not go away. You need to know what you must do — what you must absolutely do. Above all, you do not want to make things worse. You check your records. What should you do with them? Who should you confide in? This chapter will provide suggestions to help you chart a safe and reasonable course of action that includes talking with your insurer and working with your attorney as you begin working to resolve the problem.

It is a wonderful morning and you arrive at your office ahead of everyone else, eagerly anticipating the day. You feel energized. As you begin making the first pot of coffee, the doorbell rings and you see a person standing in the foyer. You approach him and he asks for you by name. You extend your hand, introduce yourself and he hands you an envelope. On it are the words, "You are served." When you open the envelope the cover sheet reads in large print, *"Summons. You are being sued."* Your stomach tightens as you read the allegations against you and your company. So ends your wonderful day (and begins a wonderful day for your lawyer).

340

Being sued is always a significant event. Few people are prepared for it. Being sued can deliver a disturbing psychological blow to your professional psyche. A lawsuit usually means your professional judgment, care, policies and procedures are being challenged. It can also mean that years of hard work to build your reputation are on the line.

Handling Complaints to Reduce Lawsuits

Many factors lead to lawsuits. The reasons for filing one are complex. In almost every lawsuit, a client family feels they have been damaged, harmed or mistreated in some way and have experienced a loss of some type. Rising customer expectations - sometimes referred to as the "expectation gap" – can make it more difficult to maintain client-family satisfaction. Society has high expectations for people working in funeral, cremation and cemetery service. While there is no magic formula for dealing with complaints, poor communication, avoidance of issues and defensiveness by the funeral-cremation provider can help turn a manageable complaint into a lawsuit. Complaint management can save a business from dealing with a lawsuit and turn angry, frustrated clients into loyal customers.

Some funeral-cremation providers find it difficult to accept and admit that things occasionally go wrong. They may not be sensitive to a client family's need to hear the words, **"I am sorry"** from their funeral director. The value of these three words cannot be underestimated in situations like this. Saying this should not be construed as any admission of guilt. "I am sorry" is an expression of empathy offered from one human being to another and helps to retain a personal connection. Saying it to an unsatisfied client can mean not having to say it to an attorney.

At first, unhappy clients might only be seeking an opportunity to voice their displeasure and receive a genuine explanation or apology. When they do not receive satisfaction, they decide to sue. Whether true or not, funeral professionals are seen as highly paid people with substantial assets and lots of insurance. Having safe **Best Practice** in place to deal with complaints or adverse situations helps minimize risks inherent in funeral practice today.

From a risk-management perspective, when a mistake occurs and is identified early on - or a complaint is properly handled - a lawsuit might be prevented. Open and honest dialogue (without openly admitting liability) is essential to reducing client disappointment and anger.

Allowing people to voice their displeasure as you give them your **total** attention is therapeutic and often helps resolve the problem. Focus your attention on steps to correct the unhappiness or problem rather than respond defensively or discuss what led to the unhappiness.

Sometimes all that is needed to diffuse a potential landmine from exploding into a lawsuit are the words, "I am sorry for any discomfort this has caused you. What would make you happy? What would you like me to do?" It is not a question of capitulation. Honesty remains the best policy; the key to dealing with adverse situations lies in your ability to maintain the trust of the client family.

Case Example: A Disturbing Disinterment – Tell or Not Tell?

The funeral director was serving his friend, whose father died. Against the advice of the funeral director, no burial vault would be used for the wood casket that the son selected. After the burial, and over a period of several months, a series of rainstorms occurred. This caused the son to become concerned, knowing that his father's casket was not in a vault. He met with the funeral director to discuss this. It was decided that the casket would be disinterred and placed in a vault after the soil was given time to dry.

With the son, the funeral director arranged for disinterment at the cemetery and for a vault. The section of land where the grave was located was in terrible condition from the storms and was in an area where the natural flow of water took place. When the grave was opened, the funeral director saw that the casket was ruined and in pieces. The body had been exposed to the elements. The condition of the casket and the remains of the deceased person had deteriorated substantially, and were in such terrible condition that the funeral director could not use the vault. The grave was closed. The funeral director struggled as to whether or not he should tell the son about the condition of the grave and his father's casket. He feared being sued, because the casket had deteriorated so quickly and he was unable to place the contents of the grave into a vault. The funeral director took the risk and met with his friend. He told him about the condition of the grave and the casket, and that conditions did not allow him to use the vault. To the funeral director's surprise, the son was not threatening, but understood. He thanked the funeral director for coming forth and being honest. He sympathized with the funeral director, only guessing as to how difficult it must have been for him to view the grave and share the facts with him. Instead of a lawsuit, the man gladly paid the funeral director for his services and admired him for his integrity.

Funeral directors provide many services and perform their duties under the emotional pressures associated with loss and grief. Sometimes, no matter how hard you try, things do not always go as well as they did in this situation. Still, people need to know the truth even when it involves delicate matters. Most people will respect you for your honesty. Above all, you don't have to worry if and when the "other shoe will fall."

I once heard a minister say about honesty, "Being honest is a work of a lifetime. It is much more than not lying to my neighbor. Honesty asks me to be open to the truths of the world, to be true to myself and to be truthful to the people I know and serve." Being truthful and honest is not always easy because of the pain and embarrassment that might be associated with it. But, in the long run, it is usually worth it.

All employees in the company must be sensitive when caring for bereaved people and be alert to complaints, especially when they involve quality-of-care issues, or in instances when quality-of-care issues could be raised, even later on. Employees must know whom to contact in management when they learn of complaints. **Best Practice** means having a process in place for reporting and responding to complaints and ensure that all employees understand the process. In all cases, complaints of any nature should be responded to immediately and, ideally, by the person with the highest level of responsibility in the company.

Allegations of poor quality care might lead to claims of emotional distress – an increasingly popular basis for lawsuits. When complaints are followed by a demand for monetary adjustment or financial compensation, it should be recognized as a precursor to a lawsuit.

Avoiding the issues or concerns of the client family are a sure way to add to their unhappiness, escalate other emotions, especially anger, and cause a lawsuit.

When a firm's owners, managers and employees ignore customer complaints, they and the company are often perceived as arrogant and indifferent. Especially when buying personal services, no one wants their concerns or feelings disregarded or ignored. It is like pouring gasoline on a fire. Anger develops, leading to a lawsuit.

Three-Step Approach to Resolving Complaints

At my funeral home, I was both owner and front-line employee, engaged on a day-to-day basis in all facets of the business. Over time, I have received critical letters, listened to verbal tirades and read negative comments on client surveys. Very little training is offered by most mortuary schools or college business programs on dealing with unhappy clients. Even advice from your mother may not do much to prepare you for the challenge and difficulty of minimizing or turning around dissatisfaction. Yet, dealing with a client family's concerns in a timely and courteous manner is often the deciding factor in their decision not to seek legal counsel.

My friend, fellow professional speaker and business consultant, James Feldman, taught me a three-step, **Best Practice** approach to handling unsatisfied customers that has produced remarkable results in dealing with complaints. The steps are:

1. Focus on discovery.

2. Reaffirm your discovery.

3. Create a joint resolution.

Focus on discovery means getting all the information; listening and looking at the customer; not talking but taking notes; devoting all of your attention to the customer; not other calls or doing other work.

Reaffirm your discovery means reiterating the critical issue or problem; maintaining a pleasant demeanor; not agreeing or disagreeing but **identifying** all issues; asking the customer for their desired resolution; clarifying their needs and wants; offering a resolution amenable to both parties.

Create a joint resolution means getting acceptance, commitment and resolution from the customer, and jointly developing a plan of action to resolve the dispute or unhappiness.

If you are not the decision-maker in the company but are confronted with a complaint, the manner in which you respond is critical. Your body language, facial expressions, attentiveness and courteous manner can serve as an all-important indication to the family as to how their concerns will be addressed. Having a solid understanding of the complaint is vital. If necessary, write down what the family tells you. Write down the resolution proposed by the family and take it to your supervisor or manager. Employees who give the appearance of taking control and acting responsibly can greatly affect the outcome. Your goal is to keep the customer your customer. The way in which you come across can mean the difference between keeping a client family forever instead of having someone spreading ill will and filing a lawsuit.

Best Practice to Reduce Lawsuits

Combinations of these **Best Practices** help reduce the likelihood of lawsuits, and/or minimize loss when you are sued. They include:

1. **Establish communication and rapport with all client families.** Poor communication or lack of rapport may cause more lawsuits than actual mistakes.

2. **Learn to listen well.** Allow the client family time to voice their concerns without interrupting them. When necessary, ask for clarification. Do not write needlessly; look at the person who is talking.

3. **Do not avoid the client family or miss an opportunity to address the adverse situation early on.** You might also call the client family or make a personal visit to their home to discuss the matter. Above all, do not put off discussions with them.

4. **When a mistake is made, do not try to conceal it.** Serious errors are almost impossible to hide. It is better that the mistake is brought forward by you than to have it discovered later by the client family or someone else.

5. **During the arrangement conference, reach informed consent - Inform before you perform.** Many services we provide have a degree of uncertainty associated with them. Both satisfactory and unsatisfactory outcomes should be discussed ahead of time especially if requests seem unusual. Over explanation is safer than partial explanation. Informed consent is discussed in Chapter Four.

6. **Document all of the facts.** This is most important. Do not wait until the end of discussions with an unsatisfied client to begin documenting the facts. The

sooner you begin documenting the complaint, the better. Written notes that accurately reflect what was said can be an important part of complaint resolution and your defense in the event of a lawsuit. Maintain copies of all signed forms and receipts. Document all dates and times and the names and relationships of people involved. Some companies log complaints on a form specifically for this purpose. It also includes recording any resolution agreed upon. This form should be retained in the file.

7. **Do not become impatient or curt with the client family when listening to a complaint.** Be open to their questions and comments. Maintain eye contact; remain calm and composed no matter what is said. Allow adequate time to meet with them. Do not allow a complaint to become a lawsuit.

8. **Do not hesitate to use a specialist to assist with particularly challenging situations.** Be honest with yourself in assessing your ability. If, for instance, a restorative arts procedure is especially challenging, consider calling in a specialist. If you are unfamiliar with a family's rituals and customs, talk to their clergyperson or a family member who can explain their customs and rituals. This is a sign of respect. Do not presume to be an expert in everything.

9. **Use interpreters when needed.** In many areas of the country, funeral directors often deal with non-English speaking people. Because of the intricacies and legalities of the business, whenever possible, find an interpreter to help you and the client.

10. **When possible, review the file before responding.** When confronted with a complaint, it is alright to ask for time to review the case file or conduct an

interview of persons involved. Review all notes and documents while they are fresh in your mind. Other important documents associated with the deceased person – for example the embalming-care report – should be completed immediately after the embalming is done...not days later when important details might be forgotten. If questions arise later on, you will have accurate information about the care rendered.

11. **Ask the client family what they would like to have happen to make things right.** You might be surprised to learn that the resolution can be simple and quick.

It is impossible to prevent all claims. But following these guidelines will reduce allegations of negligence and help in defending against such claims. Some client families give you an opportunity to make things right. They can understand. Some will not. To some people, the words, "I am sorry," said and meant genuinely, can be like a soothing balm. I can assure you that avoiding issues raised by a client family, being defensive or arguing **never** keeps a customer! In talking with families that have filed a lawsuit, I have learned that there is a big difference in being disappointed in the *services* provided and being angry at the *attitude* of employees or management as to how they were treated. In many instances, you can diffuse many explosive situations by communicating understanding and compassion while showing a willingness to act.

How a Lawsuit Develops

A client family may feel they have been damaged or harmed and/or have experienced a loss. They might or might not try to contact you to discuss and resolve matters. For whatever reasons - in their opinion - they have not received the service, care or product they feel they deserve. Sometimes the client family never contacts you but instead, seeks an attorney. There can be many variations to the following steps as to how a lawsuit develops, but in general:

1. **A client family consults with an attorney, tells their "story"** and provides their recollection of the facts. This might occur while the remains of the deceased are still in your care, custody and control.

2. **To assess whether or not there is basis for further action, the attorney begins doing research and investigation** in order to gather additional facts, witnesses and evidence. As part of such research and investigation, the plaintiff attorney might take several steps, including but not limited to these:

   a. Collect and review the documents in possession of the client

   b. Obtain the names and telephone numbers of witnesses who might have first-hand knowledge of events and speak with them

   c. Have investigators take tape-recorded / video-taped statements of your employees, witnesses and others involved in the handling of the deceased

   d. Video-tape or photograph the remains of the deceased during the time the situation of a potential claim is occurring

   e. Have samples taken for forensic analysis of the materials before you know of a potential claim

   f. Speak with other attorneys experienced in such cases

   g. Speak with an industry expert

   h. Research legal sources for recent or similar cases

3. **Prior to filing the lawsuit, the attorney might send a *Letter of Demand*** to the funeral-cremation provider, cemetery, et al. This letter outlines the grievance, might ask you to identify your insurer and policy limits and might or might not demand from you an amount of money to resolve the grievance. The letter also demands that the recipient contact the attorney directly.

4. **Either with a demand letter or not, eventually the lawsuit is prepared and filed with the court.** It names the organization, company and individuals being sued (defendants) and the names of the client family members (plaintiffs). When filed, the lawsuit becomes a matter of public domain and becomes available to reporters and others who monitor court filings.

5. **Before a process server delivers or "serves" a copy of the lawsuit to each defendant, your first contact might be a call from a news organization about the lawsuit they just picked up from their independent monitoring of court filings.** If not, your first notice beyond client complaints, or lawyers' inquiry letters or demand letters, may be when you are "served" with the Summons and Complaint.

Steps in a Lawsuit

The legal system in our country is based on the adversary system that allows opposing parties to present their case to a third party (jury or judge) who is hoped to be impartial, when he/she renders a verdict or decision. When a lawsuit is filed, it does not automatically mean there will be a trial. The majority of lawsuits are settled before the trial. Disputes might be resolved any time along the timeline of the life of the claim:

1. Before legal action is filed
2. After legal action is filed in court
3. While a trial is in process but before the judge or jury renders a decision
4. After a trial-court verdict has been rendered but before the defendant files an appeal

Settlement is a legal stratagem that allows a case to be terminated without trial, usually on payment of a certain amount of money to the aggrieved person or plaintiff. **Only if your policy specifically provides for it,** you, as defendant, may have a right to consent or refuse to consent to a settlement. Generally, the insurer controls the suit, unless their policy specifically provides that right, unless there is either a **reservation of rights,** conflict of interest in the defense of the case between the insurer and insured, or in a situation in which the damages are in excess of all available policy limits, or the kind of incident is not covered by insurance (in a situation where an "intentional" act occurred, such as where an employee may be involved in necrophilia-related molestation of the body). **It is important to know your insurance policy on this point, before you are sued.** In most instances, there is little disagreement between you and your attorney as to whether a settlement should be made or you should proceed to trial.

Types of Legal Cases

Legal cases are identified as either civil, criminal or administrative. **Administrative cases** involve a government licensing agency pursuing a claim that might result in the loss of the license of the organization or an individual for their handling of one or a series of complaints about how remains of a decedent were handled. There might or might not be fines associated with the conduct or pattern-practices of the organization. **Criminal cases** involve the enforcement of laws by the government in most situations. In a criminal case, you can lose your freedom by being placed in jail or prison and might or might not be fined. There are occasions when funeral-cremation-cemetery cases are tried in criminal court; however most cases take place in civil courts where plaintiffs seek financial compensation for damages. This kind of money damage case may seek to recover one or more of the three kinds of damages available for plaintiffs:

1. **Economic damages** are purely monetary expenses, such as for the cost of exhumation, re-burial, reimbursement for the costs of funeral services, etc.

2. **Non-economic damages** are for the pain and suffering of the family members when, for example, they

experienced viewing of poorly handled-prepared remains or bungled funeral services.

3. **Punitive damages** are an amount of money awarded to "punish" or "deter" the defendant(s) from such conduct as is thought to have been done with "malice, oppression or fraud" in some states.

Early Stages of a Lawsuit

There are variations to the following steps in a lawsuit depending on state jurisdiction and state and federal laws. In general they are simplified as:

1. The Complaint
2. The Summons
3. The Answer
4. Dismissal attempts
5. Discovery – the basics
6. The Mechanics of Discovery
7. Setting of Trial Date
8. Settlement attempts
9. Trial Preparation
10. Jury Selection
11. Opening Statements
12. Presentation of Evidence
13. Closing Arguments
14. Jury Instructions
15. The Verdict

1. *The Complaint.* This document lists the allegations, why the defendant is responsible, how your firm's performance fell below the standard of care and asks for damages. The Complaint might be very general in its allegations, providing only enough detail to inform the defendant of the nature of the claim. The Complaint can also be very detailed, setting forth allegations or facts that will inflame others reading it. During subsequent phases of the litigation process,

more specific details will be brought to light during the "discovery" phase of the case. But, by themselves, allegations listed in the Complaint do not win lawsuits. Regardless of the number of allegations listed, plaintiffs bear the responsibility to produce evidence proving their case and supporting their demand for damages.

2. ***The Summons.*** The complaint, along with the summons, is served on the defendant in the lawsuit. A summons is a written order requiring the defendant to answer the plaintiff's complaint. Among other things, it contains the case number assigned by the court, names of each defendant and plaintiff and **specifies a period of time in which you, as the defendant must file a responsive pleading.** This means that you must be very prompt in tendering your defense to your insurer and/or arrange to have your attorney (or those hired by the insurer) to file the paperwork with the court in a timely manner.

3. ***The Answer.*** This document usually sets forth a general denial of the allegations and might also set forth "affirmative defenses" as are appropriate for the given case. **Defendants must provide answers within the time limit or plaintiffs can win the case by obtaining a judgment against you by default.** The law usually requires an answer between 20 to 30 days from the date the Summons and Complaint are served, depending on which state the case was filed in or whether you are in federal court. This does **not** mean that you should wait 20 to 30 days to act. **The lawsuit will not go away on its own.** It is critical that your insurance company and/or attorney be notified immediately so (insurance) defense can be arranged. Insurance companies have been successful in many states in obtaining court approval to deny a defense or

coverage when not notified on a timely basis. Without insurance defense, your own personal attorney must be notified to ensure a timely answer and defense on your behalf.

4. Dismissal attempts. After the defense attorney has discussed the case with you and conducted his/ her own research, even including discussions with plaintiff's attorney, your defense counsel might or might not choose to use one of several methods of defending you by way of pleadings filed with the court to seek an early dismissal of the case. For example, your attorney might or might not seek to file a motion to strike, a demurrer or motion to dismiss. Depending on the case, your attorney might see the benefit for a **motion for summary judgment**, stating there is no triable issue of fact remaining to be resolved or that some legal ground bars the suit from getting to trial. Your attorney might also see the benefit of filing a **motion for judgment on the pleadings or motion to dismiss** the entire case as the specifics of your case dictate. If a motion is granted the proceedings in the lower court will terminate. However, it is probable that the losing party (and sometimes both parties) will appeal the decision to a higher court.

Middle Stages of a Lawsuit

5. Discovery – the basics. If the motions are not granted, the process of **discovery** by each side begins. Think of this as the formal, binding method of obtaining testimonial evidence from lay and expert witnesses and parties. During the investigative discovery phase, the parties learn about the information the other side has and gather information and evidence on their own for their respective case. Different activities to elicit discovery will be used by attorneys, depending on the case. Discovery is time-consuming. It is critical for your case. This is the very foundation of what will be able to transpire during settlement meetings, arbitration, trial and appeal. In some instances, it can be more important than the trial itself. Based on the strengths and weaknesses of the information and evidence discovered, for instance, it can result in a settlement. In every lawsuit, information is power. Discovery is vital to winning or losing a case. Failure to respond on time during discovery can have devastating consequences for the party who fails to serve their responses within the time limits that govern discovery. In general, the scope of discovery is quite broad. It usually permits the parties to obtain any information that might be considered relevant to the subject matter or information that may lead to discovery of further evidence. What you might feel as being relevant could be much more limited than what a court deems relevant and discoverable. For instance, some information might identify witnesses who have first-hand knowledge of events. In other instances, you might be asked to produce records of other facets of the business or provide information detailing certain processes (such as embalming) that you have done for a number of years. It might include some kind of "business records" including invoices; billings for different services; cell phone records; and all kinds of computerized information. If these things are not organized during the ordinary course of your business, gathering this information can be extremely time-consuming and expensive. **It is strongly recommended that you organize and maintain your records and documents properly.** This will save you much in attorney's fees incurred when searching for old records. Computer files become an added job for your defense counsel, staff and computer experts.

6. *The Mechanics of Discovery.* There are various tools used to obtain valuable information about information the other side has. Depending on what the attorney deems appropriate, discovery might include:

a. Subpoenas for records, documents or other materials

b. Requests for Production of Records and Documents

c. Requests for Inspection of things

d. Interrogatories

e. Depositions of individuals or of the Person(s) Most Knowledgeable about a specific issue or topic – with or without the Production of Records

f. Mental or physical examinations of persons who claim emotional distress

a. Subpoenas for records, documents or things concern the service of a subpoena or court order to produce such items as specified in the subpoena. This requires a timely response and a verification or signature on an oath that the documents produced are responsive to the request. This kind of device can be received during a suit in which you are a party or when an existing suit is probing and exploring for evidence that your company might be in control of **before** the company is brought into the lawsuit. This situation requires great care. It is strongly recommended that you produce documents of this nature if you sense that your company might be named within the Complaint after seeking the counsel of your attorney, and perhaps your insurer.

b. Requests for production of records and documents relate to tangible evidence including the **complete** contents of the decedent's file (documents, notes-notations, receipts, signed authorizations, contracts, disclosures, reports, photographs, etc) and might also include company or individual computer records, computer discs, memos, correspondence, invoices and telephone records pertaining to the case. The Evidence Code in many states and in federal court define writings very broadly, so as to include all of the above. Requests for production of documents involve all parties to the lawsuit.

The kinds of information requested from you may be very broad. For example, you might be asked to produce such writings as outside service providers or independent contractors, who might be involved in the case and/or involved in the entire chain of custody of the decedent from the notification of death to disposition and can include cell phone records and security video camera recordings. When the Response to the Requests to Produce is prepared by your defense attorney, someone within the organization other than the in-house attorney will be required to testify that the response is correct by signing an oath or verification. This is a weighty moment: If documents are not produced that should be produced, credibility is delivered to the other side. The testimony of the company is at risk unless the response is full and complete and truthfully responds to the request for document production. Failure to do so sets up the person signing the verification and his/her company for an attack that will likely come from plaintiff's counsel, alleging that things were hidden, evidence was allowed to spoil or evaporate or be destroyed. Should such evidence be destroyed, it usually causes problems within the lawsuit and may create immense consequences beyond the lawsuit itself.

c. Requests for Inspections of Things. This relates to a physical inspection of items deemed pertinent to the lawsuit. This request must be specific and state what exactly is being sought for the inspection. Depending on the nature of the lawsuit, for a funeral home it can mean inspecting specific rooms (chapel areas, entry and exit ways, preparation room, etc.); for a crematory, it can mean inspecting exterior grounds, trash containers, cremation chambers, storage and processing areas, etc.); for a cemetery it can mean inspecting the grounds, equipment storage areas, graves, mausoleum crypts, lowering devices, etc.).

d. Interrogatories are a formal set of written questions prepared by the attorney that require a written response, also under oath. Interrogatories, like Responses to Subpoenas or Requests for Production, are a form of testimony in their own right. Interrogatories must be treated seriously. Responses to questions posed can be used as evidence against the answering party. Therefore, it is important to take one's time in reviewing the questions or interrogatory, and thinking of how each response will appear to the jury. Interrogatories are helpful in providing details such as dates, times, locations, specific actions taken, naming witnesses, ascertaining legal positions, opinions and contentions. However, they are exacting and time-consuming. A sufficient period of time must be afforded for a response that might also require assistance from your own attorney in preparing the answers. There is no opportunity for a follow-up question to the answer and if a question is poorly asked, it often elicits a poor or meaningless answer. In federal court, and some states, there is a requirement that the party supplement their answers if new information is learned that should be added to the answer. In some states, "follow-up" interrogatories may be asked that specifically require the party to add new information to update the answers.

e. A deposition is oral testimony taken before trial takes place in the presence of a court reporter, who makes a verbatim transcript of everything that is said during the deposition. Depositions might or might not be videotaped. Where appropriate, the deposition might be taken by telephone, satellite or internet camera. Such videotaped depositions are admissible at trial. Your own facial expressions and demeanor are more readily perceived by a jury from video-recorded deposition than if the deposition was taken without such a recording. Attorneys for the respective parties in the case are almost always present. When your deposition is taken, you should insist that your own attorney be present to help guide you. But, more significant is that the attorney might make objections to questions and instruct you not to answer certain kinds of offensive questions, such as ones that invade the right of privacy, attorney-client or trade secret privileges. A deposition usually takes place at one of the attorney's offices, court reporter's office or your own office.

Your deposition, or that of one of your employees, is just as important as responding to interrogatories - and demands for production of documents and/or subpoenas for records. **During your deposition, you are the central focus of the attorneys.** While you might feel you are the star of the show, this is a very important event that demands adequate preparation of you and your attorney well before you enter the deposition room. During the deposition, you will receive very little help from your attorney since he/she cannot tell you what to say. If depositions are not taken, it makes it more difficult for attorneys to represent their clients.

A deposition is the heart of the case for several reasons:

- It is the opportunity for the other attorneys (including your own) to evaluate the strengths/ weaknesses of the person, face-to-face.

- It is taken under oath.

- The deponent is subject to cross-examination by *all* counsel present for the deposition.

- It is helpful in establishing favorable evidence for either side of the case.

- It "locks in" adverse or harmful testimony against the defense.

Advantages to taking a deposition include:

- It is an effective questioning opportunity for both sides.

- It obtains the deponent's personal knowledge.

- Documents, photos and other things can be shown and interpreted by the witness.

- It uncovers credibility of witnesses (either their believability or lack thereof) and their demeanor.

- It preserves testimony of helpful witnesses (in the event witnesses change their testimony or are "unavailable" by death, illness or distance from being able to attend the trial).

Disadvantages to taking a deposition include:

- They are expensive and time-consuming because of attorney's fees, your time and the cost of the transcript and/or video of the deposition.

- There is generally no control over their duration except in federal court, other than a reasonable amount of time.

- Witness fees and other expenses might be involved.

- While a deposition elicits only deponents' personal knowledge, it might also educate opposing counsel of policies and procedures that are generally known but not specifically utilized by the witness – leading to additional witnesses being deposed.

- It preserves testimony of adverse witnesses.

f. **Mental or physical examinations** might take place if a party's mental or physical condition is at issue in the litigation. This usually only involves the plaintiff(s) rather than the defendant(s). Because claims of mental anguish and emotional distress are often part of funeral-cremation-cemetery litigation – along with treatment bills from mental health providers – your counsel might call for an examination by a psychologist or psychiatrist. Material revealed in psychological-psychiatric examination is **not** confidential and may be revealed at trial.

Last Stages of a Lawsuit

7. *Setting of trial date.* Depending on the jurisdiction, a **trial date** is assigned at some point in the case. All discovery must be completed before the trial. All motions that dispose of the case are required to be filed and heard at specific dates before the trial. Generally, some time between the early and middle stages of a lawsuit, a trial **date** will be assigned to the court's calendar. In federal court, this is done through a Scheduling Conference; a Scheduling Order sets forth all appropriate dates for trial, settlement conference, discovery cutoffs, last dates to hear discovery motions and last dates to hear "dispositive motions." Depending on jurisdiction and the volume of other cases on the court's calendar, the trial date can be several months to a year or more away. The process of discovery and conflicts of time with attorneys or the parties involved can cause delays or prompt re-scheduling from the original date.

8. *Settlement attempts.* A **settlement conference** is frequently requested prior to trial and, in some jurisdictions, is often ordered to occur by the court. The purpose is to ensure that good-faith efforts to settle the case have taken place prior to committing the court's resources to the trial. A judge, who meets with both

parties and their attorneys, will actively participate to get the parties to a negotiated settlement by suggesting compromises. Some attorneys and insurers are taking advantage of Alternate Dispute Resolution (ADR) methods. This usually involves mediation or settlement meetings before an agreed-upon mediator who helps facilitate the Mediation. Some courts mandate that the parties mediate before attending any of the mandatory settlement conferences set to occur at the court. Such settlement conferences are important to prepare for properly. They usually require the parties or the representatives controlling whether money will be paid. The negotiation determines how much will be paid. It is always a good idea for you to attend personally, even though your insurer also attends. This might, at times, require your own participation, even if you have insurance attorneys defending you. Such situations usually involve a reservation of rights, conflict of interest in the defense of the case between the insurer and insured, or a situation in which the damages are in excess of all available policy limits or when the kind of incident is not covered by insurance (ie., such as in a situation where an intentional act occurred or if punitive damages are at issue).

9. **Trial preparation.** Both you and your employees should expect to spend considerable time and energy on preparation before the trial even begins. This usually involves time spent on your own reviewing the discovery responses, records, photos, and other evidence, along with deposition transcripts of the testimony of witnesses and parties. Trial preparation also involves working with the attorney on issues that need to be raised in your defense, and those that you must be ready to defend against. It also should involve discussion of the jury pool from which jurors are selected, should you or your employees know of peculiarities known to the community about the company and involved parties, including the plaintiffs. You and

your employees will likely have been more sensitive to the on-going reports of developments in the community and in the news. Your assistance in gathering this kind of information is important to your attorney's preparation for jury selection.

10. *Jury Selection.* In a jury case, **jury selection** comes from people in the local area who are asked to be fair and impartial to hear the case. From a panel of a number (40 to 80, or more) of potential jurors, the attorneys and judge have the right to question prospects about their background, employment, education, knowledge of the case at hand, prior experiences, and more. The goal is to determine bias or other factors that might indicate an inability to be fair. During jury selection, there is usually an opportunity for your attorney to use preemptory challenges. These are generally few in number (two to four) that allow your attorney to dismiss from the panel potential jurors who have been through the questioning during jury selection. You might have developed feelings or observed things during trial which could be helpful to your attorney. Your participation, or that of the company representative designated to attend the trial, can be of great benefit to the attorney and your defense. How and when to pass on information you have about the prospective juror(s) should be worked out between you and your attorney well in advance of jury selection.

11. *Opening statements.* These provide each attorney with the opportunity to present a description of the case, a preview of the evidence and basic issues of the case to the jury. While it is not to be an opportunity to argue the case to the jury, several attorneys have told me some research indicates that if jurors have not made up their minds about the case by the time jury selection has ended, many will have made up their minds about

the case by the end of opening statements – despite admonitions from the court to the contrary and swearing that they will not pre-judge the case until it has been delivered to them for actual jury deliberation. **Note:** In some jurisdictions, the defendant's attorney may choose to delay his or her opening argument until the plaintiff's attorney has finished presenting the plaintiff's case-in-chief. In other words, the defense attorney may elect to stage his or her opening statement immediately before presentation of the defendant's case-in-chief. This approach is the exception rather than the rule. Your attorney should offer you a cogent and compelling rationale for choosing to delay his or her opening statement.

12. ***Presentation of Evidence.*** During this stage of the trial, the plaintiff's attorney goes first and presents their case-in-chief with what should be legally admissible testimony from witnesses and exhibits for admission into evidence. Each side may retain their own **expert witnesses.** Experts are people who have special knowledge, training and experience in the matters of the case. For example, an experienced crematory operator, funeral director, embalmer, or cemeterian, among others, is asked (and often paid for his/her time and knowledge) to provide to the jury or judge expert testimony about specific aspects of the case. This kind of testimony provides the basis for the jury to know, for example, the standard of care and whether it was or was not met in a given situation. The plaintiff has the burden to provide evidence to support his/her claims. Defendant's attorney might or might not, at the end of the plaintiff's case-in-chief, ask the judge to dismiss the case if it appears insufficient evidence has been presented by plaintiff's attorney. After plaintiff's attorney has presented his/her case, the defendant's

attorney must then present the defendant's case-in-chief by presenting the testimony of the defense witnesses and such documentary and other evidence to disprove the claims made against them, and proves the defendant's Affirmative Defenses.

13. **Closing Arguments.** Once all sides of a case complete their case-in-chief, each party to the case is entitled to then present **closing arguments** to the jury. This is a final attempt to influence the jury by reviewing the evidence and trying to persuade the jury to vote for their client's position. Closing arguments can be made before or after the judge reads the jury instructions to the jury.

14. **Jury Instructions.** These are provided by the judge, informing the jurors of applicable laws pertaining to the case and how they might apply the facts in reaching a verdict. Your attorneys will have met with other counsel and argued about which of the instructions are appropriate for use in the given case.

15. **The Verdict.** In a jury trial, the jurors reach a **verdict** after the case is submitted to them for deliberation. This is after the jury has heard testimony, seen all the evidence and exhibits, heard arguments of the attorneys and been instructed regarding applicable laws by the judge. In most civil cases, the judge normally decides as to the number of jurors who must agree to reach a verdict. In a private room, members of the jury discuss the case among them and deliberate the facts to reach a consensus. Their decision is presented to the judge in open court. In a trial before a judge, the judge takes the closing arguments (orally or in writing) and then issues the decision from the bench, or more likely in writing some days/weeks after the case has been submitted for decision.

Alternate Dispute Resolution (ADR) - Other Ways to Decide Disputes

For the purpose of avoiding court - the most time-consuming and costly way of resolving disputes – more and more businesses look to implement in their funeral purchase agreements and contracts that, in the event of any dispute, the parties agree to settle disputes through **mediation or arbitration.** Before implementing any ADR provision in your funeral purchase agreement forms or contracts, consult with an attorney. As you do with all service and merchandise selections contained in a contract, any ADR clause should be disclosed to the client family during the arrangement conference.

Having an ADR clause is no guarantee that a lawsuit will not develop, nor does it guarantee that the costs for resolving disputes will be low. While it can help on the defense side, **more importantly it provides the mechanism for the client family to stay in communication with the funeral-cremation-cemetery provider.**

Fresno, California, trial attorney David Overstreet refers to this mechanism as the "golden opportunity of risk-management, to seize upon this opportunity to settle potential claims before they grow into something else." Overstreet goes on to say, "that besides damage control, ADR is even the opportunity for the funeral-cremation-cemetery provider to use the contract terms to implement improved relations and word-of-mouth advertising with that client family."

There are three ways to consider implementing an Alternate Dispute Resolution:

1. Informal Discussions
2. Mediation
3. Arbitration

1. As a good faith, first-step effort to resolve the controversy, an **informal discussion** takes place among representatives of the parties who have the **authority to bind their respective party to an agreement.**

2. If the parties can not reach agreement through informal discussions, the parties agree to **mediation**. In mediation, a neutral-intermediary, or mediator, is mutually-agreed upon and selected. If the parties are unable to mutually agree to a mediator, parties agree to petition the local court for an appointment of a mediator. The parties appear at the mediation with individuals who have the **full authority** to enter into a full and final settlement of the dispute. Any settlement of the dispute will be written down and signed by the parties to become an enforceable contract.

3. In the event informal discussions and mediation fails to resolve a controversy, **arbitration** takes place. Arbitration can be binding or non-binding. In binding arbitration, any and all arbitrations are binding, and final. There is often a clause that stipulates that if any party refuses or neglects to appear or to participate in arbitration proceedings after reasonable notice, the arbitrator is empowered to decide the controversy in accordance with whatever evidence is presented by the participating party or parties. Arbitrators are usually retired judges or lawyers. Depending on the case, the arbitrator and rules of arbitration in the jurisdiction, some arbitrations are much less difficult and a less expensive way of resolving a case than going to trial. However, daily fees of $4,000 to $8,000 or more for the arbitrator are not rare. Since arbitration and mediation are usually "private," the names of defendants and details of the settlement are usually not publicly disclosed.

If your case had been actually litigated, the last documents filed will be some kind of dismissal of the case from the court's docket. This ends the court's jurisdiction of the matter unless the court's jurisdiction is reserved for some purpose, such as continuing to enforce the terms of a settlement or court-order for an injunction.

Steps You MUST Take If You Are Sued

Despite your best efforts to satisfy every client family, it is very likely that at some point in your career you will be sued. When it happens, knowledge of basic risk-management procedures for **responding to the lawsuit** can prove critical to protecting your interests and those of all parties that may be involved. **Best Practice** requires the following steps:

1. **Recognize that once served, you have been sued and the lawsuit will not go away by itself**. Be proactive and deal with it immediately. You may feel distress, disbelief and embarrassment. Do not panic and control any feelings of anger.

2. **Carefully read the summons and complaint in private**. Record the date and time it was served. Keep your reactions to yourself, only shared in the confidence of the attorney-client privilege. Remember, there is a specified number of days in which your attorney must file responsive pleadings or file an Answer to the Complaint with the court. Once you have been served, the clock is ticking.

3. **Notify your insurance carrier in writing**. Most insurance policies require a claim to be reported immediately. Not doing so can result in a default judgment and a loss of insurance coverage. The claim might come before you are served with the lawsuit. It may become something you learn of even before you receive notice by a letter or other inquiry from the plaintiff(s), their counsel or investigators. Follow the directions of your insurance company when there are no reservations of rights issued by the insurer in your policy. If you are asked to mail the summons and complaint to their office, mail it via certified mail with a return receipt required. In most cases, your carrier will arrange for a lawyer to represent you and respond with the appropriate papers to the

lawsuit. Be prepared to provide the insurance carrier with the following information:

a. Your name, your title, company name, address, telephone numbers and insurance policy number

b. Name of decedent; date and place and kind/manner of death; date, type and place of disposition of the remains; name(s), address(es) and telephone number(s), facsimile number(s) and email address(es) of the next of kin or person with authority

c. Name of plaintiff's attorney, name of law firm, address and telephone number

d. Date and time you were served.

e. Brief description of the case and your assessment as to the basis of the claim. Also, be prepared for the insurer to have an investigator or claims representative request appropriate documentation from the company and to take tape-recorded statements of the significant employees involved with the case.

4. **Only discuss the lawsuit with your insurance company where there are no reservations of rights and/or the attorney retained by the carrier for your defense where there is no reservation of rights**. Do not discuss it with employees or colleagues at this time even if they may be involved. Do not discuss the case with your spouse. Seek independent counsel if there is any hint the insurer will be reserving rights for the payment of the defense or indemnity (settlement or judgment money paid to resolve claims/cases).

Important: Do not contact the opposing (plaintiff) attorney or any members of the plaintiff family. Any statements or actions can and will most likely be used against you at trial. There is an intuitive desire to want to talk to someone, but unprotected conversations with anyone other than your insurance company and attorney (as noted above) at this time can harm your defense. Conversations with your attorney are protected from being disclosed under attorney-client privilege; all others are subject to discovery. If you communicate with others outside that attorney-client privilege of what was discussed with your attorney, the privilege is potentially lost and the information able to be discovered. **Protect and maintain your privacy regarding all types of communication with your attorneys.**

5. **If you fail to comply with the strong admonition to *not* discuss the case with your spouse or business partner,** caution them not to communicate about the case with anyone else. You do not know who might become involved in the lawsuit and asked to testify.

6. **If you encounter the plaintiff or members of the family away from your office,** be pleasant, professional and polite. Do not confront them or initiate a conversation with them.

7. **Sometimes, plaintiff's attorney will suggest an "off the record" discussion or meeting with you. *Do not do so*.** If such an offer is made, report it to your attorney or insurance company. Refer all discussions to them only. Should you have public-information officers or in-house attorneys, certainly inform them of the lawsuit and the contact made by the opposing counsel. Anything that you may say to opposing counsel or the family, no matter how innocent or well intended, may be misunderstood or misused by them. Additionally, you do not know who will be called to testify and speaking to the wrong people can become a damaging situation.

8. **Retrieve the decedent's case file.** Gather it all, without leaving any source of material behind, so a full and

complete file is preserved. Place it in a separate and secure location. Familiarize yourself with the contents. It is critical that the file is kept in a private place where no one, other than yourself, has access to it at this time. **It is imperative that no changes, alterations, deletions or corrections be made to anything in the file.** Keep all of the contents intact. Plaintiff's attorneys are highly skilled in inspecting documents and records. **Even the appearance that an alteration might have been made can have serious implications for your defense.** An allegation of fraud can become a fact when documents are altered. In reviewing the contents, do not correct misspellings, change words or make any additions or marks to the original file. **Do not destroy any documents.**

9. **Start a totally separate correspondence file concerning the claim/lawsuit.** Handle all legal papers yourself. Do not depend on office staff to do this. **This file should be treated as a confidential, attorney-client communication file.** Record the name, date and time that you reported the claim. Make a photocopy of everything in the decedent's original file and keep the copies and all subsequent claims-related correspondence separate from the original file. All items in the decedent's original file are discoverable and will be requested by plaintiff's attorney. **You do not want correspondence between you, the insurance company or attorney (inadvertently) placed in the original file and discovered by plaintiff's attorney during the inspection of the file.** In the correspondence file, maintain accurate records of all discussions and correspondence you have from this point forward. **Do not release the contents of this file to anyone without approval of your attorney.**

10. **Cooperate fully with your insurer and defense attorney**
in handling the lawsuit. (Consult with independent,
private attorneys should the insurer issue a
reservation of right). Being proactive with them helps
your case. After reporting the claim to your insurance
company, if you do not hear from the assigned
attorney who will represent you in a few days, initiate
proactive follow-up by communicating and/or calling
the insurance company again.

Record in writing your follow-up communications.
The insurer is to assign an attorney who has been
approved by them to work on its cases. But, if they
fail to do so in a timely manner, your record might
preserve rights you will have against the insurer and
provide you the opportunity to ensure the case is
responded to in a timely manner if your insurer fails
to do so. You might also have the right to additional
privately selected counsel to represent you, and at
your own expense, you may also retain a personal
lawyer. There might also be insurance-defense
retained counsel representing the interests of the
insurer, separate from your own private counsel.

The costs of the private counsel under such
circumstances might be borne by the insurer. The
effectiveness of the relationship and your defense
hinges on your total honesty and candidness about all
events surrounding the claim. All conversations with
your attorney are protected as confidential. Under no
conditions should you lie to your attorney. Doing so
can invalidate your coverage. Make yourself available
to your attorney even if it means changing your daily
routine or giving up evenings and weekends. Your
attorney cannot defend you without your help. It
should not surprise you to learn that the attorney
assigned to represent you does not have experience in

funeral-cremation or cemetery matters. The attorney might be unfamiliar with funeral-home procedures, the arrangement-planning process, as well as terms and standards of care pertaining to funeral-cremation service, embalming, funeral, burial, cremation, shipment, cemetery and memorialization. **Just as the attorney will educate you about the legal and lawsuit process, you too, will need to educate the attorney about your business and details of the case.** A spirit of cooperation helps assure the best defense and a smooth working relationship. After familiarizing your attorney with the case, ask about using an expert. Retaining an expert early on can help identify areas of potential concern. Sometimes, it might be necessary to have different experts for different aspects of the case.

11. **Deal with your feelings**. You will be angry and disillusioned at some points along the life of your claim or lawsuit. You might become depressed and even begin doubting yourself. Be prepared for these emotions. Be prepared to handle the additional stress and anxiety the claim has placed on you, your employees and your family. Do not be afraid to address these concerns with your attorney and seek such medical/mental health care as required.

Things You Should NEVER Do When You Are Sued

1. Do not correspond or speak with the complainant family or others who could be called as witnesses.

2. Do not correspond or speak with plaintiff's attorney.

3. Do not discuss the lawsuit with your employees, colleagues or others until instructed to do so by your attorney or without being in the presence of your attorney.

4. Do not change or alter documents or records in your possession.

5. Do not abandon your business or professional responsibilities.

6. Do not abuse alcohol or drugs, especially when trying to cope with the pressures the lawsuit generates.

7. Do not admit guilt or place blame on anyone, other than when in the presence of your own attorney.

8. Do not hold back any information or details about the case from your attorney.

9. Do not place correspondence about the case in the decedent's original file.

10. Do not shy away from involvement with your attorney during your defense.

Basic Courtroom Behavior

For most people, being sued is unsettling. Even if you have visited a courtroom before, appearing as a defendant is altogether different. It can be intimidating and unnerving. The legal process and mechanics of a lawsuit can present a new dimension to a person's life. It can be difficult and harrowing, even for the most mature person, to know that you and your actions are being judged openly and likely in public; to face plaintiff's attorney during a deposition or testimony in court; to sit in front of a jury and listen to witnesses and adverse testimony. Your attorney will do his/her best to prepare you ahead of time for every step in the process.

Best Practice guidelines to follow in court or during a deposition are:

1. **Get plenty of rest** the night before testifying or giving a deposition.

2. **Dress conservatively and professionally.** Keep jewelry and other accessories at a minimum. In particular,

leave earrings, pinky rings and bracelets at home. Cosmetic application should be conservative and minimal.

3. **Arrive early for court appearances,** depositions or inspections. Arrange in advance where to meet your attorney.

4. **Once you enter a courtroom building or place of the deposition, speak *only* to your attorney.** This is not a social visit. You do not know who might be a potential juror, witness, family member or assistant to opposing counsel. Be especially careful with conversations or remarks in any area not made private and free from bystanders who could overhear conversations such as in public restrooms, elevators, cafeterias or parking areas.

5. **Do not act flamboyant, arrogant or flippant.**

6. **Act friendly. Be polite. Be likeable. Be pleasant.** Be optimistically cautious without being "guarded" or paranoid.

7. **Take advice only from your attorney** and do not argue with or confront him/her in public.

8. **Do not be curt, contentious or argumentative** with anyone.

9. **Talk with your attorney about issues of the case** when you are away from other people. Any conversation overheard by anyone is open for jurors and other parties to observe and report to their counsel.

10. **Do not make jokes or any hand or facial gestures.** Do not roll your eyes or show reactions during testimony of other witnesses – even ones you like, let alone the ones you do not.

11. **Be attentive to the proceedings.** Do not doze, scribble or act nervously.

12. **Stay in control at all times.** Do not make any audible or verbal outbursts.

13. **Look at members of the jury,** but make no gestures toward them. Do *not* ogle or stare at jurors. Do *not* attempt to "make eyes" at or flirt with jurors.

14. **Address the judge *only* as "your honor."** Others may be addressed by "Mr.," "Mrs.," "Ms." or "Miss."

15. **Use appropriate grammar, syntax and language.** Avoid use of "slang." Speak slowly and clearly, deliberately and audibly.

16. **Think before answering.** (Read that once more: Think before answering). After being asked a question, pause for a moment before answering it.

17. **Shut off cell phones** and leave pagers in the car.

18. **Do not leave personal items** such as briefcases or notepads lying around.

19. **Do not guess at any answer.** If you do not know, say so.

20. **Only tell the truth, even if it hurts.**

21. **Know what the themes of the case are that are against you** and those that are the basis for your defense. This only comes from working with your attorney.

Choosing an Attorney

As previously mentioned, if you are covered by insurance, an attorney will be assigned to represent you by the insurer. If the claim is not insurance-based or you do not have insurance coverage, it will be necessary for you to retain your own attorney.

It might also be necessary to retain an attorney if the insurance company agrees to defend the claim but states in the insurance policy that it "reserves" its right to cancel coverage.

In many states, insurance companies may deny claims where the defendant is judged to have committed intentional wrongdoing. In such circumstances, an attorney is assigned by your insurance company to represent the case. If employees are interviewed by the attorney to ascertain facts of the case, and employees tell the attorney, "the boss told me to do it," this can be judged as intentional wrongdoing. Under this circumstance, it would be wise to seek the advice of a personal attorney.

Like other professions, law is a diverse field. Deciding what type of lawyer you need is your first consideration. Lawsuits that allege negligence, errors and omissions of professional care - and that involve damages claiming emotional distress - are unique specialties and require competent, experienced defense counsel. You need a seasoned, skilled litigator. Your long-time company counsel probably will not be up to the task unless he / she is an experienced trial attorney.

It is always advisable to interview more than one lawyer before retaining the one you feel most comfortable with. You might not know a defense attorney personally or socially. If you do, you might not feel comfortable in becoming professionally involved with him or her and might decide to look elsewhere. Merely knowing of an attorney socially is perhaps not the best way to select counsel needed to defend you and the company. There are several things you can do to find a defense attorney to handle your case. Bar associations make these suggestions:

1. If you have a corporate attorney, ask for a referral or recommendation.

2. Ask your state association office for a referral. If the association provides insurance to its members, get the name of the insurance company and call the carrier for a referral.

3. Call the city, county or state bar-association office.

4. Contact colleagues in your area that might have had similar experiences. This might help you avoid some less-than-stellar lawyers.

5. Go to a law library and read the book, *O'Brien's Evaluator* or another jury verdicts report such as "Westlaw on Line," which lists all cases in the past 12 months in your state, along with the names of attorneys involved and a brief case description. Search for cases related to funeral-cremation, et.al.

Just because a defense attorney is not experienced or familiar with funeral, cremation or cemetery litigation does not mean he or she will not be capable of providing you with competent defense services. **Choosing a defense attorney to represent you is similar to selecting a physician. The decision should be similar to how a discerning, quality-focused consumer might choose a funeral-cremation provider.** At the end of the day, you want a skilled professional with the human qualities you admire.

Interview the attorney and watch how he/she responds. Does the lawyer show a genuine interest in your case? Is the attorney engaging or does he/she appear preoccupied or distracted? Is it easy to establish rapport? What is your comfort level with this person? Ask about his/her education and any previous experience in professional liability and errors-and-omissions cases. Learn about previous cases litigated and the outcomes of the cases. Does this person communicate clearly? Does he or she appear to be organized? Does the attorney show a willingness to learn about your profession? Do you feel that the two of you can work together in a cooperative effort? Does the attorney have what it takes to competently defend and represent your interests?

Prevention: Your Best Strategy

Some second- third- and fourth-generation funeral-cremation providers say, "My firm has never been sued. We have nothing to worry about." This is not prudent strategy. It is flawed, wishful thinking. Do not think for a moment that you are immune from a lawsuit. Do not mistakenly believe that you are totally protected just because you carry a high limit of insurance coverage. Lawsuits, even those without merit, are stressful and potentially damaging to one's reputation. Funeral-cremation providers and cemeterians are much better off avoiding lawsuits in the first place. Funeral-cremation providers and cemeterians and courtrooms are not a good mix.

Michael Josephson, president of the Josephson Institute and radio commentator, speaks about reducing the risk of legal action, eliminating deception and fraud and promoting trust and responsible behavior by adhering to four basic principles:

1. Trust and credibility are the company's most vital and valuable assets.

2. Assume all critical facts (or mistakes) will eventually be known. Make decisions that support and enhance trust.

3. Avoid any behavior, legal or not, that obscures, conceals, distorts, misrepresents, misleads or otherwise undermines trust.

4. Fulfill your responsibilities with diligence, good professional judgment and an unwavering commitment to honesty, responsibility, fairness and good citizenship.

An atmosphere of trust, respect and open communication represents a win-win scenario for the client family and funeral-cremation-cemetery provider. In talking with people who are dissatisfied, most complaints are simple and straightforward. Any reluctance on your part to deal with their issues can be a reason for being served with a lawsuit.

General Questions Concerning Lawsuits

How long does a lawsuit take?

In most states and most courts, a trial can be scheduled within a year after the filing of the lawsuit. Depending on the state, the jurisdiction of the court, as well as the zeal of the attorneys, the range of time can be extreme, from less than a year to as much as five years. If the case is appealed, the time may double. Some states have laws that may also allow for an extension, or continuance of the trial.

What is a verdict?

A verdict means the case has gone to trial and the jury has made a decision as to whether or not you met standards of care or fell below standards of care. If you fell below the standards of care, the verdict will also determine whether you caused an injury; and finally, the amount of money damages you will pay as a result of the injury. Whether the jury must decide by unanimous vote or simple or two-thirds majority, is decided by the jurisdiction of the court. How many jurors will be selected to hear the case is normally set by state statute. For instance, in Federal Court there are six jurors. But, in California and some other states, to conserve on the time it takes to select a jury, some counties are seeking to have the parties stipulate to smaller juries than those made of twelve, plus one or two more alternate jurors.

What can I tell my attorney?

Tell your attorney everything you know about the case. Anything you tell your attorney is privileged and cannot be disclosed to any third party by your attorney. Tell your attorney about any problems that may exist regarding the case or any problems that may exist with other people who are also named as defendants in the case. **What your attorney does not know can hurt you.**

What is an expert witness, and can I participate in the selection of a defense expert witness on my behalf?

Yes, you can participate in the selection of an expert witness. An expert witness is a person, who by reason of education or specialized experience, is allowed to testify at a trial. The expert may testify about the facts of the case and also about the professional conclusions he/she draws from the facts. Medical, scientific and technical experts are commonly used, but other types of experts can be used depending upon the facts of the case.

Attorney David Overstreet explains the parameters when an expert witness is called: "To be able to express an expert opinion, one does not have to be certified, or go through a certification hearing. Usually the foundation is presented about the qualifications of the person, so that they have testified that they have special knowledge, skill, experience, training or education on a certain issue. Then, if the issues are sufficiently beyond the common experience of people (the jury), the opinion must be helpful for the trier of fact (judge and jury) to hear such an expert opinion."

Overstreet goes on to say, "But, if challenged, there can be a hearing to determine if (1), if the issue is sufficiently beyond the common experience of people generally; and, (2), whether the particular person has the qualifications for rendering such an opinion, including upon what the person based their opinion. If so, then the court may "certify" the person as an expert for that particular case, on that particular issue. If one failed to gain the court's approval, then the court may have ruled that the expert was prohibited from rendering opinions, or be disqualified from testifying."

Your defense expert witness cannot be a relative or person you have regular contact with. Your attorney may not ask you about expert witnesses, but it is important for you to remember that this is **your** case. If you know a person who is a leader in the field and makes a good witness, tell your attorney. Participate with your attorney in your defense from the beginning to the end.

Should I ever consider hiring my own personal attorney?

You should consider hiring your own personal attorney if it appears there might be a verdict in excess of your policy limits and/or the insurance carrier reserves rights. It is wise to have your personal attorney review the case and provide you with an independent determination as to your exposure. You should also consider hiring a personal attorney if it appears you are receiving ineffective representation from the lawyer furnished by the insurance company, or if you need another attorney to help negotiate a settlement.

How does being sued affect my insurance premiums?

Insurance companies profit from collecting premiums. They do not like to pay settlements or judgments. You have certain contractual rights with your insurance carrier while you are insured. More than likely, you can expect your premium rates to increase. In some instances, your insurance company can deny renewing coverage upon expiration of the dates of coverage. **Since the costs of defending cases are often many times more than one year's insurance premium, having insurance coverage is a very wise risk management, loss prevention method to conserve your assets and the company's resources.**

What are some personal issues I need to be aware of if I am ever sued?

No question – lawsuits are stressful. You will likely feel shock, anger, disbelief, perhaps fear, sleeplessness, anxiety and possibly have bouts of depression. You might feel physical as well as psychological symptoms. Lawsuits are not resolved overnight; they usually take two or more years to be settled, tried or otherwise brought to conclusion. During this period of time and the stages of the lawsuit, there are deadlines scheduled and deadlines missed; events are postponed and need to be rescheduled; people may become ill, move or otherwise be unable to appear for depositions, and more. Each time you revisit the case after being away from it for a period, you might experience distress all over again. You might notice that some business relations change and that you will lose a sense of trust in many areas of life. It is not unusual to experience a slump in vitality in promoting your business or participating in sport activities. A lawsuit can affect your most personal relationships with your wife and children, as well as attending holiday gatherings with relatives. You might lose your appetite and have difficulty sleeping. Your sex life might not be the same as it was before the lawsuit. Social functions may not be as enjoyable as they once were. You may be guarded and feel humiliated.

Should I ever seek professional help?

For a caregiver and personal-service provider, a lawsuit

is a difficult emotional experience. Do not underestimate the possible negative impact it can have on your emotional well being. A lawsuit is a very appropriate reason to seek professional help. If fear or depression has begun to affect your personal or professional life, it is time to reach out for support. Counseling can be lifesaving.

What can I do to prepare for my testimony?

Become an expert about your case. Discuss with your attorney how much expertise you need to acquire. While you do not want to educate the opposing lawyer during your deposition, you need to be knowledgeable about the case at hand and be able to educate your attorney as much as possible. You want to come across as a likeable, knowledgeable witness. You should try to be the most knowledgeable person in the case about funeral-cremation service or the cemetery. Some juries will often equate your knowledge of the case and your concern with details with your care and concern for the bereaved. Knowledge is power and the more familiar you are with all aspects of the case, the more comfortable you will be when you are questioned.

How important are diet, relaxation, exercise and other wellness techniques?

These things are more important now than ever before in your life. If possible, pamper yourself with nutritious, satisfying foods. Spend time with people you feel comfortable with.

Are juries influenced by how I look, dress, talk and act?

Most definitely. Your attorney will advise you about these things ahead of time. In general, dress conservatively. Wear clothes that fit and be properly groomed. Leave expensive watches and flashy jewelry at home. Acting arrogantly is the kiss of death. When you give testimony, look the jurors in the eye and talk to them, not as a funeral director, but as a human being; choose your words carefully and always use professional language, not slang. Be polite and maintain your composure at **all** times. Avoid making disturbing, inappropriate facial expressions or noises.

Michael W. Kubasak

Mike has a life long career in funeral service. Born and raised in Chicago, Illinois, where his father and mother owned a funeral home, he moved to Burbank, California in 1955 where his parents started The Valley Funeral Home. With his brother, Mike became the owner in 1972. In 1997 Mike sold the funeral home but remained active with the business. Known as the "funeral director's coach," he is president of Kubasak Associates Inc., a management performance and personal coaching-consulting company for funeral-cremation service and allied industries.

Mike is a licensed funeral director, embalmer and a certified crematory operator. He is a graduate of the California College of Mortuary Science and attended Arizona State University. He is a member of the National Funeral Directors Association, International Cemetery, Cremation and Funeral Association; National Hospice Association; a member of the Board of Advisors for Cypress College Department of Mortuary Science.

Mike is a recipient of the coveted Pursuit of Excellence "Eagle" Award from the National Funeral Directors Association. He is the author of the best-selling book, *Cremation and the Funeral Director - Successfully Meeting the Challenge*. Mike lectures nationwide and coaches funeral service professionals and personal service businesses about leadership, innovation and personal service in the marketplace, liability exposure and risk reduction, new product and service development, and creating value for the consumer. A frequent contributor to funeral service publications, Mike publishes the *Kubasak Line*, an electronic newsletter sent to funeral-cremation providers and businesses worldwide. With his background and experience, Mike also serves as an expert witness in funeral, cremation and cemetery litigation cases.

Mike and his wife of 38 years live in Mesquite, Nevada, and have two daughters.

William M. Lamers, Jr., M.D.

Dr. Lamers was born and raised in Milwaukee, Wisconsin, where he attended Marquette University and graduated from the Marquette University School of Medicine. Following internship in San Francisco he completed a residency in psychiatry at Cincinnati General Hospital followed by a fellowship in child psychiatry. During the Viet Nam war he served in the U.S. Naval Medical Corps at the U.S. Naval Hospital, Oakland. He practiced psychiatry in Marin County and taught on the clinical faculty of the University of California Medical School in San Francisco.

In the early 1950s, he assisted in researching and writing *The History of American Funeral Directing*. In 1965 he became a consultant to NFDA which led to involvement in funeral service seminars in all areas of the country. He became active in the International Work Group on Dying, Death and Bereavement and researched customs related to dying and death in a number of foreign countries. This interest led to him founding the Hospice of Marin, one of the earliest hospice programs in the United States.

Dr. Lamers has written and co-authored numerous books, chapters and papers in the fields of medicine, psychiatry, child psychiatry, hospice, thanatology and funeral service. He testified on behalf of funeral service before the Federal Trade Commission. His paper, "Death, Grief, Mourning, the Funeral and the Child" served to define the value of children being involved in funeral services. His paper, "Funerals are Good for People, M.D.s Included," was published in a medical magazine that was distributed to every doctor in the United States. He edited and published the book by Michael W. Kubasak, *Cremation and the Funeral Director: Successfully Meeting the Challenge*.

Because of his extensive experience in psychiatry and his work with dying and bereaved persons plus his experience as a medical-legal expert in many criminal cases, Dr. Lamers has been called as an expert witness in numerous individual and class action cases involving funeral, burial and cremation issues.

Dr. Lamers resides in southern California.

Emotional Distress

By William M. Lamers, Jr., M.D.

A century ago, people rarely sued providers of funeral and burial services. Cremation was a rarity. Shipment of human remains was uncommon. Times have changed and funeral service, like other professions that serve a demanding public, is not exempt from lawsuits. Some claims for damages related to the conduct of a funeral, burial or cremation are justified. Others are not. Today, experts from disciplines outside of funeral service are often used to evaluate claims for damages and to explain to a jury the validity or lack of basis of the claims. The process of arriving at a just resolution is often complex, costly and time consuming.

Trials evolved over the centuries to help determine the guilt or innocence of persons accused of a crime. Anthropologists inform us that in earlier civilizations trial by 'ordeal' was common. In such trials, the accused swallowed a solution prepared by the shaman or medicine man. The solution contained an irritating substance that was toxic to the nerves controlling the beating of the heart. The accused person was instructed to swallow the liquid in front of the senior members of the tribe. If the accused sipped the solution slowly, as the elders believed a guilty person would do, sufficient toxin was absorbed through the upper gastrointestinal tract to stop the heart, and the subject died. This was interpreted as evidence of guilt. However, if the accused swallowed the solution rapidly, as the elders believed an innocent person would do, the accused would reflexively vomit all the toxin before it could be absorbed, and survive.

Witnesses

There are usually two major types of witnesses: **fact witnesses** and **expert witnesses**. Fact witnesses are used to help determine the facts of the matter. They testify as to what they know, what they observed, heard or otherwise sensed. Expert witnesses have special knowledge, expertise and training in some field that has relevance to the case at hand. After becoming acquainted with the facts of the case, they conduct examinations, examine evidence and make use of their specialized knowledge, experience and background to provide evaluations, opinions, and prognosis.

During the 1970s, the Justice Department encouraged the use of expert witnesses to help clarify issues in a case that were deemed to be too complex for the average juror. A number of states have now set standards for the use of expert witnesses. Massachusetts established the Briggs Rule that led to the hiring of expert witnesses by the court rather than by plaintiffs or defense attorneys. In Chicago, one judge allowed jurors to question experts themselves to help clarify confusing testimony. The American Medical Association proposed barring experts who were hired on a contingency basis.

Expert Witnesses

The use of expert witnesses in funeral, burial and cremation litigation is now fairly common. The account of a case involving a funeral home in Milwaukee, Wisconsin, serves as an introduction to the subject of emotional distress and the use of expert witnesses. In February, 1994, the Wisconsin Appellate Court considered a case (Holsen v Prasser-Kleczka) involving claims for emotional distress following the mix-up of bodies. By a 2-1 vote, the court denied plaintiff claims for emotional distress. The Appellate Court ruled:

> It is outside the realm of the assumed ordinary experience of the jurors for them to be able to determine without expert testimony which, if any, of these alleged symptoms were caused by the conduct of the funeral home rather than as a natural consequence of the trauma that generally results from the loss of a loved one, and the other circumstances of the plaintiff's lives.

Further details of the case are revealed in a story that appeared in the Milwaukee Journal on February 22, 1994:

A funeral home that placed the wrong man in the casket is not obligated to compensate the man's family for the anguish that the family said it suffered, the Wisconsin Court of Appeals ruled Tuesday by a vote of 2-1.

When the family of Charles Holsen, Sr., arrived at the Prasser-Kleczka funeral home, 3275 S. Howell Ave., on August 28, 1989, they found that it was not Holsen in the casket. The error was not discovered until 15 minutes before the scheduled public viewing of the body, so the casket was closed.

It turned out that Holsen, of Milwaukee, had been buried a day earlier by the funeral home. The family at the earlier funeral had never noticed the mistake. The funeral home eventually had to dig up the first grave and make a switch.

Appeals Court Judge Ralph Adam Fine and Michael T. Sullivan ruled Tuesday that the family's lawsuit against the funeral home should not be allowed to go forward because the family failed to provide expert testimony on how they were affected by the discovery. In making that ruling, Sullivan and Fine upheld a dismissal of the case by the late Milwaukee County Circuit Judge Joseph P. Callan.

The six family members claimed that because of the error, they suffered such symptoms as extreme anger, obsessive thoughts about the funeral, nightmares, weight gain, paranoia, headaches, diarrhea, frequent colds, and, as one son said, "feeling guilty because he lied to people as to why the casket at his father's funeral was closed."

The two judges said: "We conclude that it is outside the realm of the assumed ordinary experience of the jurors for them to be able to determine without expert testimony which, if any, of these alleged symptoms were caused by the conduct of the funeral home rather than as a natural consequence of the trauma that generally results from the loss of a loved one, and the other circumstances of the plaintiff's lives."

"The plaintiffs have not submitted an affidavit or any statement under oath by a qualified expert witness linking their alleged physical or emotional illnesses to the funeral home's actions," the judges said.

Appeals Court Judge Charles B. Schudson dissented, saying:

"Expert testimony is unlikely to define where death-stress stops and corpse-mishandling stress begins. Would a jury really be incapable of assessing the credibility of witnesses and weighing the evidence in order to demarcate the line between death-stress and corpse-mishandling-stress?"

There is a certain amount of tension associated with a funeral service, even when all goes as planned. It is a time of heightened sensitivity, especially on the part of the bereaved family. Minor mishaps that might be overlooked under other circumstances can be misinterpreted as disrespect or an affront or even as an insult or breach of contract. It is easy to understand how a mishap might serve to aggravate grief.

Plaintiffs might associate unpleasant incidents that occur during or shortly after the funeral with normal feelings of grief that accompany the death of a loved one.

Incidents that occur at some time following the course of the funeral, burial and cremation might serve to reawaken and perhaps even intensify feelings of loss and grief that may have been quiescent. Even the development and filing of a formal complaint (lawsuit) can be a source of stress for a bereaved person.

Determining the validity of a claim for emotional distress is often a complex process. In this chapter, we will look at the factors that contribute to both emotional distress and normal grief. Grief is usually stressful. Yet not all stress experienced at the time of death is due to grief.

The decision of the Wisconsin Appellate Court in Holsen v Prasser-Kleczka affirms the need for expert testimony to aid the Court (jurors) in differentiating between emotional distress caused by the conduct of funeral practitioners and the normal grief (trauma) that generally results from the loss of a loved one.

The decision highlights the need to identify and consider "other circumstances" in the plaintiff's life that may affect or influence the validity of a claim for damages based on emotional distress.

It is essential, therefore, to have a person skilled in performing psychological examinations and evaluations carefully review the multiple dimensions of the plaintiff's life - physical, social, psychological and spiritual - to discern any influences that might affect the validity of a claim for emotional distress **secondary** to learning of alleged irregularities in the funeral-burial-cremation sequence of a loved one.

Role of the Expert Witness

Among other things, the expert witness in funeral, burial and cremation litigation must:

1. Differentiate between normal grief and the emotional distress that developed subsequent to learning of the alleged mishandling.

2. Define and describe normal grief and show its influence on the plaintiff.

3. Define and describe emotional distress secondary to the alleged incident and show how it affected the plaintiff.

4. Show the differing impact of grief and emotional distress on the plaintiff.

In certain cases, experts from other disciplines are called to help clarify crucial issues as well as to offer expert opinions. Forensic anthropologists are sometimes called to examine evidence and testify concerning the identification of human remains. Sociologists with special experience in customs and practices related to dying, death and the care of human remains are sometimes called to provide expert opinions. Dentists and anatomists with special training and experience might also be called to testify regarding the identification of human remains.

When a claim for damages arises out of the actual or alleged mishandling of some aspect of care of a deceased person, the focus is on the impact on the survivor, the one who contracted for the services of a funeral director. Claims for damages might also extend to others who were involved in handling the body - for example the embalmer, the cemeterian and the cremationist.

Claims for damages may include the monetary value of involved services - the cost of the funeral and its various elements - as well as merchandise and materials involved in preparation of the body,

What is Emotional Distress?

The major element of most claims for alleged mishandling during the course of funerals, cremation and disposition fall under the category of **emotional distress** resulting from failure to perform according to the explicit or implicit terms of the funeral contract.

Most claims are based on the assumption that the survivor experienced emotional distress from learning of the alleged mishandling.

The psychological term, "emotional distress" probably means little to the average funeral director. When a plaintiff enters a claim for damages on the basis of emotional distress there is usually an accompanying list of symptoms (anxiety, depression, insomnia, anger and so forth) that expands on the basic claim of emotional distress.

A claim for damages based on emotional distress automatically raises several basic questions that need to be answered:

- **What is the basis of the claim for damages?** Is the description of the incident (an act, or perhaps a failure to act) serious enough to result in the damages as claimed?
- **Is there a reasonable temporal relationship between the incident and the development of symptoms as enumerated in the complaint?**
- **Are the claimed symptoms of distress due to an act or failure to act on the part of the funeral, burial, cremation provider?** Or are the symptoms primarily related to grief over the death of the loved one?
- **Is the plaintiff presenting the symptoms of distress in a straightforward, reasonable manner** or are the symptoms being exaggerated?

These are but a few of the questions that must be addressed whenever a claim for emotional distress made. Each of these questions - plus some related questions - will be examined later in this chapter.

The nexus between what actually happened and the later development of emotional distress is clear and becomes obvious when, for example, the body is lost, when the wrong body is cremated or when something goes awry during the conduct of the funeral, burial or cremation. In these instances, the cause of emotional distress is obvious.

Emotional distress has been called "mental distress," "mental suffering," or "mental anguish." It can result in phenomena such as fright, nervousness, grief, anxiety, worry, mortification, shock, humiliation and indignity, as well as physical pain.

It is important to determine the intensity and duration of the distress. Was it mild or severe? Was it transient or enduring?

Intensity of distress is quantified on a scale from mild to moderate, severe or even excruciating. Intensity is important in litigation as there usually is no monetary compensation (award) for emotional distress rated less than severe by the court. The **duration** of distress can extend from merely transient to persistent or enduring.

Stress and Distress

Stress, in itself, is not always a bad thing. Many persons live with a certain amount of stress because of their occupation, family life, state of health or even their economic situation. Hans Selye, the person who developed the concept of stress in humans, said that up to a certain level, stress can be a good thing; it can help us remain alert and aware of our surroundings. He called this "eu-stress," the prefix 'eu' derived from the Greek word meaning 'good.' However, excessive amounts of stress have been classed as 'distress,' and have been shown to have a negative effect upon physiologic processes.

Psychosocial Stressors

The most commonly used method of evaluating the **intensity** of stressors is to compare them to a scale included in the Diagnostic and Statistical Manual of Emotional Disorders (DSM-IV) developed by the American Psychiatric Association. Following is an example of 'stressors' that are used to provide a basis for evaluating (in adults) both the intensity and duration of psychosocial stressors:

Code Term		Acute Events	Enduring Circumstances
1	**None**	no acute events related to the disorder	no related enduring circumstances
2	**Mild**	breakup with boy or girlfriend; start or graduate from school; child left home	Family arguments; Job dissatisfaction; Residence in high crime neighborhood

3 **Moderate**	Marriage; Marital separation; Loss of job, Retirement; Miscarriage	Marital discord; Serious financial problems; Trouble with boss; Being a single parent
4 **Severe**	Divorce; Birth of first child	Unemployment; Poverty
5 **Extreme**	Death of Spouse; Diagnosis of serious; illness Victim of rape	Severe chronic illness in self or child; Ongoing physical or sexual abuse
6 **Catastrophic**	Death of a child; Suicide of spouse; Devastating natural disaster	Captivity as a hostage; Concentration camp experience
7 **Inadequate Information** or no change in condition	N/A	N/A

Note that the above examples of psychosocial stressors provide a gradation of intensity. Individual variations in response to psychosocial stressors depend on a number of factors including, age, physical health, internal and external sources of support. No two people will react in exactly the same way to the same stressor. Members of the same family often react differently.

If there are direct physical damages or physical injuries of any sort arising from the incident, they should be noted and described in terms of severity and duration. The word 'severe' in the phrase "severe emotional distress" means: substantial or enduring as distinguished from trivial or transitory.

Levels of Stress

Severe emotional distress is: emotional distress of such **substantial quantity** or **enduring quality** that no reasonable person in a civilized society should be expected to endure it. Substantial, in this sense, refers to a considerable rather than a trivial quantity. Enduring refers to a lasting rather than a merely transitory quality.

In California, judges may use a manual, *Book of Accepted Jury Instructions* (BAJI) as a guide in instructing jurors who will deliberate cases involving allegations of emotional distress. Jurors are advised to evaluate the intensity and duration of physical problems in plaintiffs resulting from the alleged mishandling. Physical problems that can arise as a result of continuing stress include things like hypertension, insomnia, and reactivation of prior physical conditions. Emotional effects must also be evaluated re: intensity and duration and can include symptoms like shock, fright, outrage, anxiety, extreme anxiety, nervousness, worry, distress, mortification, embarrassment, humiliation, indignity, grief and sorrow.

Infliction of Emotional Distress

There is yet another aspect to evaluating damages due to claims of emotional distress: Namely, was the emotional distress caused by negligence or was the action or failure to act performed in a way that was intended to cause emotional distress? Damages therefore, may be considered to have been caused by:

> **Negligent** infliction of emotional distress (NIED) or,
> **Intentional** Infliction of Emotional Distress (IIED)

To qualify as intentional infliction of emotional distress it must be shown that:

- The extreme and outrageous conduct of the defendant was **intended** to cause emotional distress, or was performed with **reckless disregard** of the probability of causing emotional distress

- The plaintiff suffered **severe** or **extreme** emotional distress

• The defendant's outrageous conduct was the actual and proximate cause of the plaintiff's emotional distress

Outrageous conduct must be so extreme as to exceed all bounds of that usually tolerated in a civilized community. The defendant must have engaged in "conduct intended to inflict injury or engaged in with the realization that injury will result." In one instance, a defendant used the excess cremated remains in his cat's litter box. In other instances, defendants removed body parts without authorization and sold them for use in anatomical dissections.

Anguish

It is essential to determine whether or not the claimed emotional distress was actually **caused** by the untoward incident and not merely **attributed** to it when, in fact, the distress was caused by another factor or factors. Levi's description of the phenomenon known as 'anguish' helps to illustrate this point:

Anguish is known to everyone, even children, and everyone knows that it is often blank, undifferentiated. Rarely does it carry a clearly written label that also contains its motivation: any label it does have is often mendacious. One can believe or declare oneself to be anguished for one reason and be so due to something totally different. One can think that one is suffering at facing the future and instead be suffering because of one's past: one can think that one is suffering for others, out of pity, out of compassion, and instead be suffering for one's own reasons, more or less profound, more or less avowable and avowed, sometimes so deep that only the specialist, the analyst of souls, knows how to exhume them.

Therefore, the evaluation of a claim for emotional distress, mental suffering or anguish must include a review of the plaintiff's history to determine if there are other factors (incidents, experiences) that might account for the current complaint (symptoms). This evaluation must include a review of the medical and employment history of the plaintiff. Prior or concurrent legal involvement must be noted. Educational and military history, plus family and marital history, must be included.

Grief

The subject of grief is a common element in almost all legal cases involving funeral, burial or cremation. In some cases, grief from the death of a loved one is still prevalent or has been prolonged or, intensified because of alleged mishandling in the overall disposition (burial, entombment, cremation) process. In other cases, grief that might have previously been resolved has been re-activated through involvement in the development or process of a lawsuit, including interrogatories, examination by expert witnesses, deposition, and direct testimony in a court hearing.

Grief means different things to different people at different times. When we speak of grief, we have to differentiate between grief as an individual's emotional reaction to loss and grief as an abstract, psychological concept. Most persons believe they know what grief is. Yet when asked to define grief, even health care professionals who deal repeatedly with grieving persons are hard-pressed to offer a concise definition.

Grief is, "deep and poignant distress caused by or as if by bereavement." *(Webster)*

"Grief is a universal human response to loss that occurs across all age groups and throughout all cultures. It is characterized as a dynamic, pervasive and highly individualized process with a strong normative component. *(Cowles and Rogers, 1991)*

"Although grief is a common core, grief is determined by a variety of social and other factors and is rooted in the attachments people form with each other and with the objects around them; thus the effects of grief are multidimensional when people experience a significant loss." *(Parkes, 2001)*

"Grief is a liminal phenomenon, existing at the interface between the individual and society." *(Fulton, 2004)*

Grief: "A crucifying loneliness; a silent screaming slide into the bowels of despair. *(Funeral Director, Minneapolis, MN, 2003)*

The importance of understanding grief and of gaining some understanding of the timing, intensity and duration of grief in a case alleging damages secondary to the mishandling of the remains of a deceased person relate to the fact that an award for damages is generally not provided merely for grief related to the death of a loved one. Damages are awarded on the basis of the intensity and duration of emotional distress stemming from knowledge of the mishandling (negligent or intentional) of the remains of a deceased loved one.

As mentioned above in the Wisconsin Appellate Court decision (Holsen v Prasser-Kleczka, February, 1994)

"...it is outside the realm of the assumed ordinary experience of the jurors for them to be able to determine without expert testimony which, if any, of these alleged symptoms were caused by the conduct of the funeral home rather than as a natural consequence of the trauma that generally results from the loss of a loved one, and the other circumstances of the plaintiff's lives."

The expert witness, through careful examination of the plaintiff, including review of all pertinent records plus psychological testing, is in a position to offer an opinion on the quantity and intensity of grief versus the quantity and intensity of emotional distress secondary to the alleged mishandling of the remains of the deceased person.

Psychological Testing

Psychological testing is a necessary part of the evaluation of a claim for damages based on emotional distress. Among the test instruments commonly used in legal actions alleging emotional damages, the MMPI 2 (Minnesota Multiphasic Personality Inventory) is most revealing. As my associate, Dr. David Levy, points out:

"...the plaintiff's MMPI profile almost invariably indicates an appreciable degree of psychological distress. The critical question, of course, concerns the validity of these results. Are they an accurate indication of genuine emotional disturbance? Or do they reflect an attempt to deliberately exaggerate, or even falsify, one's problems and symptoms with the intent of appearing worse off than is, in fact, the case? In other words, are the plaintiff's emotional problems authentic, or are they due to conscious malingering (clinically referred to as 'faking bad')? Conversely, what if an examinee's MMPI profile shows an *absence* of emotional disturbance? Is this an accurate reflection of his or her psychological status? Or did the examinee, wishing to appear in a positive light, falsely slant his or her responses in a 'socially desirable' direction? And if so, to what extent was this attempt conscious (that is, intentional 'faking good'), or relatively unconscious? The MMPI is now capable of providing accurate answers to these most important questions. The ability of the MMPI to ascertain such crucial distinctions thus makes it an invaluable and indispensable tool in forensic settings and courtroom proceedings."

Other factors should also be taken into account by the expert witness retained to analyze and offer an opinion on emotional distress, namely the variability of response to loss. Not everyone responds to loss the same, even members of the same family. There are a number of questions to be asked and answered before offering an opinion on an individual's response to the death of a loved one:

- Who died?
- When did the death occur?
- How did the death occur?
- Where did the death occur?
- Was the death anticipated or unanticipated?
- Was the death violent? Or was it tranquil?
- Was the survivor involved in care of the decedent?
- Were there any unusual circumstances surrounding the death?

- What was the age of the decedent?
- What is the age of the survivor?
- Was this loss sanctioned? or unsanctioned?
- What prior losses has the survivor experienced?
- What was the impact of the funeral on the survivor?
- Was this the "straw that broke the camel's back?"
- What was the quality of the relationship with the decedent?
- What is the impact of this death on the survivor?
- Was the survivor dependent on the decedent?
- Was the survivor involved in the funeral planning?
- Was there "unfinished business" with the decedent?
- What are the long-term implications of this death?
- What financial and legal matters remain unsettled?
- Did the survivor observe the alleged mishandling of the body?

These are but a few of the many areas that have to be explored in order to gain an understanding of the plaintiff's reaction to the death. The reason an expert witness must explore questions like this is to ascertain and be able to testify to the intensity and duration of feelings related to the death of the person as compared and contrasted to the intensity and duration of feelings related to the alleged mishandling of the remains of the person who died.

Variable Responses to Loss

Following is a diagram developed by the Lamers Medical Group to show the range of variability of reactions to loss based on pre-existing (before the loss) personality, needs during bereavement, and anticipated outcome. In terms of current vocabulary, persons with innate strengths would be described as "resilient." Such persons are strong and adequate. They have adequate internal resources (ego strengths) and usually have external support systems (family, community, social groups) to help sustain them through a period of bereavement. As a result, their needs during bereavement are usually met through the support of friends and family. They can rely on their own inner strengths (intelligence, education, employment, physical and financial resources). Traditionally, such persons survive a loss without undue hardship. They make a successful adaptation to loss.

Persons with lesser strengths will need more support during bereavement as their internal and external resources may not always be adequate to their perceived needs. They may require assistance in the form of therapy, especially supportive group therapy which will provide a constructive outlet for their reasonable fears, concerns and feelings of loss. With assistance, they will usually do quite well and can experience growth from the knowledge and experience of working with peers in a trusting, honest interchange of feelings.

The outlook for persons who were maladjusted and needy before the loss is not bright. They generally do not make successful use of supportive group therapy as their challenges seem, to them, to be overwhelming and resources seem unable to fill the void in their life. They might require long-term, one-to-one therapy and might not make a successful adjustment to the loss, even after prolonged supportive or even insight-focused therapy. One important point to consider is that persons in this latter category are likely to have "feelings of entitlement." They might consider the slightest affront or misstep in the conduct of the funeral-burial-cremation sequence as proof that the world owes them a living. Such persons seem to feel that class-action funeral, burial and cremation suits were designed just for their benefit. Of course, there are exceptions to that observation, but such personality types are rarely seen in individual lawsuits.

Responses to Loss

	Pre-Existing Personality	Bereavement Needs	Outcome
A	Strong, adequate Innate strengths +++ (internal and external)	Temporary Social Support	Successful Adaptation
B	Variable adjustment Medium strengths ++ (internal and external)	Ongoing social support Perhaps psychotherapy	Prolonged Adjustment with eventual+outcome
C	Inadequate coping Deficient strengths	Unable to make good use Of conventional therapies	Still maladjusted long after period of bereavement

(Lamers, 1991)

Grief: A Brief Overview

Erik Erikson, widely assumed to be one of the outstanding psychologists of the past century, had a benevolent attitude the long-term impact of grief. He wrote,

> "Grief can serve as the basis for new social and psychological growth."

Erikson saw that it was possible for people in the midst of their grief to take a new look at their own lives; to recognize their finity; to recognize patterns that they no longer wanted to follow. Of necessity, they had to take a hard look at what was truly important to them. Out of this process, it was possible to consider establishing new objectives and new priorities. The fact that Erikson could speak of the potential of "new growth" coming out of the death of a loved one is truly paradoxical. In some ways it parallels the Buddhist maxim, "Out of the mud grows the lotus."

Involvement in a lawsuit that claims damages for emotional distress arising from charges of mishandling the funeral (burial, cremation, entombment) of a deceased person, it is as important to consider both normal grief and the impact of litigation on the phenomenon of grief. During the overall process of this sort of litigation, it is crucial to remember that grief is a normal combined social and psychological process. There is a spiritual dimension to grief as well. Following resolution of litigation, it is possible for grief to be resolved, though in some instances it may take time and perhaps some psychological therapy to assist the bereaved person to make a satisfactory adjustment. I believe it is inappropriate to speak of closure, as the sense of loss and its attendant feelings never completely resolve. They merely become less intense over time.

Summary and Conclusions

The concept of emotional distress is central to funeral, burial and cremation litigation.

Issues related to grief emotional distress can be like a powder keg, waiting to be ignited.

Persons claiming damages during the course of care of their deceased loved one often develop feelings of entitlement that can contribute to intense feelings that they, along with their deceased loved one, have been recklessly abused. Therefore, it is not unusual to find plaintiffs who conflate their feelings of grief with what they believe to be emotional distress. The major role of the psychological or psychiatric expert witness is to determine the intensity and duration of both emotional distress and grief. To do this it is necessary to conduct a thorough review of all of plaintiff's relevant history and experience. In this manner, the expert will be able to develop and present an accurate evaluation of the influence of the alleged mishandling to the court. Psychological testing, especially the administration and analysis of the Minnesota Multiphasic Personality Inventory, is a standard method at helping determine a number of aspects of plaintiff's state of mind regarding the case and can help determine if the plaintiff is exaggerating or even minimizing symptoms. The work of the psychological expert witness is often central to a thorough presentation of the facts through the process of deposition and court hearings.

References: Emotional Distress

American Psychiatric Association (1994). Diagnostic and Statistical Manual of Mental Disorders, Fourth Edition. (DSM-IV)

Bonanno, G, Wortman, C, Lehman, D. et al (2002) Resilience to loss and chronic grief; a prospective study from pre-loss to 18 months post-loss. J Personal Soc Psychol; 83:1150-1164.

Bowlby, J. Processes of Mourning. Int. J Psychoanal. 1961;42:317-339.

Fulton, R, Gottesman, D, & Owen, G. (1982) Loss, social change and the prospect of mourning. Death Education. (6); 137-153.

Lamers, W. M., Jr. (1991) Grief in Dying Persons. In Rando, T (ed.) in Clinical Dimensions of Anticipatory Mourning.

Levi, Primo (1988) The Drowned and the Saved. New York: Simon and Schuster.

Parkes, C. (1972) Bereavement: Studies in Grief in Adult Life. London, England. Tavistock Press.

Superior Court, State of California (1996). Book of Accepted Jury Instructions (BAJI).

Wisconsin Appelate Court (Febr. 1994): Holsen v Prasser-Kleczka, in *The Milwaukee Journal*, February 22, 1994

References: Psychological Assessment

1. Korchin, S. J., & Schuldberg, D. (1981). The Future of Clinical Assessment. *American Psychologist, 36*(10), 1147-1158.

2. Cofer, C. N., Chance, J. E., & Judson, A. J. (1949). A Study of Malingering on the MMPI. *Journal of Psychology, 27,* 491-499.

3. Dahlstrom, W. G., Welsh, G. S., & Dahlstrom, L. E. (1972). An *MMPI Handbook: Vol.I, Clinical Interpretation.* Minneapolis: University of Minnesota Press.

4. Dahlstrom, W. G., Welsh, G. S., & Dahlstrom, L. E. (1975). *An MMPI Handbook: Vol.11, Research Applications.* Minneapolis: University of Minnesota Press.

5. Gilberstadt, H., & Duker, J. (1965). *A Handbook for Clinical and Actuarial MMPI Interpretation.* Philadelphia: W. B. Saunders.

6. Graham, J. R. (1987). *The MMPI: A Practical Guide* (2nd ed.). New York: Oxford.

7. Greene, R. L. (1980). *The MMPI: An Interpretive Manual.* NewYork: Grune & Stratton.

8. Hathaway, S. R., & Meehl, P. E. (1951). *An Atlas for the Clinical Use of the MMPI.* Minneapolis: University of Minnesota Press.

9. Marks, P. A., & Seeman, W. (1963). *The Actuarial Description of Personality: An Atlas for Use With the MMPI.* Baltimore: Williams & Wilkins.

10. Morey, L. C., Waugh, M. H., & Blashfield, R. K. (1985). MMPI Scales for DSM-III Personality Disorders: Their Derivation and Correlates. *Journal of Personality Assessment, 49*(3), 245-251.

11. Hathaway, S. R., & McKinley, J. C. (1983). *The Minnesota Multiphasic Personality Inventory Manual.* New York: Psychological Corporation.

12. Caldwell, A. B. (1988). *MMPI Supplemental Scale Manual.* Los Angeles: Caldwell Report

Professionalism

*Is funeral service a profession? Or is it, as some claim,
an occupation, a business? The terms, 'profession' and
'professional' are applied loosely these days as seen in the
lengthy lists of professions on the website, Wikipedia. This
section reviews the term 'profession' as it relates to funeral
service and offers some suggestions about how to resolve the
continuing confusion.*

Historical Background

During the middle ages there were three initial professions
among many trades, occupations and guilds: the priesthood,
the law and medicine. Members of these professions wore
robes as a sign of their authority and noble origins and, as such,
they stood above the common man. They were educated at a
time when formal education was not common. They dedicated
themselves to a lifetime of ethical service to the community.
Even today the graduation ceremony for physicians includes
reciting of the Oath of Hippocrates. This tradition dates back
two thousand years. It details standards of ethical behavior that
guide the physician's lifetime service to humanity.

Some early professional traditions persist today for priests,
lawyers and physicians. Judges don formal robes when presiding
in court. Priests and some other clergypersons wear vestments
or robes as hallmarks of their religious authority. Physicians and
lawyers in this country have forsaken the custom of wearing
formal robes, yet, they undergo extensive, formal training.

Over the centuries, other professions have evolved in
response to changing needs of an increasingly complex society.
Physicians, lawyers and priests are aided by other dedicated
workers who pursue the same professional goals. Newer

professions like surgery, dentistry, psychology, nursing, accounting and engineering have arisen. Within the legal profession there are paralegals, investigators, arbitrators, analysts and researchers. Technicians, researchers, sanitary workers, administrators, medical record technicians, and biochemists are but a few of the professionals who augment the work of the physician. Similarly, new professional disciplines – deacons and lay ministers, among others – complement the work of the priest, rabbi and minister.

A comparable evolution occurred in funeral service. Initially, the family and religious community assumed responsibility for care and disposition of the body of a deceased member. Later, the carpenter who made the coffin, the sexton who dug the grave, and the embalming chemist, were subsumed in the evolving role now known as the funeral director. Habenstein and Lamers described the situation a century ago:

> ...at the turn of the century while funeral directing in
> America had managed to organize, to establish itself,
> and to gain public recognition as a distinct occupation,
> it still had a very long distance to go in becoming a full-
> ledged profession. For one thing, even among its own
> practitioners, its aims and interests were by no means
> universally agreed upon. For another, the procedures
> or controls whereby any profession secures its aims and
> brings its members into conformity by social and legal
> pressures were only partially developed. (497-499)

These challenges were not unique to funeral service but were common in the development of any profession. Habenstein and Lamers characterized the problem that is still unresolved today:

> Perhaps the most difficult problem still facing the
> funeral director at the turn of the century (1900) was the
> all-encompassing question of professionalization itself.
> How far should the effort to professionalize the group

be carried? By its very nature the occupation could have swung sharply and far toward one or the other of opposites, or remained in some intermediate position. It faced the choice of becoming either an out-and-out trade or business, or a profession, or of compromising these extremes. It merits repeating that the personal service elements in funeral directing have a natural 'professional' orientation; the impersonal service or merchandizing elements a natural 'trade' orientation. (Page 500)

The role of the funeral director also derives from the quasi-priestly activities of those who for many centuries have prepared the bodies of deceased leaders – pharos, popes, emperors and kings – for the eternal journey that continues after physical death.

The role of the funeral director, then, is not something that arose in recent years simply as a way to earn a living. True, there is a business (commercial) aspect to funeral service. Yet that is not the sole objective of the occupation. Funeral service is not simply a trade, which Webster defines as "business or work in which one engages regularly. An occupation requiring manual or mechanical skill." Funeral service more closely matches the definition of a profession, namely, "a calling requiring specialized knowledge and often long and intensive academic preparation; a principal calling, vocation or employment." The funeral director also meets the definition of a professional, namely, "...one who is involved as a lifelong career in one of the learned professions, conforms to the technical and ethical standards of a profession, and exhibits a courteous, conscientious and businesslike manner in the workplace and in all steps of performing his/her obligations."

There is another important dimension to professionalism that pertains to the funeral director, namely the matter of authority. A professional acquires authority as a result of specialized education, training, dedication and experience. This authority is neither granted nor assumed, but is earned. It consists of three elements: sapiential authority, moral authority and charismatic authority.

Sapiential authority comes from the body of specialized knowledge that a funeral director possesses. It consists of extensive knowledge not known by the general public including knowledge regarding care of the body after death. It includes knowledge about grief needs of bereaved person as well as awareness of laws and procedures that govern disposition. Because of this special knowledge, the funeral director plays an important role in the management of difficult situations including violent death and disasters. The funeral director has specialized knowledge in subjects including anatomy, chemistry, microbiology, toxicology, mortuary law, ethical business practices, vital statistics, embalming, cremation, coroner policies, local, state and international regulations regarding the preparation and shipment of the bodies of deceased persons, as well as communication skills, knowledge of the psychology of grief and awareness of cultural, ethnic and religious variations of funeral customs. This knowledge is not generally in the possession of the average person and it therefore enables the funeral director to instruct, advise and direct others in the respectful and timely performance of necessary procedures and practices.

Moral authority of the funeral director derives from the central, responsible position of the funeral director in performing duties concerning the body of the deceased person and conducting activities that involve survivors and the general community. It is a high and important responsibility, not to be taken lightly. The funeral director and related staff must function in an ethical manner while enabling a seamless, satisfying service, whether religious or secular, that meets the needs of the bereaved family and friends. There can be no compromise in the conduct of all aspects of funeral service, from first-call to final disposition.

The significance of moral authority and the high calling of

the funeral director can be validated in the way others look at funeral service. In a complaint filed several years ago in California, a plaintiff attorney offered the following description of the nature of the relationship between survivors and funeral-cremation service providers. While the author of this extended complaint (this is but number 61 of a long series of complaints) resorts to hyperbole, there can be no escape from the fact that irregularities in handling the remains of a deceased individual can have serious repercussions:

"A culturally, socially and religiously accepted fiduciary relationship existed between relatives of decedents and mortuaries, crematoriums, and other decedent care providers in that the death of the loved one is the time in life that causes the family the utmost emotional turmoil, bereavement, feeling of helplessness and loss, need for consolation, comfort, compassion and assurance that the beloved will receive a proper, respectful and dignified cremation without further family supervision or involvement once the beloved decedent is given to the custody and control of the mortuary, crematorium or other decedent care providers. It is a relationship of utmost trust. It is a sacred trust."

Charismatic authority derives from the serious nature of the work of the funeral director. Death is serious and the remains of the deceased person must always be treated with respect. The funeral director must perform his/her duties with the utmost seriousness; anything less is a violation of the sacred trust placed in the funeral director and all others who assist in the course of the funeral and disposition. The ultimate responsibility for doing things right lies with the funeral director. There is no escape from the need for excellence in all aspects of the funeral. The funeral director takes the lead, must be aware of all that is going on, must anticipate anything that might disrupt the smooth flow and do whatever is needed to reduce the possibility of error in the complex sequence of events that constitute the modern funeral. As the one who takes the lead in the direction of funeral services as well as in care of the body, the funeral director takes on charismatic authority.

The sapiential, moral and charismatic authority of the funeral director are clearly reflected in the following commendation describing the work of volunteer funeral directors in a Disaster Mortuary Operational Response Team (DMORT) following Hurricane Katrina.

"Your work, while removed from the public eye
due to its sensitivity, is often the only thing that can
bring certainty and closure to a family searching for
a lost relative or spouse. I know the tasks involved in
completing your assignments can push your human
sensibilities to their limit, but time and time again you
all rise to the occasion and conduct yourselves with
a professionalism and character that reflect the best
qualities of this country."

The funeral director is generally considered to be a member of the helping and healing professions. Like physicians, social workers, clergy, and psychologists, funeral directors provide service in a manner that reflects their commitment to a worthy cause that transcends self-interest. The business aspect notwithstanding, the altruistic nature of the funeral profession elevates funeral service above that of a purely economic enterprise. In my fifty years as a physician including the last thirty years working as a hospice physician, I knew that, if a patient died and the family was economically challenged, I could ask a funeral director to help, knowing that the family would receive dignified service without question. To me, altruism is one of the hallmarks of a true professional. Lundberg made the same point when he wrote:

"The fundamental purpose of a business is to make
money. On the other hand, the fundamental purpose of a
profession is to provide a service that reflects commitment
to a worthy cause that transcends self-interest."

Apart from the area of popular sports where one acquires

professional status based on how fast one can run or throw a ball, it is not sufficient for an individual to simply declare oneself to be a professional. In the sense we are discussing here, professionalism is acquired and demonstrated through a combination of factors including recognition as a professional by one's community, peers and other professionals. Professionalism is also expressed through:

- **Clinical competence**: The professional knows what must be done to meet the needs of the client and has the education, training and experience to handle a wide variety of real life situations.

- **Communication skills:** The professional is skilled at listening as well as speaking, and recognizes the importance of non-verbal as well as verbal communication. The professional does not 'talk down' to persons who are unfamiliar with the practices of a particular discipline.

- **Ethical standards**: The practice of the professional is guided by a clear set of ethical principles that have evolved over time in his/her particular discipline and are an integral part of everyday practice.

- **Educational standards**: The educational standards of professions are generally set high, rather than low, out of the common assumption that practitioners with more education will perform better than those with less education.

One deterrent to funeral service being recognized as a profession is that educational standards have not significantly improved despite continuing sporadic efforts by some leaders and selected colleges of mortuary science. Education and licensing standards vary widely from state to state. Some have made significant positive changes including requiring a baccalaureate degree prior to licensure. While entry requirements for other helping and healing professions are rising, the same cannot be said for funeral service overall.

I have seen excellent people leave funeral service and seek employment elsewhere. Reasons cited for leaving include inadequate compensation, long hours and limited opportunity for advancement.

There is no quick or easy solution to remedy these deterrents. The various groups and organizations at local, state and national levels must work together to develop uniform standards for education and licensure as well as nationally recognized standards of practice.

Funeral service is not alone in facing these challenges. Other caregiving professions, especially nursing, also face the problem of recruiting adequate numbers of qualified applicants. The high calling to serve one's fellow man is not enough. Career choice always includes balancing altruism with reality. Low entry requirements will not attract quality candidates to funeral service. Other professions have united to address difficult issues like compensation, advancement opportunities, ownership potential and retirement benefits.

Positive action now will ensure that funeral service will continue to be seen as a career and a calling, not merely a job or occupation, and funeral practitioners will retain their rightful place among the caregiving professions.

- References -

Cruess, RL, Cruess, SR. Teaching medicine as a profession in the service of healing. Acad Med 1997; 72:941-952.

Dewey, J. Experience and Education. New York, N.Y.: Collier Books, 1963.

Funeral Service Insider. March 5, 2007; 32:9, p. 3 (sidebar).

Habenstein, R.A., Lamers, W.M. The History of American Funeral Directing. Milwaukee: Bulfin Publishing 1955, 497-500.

Hafferty, FW. Professionalism: the next wave. New Engl J Med. 2006;355:2151-2.

Inui, TTS, Cottingham, AH, Frankel. RM, et al. Educating for professionalism at Indiana University School of Medicine: Feet on the ground and fresh eyes. In Wear, D, Aultman, JM, eds. Professionalism in medicine: critical perspectives. New York: Springer, 2006:165-184.

Kerry, John. Commendation to Commander Mike Neal and the volunteer funeral director members of Region 1 DMORT Team (Disaster Mortuary Operational Response Team).

Lamers, W.M. Jr. The Hippocratic Oath ....in The Encyclopedia of Death.

Leach, DC.. Professionalism: The formation of physicians. Am J Bioeth 2004; 4:11-12.

Lundberg, G. The failure of organized health system reform. JAMA 1995;273:1539-1541

Parsons, T. The Social System. Glencoe, IL. Illinois Free Press, 1951, 435.

Stern, DT, Papadakis, M. The developing physician – becoming a professional. N Engl J Med. 2006;355:1794-9.

Webster, Merriam. College Dictionary 10th Ed 1994.

Wikipedia – accessed July 9, 2007 re: 'Profession" and 'Professional'.

Bibliography
Books, Periodicals and Articles

The following list indicates numerous resources important in the development of this book:

A "Sorry" Strategy. *HR Magazine*, March, 2006.

Adams, J.A. *Project Understanding: A National Study of Cremation*, Des Plaines, IL. National Foundation of Funeral Services, 1986.

Associated Press. *Unclaimed ashes creating problems for funeral directors*. Portsmouth Herald News. Accessed 3/7/2007. http://www.seacoastonline.com/2001news/6_17_sbl.htm.

A Guide to Scattering Cremated Remains. *Funeral Service Insider's Cremation Report*, May, 2006.

Be Informed About Informed Consent. *SCPIE Safe Practice Publication*, May, 1999.

Berg, Jessica W., Applebaum, Paul S., Parker, Lisa S., and Lidz, Charles W. *Informed Consent – Legal Theory and Clinical Practice*. NY: Oxford University Press, 2001.

Carlson, Richard, Ph.D., *Don't Sweat the Small Stuff...and It's All Small Stuff*. NY: Hyperion, 1997.

Communication: The Key to Minimizing Liability in Limited Relationships. *SCPIE Safe Practice Publication*, August, 2001.

Cobb, Augustus G. *Earth-Burial and Cremation*, NY: G.P. Putnam's Sons, 1892.

Cremation – Its Ethical Issues. *Funeral Ethics Association*, Volume IV, Number X.

Cremation Association of North America. *Crematory Guidelines*. Accessed December 2006. http://www.cremationassociation.org

Culley, Carl A. So You're Being Sued: Do's and Don'ts for the Defendant, *Cleveland Clinic Journal of Medicine*, October, 2002.

Deposition Goals – Develop a Plan to Get What You're After from Witnesses in Discovery. *American Bar Association Journal*, August, 2003.

Distinguishing independent contractors. *Internal Revenue Service.* Accessed September, 2006. http://www.irs.gov/business/small/article/0,,id=99921,00.html

Dramatic Market Change Hits Professional Liability. *Insurance Journal,* November, 2002.

Eisenberg, Daniel. When Doctors Say, "We're Sorry." *Time Magazine,* August 15, 2005.

Feldman, James. *Shift Happens,* Chicago, IL: James Feldman Associates, Inc. 2004.

Funeral Rule. *Federal Trade Commission.* Accessed 4/22/2007. http://www.ftc.gov/funeral.shtm.

Garner, Bryan A. and Garner, Braun A. *Black's Law Dictionary,* 8th Edition, Eagan, MN: 2004

Gilligan, T. Scott. *Funeral Procession Liability: A Growing Concern.* The Director Magazine, May, 2007.

Gilligan, T. Scott and Stueve, Thomas F.H. *Mortuary Law,* Tenth Revised Edition, Cincinnati, OH: The Cincinnati Foundation for Mortuary Education

Glannon, Joseph W. *Law of Torts,* NY: Aspen Publications, 2005.

Habenstein, Robert W. and Lamers, William M. *Funeral Customs the World Over.* Milwuakee: Bulfin, 1960.

Hast, Ron. The Art of Embalming and Its Purpose. *Mortuary Management Magazine,* October, 2006.

Hays Affinity Solutions. *Hays Companies.* Accessed June 2006. http://www.hayscompanies.com

Howarth, Glennys. *Last Rites: The Work of the Modern Funeral Director.* NY: Baywood, 1996.

How Do I Choose An Insurance Company? *Insurance Information Institute.* Accessed 10/25/2006. http://www.iii.org/individuals/choosing.

Ihara, Toni, Warner, Ralph and Hertz, Frederick. *Living Together: A Legal Guide for Unmarried Couples,* Berkeley, CA: Nolo Press, 2006
Independent Contractors: The Pitfalls of False Perceptions. *SCPIE Safe*

Practice Publication, June, 2000.

Informed Consent. *American Medical Association*. Accessed 11/21/2003. http://www.ama-assn.org/ama/pub/category/4608.html.

International Cemetery and Funeral Association. *Handling of Human Remains in Conjunction with the Cremation Process*. Accessed 12/11/2006. http://www.icfa.org/cremationguidelines1.htm.

Iserson, Kenneth V., M.D. *Death to Dust*, Tucson, AZ: Galen Press, 2001.

Josephson, Michael. *Character Counts Commentary*. Accessed June, 2006. http:// www.josephsoninstitute.com

Kershaw, Sarah. *Long-Forgotten Reminders of Oregon's Mentally Ill*. The New York Times, March 14, 2005.

Kroboth, Alan. *Human Body Weight and Its Effects on Cremation*, Cremation Association of North America. Accessed 12/06/2006. http://www.cremationassociation.org/html/article-weight.html.

Kubasak, Michael W. *Cremation and the Funeral Director: Successfully Meeting the Challenge*, Malibu, CA: The Avalon Press, 1990.

Lapin, Harvey, I. Cremated Remains Cannot Be Sent By Express Mail. *Cremation Association of North America*. Accessed 11/5/2006 http://www.cremationassociation.org.

Lynch, Thomas. *Undertaking: Life Studies From the Dismal Trade*. NY: Penguin, 1998.

Mackenzie, Roger. How to Deal With Complaints, *The Journal Magazine*, February, 1999.

Matthews Cremation Division. *About Matthews*. Accessed February 2007. http://www.matthewscremation.com/aboutUs/index.asp

Mayer, Robert G. *Embalming History, Theory, & Practice*, Third Edition, NY: McGraw-Hill, 2000.

Mayer, Robert G. *Embalming History, Theory, & Practice*, Fourth Edition, NY: McGraw-Hill, 2006.

Negligence. *The Columbia Encyclopedia*, NY: Columbia University Press, 2003.

Negligence. *West's Encyclopedia of American Law,* Farmington Hills, NJ: The Gale Group, Inc., 1998.

O'Connor, Naoibh. Gone, Cremated, Then Forgotten, The Vancouver Courier. Accessed December 1, 2006 http://www.vancourier.com/issues04/112104/newshtml.

Poynter, Al. Unclaimed Cremated Remains, *Poynteronline,* May 18, 2006.

Prothero, Stephen. *Purified By Fire,* Berkeley and Los Angeles, CA: University of California Press, 2001.

Raether, Howard C. *The Funeral Director's Practice Management Handbook,* NJ: Prentice Hall, 1989.

Rando, Therese A., Dr., *Grief, Dying and Death: Clinical Intervention for Caregivers,* Champaign, IL: Research Press, 1984.

Receiving Remains from Abroad. *International Blue Book of Funeral Service*

Recommended Procedures For Handling Dead Human Bodies By An Authorized Crematory Authority. *Cremation Association of North America.* Accessed 12/6/2006 http://www.cremationassociation.org/html/article-procedures.

Rupp's Insurance and Risk Management Glossary. NILS Publishing, 2002.

Sloane, David Charles. *The last Great Necessity: Cemeteries in American History,* Baltimore: Johns Hopkins University Press, 1991.

Solot, Dorian, and Miller, Marshall, *Alternative to Marriage Project,* Brooklyn, NY: 1998. Accessed November, 2006. http://www.unmarried.org
The Wirthlin Group. *1995 Study of American Attitudes Toward Ritualization and Memorialization,* McLean, VA: The Wirthlin Group, 1995.

Transporting the Deceased – Crematory Containers. *Transportation Security Administration.* Accessed 11/12/2006 http://www.tsa.gov/travelers/airtravel/specialneeds/editorial_1296.shtm.

United States Army. *Arlington National Cemetery, Regulations AR-290-5.* Accessed May 11, 2007 http://www.arlingtoncemetery.net/ar290-5inspect4.0html.

Use of Dental Information in Missing Person and Unidentified Body Cases. *American Board of Forensic Odontology.* Accessed 1/8/2007 http://www.abfo.org/MissUnID.htm.

Williams, Melissa Johnson. Proper Use of an Embalming Care Report Form. *Funeral Ethics Association,* Volume V, Number 1.

Williams, Melissa Johnson. Receiving Remains from Abroad. *International Blue Book of Funeral Service,* 2006.

Williams, Melissa Johnson. Shipping Human Remains To Foreign Countries. *International Blue Book of Funeral Service,* 2006.

Young, Phillip J. The Independent Contractor Dilemma. *Moss-Burnett Legal.* Accessed 6/12/2004 http://www.moss-burnett.com/CM/Articles.

Resources

American Blue Book of Funeral Service
Published by Kates Boylston Publications
11300 Rockville Pike, Suite 1100, Rockville, MD 20852
800-500-4585
Web Site: www.kates-boylston.com
A comprehensive resource guide for funeral service and related industries.

American Board of Funeral Service Education
38 Florida Avenue, Portland, ME 04103
207-878-6539
E-mail: gconnic1@maine.rr.com
Web Site: www.abfse.org
"The ABFSE is organized for educational purposes in the interests of the public and of the funeral profession. Its purpose is to cooperate with all groups and agencies having an interest in advancement of the principles and standards of funeral service education."

CB Legal Publishing Corp.
P.O. Box 1327, Northbrook, IL 60065-1327
847-509-0501
Specialty release and legal forms for funeral homes, cemeteries, and crematories, developed by Harvey Lapin, Esq., specialist in mortuary and cremation law

Cremation Association of North America
401 North Michigan Avenue, Chicago, IL 60611
312-245-1077
E-mail: CANA@smithbucklin.com
Web Site: www.cremationassociation.org
"The objectives and purposes of CANA are to further the high standards of cremation service, to present the concept of cremation on the highest level of integrity and to emphasize the importance of proper memorialization."

Facultatieve-Technologies The Americas
Tom Snyder, Vice-President, Sales & Marketing
330-723-6339
734 N. Progress Drive, Medina, OH 44256
E-mail: Ths1114@aol.com
Web Site: www.facultatieve-technologies.com
Facultatieve-Technologies is the world wide leader in the manufacturing and operating of high technological, process-monitored cremation equipment.

Federated Insurance
121 E. Park Square, Owatonna, MN 55060
800-533-0472
Web Site: www.federatedinsurance.com

Fountain National Academy of Professional Embalming Skills
Vernie R. Fountain, Founder
2211 West Norton Road, Springfield, MO 65803
417-833-5130
E-mail: vrfountain@earthlink.net
www.fnacademy.com
The most complete Embalming-Care Report available

Funeral Ethics Association
Robert Ninker, Executive Director
215 S. Grand Avenue West, Springfield, IL 62704
217-525-1520
E-mail: info@fea.org
www.fea.org
This association helps resolve problems for people having difficulty getting
a fair response from funeral directors who served them and works to
educate the funeral professional about ethical practices.

Scott Gilligan, Esq.
3734 Eastern Avenue, Cincinnati, OH 45226
513-871-6332
E-mail: scott@gilliganleagal.com
Private law practice and General Counsel to the National Funeral Directors
Association.

Inman Nationwide Shipping
Robert Inman, CEO
1605 Merwin Avenue
Cleveland, OH 44113
800-321-0566
E-mail: rjinman@inmanshippingworldwide.com

Innovative Supply, Inc.
41085 State Hwy #11, Roseau, MN 56751
800-890-0558
Universal identification system
E-mail: phelgeson@mncable.com
www.universalidsystem.com

International Cemetery, Cremation and Funeral Association
107 Carpenter Drive, Suite 100, Sterling, VA 20191
800-645-7700 or 703-391-8400
E-mail: gen4@icfa.org
Web Site: www.icfa.org
"ICCFA is committed to fostering positive consumer relationships by promoting high ethical standards; providing services, products and educational opportunities for members; proactive leadership on legislative, regulatory and legal issues; creating mutually beneficial relationships with state, regional, international and allied associations; encouraging members to promote the celebration of life, remembrance and memorialization." Sponsors **ICCFA College of Cremation Services** for funeral, cremation and cemetery professionals.

International Order of the Golden Rule
13523 Lakefront Drive, Earth City, MO 63045
314-209-7142 or 800-637-8030
Web Site: www.ogr.org
"OGR provides a forum for interaction and information; affords members the highest quality professional development and continuing education programs, products and services related to the death care profession; and serves as a resource to the public through members on death care issues."

Jewish Funeral Directors of America
150 Lynnway, Suite 506, Lynn, MA 01902
781-477-9300
E-mail: JFDAMER@aol.com
Web Site: www.JFDA.org
"JFDA strives to preserve the finest traditions and customs of Jewish funeral service as recognized and practiced by those of the Jewish faith; to formulate and advocate, with dignity and honor, the highest principles, ideals and ethics of the funeral profession."

Kubasak Associates, Inc.
Mike Kubasak, President
531 Calais Drive, Mesquite, NV 89027
702-345-3212
E-mail: mkubasak@aol.com
www.kubasak.com

Lamers Medical Group
A Professional Corporation
9515 Seabreeze Terrace, Malibu, CA 90265-2279
310-457-3055
E-mail: william.lamers@gmail.com

Harvey I. Lapin, Esq.
Harvey I. Lapin, P.C.
P.O. Box 1327, Northbrook, IL 60065-1327
847-509-0501
E-mail: harv4law@aol.com
Law practice specializing in funeral, cremation, cemetery affairs.

Matthews Cremation Division
Paul Rahill, President
2045 Sprint Blvd., Apoka, FL 32703-7762
800-327-2831 or 407-886-5533
www.matthewscremation.com
The leader in the design and manufacturing of cremation systems and the
most sought trainer for cremation professionals.

National Funeral Directors Association
13625 Bishop's Drive, Brookfield, WI 53005-6607
800-228-6332 or 262-789-1880
E-mail: nfda@nfda.org
Web Site: www.nfda.org
"The mission of NFDA is to enhance the funeral service profession and
promote quality service to the consumer."

National Funeral Directors & Morticians Association
3951 Snapfinger Pkwy, Suite 570, Decatur, GA 30035
404-286-6680
E-mail: NFD&MA @NFDMA.com
Web Site: www.nfdma.com
"The Association is charged to enlighten and inform its members of the
changing laws that govern the profession, share knowledge that will
empower our firms and preserve the heritage of the African-American
funeral industry, with compassion and business expertise."

Overstreet & Associates
David Overstreet, Esq.
1530 E. Shaw, Suite 102
Fresno, CA 93710
559-221-2771
E-mail: dmo@oa-law.net

Preferred Funeral Directors International
1501 Belcher Road. S., Bldg. B, Largo, FL 33771
727-524-8100
E-mail: info@pfdi.org
Web Site: www.pfdi.org
"PFDI encourages and fosters the ideal of service as a basis of worthy enterprise, to encourage the highest standards as an opportunity to serve society, to exchange views and ideas and accurate information on subjects pertaining to our industry that we may be united in the ideal of service."

Selected Independent Funeral Homes
500 Lake Cook Road, Suite 205, Deerfield, IL 60015
847-236-9401 or 800-323-4219
Web Site: www.SelectedFuneralHomes.org
"The purpose and objective of SIFD is to study, develop and establish the highest standards of service for the benefit of the public; to provide a continuing forum for the exchange, development, and dissemination of knowledge and information beneficial to members and to the public regarding all aspects of funeral service."

The Red Book
The National Directory of Morticians
P.O. Box 73, Chagrin Falls, OH 44022
440-247-3561
Web Site: www.funeral-dir.com
Listings of 27 sections pertaining to the funeral industry.

The Yellow Book
A publication of Nomis Publications, Inc.
P.O. Box 5159, Youngstown, OH 44514
800-321-7479
Web Site: www.yelobk.com
A directory of funeral homes, related funeral service businesses and resources.

The Whitmore Group Insurance
James Metzger, Chairman0 & CEO
370 Old Country Road, Garden City, NY 11530
888-747-3343 or 516-746-4141
www.whitmoregroup.com
Specialty insurance for funeral homes, crematories, cemeteries, and allied manufacturers and suppliers

FIRST CALL RECORD

Name of Deceased: _____ Date of Death: _____

Person Receiving Call _____ Date _____ Time _____

Place of Death _____ Phone: _____

Address _____ City _____ State _____ Zip _____

Time of Death _____ A.M./P.M.

Person Calling: _____ Phone: _____

Relationship to the Deceased: _____

Next of Kin_____ Relationship_____

Address _____ City _____ State _____ Zip _____

Phone_____ Cell/Pager_____

Doctor _____ Address_____

City _____ State _____ Zip _____ Phone_____

Date last seen by Doctor _____;Coroner ___Yes ___ No; Hospice ____Yes ____No

Transfer Personnel Dispatched: Date _____ Time _____

Were any of the following expressed? ____Burial _____ Cremation _____ Shipment

____Undecided

Was authorization for embalming received? _____ Yes _____No

Name of Person authorizing embalming: _____

Relationship to deceased: _____

Date & Time of Authorization: _____

Form 03-01 ©2003 Kubasak Associates

ORDER FOR RELEASE

Name of deceased: _____ Date of death: _____

To: _____

The undersigned represents and warrants to be the next of kin to the decedent or the person(s) with the legal right and authority by law to control the disposition of the above-named decedent and directs the above-named decedent be released to:

_____

Name of Funeral Home

The above-named funeral home, including its designated agents, is hereby authorized to sign on my/our behalf, any and all other authorizations that may be required in order to secure the release of the above-named decedent.

Signed this _____ day of _____, 20__ at _____.

Signature: _____

Relationship to the Deceased: _____

Signature: _____

Relationship to the Deceased: _____

Representative of Funeral Home: _____

CONFIRMATION OF DELIVERY OF DECEASED TO FUNERAL HOME

Name of deceased: _____ Date of death: _____

The undersigned certifies the remains of the above-named decedent were transferred

from _____ to the _____ funeral

home on _____ and the arrival time was _____ A.M./P.M.

Describe condition of remains upon arrival at funeral home: _____

_____

_____

_____

Describe where the remains were placed in the funeral home: (e.g., refrigeration,

embalming table, etc.) _____

_____

Signed this _____ day of _____, 20__ at _____.

Signature of person(s) making transfer: _____

Print name of funeral home employee: _____

Name of Transfer Company: _____

Address & Phone Number: _____

Print name of transfer company employee: _____

GENERAL RECEIPT OF DECEDENT FROM FUNERAL HOME

Name of deceased: _____Date of death: _____

Name of Person and/or Company Receiving Deceased from the funeral home:

_____

Relationship to deceased: _____

Address_____

City_____State_____Zip_____

Telephone #_____

The recipient named above, acknowledges and warrants that the funeral home released custody of the decedent on the date and time herein listed. The decedent was received in the following condition:

_____

.

Signed this _____day of _____, 20___ at _____.

Signature of recipient of the decedent: _____

Relationship to the decedent: _____

Representative of Funeral Home: _____

Form 03-27   ©2003 Kubasak Associates

428

AUTHORIZATION FOR REMOVAL OF MEDICAL DEVICES

Name of deceased: _____ Date of death: _____

The undersigned hereby represents and warrants to be the next of kin and/or the person(s) with the legal right to control the disposition of the above-named decedent.

The following medical devices have been implanted or attached to the deceased:

_____

_____

The undersigned fully acknowledges the funeral home has explained the need for removal of all devices prior to cremating the body. In the event medical devices are not removed they can cause injury to personnel, damage to equipment and damage to the cremation chamber. Failure to remove the medical devices before cremation makes it impossible to retrieve them after cremation. The undersigned hereby authorize the removal of the above-listed medical devices and/or implants by the funeral home or their designated agent.

The undersigned releases and discharges the funeral home, its affiliates, officers, employees, agents, and representatives from any and all liabilities, losses, damages, and injuries resulting from non-disclosure of medical devices or implants on or in the above-named decedent and agrees to indemnify the funeral home from any costs, damages, causes of actions or claims arising out of this authorization.

Signed this _____day of _____, 20___ at _____.

Signature: _____

Relationship to the Deceased: _____

Signature: _____

Relationship to the Deceased: _____

Representative of Funeral Home: _____

VERIFICATION OF IDENTITY OF DECEDENT

Name of deceased: _____ Date of death: _____

The undersigned hereby attests to the identity of the above named decedent, which took place on _____, 20____, at _____ A.M./P.M.

The undersigned represents and warrants to be the next of kin to the decedent or the designated representative of the next of kin or the person(s) with the legal right and authority by law to identify the decedent.

The undersigned acknowledges he or she has had adequate and sufficient time and opportunity to properly identify the decedent before final disposition of the deceased's remains. The undersigned acknowledges there is no doubt or question about the identity of the decedent that is in the custody of the funeral home.

If verification of the identity of the deceased was performed by means other than visual identification (e.g., photograph, scars, tattoos, etc.), specify the means used:

_____

_____

The undersigned releases and discharges the funeral home and agrees to indemnify and hold harmless the funeral home, its affiliates, officers, directors, employees and agents from any and all liabilities, obligations, losses, damages, claims of mental or physical distress or anguish, costs or expenses of any nature whatsoever relating to or arising out of the misidentification of the decedent.

Signed this _____ day of _____, 20___ at _____.

Signature: _____

Relationship to the Deceased: _____

Signature: _____

Relationship to the Deceased: _____

Representative of Funeral Home: _____

MINIMUM CARE AUTHORIZATION WHEN EMBALMING IS DECLINED

Name of deceased: _____ Date of death: _____

The undersigned represents and warrants to be the next of kin to the decedent or the person(s) with the legal right and authority by law to control the disposition of the above-named decedent.

The undersigned has declined embalming of the above-named decedent and authorizes the funeral home, or its designated agent, to provide shelter to the body and minimum care.

The undersigned understands minimum care may include, but not be limited to, sheltering the body in a clean, private environment; refrigeration; positioning the body; removing exterior tubes, catheters, or other medical devices deemed necessary; closing of eyes and mouth by accepted mortuary practices; aspiration of excess fluids and gases from the body; inventory of personal effects from the body; use of surface disinfectants or deodorants; wrapping or covering the body in suitable material. Minimum care does not include chemically treating the body by arterial injection of chemicals and does not retard organic decomposition. Minimum care will not ensure any time for presentation of the body for viewing or preservation as a replacement for arterial embalming.

The undersigned have been provided with the opportunity to ask any questions pertaining to minimum care.

The undersigned releases and discharges the funeral home, its affiliates, officers, directors, employees and agents from any and all liabilities claim, losses, damages, costs, or causes of action arising from the decision to not embalm the body, or arising out of any other decision indicated by this authorization which may result in mental or physical distress or anguish or harm or financial loss to the undersigned or others.

Signed this _____ day of _____, 20__ at _____.

Signature: _____

Relationship to the Deceased: _____

Signature: _____

Relationship to the Deceased: _____

Representative of Funeral Home: _____

Form 03-14   ©2003 Kubasak Associates

AUTHORIZATION TO PHOTOGRAPH THE DECEASED

Name of deceased: _____Date of death: _____

The undersigned hereby represents and warrants to be the next of kin and/or the person(s) with the legal right to control the disposition of the above-named decedent and hereby authorizes the funeral home to photograph the deceased person for the following purpose:

_____

The undersigned agrees and understands the photograph(s) taken by the funeral home will be presented to the next of kin or the person(s) with the legal right to control the disposition, who will be asked to sign, date, and affix the time it was examined, for the purpose listed above, and that the photograph(s) will remain in the custody of the funeral home in the decedent's file on a confidential and permanent basis.

Additionally, except for the sole negligence or willful misconduct of the funeral home, it is agreed that the undersigned agrees to indemnify and hold harmless the funeral home, its affiliates, officers, directors, employees and agents from any and all liabilities, claims, losses, damages, costs, or causes of actions arising or relating in any manner from photographing the deceased for the above-listed purpose.

Signed this _____day of _____, 20___ at _____.

Signature: _____

Relationship to the Deceased: _____

Signature: _____

Relationship to the Deceased: _____

Representative of Funeral Home: _____

AUTHORIZATION FOR OVERNIGHT STAY OF DECEASED

Name of deceased: _____ Date of death: _____

The undersigned hereby represents and warrants being the next of kin and/or the person(s) with the legal right to control the disposition of the above-named decedent.

The undersigned authorize and direct the funeral home to leave the above-named decedent overnight in the following facility:

_____.

It is understood that during the period of time the decedent is at this facility, it is out of the custody or care of the funeral home. The funeral home is not responsible for the security of the facility or for providing care to the decedent at the facility. The undersigned acknowledge they have been advised by the funeral home to speak directly with the facility to determine any security concerns, or to have questions answered.

Additionally, except for the sole negligence or willful misconduct of the funeral home, it is agreed that the undersigned hereby releases and discharges the funeral home, its officers, affiliates, employees and agents from any and all liabilities, losses, damages, injuries, theft, known or unknown, including claims of mental or physical distress or anguish, financial loss to the undersigned or to others, in directing the funeral home to leave the decedent overnight in the above-listed facility. The undersigned agree to indemnify the funeral home, its officers, affiliates, employees and agents from any causes of action or suits of any kind arising out of this authorization.

Signed this _____ day of _____, 20___ at _____.

Signature: _____

Relationship to the Deceased: _____

Signature: _____

Relationship to the Deceased: _____

Representative of Funeral Home: _____

RELEASE OF LIABILITY FOR PERSONAL PROPERTY
USED <u>DURING</u> FUNERAL ACTIVITIES

Name of deceased: _____Date of death: _____

The undersigned represents and warrants to be the next of kin to the decedent or the person(s) with the legal right and authority by law to control the disposition of the above-named decedent and directs the funeral home to place the following personal property on the body or in the casket/container of the above-named decedent.

Property Description	To Remain	To Be Returned

In placing personal property on the body or inside the casket/container, the undersigned understand and agrees to assume complete responsibility for the personal property even while the decedent is in the custody of or on the premises of the funeral home. The undersigned has the right to provide security for the personal property at their expense

Additionally, it is agreed that the undersigned assumes all responsibility and releases and discharges the funeral home and agrees to indemnify and hold harmless the funeral home, its affiliates, officers, directors, employees and agents from any and all liabilities, obligations, losses, theft or removal, damages, costs or expenses of any nature whatsoever relating to or arising out of the placement or use of the above-listed personal property during any funeral-memorial, wake observances or practices held or to be held for the burial, entombment, cremation, shipment or transfer of the deceased.

Signed this _____day of _____, 20__ at _____.

Signature: _____

Relationship to the Deceased: _____

Signature: _____

Relationship to the Deceased: _____

Representative of Funeral Home: _____

Form 03-11   ©2003 Kubasak Associates

RECEIPT FOR PERSONAL PROPERTY
RETURNED <u>AFTER</u> FUNERAL ACTIVITIES

Name of deceased: _____Date of death: _____

The undersigned represents and warrants to be the next of kin to the decedent or the person(s) with the legal right and authority by law to control the disposition of the above-named decedent and the designated person to receive the personal property.

Property Description	Returned Date & Time

The undersigned acknowledges receipt of the above-listed personal property and assumes all responsibility for the personal property and releases and discharges the funeral home and agrees to indemnify and hold harmless the funeral home, its affiliates, officers, directors, employees and agents from any and all liabilities, obligations, losses, theft or removal, damages, costs or expenses of any nature whatsoever which relates to or arises out of the removal of the personal property which may result in mental or physical distress or anguish or harm or financial loss to the undersigned, myself, or others.

Signed this _____day of _____, 20__ at _____.

Signature: _____

Relationship to the Deceased: _____

Signature: _____

Relationship to the Deceased: _____

Representative of Funeral Home: _____

Form 03-12   ©2003 Kubasak Associates

435

CREMATION and DISPOSITION AUTHORIZATION

This Cremation and Disposition Authorization form must be completed in its entirety for each cremation of human remains prior to the scheduling and/or starting of the cremation process. THIS IS A LEGAL DOCUMENT. READ IT CAREFULLY. Cremation will take place in accordance with all rules and regulations of the Crematory and in accordance with all applicable Federal, State and County laws. We want you to fully understand the information in this Form and we are pleased to answer any questions concerning the contents of this Form, the cremation process or other information that will be helpful to you.

This Cremation and Disposition Authorization form is not a contract for cremation services. A separate contract or contracts will be required to purchase the services of a funeral home or other provider.

1. IDENTIFICATION OF DECEDENT

Name of Decedent: _____

Date of Death: _____ Time of Death: _____ Place of Death: _____

Sex: _____ Age: _____ Date of Birth: _____ Social Security No.: _____

Cremation is irreversible and verification of the identity of the decedent is required before it can take place. The following method was used for this purpose:

_____ The Authorizing Agent has viewed the remains and positively identified them as the decedent named above. Date & Time: _____

_____ The *designated-in-writing* personal representative of the Authorizing agent has viewed the remains and positively identified them as the decedent named above. Date & Time: _____

_____ Other (specify in detail) _____
_____

Cremation Authorization Form – Page 1 of 10

436

2. FUNERAL HOME INSTRUCTIONS

The Authorizing Agent instructs the Funeral Home and Crematory to carry out all instructions set forth in this Cremation and Disposition Authorization form.

Name of Funeral Home: _____ Tel. #: _____

Address: _____ City: _____ State: _____

The Funeral Home represents to the crematory that the following documents are attached to this Cremation and Disposition Authorization form:

_____ A signed statement attesting to the identification of the Decedent, and

_____ A copy of a completed death certificate and/or filed with the local registrar where the Death occurred, and

_____ Written authorization from the medical examiner/coroner or physician to permit Cremation

Name of Funeral Director in charge: _____

Signature of Funeral Director in charge: _____

3. AUTHORIZING AGENT REPRESENTATION

I (we) certify that the decedent is survived by the following heirs:

Spouse: __Yes __No Name of surviving spouse: _____

Children: __Yes __No Names of all surviving children: _____

_____

Parents: __Yes ___No Names of surviving parents: _____

If all responses are NO, the person(s) in the next degree of kinship to the decedent is (are):

Name: _____ Relationship: _____

Name: _____ Relationship: _____

Name: _____ Relationship: _____

4. AUTHORIZING AGENT CERTIFICATION

Authorizing Agent certifies that the relationship between the Authorizing Agent and the Decedent is as follows:

_____ Surviving spouse of Decedent at time of death

_____ The adult children of the Decedent

_____ The parents or sole surviving parent of the Decedent

_____ The siblings or sole surviving sibling of the Decedent

_____ The legal guardian of a minor aged child to the Decedent

_____ A person with the next degree of kinship to the Decedent not listed above

_____ A person, other than a surviving heir, who possesses legal authority and power to control disposition and cremation according to the laws of this state

Name of Authorizing Agent: _____

Relationship to the Decedent: _____

Address of Authorizing Agent: _____

City: _____ State: _____ Zip: _____

Home Telephone: _____ Cell Phone: _____

I certify that I (we) am (are) the person(s) who have the legal right to authorize the cremation and disposition of the Decedent and represent that <u>no other living person or persons has equal or superior rights</u>.

Signature of Authorizing Agent(s):

Name: _____ Relationship: _____ Date & Time: _____

Name: _____ Relationship: _____ Date & Time: _____

Name: _____ Relationship: _____ Date & Time: _____

Separate authorizations, if necessary, shall be attached to this Cremation and Disposition Authorization form and considered a part of this form.

Cremation Authorization Form – Page 3 of 10

438

5. PACEMAKERS, IMPLANTS, PROSTHESES, MECHANICAL DEVICES

These and other similar medical devices may create a hazardous condition when placed into a cremation chamber and subjected to heat and direct flame and must be removed prior to making delivery of the Decedent to the crematory. If the presence of any such device is not disclosed, Authorizing Agent will be liable for damages to the crematory and/or crematory personnel. The following list describes all devices and materials which may have been implanted or attached to the Decedent:

Description: _____

____ The Decedent does not contain any of the devices-materials described above

OR

____ As Authorizing Agent, I (we) instruct the Funeral Home to remove or arrange for the removal of each device listed above and acknowledges that a charge may be made for services in removing said devices.

____ Devices will be disposed of by Funeral Home

____ Devices to be returned to the possession of Authorizing Agent, if permitted

6. CASKET or APPROVED CONTAINER

Each Decedent to be cremated shall be delivered to the crematory in a cremation container composed of a combustible material, resistant to the escape of bodily fluids, and further, the crematory requires the container to be completely closed, of rigid construction for handling, that provides protection for the health and safety of funeral home and crematory personnel while respecting the privacy of the deceased. The crematory is authorized to inspect the casket or container, and if opening the casket is necessary, it will be opened only in the presence of a license funeral director representing the contracting funeral home. Any container not meeting the above requirements or that poses a hazard, will be refused by the crematory. Some caskets or containers that contain exterior decorative parts (handles, rails, etc) that are not combustible may cause damage to the cremation equipment. The Authorizing Agent hereby instructs the crematory, in its discretion, to remove and discard non-combustible parts from the casket or container. The crematory does not accept metal, fiberglass or plastic caskets or containers for cremation. As Authorizing Agent, I understand that the casket or container will be totally consumed as a part of the cremation process.

____ Authorizing Agent

7. WITNESSES

Witnessing a cremation can be an emotional experience. Witnessing must take place while a licensed funeral director is present. Witnesses assume all risks involved and fully release the funeral home and crematory from any liability, claims of mental or emotional distress, loss, harm or other claims. Witnessing can only take place with the written permission of the Authorizing Agent and may include witnessing the delivery of the Decedent to the crematory, placing the Decedent in the cremation chamber and the removal of the Decedent from the cremation chamber.

As Authorizing Agent:

____ Permit witnessing, or

____ No witnessing

8. THE CREMATION PROCESS

Please initial each section as confirmation of understanding

Cremation will occur only after all ceremonies and visitations have taken place. Only human remains will be cremated by the crematory, on an individual basis.

___ The deceased is placed into a casket or container which is then placed into the cremation chamber. Through the use of a suitable fuel, the Decedent and the container are subjected to intense heat and direct flame with all contents incinerated with the exception of bone fragments (calcium compounds) and metal (including dental gold or silver and other non-human materials) as the temperature is not sufficient to consume these materials. During the cremation process, it may be necessary to open the chamber and reposition the Deceased in order to facilitate a complete and thorough cremation.

___ Due to the nature of the cremation process any personal possessions, either valuable or of a sentimental value, left with the Decedent and <u>not removed</u> from the casket or container <u>prior</u> to the start of cremation will be destroyed or otherwise not be recoverable (this includes such things as body prostheses, dental bridgework, dental gold or silver, jewelry, clothing, photographs, letters, and more) and will be disposed of by the crematory. The Authorizing Agent understands and agrees that <u>arrangements must be made with the funeral home</u> in advance of delivering the Decedent to the crematory to remove any such possessions or valuables. Crematory personnel will not open any casket or container and will not remove any personal possessions inside the casket or container. Possessions of the deceased shall not be removed or disposed of without the express written permission of the authorizing agent.

___ Following a cooling period, the cremated remains, which normally weigh several pounds in the case of an average size adult, are collected from the cremation chamber by sweeping and/or raking. The crematory makes a reasonable effort to remove all of the recoverable cremated remains from the cremation chamber but some dust and other residue from the process will remain in cracks and crevices inside the chamber. In addition, while every effort is made to avoid commingling, inadvertent and incidental commingling of minute particles of cremated remains from the residue of previous cremations will occur.

___ After the cremated remains are removed from the cremation chamber, all non-combustible materials (insofar as possible) such as bridgework, prostheses and materials from the casket or container (hinges, latches, screws, nails, etc) to which some bone residue will be affixed, will be separated and removed from the human bone fragments by visible or magnetic selection and disposed of by the crematory with similar materials from other cremations in a non-recoverable manner, so that only human bone fragments will remain. Foreign materials removed may be commingled with other like material and shall be disposed of by burial in a cemetery.

___ When the cremated remains are removed from the cremation chamber, the skeletal remains often contain recognizable bone fragments. Unless otherwise specified by the authorizing agent, after the bone fragments have been separated from the other material, they will be mechanically pulverized. This includes a process of crushing and grinding the skeletal fragments into granulated particles of unidentifiable dimensions that renders them virtually unrecognizable as human remains. This process may also cause inadvertent and incidental commingling of the remains from the processing of previously cremated and pulverized remains. When completed, the pulverized cremated remains will be placed into designated urn container.

As Authorizing Agent, I have read and understand the description of the cremation process, have had ample time to ask questions and hereby authorize the funeral home to deliver the Decedent to the crematory for the purpose of cremation.

Signature of Authorizing Agent: _____

Date: _____ Time: _____

9. URNS

After the cremation process is completed, the crematory will place the cremated remains into a cremated remains container called an urn. The crematory requires that all urns to be used for placement of cremated remains be resistant to deterioration and breakage and be suitable for shipment. For the average size adult, urns must accommodate a minimum of two hundred (200) cubic inches. In the event the urn is of insufficient size to accommodate all of the cremated remains, the excess remains will be placed in another separate receptacle and will be kept with the primary receptacle and handled according to the final disposition instructions listed below. The Authorizing Agent specifies the following urn to be used:

Description of urn: _____

Provided by: ___ Funeral Home ___Authorizing Agent

10. DISPOSITION OF CREMATED REMAINS

Cremation may only occur when a provision for final disposition of cremated remains is made and included on this form. The crematory will not hold or store cremated remains for more than _____ days following the actual cremation.

When Authorizing Agent directs the funeral home and crematory to ship cremated remains, crematory or funeral home can only utilize registered United States mail with a return receipt or a service that provides an internal system for tracing the location of the cremated remains at all times during the shipment and that requires a signed receipt of the person taking delivery of the cremated remains.

Authorizing Agent instructs that disposition shall be as follows:

___ Deliver to _____ Cemetery with which arrangements have already been made.

___ Deliver cremated remains to the US Postal Service for shipment by registered, Return receipt mail to: _____

_____.

___ Deliver the cremated remains to the funeral home

___ Deliver or release the cremated remains only to:

Name: _____ Relationship: _____

Address: _____ City: _____

State: _____ Telephone: _____

___ **Note: Photo identification will be required before cremated remains are released to any designated person or persons.**

In the event that Authorizing Agent directs that cremated remains be proportioned and placed into multiple cremated remains containers (usually referred to as keepsake urns), this will not take place at or by crematory personnel but will take place at the funeral home by funeral home personnel.

___ The Authorizing Agent understands that the services of the crematory will have been fully completed when the cremated remains are delivered to the place of disposition or designated receiver or US Postal Service. The crematory only acts as an agent for accommodation in carrying out disposition instructions. The Authorizing Agent assumes all liability for any damages or loss that may arise from such disposition instructions and/or delivery and/or release and agrees to indemnify and hold the crematory harmless from any and all claims arising from these instructions.

In the event that Authorizing Agent desires scattering of cremated remains, it is understood that scattering can only be done by funeral home personnel, not crematory personnel. Additionally, Authorizing Agent understands that scattering is irreversible and makes the cremated remains unrecoverable in whole or in part.

11. VISITATION AND FUNERAL CEREMONIES

Cremation may only take place after all ceremonies and visitation has occurred. Prior to the cremation of the Decedent, the Authorizing Agent or Decedent's family acting with the consent of the Authorizing Agent, has arranged for a visitation and/or funeral ceremony as set below:

Date(s): _____ Time(s): _____

Place of ceremony: _____

12. TIME OF CREMATION

Cremation may only take place after all legal documents have been secured and this form has been completed and signed in its entirety and delivered to the crematory. The Authorizing Agent requests that one of the following take place:

____ The crematory may perform the cremation of the Decedent at a time and place as its work schedule permits and without any further notification to the Authorizing Agent,

OR

____ The crematory is to use its best efforts to schedule the cremation of the Decedent in accordance with the schedule set forth below:

Date of cremation: _____ Time of cremation: _____

13. CERTIFICATION AND INDEMNIFICATION

___ The Authorizing Agent acknowledges that the funeral home and crematory are relying upon the representations being made by the Authorizing Agent(s). The Authorizing Agent(s) certify that all of the information and statements contained in the Cremation Authorization and Disposition document are accurate and no omissions of any material fact have been made.

___ Authorizing Agent(s) understand and agree that the obligations of the crematory shall be limited to the cremation of the Decedent and the release and/or disposition of the Decedent's cremated remains as specified and authorized on this form. No warranties express or implied are made and damages shall be limited to the amount of the cremation fee paid.

___ The Authorizing Agent(s) agrees to indemnify, defend and hold harmless the funeral home and crematory, its officers, directors, employees and agents from any and all claims, cause of action, suits of any nature, in law or in equity, cost or expense of litigation, arising as a result of, based upon or connected with the instructions in this form, including the failure to properly identify the Decedent, the failure to take possession of the cremated remains, any damage due to harmful or explodable implants or devices in or on the Decedent's remains, claims by any other person(s) claiming the right to control disposition of the Decedent or the Decedent's cremated remains, excepting only acts of willful negligence by the crematory.

Executed at: _____, this ____ day of _____.

Printed Name of Authorizing Agent: _____.

Signature of Authorizing Agent: _____.

Witness: _____.

Name of Funeral Home: _____.

Signature of Funeral Home Representative: _____.

Title: _____.

CREMATORY INSPECTION FORM

Inspected by:_____ Date & Time: _____

Crematory Name: _____ Location: _____

Owner: _____ Operator on Duty: _____

1. External condition of building & grounds: _____

2. Internal condition of structure: _____

3. Date of Installation: _____ # of chambers: _____

4. Date of last service: _____ By: _____

5. Date of last regulatory inspection: _____ Agency: _____

6. Appearance/dress of crematory personnel: _____

7. State & local licenses, posted & current: _____

8. Refrigeration for remains? _____ Temperature of refrigeration @ inspection: _____
   Capacity of unit: _____

9. Describe how other decedents were held: _____

10. Are documents for each cremation attached to chamber during cremation? _____

11. Describe body identification procedure: _____

12. Describe method of processing: _____

13. Condition of processing room? _____ Equipment? _____

14. Describe policy for removing cremated remains from chamber: _____
_____

15. Describe policy for handling excess cremated remains: _____
_____

16. Describe policy for labeling cremated remains: _____

17. Is there an operational manual in the crematory? _____

18. Crematory policy on recovering, handling & disposing of: (use back of form)

    a) jewelry   d) body tissues

    b) dental gold   e) medical devices

    c) prosthetics   f) casket hardware

19. Names of crematory employees: _____

20. Names of bonded employees: _____

21. Background checks of bonded employees? _____

22. Are operators certified? _____ By whom? _____

Form 03-28

23. Are certificates posted and in view? _____

24. Policy of witnessing: _____

25. Does this crematory cremate animals? _____

26. Usual hours of operation for crematory: _____

27. Cremation Log Book inspected? _____

28. Describe if anything unusual was observed during this inspection? _____

_____

_____

29. General Comments:

_____

_____

_____

_____

Date: _____

Signature of Funeral Home Representative: _____

Signature of Crematory Personnel: _____

RECEIPT OF REMAINS FOR CREMATION

Name of deceased: _____ Date of death: _____

I hereby acknowledge receipt of a casket/container from

_____
Name of Funeral Home

Which appear to be presented for holding in good condition at the time of receipt, and

agree to hold the remains of the above-named deceased on this _____ day of

_____, 20 ___ until the date and time set for the cremation of the remains.

Crematory Representative: _____ Time: _____

Representative of Funeral Home: _____

DIRECTIVE FOR RELEASE OF CREMATED REMAINS

Name of deceased: _____Date of death: _____

The undersigned represents and warrants to be the next of kin to the decedent or the person(s) with the legal right and authority by law to control the disposition of the above-named decedent and directs the funeral home to release the cremated remains to the following people only:

Name: _____Relationship to the Deceased: _____

Name: _____Relationship to the Deceased: _____

Name: _____Relationship to the Deceased: _____

The undersigned understand the funeral home can only release or deliver the cremated remains to the person(s) specified in this directive and any changes to this directive must be made in writing by the next of kin or by the person(s) with the legal right of disposition.

The undersigned releases and discharges the funeral home, its affiliates, officers, directors, employees and agents from any and all liabilities, claims, losses, damages, costs, or causes of actions arising or relating in any manner from the release of cremated remains to any or all of the persons listed above.

Signed this _____day of _____, 20__ at _____.

Signature: _____

Relationship to the Deceased: _____

Signature: _____

Relationship to the Deceased: _____

Representative of Funeral Home: _____

Form 03-23   ©2003 Kubasak Associates

449

AUTHORIZATION TO SCATTER CREMATED REMAINS

Name of deceased: _____ Date of death: _____

The undersigned hereby represents and warrants to be the next of kin and/or the person with the legal right to control the disposition of the above-named decedent and requests and authorizes the funeral home to scatter the cremated remains of the above-named deceased. It is understood and agreed that scattering will take place as stated below in accordance with the funeral home's policies and any applicable federal, state, provincial, county, city or other local laws, statutes or regulations.

The undersigned requests and authorizes the cremated remains be scattered as follows:

   a. Scattering Garden located at_____

   b. Scattering At Sea (describe)_____

   c. Scattering At (describe)_____

It is understood the scattering will take place on _____, 20___. If no specific instructions are stated, scattering of the cremated remains will take place at the convenience of the funeral home or its designated agent or representative within a reasonable time.

It is understood scattering of cremated remains is the dispersement of the remains and once the cremated remains have been scattered, they are unrecoverable in whole or in part. Unless otherwise specifically provided for on this authorization, the funeral home, its agent or representative reserves the right to dispose of the container that held the cremated remains. The obligation of the funeral home shall be limited to scattering the cremated remains of the above-named deceased as directed on this authorization.

The undersigned hereby releases and discharges the funeral home, its officers, affiliates, employees, agents and representatives from any and all liabilities, losses, damages, and injuries, known or unknown, including claims of mental or physical distress or anguish, financial loss to the undersigned or to others in directing that scattering of these cremated remains take place. The undersigned agree to indemnify the funeral home, its officers, affiliates, employees, agents or representatives from any causes of action or suits of any kind arising out of this authorization.

Signed this _____day of _____, 20__ at _____.

Signature: _____

Relationship to the Deceased: _____

Representative of Funeral Home: _____

07/03

©2003 Kubasak Associates

450

REQUEST TO WITNESS THE CREMATION PROCESS

Name of deceased: _____ Date of death: _____

The undersigned represents and warrants to be the next of kin to the decedent or the designated representative of the next of kin or the person(s) with the legal right and authority by law to control the disposition of the above-named deceased and does hereby request to witness the cremation of the above-named decedent. The undersigned acknowledge:

      a. the funeral home representative listed below has advised and informed me of the cremation process,

      b. viewing the cremation process can be visually difficult and

      c. viewing the cremation can be emotionally distressful.

Having been thoroughly advised, the undersigned wishes to witness the cremation, which will take place on _____ at _____ Crematory at _____ A.M./P.M.

In so witnessing, the undersigned agrees to release and forever discharge the funeral home, its affiliates, officers, employees, agents and representatives from any and all liabilities, losses, damages, and injuries, known or unknown, claims of mental or physical distress or anguish, and agrees to defend and indemnify the funeral home from any claims, causes of action or suits of any kind that may arise from or in any way are related to the witnessing of the cremation process.

Signed this _____day of _____, 20___ at _____.

Signature: _____

Relationship to the Deceased: _____

Signature: _____

Relationship to the Deceased: _____

Signature: _____

Relationship to the Deceased: _____

Representative of Funeral Home: _____

Form 03-22

451

RECEIPT FROM THE CEMETERY FOR BURIAL OR ENTOMBMENT

Name of deceased: _____ Date of death: _____

I hereby acknowledge receipt of a casket/container from

_____

Name of Funeral Home

which appear to be presented in good condition at the time of receipt and said to hold

the remains of the above-named decedent for burial or entombment in

_____ Cemetery/Memorial Park on

this _____ day of _____, 20 ____ .

Cemetery Park Representative: _____Time: _____

Representative of Funeral Home: _____

Form 03-19 ©2003 Kubasak Associates

WITNESS OF TRANSFER OF HUMAN REMAINS FROM PLACE OF DEATH

Name of deceased: _____ Date of death: _____

Date of Transfer: _____ Time of Transfer: _____

Place of Death : _____

Name of Funeral Home: _____

The undersigned hereby confirms being present and witnessing the transfer of the remains of the above-named deceased by representatives of the above-named funeral home, on the date and from the place identified above. The undersigned acknowledges that an identification tag, with the name of the deceased written on it, was attached to the body of the deceased by the funeral home or their representative.

Date: _____ Signature: _____

Print Name: _____ Telephone # _____

Relationship to the deceased: _____

Name of Funeral Home Employee or Representative: _____

AUTHORIZATION FOR SHIPMENT OF REMAINS

Name of deceased: _____ Date of death: _____

The undersigned represents and warrants to be the next of kin to the decedent or the designated representative of the next of kin or the person(s) with the legal right and authority by law to control the disposition of the above-named decedent and hereby authorizes the funeral home to ship and/or transport the above-named decedent to

_____.

The shipping/transport will be done by the following common carrier or transport company: _____.

The undersigned acknowledges transporting a decedent can result in delays or inconvenience and agree the funeral home will not be held responsible for any delay, inconvenience, loss, damage, or deterioration to the above-named decedent or the casket/container holding the remains. The undersigned further agrees to release, discharge and hold harmless, absolutely and unconditionally the funeral home, its affiliates, officers, directors, employees and agents from any and all liabilities, obligations, losses, damages, costs or expenses of any nature whatsoever which in any manner relate to or arise out of the shipment/transport of the decedent and will indemnify the funeral home in the event of any claims or causes of action.

Signed this _____ day of _____, 20___ at _____.

Signature: _____

Relationship to the Deceased: _____

Signature: _____

Relationship to the Deceased: _____

AUTHORIZATION FOR SHIPMENT OF CREMATED REMAINS

Name of deceased: _____ Date of death: _____

The undersigned hereby represents and warrants to be the next of kin and/or the person(s) with the legal right to control the disposition of the above-named decedent and do hereby request and authorize the funeral home to ship the cremated remains to:

_____

Name of agency/company doing shipping: _____

Describe cremated remains container: _____

Date of shipment_____

The undersigned acknowledge that transporting-shipping cremated remains can result in delays, inconvenience, loss and damage and additionally, there can be damage to the cremated remains container.

The undersigned hereby releases and discharges the funeral home, its officers, affiliates, employees and agents from any and all liabilities, losses, damages, injuries, theft, known or unknown, including claims of mental and physical distress or anguish, financial loss to the undersigned or to others, in authorizing the funeral home to ship the cremated remains in the manner described above. The undersigned agree to indemnify the funeral home, its officers, affiliates, employees and agents from any causes of action or suits of any kind arising out of this authorization.

Signed this _____ day of _____, 20___ at _____.

Signature: _____

Relationship to the Deceased: _____

Signature: _____

Relationship to the Deceased: _____

Representative of Funeral Home: _____

Form 03-24   ©2003 Kubasak Associates

455

DIRECTION FOR DISPOSITION OF CREMATED REMAINS
OTHER THAN SCATTERING OF REMAINS

Name of deceased: _____ Date of death: _____

The undersigned represents and warrants to be the next of kin to the decedent or the person(s) with the legal right and authority by law to control the disposition of the above-named decedent.

The undersigned direct the funeral home to dispose of the cremated remains in the following manner: (describe and give details of disposition)

Burial in _____

Entombment in _____

Placement in Cemetery _____

Placement in Common Receptacle _____

Other disposition (other than scattering) _____

Shipment/mailing to: _____ Via: _____

Special Instructions: _____

_____

_____

The undersigned agree the obligation of the funeral home is limited to the disposition of the cremated remains as directed on this form. Further, the undersigned agree to release and forever discharge the funeral home, its officers, affiliates, employees, agents and representatives from any and all liabilities, losses, damages, injuries, known and unknown, claims of mental or physical distress or anguish, that may result from the disposition of the cremated remains as directed above.

Signed this _____ day of _____, 20___ at _____.

Signature: _____

Relationship to the Deceased: _____

Signature: _____

Relationship to the Deceased: _____

Representative of Funeral Home: _____

Form 03-26   ©2003 Kubasak Associates

CEMETERY-GRAVE SPACE DISCLOSURE

Name of deceased: _____ Date of death: _____

The undersigned understands and agrees that the funeral home has no connection with or responsibility for the construction, inspection or maintenance of the grave for the above-named decedent at _____
Cemetery. The cemetery has complete control and authority over the operation of facilities, equipment, personnel, and grave spaces on their premises.

The undersigned agrees and states a grave will be or has been purchased for the above-named decedent without any involvement, sale or contract, or obligation by the funeral home for the purchase of the grave. The funeral home has not been asked to inspect, nor has it inspected the grave, nor does it have information as to its construction, excavation, maintenance, preparation or condition. The funeral home recommends the undersigned inspect and clarify this information directly with the cemetery in advance of the interment of the casket or container into the grave or for maintenance or care of the grave. The undersigned agree to look solely to the cemetery with respect to any loss, injury, costs, attorney fees, or claims that may arise from the burial of the decedent in the grave.

The undersigned releases and discharges the funeral home and agrees to defend, indemnify and hold harmless the funeral home, its affiliates, officers, directors, employees and agents from any and all liabilities, claims, obligations, losses, damages, costs or expenses of any nature whatsoever, which in any manner relate to, or arise out of the purchase or use of the grave site.

Signed this _____ day of _____, 20___ at _____.

Signature: _____

Relationship to the Deceased: _____

Signature: _____

Relationship to the Deceased: _____

Representative of Funeral Home: _____

Form 03-17   ©2003 Kubasak Associates

457

MAUSOLEUM-CRYPT DISCLOSURE

Name of deceased: _____Date of death: _____

The undersigned understands and agrees the funeral home has no connection with or responsibility for the sale of, contract for sale of, construction, inspection nor maintenance of the crypt or mausoleum for the above-named decedent at _____ Cemetery-Mausoleum. The cemetery-mausoleum has complete control and authority over the operation of facilities, equipment, personnel, and crypt spaces on their premises.

The undersigned agrees and states that a crypt will be or has been purchased for the above-named decedent without any involvement by the funeral home. The funeral home has not inspected nor does it have information as to its construction, maintenance, preparation or condition. The funeral home recommends the undersigned inspect and clarify this information directly with the cemetery-mausoleum before entombment of the casket or container into the crypt, or for the maintenance or care of the crypt. The undersigned agrees to look solely to the cemetery-mausoleum with respect to any loss, injury, costs, attorney fees, or claims that may arise from the entombment of the decedent in the crypt.

The undersigned releases and discharges the funeral home and agrees to defend, indemnify and hold harmless the funeral home, its affiliates, officers, directors, employees and agents from any and all liabilities, claims, obligations, losses, damages, costs or expenses of any nature whatsoever, which in any manner relate to, or arise out of the purchase or use of the crypt site.

Signed this _____day of _____, 20___ at _____.

Signature: _____

Relationship to the Deceased: _____

Signature: _____

Relationship to the Deceased: _____

Representative of Funeral Home: _____

METAL CASKET DISCLAIMER

Name of deceased: _____Date of death: _____

The undersigned represents and warrants to be the next of kin to the decedent or the person(s) with the legal right and authority by law to control the disposition of the above-named decedent and hereby instructs the funeral home to provide and place the above-named decedent in the casket herein listed that I/we have selected and purchased from the funeral home.

Description of Metal Casket: _____

The undersigned hereby attests the funeral home made available a casket price list prior to selection, listing a variety of caskets.

The undersigned hereby attests the funeral home, its officers, employees or sellers have made no representations, warranties, claims of merchantability, fitness, protectiveness, air or water tightness or sealability or durability to me/us. **All warranties of all kinds are hereby expressly disclaimed, including implied warranties for fitness and merchantability. The undersigned hereby acknowledges receipt of said manufacturer's warranty, if any, from the funeral home.**

The undersigned releases and discharges the funeral home from liabilities, losses, damages, and injuries known or unknown to me/ourselves or others, including but not limited to claims of mental or physical distress or anguish, attorneys' fees, claims of durability, fitness, merchantability or protective qualities of this casket. **The undersigned understands the only warranties or representations, expressed or implied, in connection with goods and services sold with this funeral service, are the expressed written warranties, if any, extended by the manufacturer of the casket.**

Signed this _____day of _____, 20__ at _____.

Signature: _____

Relationship to the Deceased: _____

Signature: _____

Relationship to the Deceased: _____

Representative of Funeral Home: _____

WOOD CASKET DISCLAIMER

Name of deceased: _____Date of death: _____

The undersigned represents and warrants to be the next of kin to the decedent or the person(s) with the legal right and authority by law to control the disposition of the above-named decedent, and hereby instructs the funeral home to provide and to place the above-named decedent in the casket herein listed that I/we have selected and purchased from the funeral home.

Description of Wood Casket: _____

The undersigned hereby attests the funeral home made available a casket price list prior to selection, listing a variety of caskets. I/we have selected and purchased a casket constructed of wood or wood products and understand a wood or wood product casket of this type is not protective, not sealable, not air or water tight. This casket that I/we have selected will not prevent the entrance of outside or gravesite elements. Over a period of time, wood and wood product caskets will disintegrate.

The undersigned hereby attests the funeral home, its officers, employees or sellers made no representations, warranties, claims of merchantability, fitness, protectiveness, air or water tightness or sealability or durability of this wood casket to me/us. **All warranties of all kinds are hereby expressly disclaimed, including implied warranties for fitness and merchantability. The undersigned hereby acknowledges receipt of said manufacturer's warranty, if any, from the funeral home.**

The undersigned releases and discharges the funeral home from liabilities, losses, damages, and injuries known or unknown to me/ourselves or others, including but not limited to claims of mental or physical distress or anguish, attorneys' fees, claims of durability, fitness, merchantability or protective qualities of this casket. **The undersigned understands the only warranties or representations, expressed or implied, in connection with goods or services sold with this funeral service, are the expressed written warranties, if any, extended by the manufacturer or the casket.** The undersigned agrees to indemnify and hold harmless the funeral home, its affiliates, officers, directors, employees and agents from any and all claims, demands, damages, actions, causes of action or suits of any kind arising from or in any way related to the wood casket.

Signed this _____ day of _____, 20___ at _____.

Signature: _____

Relationship to the Deceased: _____

Representative of Funeral Home: _____

OUTER BURIAL CONTAINER DISCLAIMER

Name of deceased: _____ Date of death: _____

The undersigned represents and warrants to be the next of kin to the decedent or the person(s) with the legal right and authority by law to control the disposition of the above-named decedent, hereby instructs the funeral home to provide and to place the casketed body or cremated remains of the above-named decedent into the following outer burial container I/we have selected and purchased from the funeral home.

Description of Outer Container: _____

The undersigned hereby attests the funeral home made available an outer burial price list prior to selection, listing a variety of outer containers. The undersigned hereby attests the funeral home, its affiliates, officers, directors, employees and agents made no representations, warranties, claims of merchantability, fitness, protectiveness, air or water tightness or sealability or durability to me/us. **All warranties of all kinds are hereby expressly disclaimed, including implied warranties for fitness and merchantability.**

The undersigned hereby acknowledges receipt of said manufacturer's warranty, if any, from the funeral home. The undersigned releases and discharges the funeral home from liabilities, losses, damages, and injuries known or unknown to me/ourselves or others, including but not limited to claims of mental or physical distress or anguish, attorneys' fees, claims of durability, fitness, merchantability or protective qualities of this outer burial container. **The undersigned understands the only warranties or representations expressed or implied, in connection with goods and services sold with this funeral service, are expressed written warranties, if any, extended by the manufacturer of the outer burial container.**

Signed this _____day of _____, 20___ at _____.

Signature: _____

Relationship to the Deceased: _____

Signature: _____

Relationship to the Deceased: _____

Representative of Funeral Home: _____

Form 03-13   ©2003 Kubasak Associates

461

URN CAPACITY DISCLOSURE

Name of deceased: _____ Date of death: _____

The undersigned represents and warrants to be the next of kin to the decedent or the person(s) with the legal right and authority by law to control the disposition of the above-named decedent and has selected the following cremated remains container to hold the cremated remains of the above named decedent:

Description of urn: _____

The undersigned acknowledges that there can be instances when the urn capacity is insufficient to hold-accommodate all of the cremated remains of the deceased. It is understood and agreed any amount of cremated remains that does not fit into the cremated remains container listed above because of insufficient capacity, will be placed and contained in a different and additional cremated remains container. Both containers will be returned to the undersigned or their designated representative.

The undersigned hereby releases and discharges the funeral home, its affiliates, officers, directors, employees and agents from any and all liabilities claims, losses, damages, costs, or causes of actions arising or relating in any manner from the cremated remains not fitting into one cremated remains container or from the use of a different and additional urn to hold the cremated remains.

Signed this _____ day of _____, 20___ at _____.

Signature: _____

Relationship to the Deceased: _____

Signature: _____

Relationship to the Deceased: _____

Representative of Funeral Home: _____

Form 03-25   ©2003 Kubasak Associates

462

ACKNOWLEDGMENT OF MERCHANDISE
NOT PROVIDED BY THE FUNERAL HOME

Name of deceased: _____ Date of death: _____

The undersigned, acknowledges the following merchandise was purchased elsewhere to be used for the final arrangements for the above-named decedent:

List merchandise and supplier purchased elsewhere: _____

_____

_____

The undersigned releases and discharges the funeral home, its affiliates, officers, directors, employees and agents from any and all liability associated with any and all merchandise acquired from any source other than a direct contract for sale of goods from the funeral home. The undersigned hereby agrees to indemnify, defend and hold harmless the funeral home, its affiliates, officers, directors, employees and agents from any and all liabilities, obligations, losses, damages, costs or expense of any nature whatsoever which in any manner relate to or arise out of the purchase or use of the above listed goods used for the burial, entombment, cremation, shipment or transfer of the deceased, and for any accompanying funeral/memorial observances or practices held or to be held. In receiving the goods, on behalf of the undersigned, the funeral home makes no representation as to condition, suitability or fitness of the goods. Acceptance of the goods, as to suitability, fitness and condition of the goods can only be made by the purchaser of the goods, not by the funeral home.

All warranties of all kinds are hereby expressly disclaimed, including implied warranties for fitness and merchantability.

Signed this _____ day of _____, 20__ at _____.

Signature: _____

Relationship to the Deceased: _____

Signature: _____

Relationship to the Deceased: _____

Representative of Funeral Home: _____

Form 03-16   ©2003 Kubasak Associates

463

CASKET RENTAL
ACKNOWLEDGEMENT AND RELEASE

Name of deceased: _____Date of death: _____

The undersigned hereby represents and warrants to be the next of kin of the decedent or the person(s) with the legal right to control the disposition of the above-named decedent and is aware the casket/container being used in conjunction with the funeral services for the above-named deceased is a rental casket which may have been used previously and may be used again in the future.

The undersigned further acknowledges that at the conclusion of the funeral services for the above-named deceased, the deceased will be removed from the rental casket and placed in another casket/container and the rental casket in question will remain the property of the funeral home.

· The undersigned releases and discharges the funeral home and agrees to indemnify and hold harmless the funeral home, its affiliates, officers, directors, employees and agents from any and all liabilities, obligations, losses, damages, costs or expenses of any nature whatsoever which in any manner relate to or arise out of the rental or use of the rental casket for the accompanying funeral-memorial observances or practices held or to be held.

Signed this _____day of _____, 20__ at _____.

Signature: _____

Relationship to the Deceased: _____

Signature: _____

Relationship to the Deceased: _____

Signature: _____

Relationship to the Deceased: _____

Representative of Funeral Home: _____

Form 03-15   ©2003 Kubasak Associates

464